Stefan Gierowski

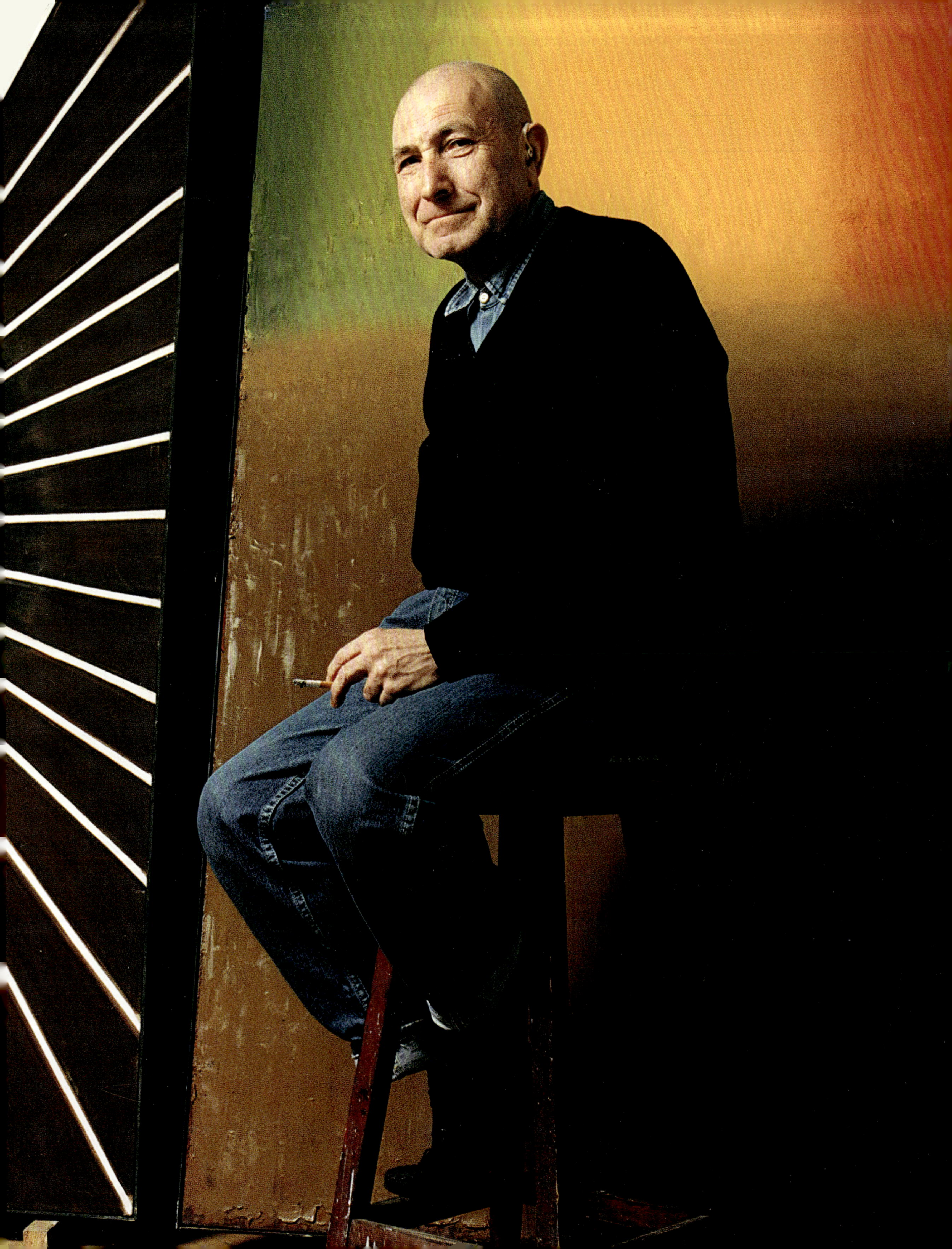

STEFAN GIEROWSKI

SKIRA

Contents

Black, White, and Everything In Between: Stefan Gierowski and His Thousand Paintings

Stach Szabłowski

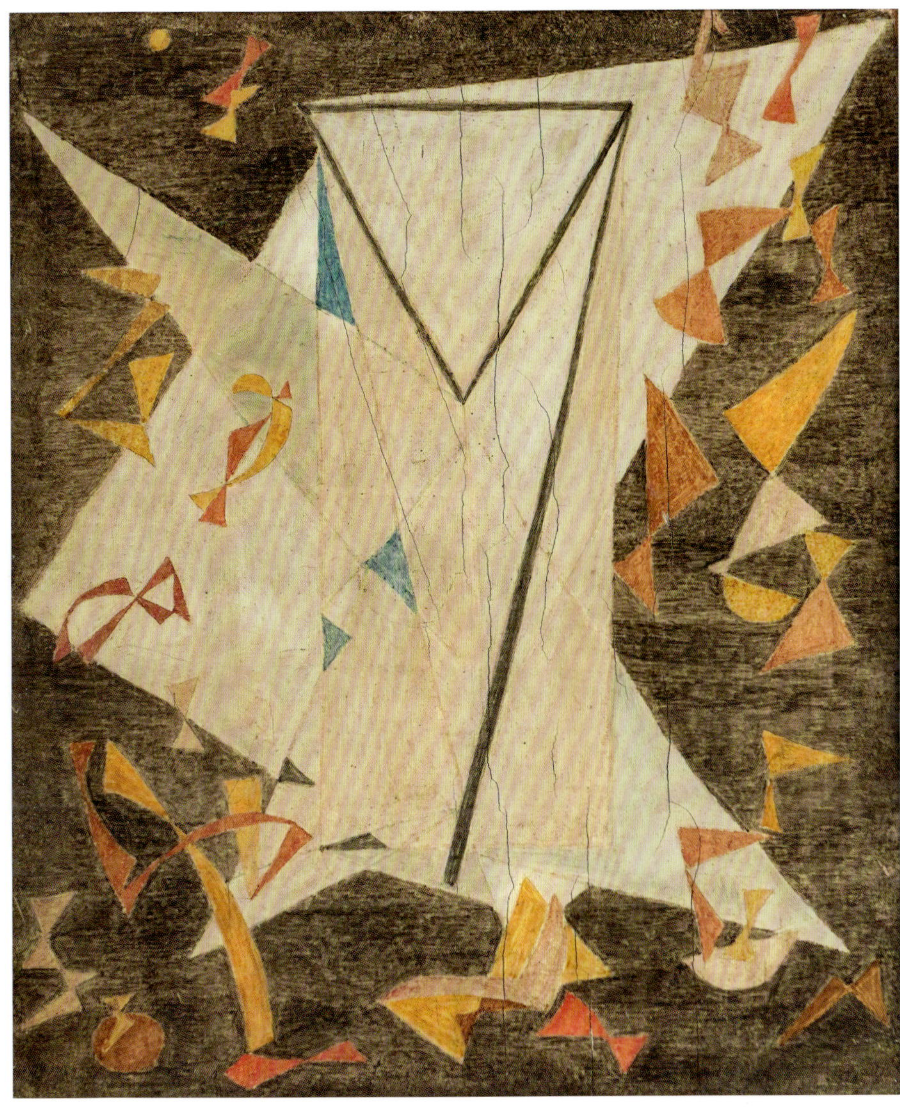

Stefan Gierowski
Falling Down, 1948
Tempera on board
41 x 34.5 cm

In 1957, Stefan Gierowski started making *Paintings* numbered with successive Roman numerals. The artist was thirty-two at the time. Today, the number of *Paintings* approaches one thousand.

This oeuvre represents not so much Gierowski's life project as a painting project based on a sense that the work can go beyond the artist and connect with the universal dimension, still without ceasing to be a personal statement. The *Paintings* are non-representational, but that does not mean they are devoid of a subject, topic, or issue. The universal issue Gierowski explores in and through his practice is the visuality of the human experience of the world. In the thousand *Paintings*, he ponders on it from a thousand different perspectives. It is also the issue of painting as one of the two keys that open the way to the very essence of the notion of visuality. One is science, which answers the question of visuality on the theoretical level; the artist does not ignore the science discourse in his practice, but ultimately leaves this key for scholars to use. The other is painting, the practical answer to the visuality question. This is the key Gierowski uses.

Gierowski's work is rooted in multiple discourses. It is a voice in the discussion, continuing well after 1945, on the essence of painting and the definition of abstraction. In the 2019 exhibition *Deep Impact* and its catalogue, Michel Gauthier of Centre Pompidou draws a convincing parallel between Gierowski's painting from the 1960s and the concurrent practices of the Zero group artists.[1] The way Gierowski's work resonates and corresponds with American painting – particularly Color Field painting – and with the painterly experiments of Mark Rothko is a subject worthy of a detailed investigation, one analogous to that carried out in *Deep Impact*. At the same time, Gierowski's painting is a practice informed by art history construed as far longer (in the chronological sense) and broader (in the sense of artistic topography) than the place and time in which he defined the key principles of his artistic philosophy. Pursuing a project of universalistic ambitions, Gierowski took into account benchmarks as diverse as nineteenth-century avant-garde art, Impressionism, Oriental painting, Orthodox religious painting, and unprofessional, outsider art. A universalistic project of this scale can hardly be imagined without learning the lessons of fifteenth- to seventeenth-century

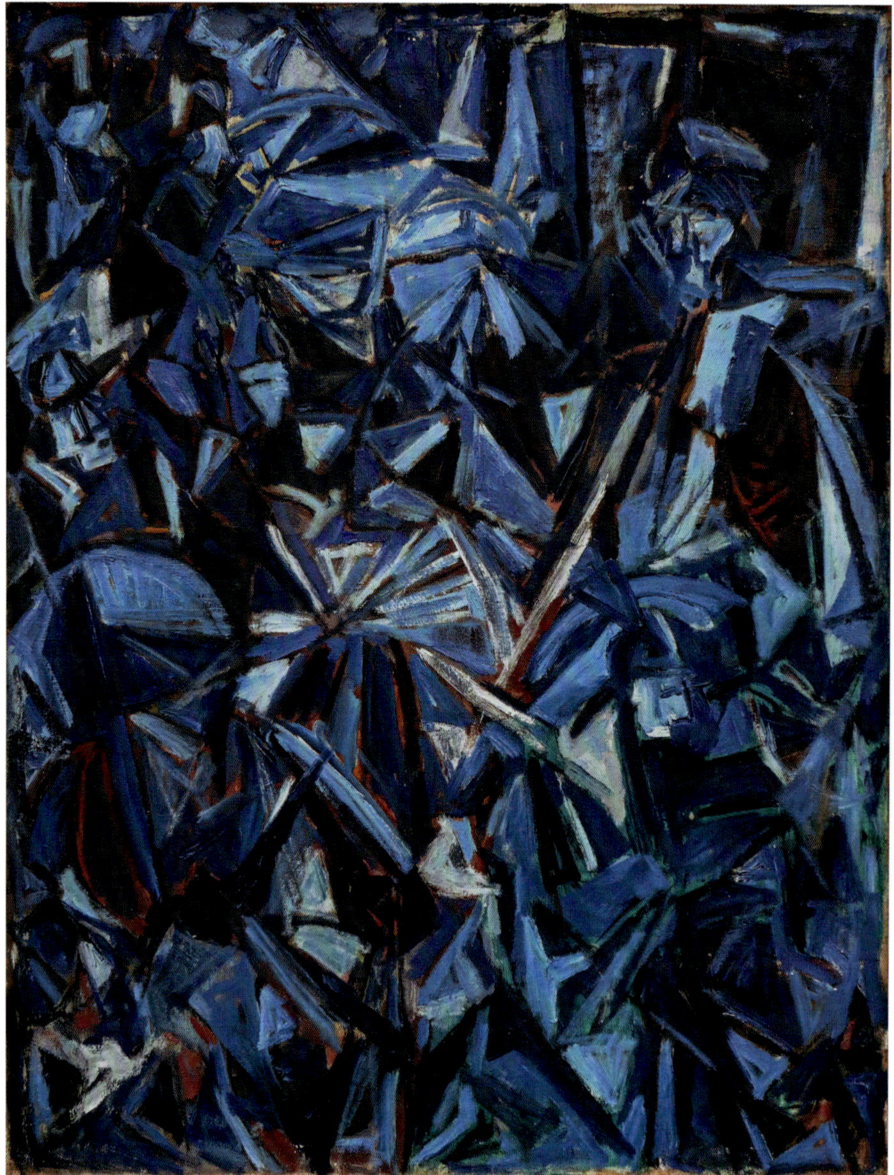

Stefan Gierowski
Trojan War, 1948–49
Oil on canvas
88 x 68.5 cm

European old masters: conclusions from their study are also embedded in Gierowski's work.

While thinking of the universal contexts in which Gierowski's artistic attitude matured and crystallised, we must not lose sight of its local components and circumstances. An heir to various painting traditions who has decided to invest this legacy in the construction of a synthesis, as it were, in his own version of the project of universal painting, Gierowski is not only a "citizen of the painting world" but also an artist from Poland, from Eastern Europe, a painter who began his career at the end of the Second World War, on the ruins of the old geopolitical order and on the threshold of a new one. Before he had a chance to make any advances on this path, he found himself on what for the West was the "other" side of the Iron Curtain. This means the context of the communist regime, its evolution, and the meanderings of its cultural policy, organized by a cycle of alternating periods of "screw-tightening" and "thaw" – that is, heightened oppression and relative liberalisation. Reflected in this cyclicality is the authoritarian system's ambivalent attitude to modern and experimental art, which could be banned, or allowed under certain conditions, or enthusiastically embraced, only to be proscribed again.

Therefore, Gierowski's work stems from roots firmly planted in specific circumstances: artistic, historical, and geopolitical. At the turn of the 1960s, his painting breaks away from those roots. Since then, Gierowski has been working beyond the context of politics and history, writing his own story, measured out by the successive *Paintings*. This declaration of autonomy applies to art history too: over the recent decades, Gierowski has been an observer of its development rather than an actor in it. Since the early 1960s, he has abstained from coordinating the vectors of his investigations with the shifts and turns of the art discourse. He neither affirms nor argues with the successive generations of painters. He does not react when the death of painting is announced time and again, nor when in the 1980s the trans-avant-garde generation and the Neue Wilde enthusiastically re-embrace the medium. He neither spars with the conceptualists or the neo-avant-garde, nor joins the latter. He adopts no painterly stance towards Post-Modernism. This does not mean that he turns his back on the changing world or on art, quite the opposite: Gierowski is an im-

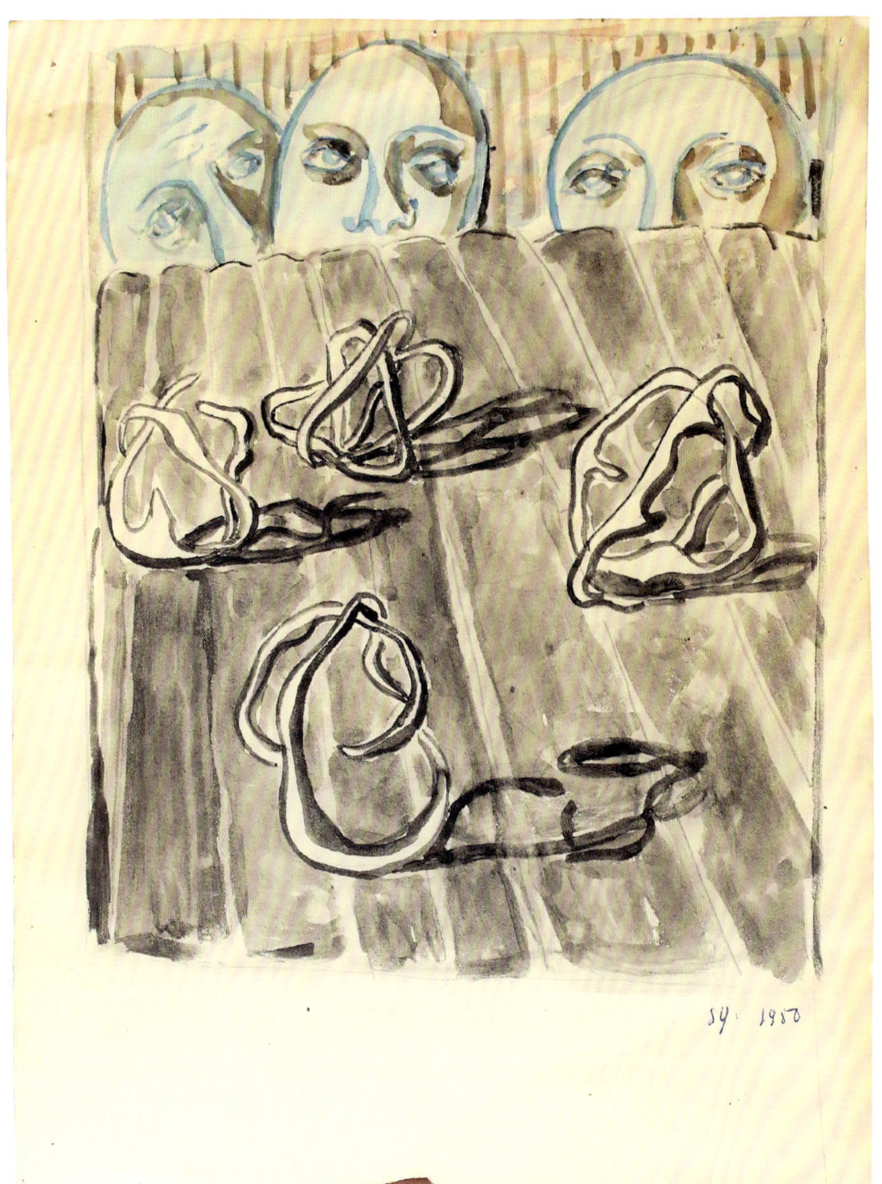

Stefan Gierowski
Untitled, 1950
Watercolour on paper
35.5 x 26.9 cm

portant public figure, an eminent academic, an active participant and organiser of artistic life, a lecturer and professor who educates in his class successive generations of artists, many of whom are classic figures in Polish painting, the most outstanding individualities of different generations. Gierowski also remains an attentive and critical observer of art.

As a painter, however, he is preoccupied with matters other than the latest trends. His main reference point is not so much art as a public discourse, a sequence of formal transitions, or an institution of social life, as painting itself, its profound grammar, its ontology, and its ability to dialogue with the world seen as a set of infinitely diverse visual events.

In other words, Gierowski at some point relocates his work beyond the flow of art-historical time. Since the turn of the 1960s, his art has been unfolding not so much in time as in space: each successive *Painting* is a broadening of the field of vision, of the sum total of the artist's visual experiences and reflections.

Situated beyond time, Gierowski's painting takes place between light and darkness, black and white. The question of what is between these extremes, and of their very nature, is a fundamental one for Gierowski, his art being based on the distinction between the invisibility of time and the visibility of space.

But before Gierowski marks that distinction by commencing work on the *Paintings*, he remains immersed in a reality that is defined by a quintessentially temporal category: modernity. The word denotes a distinct way of experiencing, organising, and conceptualising time. Let us therefore take a look at Stefan Gierowski's modernity.

Modernity

What was the modernity that Stefan Gierowski came face to face with as a young artist?

The year is 1945, Gierowski is twenty and enrols in the art history course at Jagiellonian University and, at the same time, at the Kraków Academy of Fine Arts.

The country is Poland, amid the wreckage and devastation of the old order, which lies in ruin both literally and symbolically.

Construed in Hegelian terms, history manifests itself at the time as an overwhelming causative power, a mill that grinds both individual and collective existences. War, occupation, genocides, Shoah, deportations, redefinition of social hierarchies, radical political and economic transformations: these are the means deployed by history in those days. Gierowski is one of its protagonists: together with his entire generation, he is immersed as deeply in it as anyone could ever be. He comes from a bourgeois family with roots in the landed gentry and attached to patriotic traditions. His ancestors too were active agents of history, which in Poland more often than not meant the history of the struggle for national emancipation and the re-establishment of a Polish nation-state, which had collapsed in the late eighteenth century, on the eve of modernity. Gierowski's forebears can be found among the participants of most Polish independence struggles, from the Napoleonic wars, through the nineteenth-century uprisings, to the fronts of the Great War as well as the war that the recently reborn Polish state fought against Soviet Russia in 1920.

This patriotic family has an appreciation for the arts. Some of Stefan Gierowski's ancestors were artists, and his father, a doctor by profession, paints as a hobby and collects paintings. Stefan decides to become an artist even before the war. During the occupation, as a teenager, he joins the armed resistance but continues his artistic education in clandestine courses. Under the Nazi German rules, Poles are not allowed to study art – or any other discipline, for that matter.

After the war, Gierowski enters art school straight from the armed resistance. The ruined world in which he embarks on his artistic path begs to be rebuilt. Will it be a reconstruction and continuation of modernity in its pre-war version or a radical transformation? Liberated by the Red Army from German occupation, Poland finds itself in the Soviet zone of influence and is brought back from ruin as a satellite state of the communist empire. Modernisation is one of the new regime's mainstays, but the concept is identified with a revolution decreed and implemented from the top down, regardless of social dynamics. In the political sense, the government is totalitarian. These processes directly impact the artistic reality. During Gierowski's studies, the pre-war avant-garde and modernist communities organise anew, working to develop and transcend practices begun back in the old world, but now in the light of Adorno's fundamental question: how to write poetry after Auschwitz? Pre-war artists are joined by modern art makers. The revival and

updating of modern art discourse find expression in the 1st Exhibition of Modern Art, staged in 1948 in Kraków.

In the same year, Gierowski completes his studies. He does not participate in the exhibition, which will soon prove to have been the last show in a spirit of modernity for the next few years. In 1949, the cultural authorities decree Socialist Realism as the sole officially sanctioned artistic doctrine, greatly curbing the scope of artistic licence tolerated in the public sphere and effectively expelling modern art from it. Socialist Realism not only seeks to squeeze art into a narrow ideological framework, but also imposes draconian formal rigours on artists. In practice, it means a forced return to times from before the modernist revolution – to nineteenth-century academism, now additionally harnessed in the service of political propaganda.

Objectively speaking, Socialist Realism was a relatively brief episode in Polish art history, coinciding with the Stalinist period in political life. Soon after the death of the Soviet dictator, cultural policy began to be liberalised. By 1955, Modernism, in all its hues, was no longer considered "degenerate art",[2] so modern art was possible again, and by 1956 it had been ultimately rehabilitated. Though brief in duration, Socialist Realism nevertheless left a profound impact on the Polish art world's consciousness and collective psyche. As Piotr Piotrowski writes in *Meanings of Modernism*, Socialist Realism was "a great swindle . . . Its fault was that it offered ideology in lieu of art, and Party policy in lieu of the artist's psychology; it therefore re-established not so much the picture as its substitute".[3] Art's politically decreed mendacity and its total instrumentalisation, as well as the replacement of critical discourse within a system of police reprisals against non-conformers, forced Polish artists to make dramatic existential and ethical choices. Some, like Tadeusz Kantor, chose to wait out Socialist Realism in artistic silence. Others embraced the new doctrine, but unless they were opportunists and cynics, this meant renouncing themselves, which led to disappointments and frustrations. The tragic lot of Andrzej Wróblewski, one of the most outstanding Polish painters of the post-war years, is an example of such a fateful implication in history. Still others, like the future star avant-gardist Wojciech Fangor, tried as well as they could to play a dou-

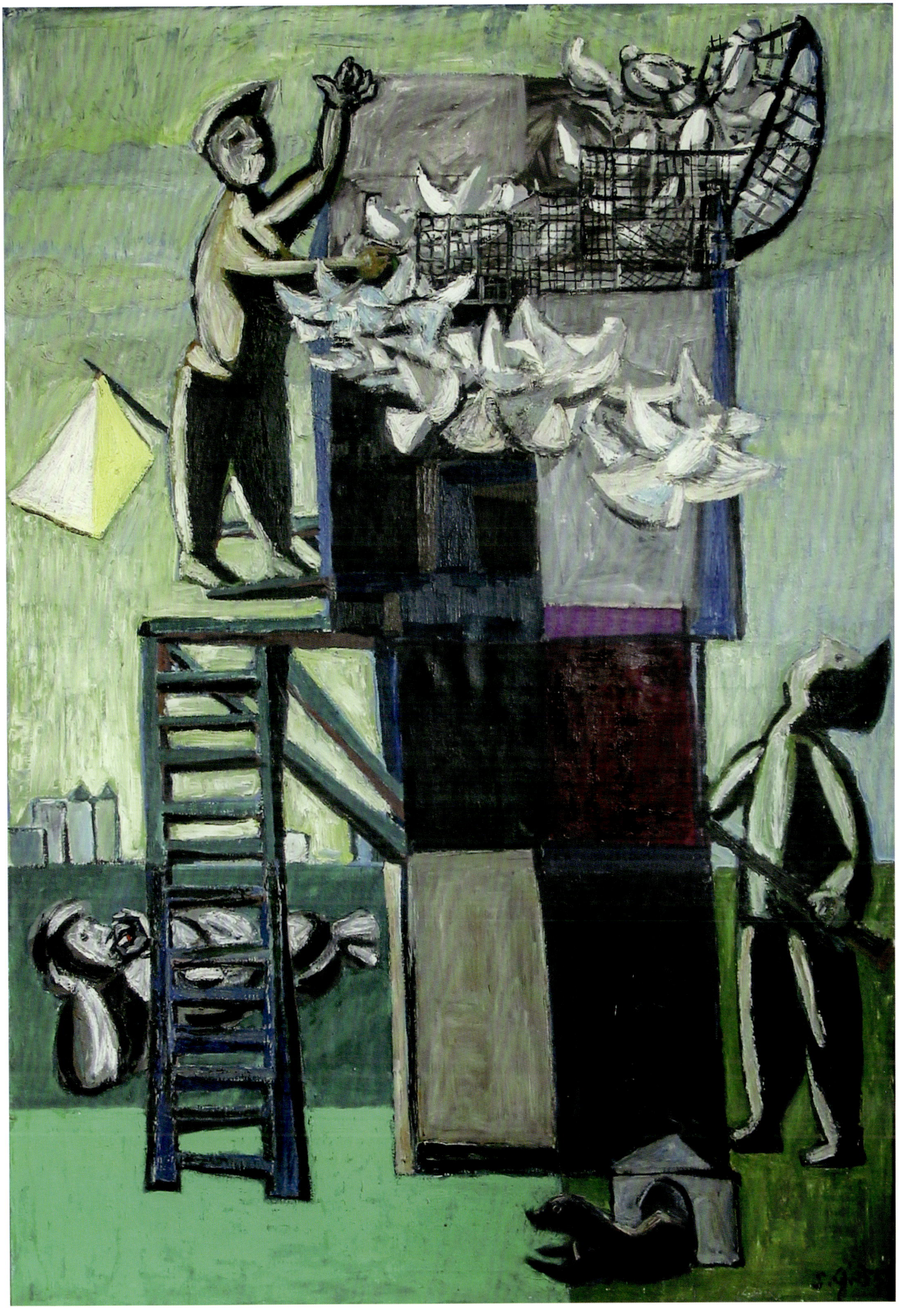

Stefan Gierowski
I Love Life, 1955
Oil on canvas
130 x 160 cm

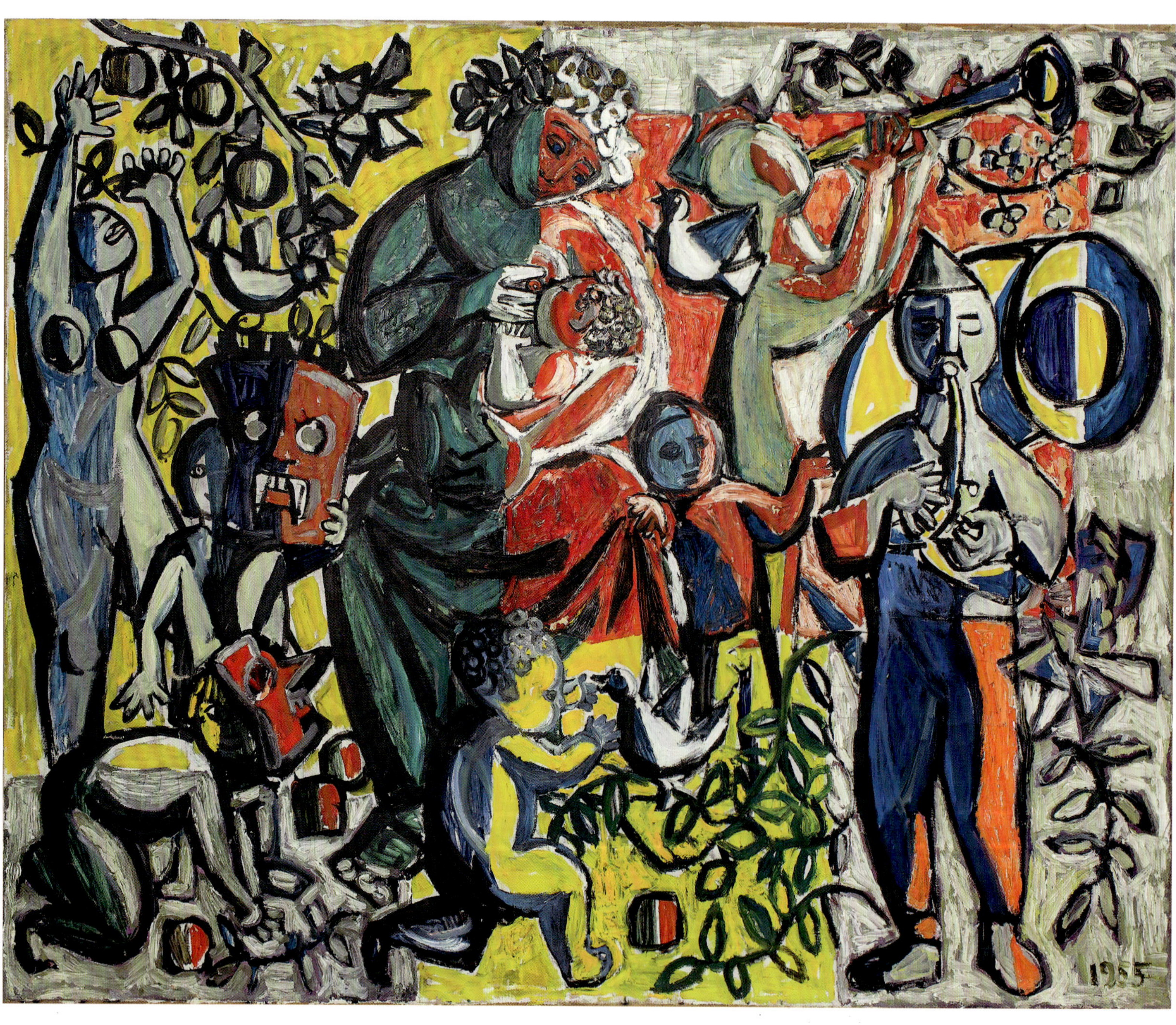

ble game, formally sticking to the Party line but challenging it in private.

With the art scene paralysed by the deadness of propagandistic visuality, Stefan Gierowski spends the socialist realist period at its fringes, working as a technical and artistic editor for periodicals and publishers. The public at large becomes familiar with him only during the "thaw", as the post-Stalinist period of liberalisation was branded in Poland. In art, the thaw brought about an eruption of hitherto stifled modernity. Gierowski was part of that revival. In 1955, he participates in the Nationwide Exhibition of Young Visual Artists *Against War – Against Fascism*, also known, from the name of its venue, as the "Arsenal Show". Polish art history recognises it as a watershed event, the symbolic end of Socialist Realism and an outspoken manifestation of modernity. But how exactly was this modernity construed?

Piotr Piotrowski suggests we look at modernity as an attempt to see the real picture, which in European culture is obscured by pictorial conventions. The modern artist rejects them and "produces autonomous visual matter, in which subject and form are not disjunct".[4] Immediately after 1945, the idea of rejecting entrenched formulas, which was foundational for modernist thought from the very outset, took on an additional meaning because conventions, and past culture in general, had lost credibility in the face of the atrocities of the Second World War. A sense of distrust in the existing legacy informed such post-war trends as Tachisme, Arte Povera, matter painting, non-professional art, and the art of children and the mentally ill. With Western civilisation – which not only had failed to prevent the gas chambers but had actually built them – lying in shambles, not only tradition was mistrusted (not excluding the admittedly quite recent pre-war modernist traditions) but even the very concept of form itself. The devastation wrought by the war, including on the symbolic level, meant that culture had not only to be rebuilt, but pretty much reinvented. It was for a reason that in the first post-war years this update of modernity was often sought beyond form: in gesture, in intuition, in the materiality of the medium.

Modern art was traumatised after the war. In Poland, modern artists were returning from hiatus in 1955 with an experience of a double trauma: the still-vivid memory of wartime horror on the one hand, and on the other the experience of Socialist Realism, a compulsory dissociation from an artistic past identified with Modernism. As a result, the main thing Polish modernists sought after 1955 was to regain artistic subjectivity. Establishing the autonomy of art, so brutally violated by the Stalinists, was almost equally important. Also the very notion of form was rehabilitated. The guardians of socialist realist doctrine had condemned the "formalism" of avant-garde art; so, in a reaction to the politicisation of formal experiments by the regime, artists saw precisely in them an area of freedom. The art of the Arsenal Show generation is a case in point. Some of that exhibition's participants presented work that dealt with wartime traumas (which under Stalinism was not allowed, since trauma was seen as defeatist and bourgeois: a totally inappropriate subject for a socialist realist artist to express). Others pursued purely formal investigations. Both strategies had their political dimension and met in the celebration of the artistic subject's independence.

Gierowski has more in common with the representatives of the latter attitude; one would search in vain for war themes in his post-1945 work. Back in the early 1950s, the artist experiments with near-abstraction, usually in watercolours, but these works are unexhibitable at the time. If he paints figuratively, then, as the post-impressionists once did, he usually chooses neutral, conventional themes, so that the narrative content of the picture does not obscure the painterly issues it takes up. He works through the lessons of the Italian and Polish futurists, explores the possibilities offered by Cubism, studies Picasso, Matisse, and, particularly, Léger, whose influence can be discerned in such works from the Arsenal period as *Pigeonhouse* (p. 11) or *I Love Life* (p. 12), which brought Gierowski prizes and critical recognition.

Two years later, in the Exhibition of Modern Art at the Zachęta gallery in Warsaw, the first numbered *Paintings* appear. Gierowski ultimately abandons figuration: he no longer needs it in the construction of his own painting reality. "From then on I went only inwards, deeper and deeper into myself, which means that I'm actually terribly conservative, towards myself at least", he remembered ironically in an interview many years later.[5]

The paradigm of artistic modernity arose as a vehicle for breaking away from tradition. Modernity places the image of perfection on the horizon of the future: the most perfect paintings are not those by the old masters, but those yet to be painted. In post-war Poland, modernity was a philosophy that allowed one to free oneself from the burden of national painting, from historicism and symbolism, from art formulas entrapping the artist in a web of political and narrative duties. A work produced by an artist so constrained becomes invisible, or rather transparent, revealing only the content it mediates. The problem with Socialist Realism is basically of the same nature, with the only difference that under the socialist realist doctrine, in keeping with the spirit of Stalinism, the issue of art's duties towards political orthodoxy was radically brutalised. In this context, one can hardly overestimate the emancipatory power of abstraction at that time. By the late 1950s, it had become virtually synonymous with progress and liberty in art.

Gierowski also heads in that direction, but always remains wary of the term "abstraction", favouring "non-representational painting" instead. Even then he was sceptical of the notion of progress in art. "There is no progress", he once told me, "Picasso isn't better than the masters of Romanesque art or Chinese art makers over the centuries. Art expands rather than progressing. It expands in our imagination".[6]

For Gierowski's generation, modernity was a discourse of artistic emancipation from an art world frozen in petrified conventions of the past. To an even greater degree, it meant liberating artistic practice from the power of discourses that, like Socialist Realism or national tradition, sought to weaponise art and subjugate its protagonists. In the first decades of the twentieth century, the polemic with tradition was crucial for the philosophy of Modernism: a dispute sometimes verging on iconoclasm and futuristic calls for museums to be burned, for the burden of the past to be shed ultimately and irreversibly. In post-war Poland, especially after the experience of Socialist Realism, what mattered most was participation in modernity, construed as the constitution of an individual, autonomous subjectivity. In the shadow of an authoritarian political order, Clement Greenberg's notion of the autonomy of modernist art assumed additional meaning. With the end of the Stalinist period, a system of penalties and compulsions was replaced with one of "panoptical supervision", to describe the situation of Polish artists after 1956 in Foucauldian terms.

Modernity, with the emancipation of the creative subject that came with it, was acceptable again, but the art community did not forget that it could be banned again by the authorities at any moment. In this context, the practice of the autonomy of art, and abstraction in particular, had a political dimension. Rather than freedom to articulate political positions, though, it was about freedom *from* politics.

To understand Stefan Gierowski's relation with the paradigm of modernity, it is important to distinguish between the concepts of pictorial convention and painting tradition. The modern artist freed himself from existing conventions of depiction, but not in order to reject with them the legacy of the past. Quite the opposite: the purpose was to resurrect the tradition and contemporaneity of painting now that they were freed from convention, to relive them anew, on one's own terms, and to involve them in a relation with the visuality of reality. In Gierowski's case, the parting with figuration did not serve to severe the ties connecting the picture with the outside world. To the contrary, the artist planned precisely to get closer to the world through non-representational painting. "I wanted to get away from nature, to break away from figurativeness", the painter says of those decisions. "Once I did, I felt more confident . . . It was an emotional rather than intellectual choice, driven by a sense that painting is autonomous and free from any constraints or obligations".[7]

In a 1968 essay, "Painting i.e. Painting",[8] Jerzy Stajuda tries to locate the place Stefan Gierowski occupies in the landscape of 1960s Polish art. To his eyes, this is a landscape that on the one hand is shaken by debates about the value of new artistic formulas streaming in from the West and, on the other, divided between "left" and "right". The "left" is of course the progressives, experimenting with increasingly open, often performative art forms, challenging ever more boldly the status of the artwork, and revolving ever more closely around the concept of anti-art. The "right" is modern too, but conservative in the sense of not entirely dissociating itself from what Stajuda terms the "Mediterranean Tradition". The author discusses the critics' difficulties applying the "left" vs "right" categorization to Gierowski. His faith in painting, the picture, and the work should situate him on the right, but Gierowski does not really fit there: his proposition is too radical. The point

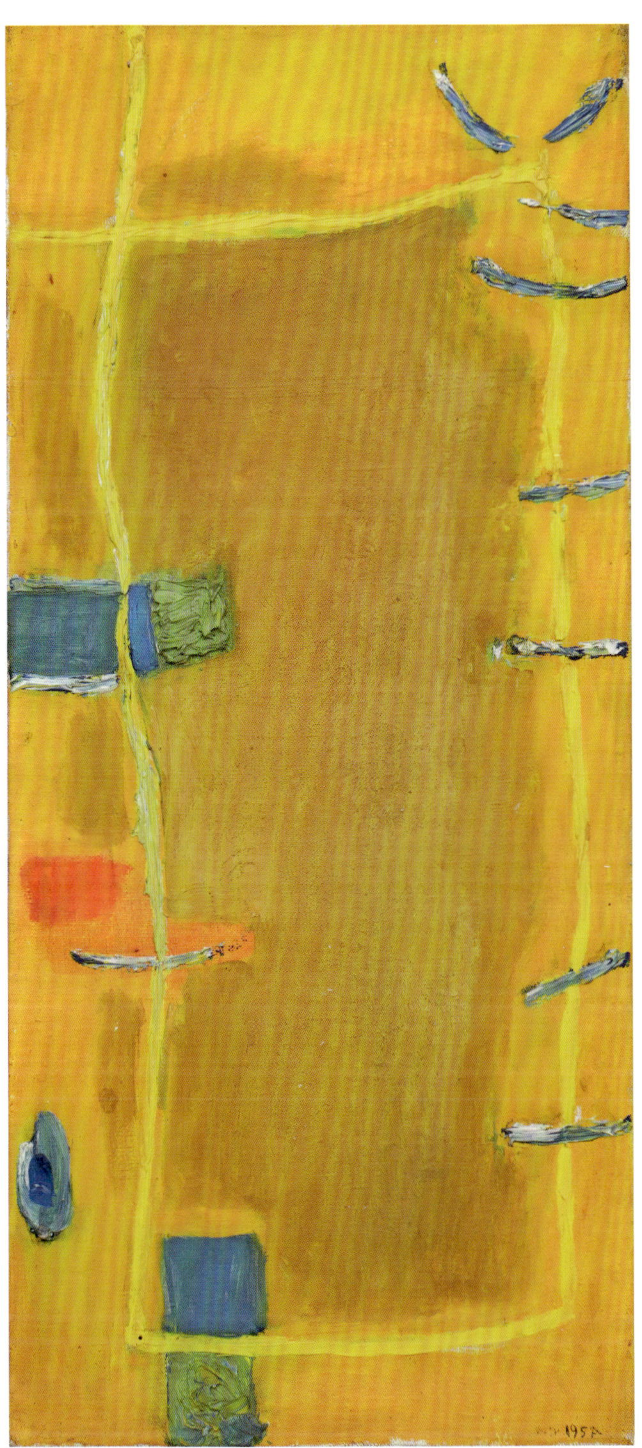

is that he evades the dialectics of the artistic right and left and instead opts for a third path, leading towards what Stajuda calls the "Great Strategy". Gierowski has on many occasions stressed the primal nature of painting and its irremovability from the horizon of human experience. He could deal with this or that topic, but not with the issue of the very matter and ontology of the picture, which is a reflection – a model – of the matter and ontology of the world. Such an issue is one to be pursued throughout one's lifetime. And that is precisely what Gierowski does.

Sky-Line

Gierowski's art is not organized by time, by the successive periods and stages of his investigations, but by the issues he concerns himself with, and which he has been returning to in ever new ways over the course of the last six decades.

One of these issues is the notion of space, which in Gierowski's art does not refer to a specific place. For him, space has no boundaries – it is tantamount to the notion of the universe. We are speaking here about the pictorial space as an event rooted in reality and nature and, at the same time, parallel and equal to it. In other words, Gierowski's ultimate objective is to produce *Paintings* the space of which will be governed by the same laws that organise the space of the universe.

"I've always been interested in the notion of space as something inexpressible yet omnipresent in our existence", the artist says, adding that he is reluctant to use the term because it has been abused in contemporary discourse, losing its semantic potency as a result: "Everybody talks about space these days", he notes.

Like the universe itself, space is for him a realm of thoughts. To see, let alone depict, space, it is necessary to think it. Thought or, more precisely, the relation between thinking, seeing, and visuality is one of the fundamental categories on which Gierowski's painting is based. At the same time, it is a category he transcends with painterly means. The space he establishes is not confined to the picture plane, nor is it identical with the surface of the canvas, but organised by painterly "light", which is a dialectic of its presence and absence. As Maria Olejarnik writes, it is "a space that goes deep into the picture, infinite, one that brings to mind outer space".[9]

When Gierowski was formulating his painting programme, the theory and practice of Władysław Strzemiński, who had worked with El Lissitzky and Rodchenko, remained the most influential statement on pictorial space ever put forward in the context of Polish art. After his return to Poland in 1922, Strzemiński animated the avant-garde movement while developing the concept of Unism, a programme of radical autonomy for painting. Gierowski met Strzemiński personally in 1949 and later took part in debates about his legacy, something that erupted with renewed strength once Stalinism came to an end. He worked through the lesson of Strzemiński (author of *Theory of Vision*) and, *pars pro toto*, of the constructivist avant-garde. He agreed with Strzemiński that the picture was a constructed event. He distanced himself from Art Informel, the lively trend of abstract painting that in the late 1950s was quickly gaining more and more adherents among Polish artists. Unlike Strzemiński, however, who postulated eliminating any and all tensions or contrasts, and therefore emotion, from the space of the autonomous picture, Gierowski firmly believed that the formal construction and intellectual dimension of painting not only did not preclude emotion, but actually formed a frame in which it could and indeed should occur. Gierowski searched for ways to visualise an expanded space, one stretching beyond the surface and confines of the picture – an infinite space. In this sense, his investigations and the cosmic quality of the spaces he produces seem to bear a far greater affinity with the work of Mark Rothko than with that of Władysław Strzemiński.

Almost from the very beginning of the *Paintings*, their space featured the line, and soon entire constellations of lines. For the artist, the line is an element introduced to disrupt space. The line is a ray of light, a diagram of forces and tensions, a record of life flowing through the picture, an event occurring in painterly space. "I was particularly intrigued by its latent dynamics and ambiguity", the artist wrote about the line, "for it is at the same time a concrete, geometric, physical set of points and a symbol of metaphysical striving. On the canvas it is a disturbance of stable space, a division, a trace of a point in motion, a token of a wave or light, a flight and a striving, a weak reflection of what cannot be seen, as if the meaning of [my] line were suspended between a graph and metaphysical infinity".[10]

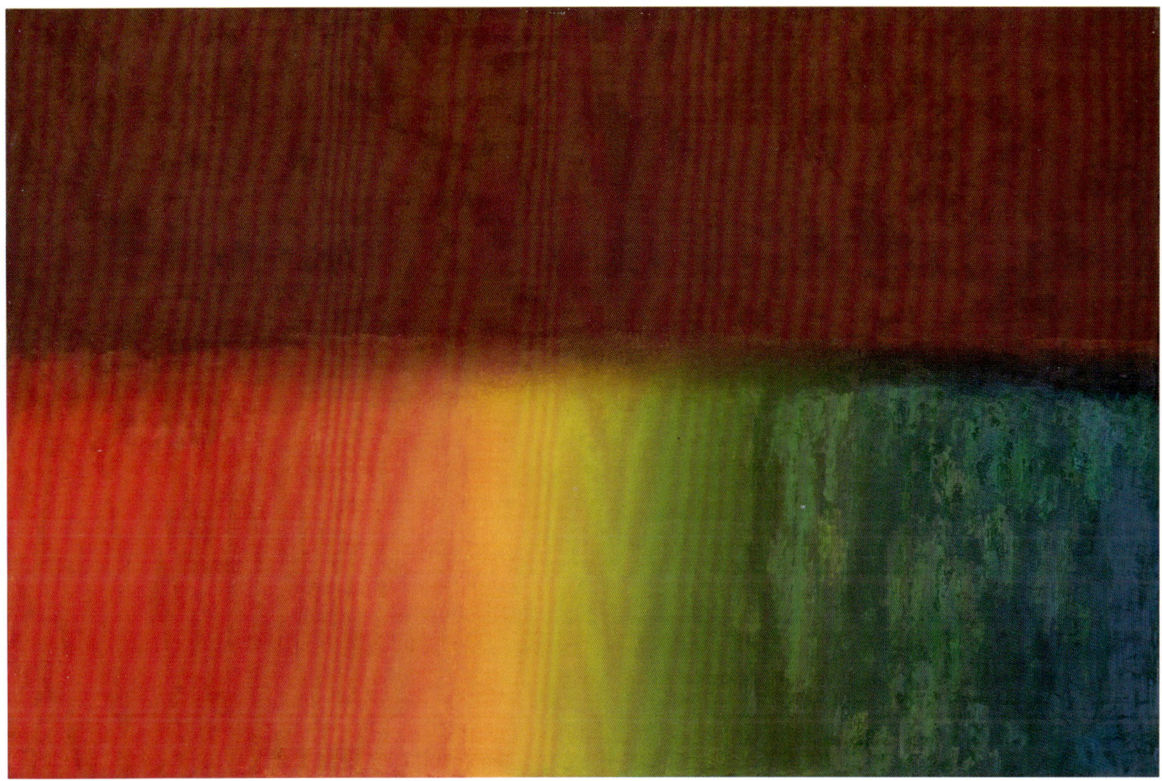

Light and Colour

The light reflected from the picture manifests itself through colour, and colour has defined painterliness as long as the discipline has existed. Like other late-modern artists, Gierowski faced the question of how to deepen his understanding of this fundamental painting category. Having become interested in the problematics of colour during his studies, his seminar essay in art history, which he studied concurrently with painting, was devoted to Impressionism. For modern painting, Impressionism was an initiation into a realism of looking which the modernists would soon begin to prefer over the ostensible realism of illusionism and representation. Moreover, Impressionism marked a milestone on the path towards the emancipation of colour in painting. Gierowski too drew conclusions from his study of the movement: "I realized", he recalls, "that neither subject matter nor figuration are as important as the picture itself, a way of seeing, something more primal and basic".[11]

Gierowski worked to develop an understanding of the nature of light as matter and, at the same time, as a theme manifested in painting through colour. Historical art provided vital clues in these investigations, to which

Strzemiński's words could be applied: "Contemporary art should be made on the basis of all previous efforts, but its beginning is at the end of all that has been created so far".[12] It is at this point that there begins for Gierowski the work on transcending "all previous efforts" in the direction of experience and emotion.

Gierowski's art is a chronicle of experiments with colour, a history of casting it in ever new roles. Sometimes, colour participates in dramatic encounters with other colours resulting in daring or truly extreme contrasts, or, conversely, producing harmonious effects. At other times, it is combined with other colours into a vibrant space reminiscent of Pointillisme. Gierowski limits one colour with other ones, or instead has it "go beyond" the frame and surface of the picture. Abstracted from the object, colour is for Gierowski a thing unto itself. His *Paintings* arrange themselves into an encyclopaedia of possibilities of the existence, perception, and "behaviour" of colour. It is of course an incomplete encyclopaedia, because the subject is inexhaustible: every colour, Gierowski says, has its own space which is infinite in itself. Still, few painters have asked so many questions of colour as he has, and come up with so many extraordinary painterly an-

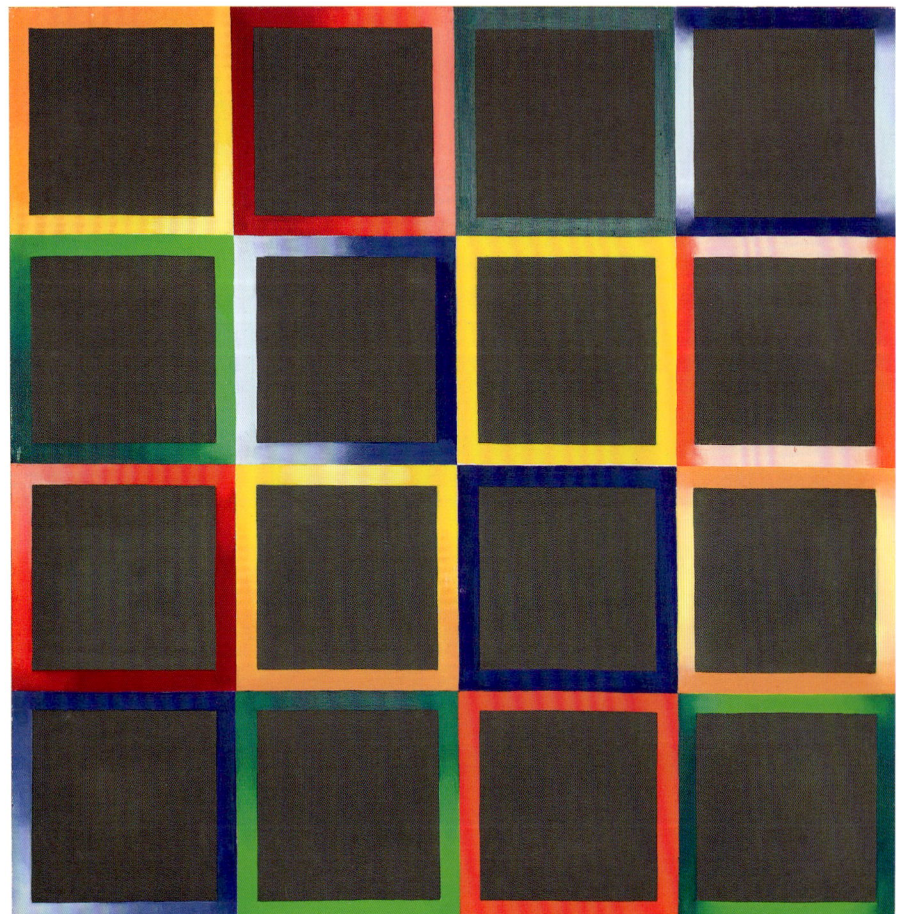

swers to them. Extraordinary as well as full of emotions, for Gierowski believes that without colours painting could hardly be thought, let alone experienced. In his art, colour is what transcends the construction of the picture and conveys emotions; but it serves not so much to express the artist's feelings as to evoke feelings in the viewer.

Earth: Divisions

"It's hard to speak of the universe and forget that you're standing on earth", Gierowski says. "What relates to earth is a bit different from what relates to the universe. What's in the universe belongs to the mind. What's on the earth is seen: fields, divisions, tensions, distances, depending on the intensity of light."

In the late 1950s, some critics drew parallels between Gierowski's work and matter painting. In hindsight, this diagnosis seems misleading and an interpretational dead end. Gierowski does not reduce painting to its matter but transcends it, striving towards what could be termed the metaphysical dimension of the picture. It is a movement beyond the painterly object and towards the picture, beyond paint and towards colour, beyond the painting surface and towards space. Its initiation does not mean, however, that the transcended painting dimensions are removed from the field of vision, lose their essentiality. To the contrary, painterly matter remains important, like paint itself. Talking about what has shaped his visual sensibility, Gierowski cites painters whose work he has studied at various stages of his creative practice, evoking figures as diverse from each other and distant in time as Piero della Francesca, Vermeer, Paul Klee, Picasso, and Strzemiński. But he also mentions the Holy Cross Mountains (Góry Świętokrzyskie), one of Europe's geologically oldest mountain ranges, where he grew up. We discuss the region's woods, and the peculiar light of the forest. And hills divided up by the variously coloured geometric figures of fields. He speaks of the way the sky glows right after a storm has passed. Gierowski's art is rooted in concreteness, even if it transcends it: paint is not just a medium for colour in the picture, it's also physical matter, like earth. Gierowski does not try to make paint "transparent", and his paintings are not ethereal, bodiless entities. These are artworks painted by the human hand, the hand of a mundane creature, flesh and blood, and the artist never tries to cover

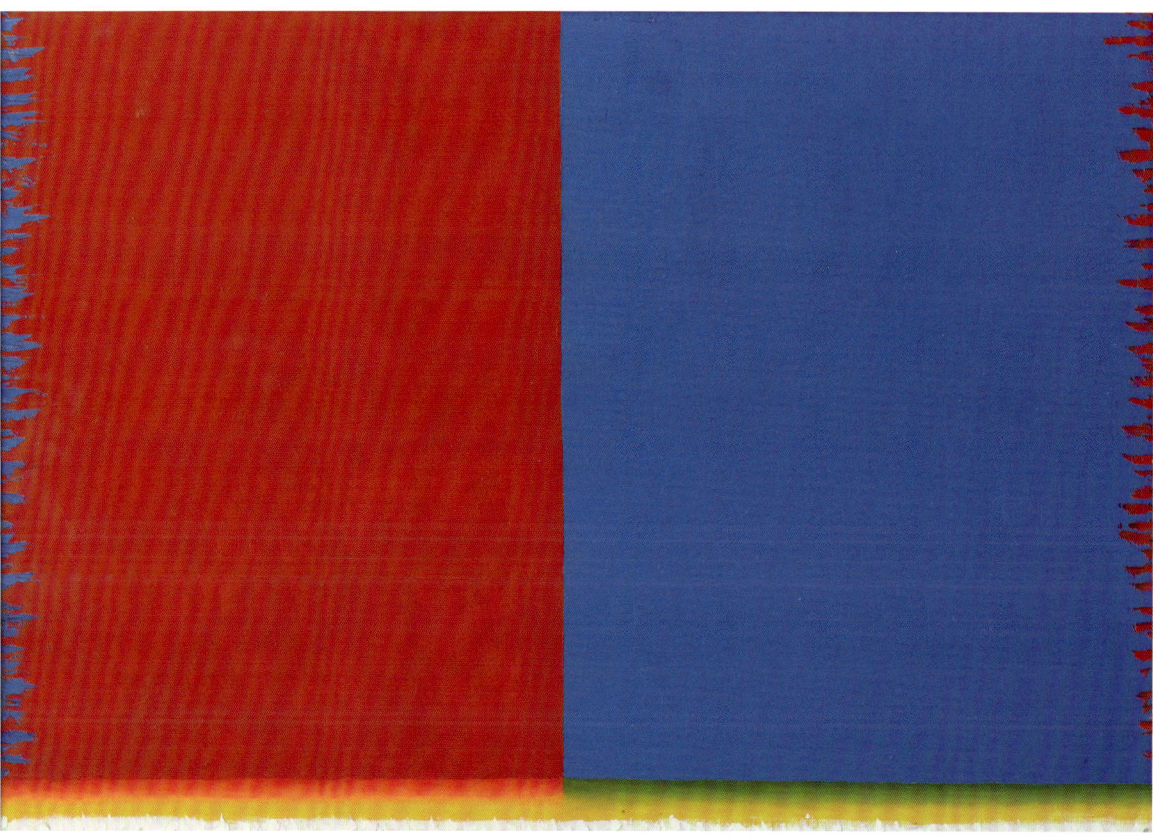

up or erase the trace his hand has left on the surface of the canvas.

Gierowski's oeuvre is an irremovable touchstone in any serious discussion of Polish abstract art. Often called Poland's most famous abstractionist, he says however that the picture is never abstract but always a concreteness. It is only the notions that a well thought-out and emotion-imbued picture evokes in the viewer's mind that can be of an abstract nature.

Gierowski's proposition is painting that realizes its potential for metaphysical speculation, but at the same time is based on facts. It is an art that opens up an insight into the universe, into what is graspable solely with artistic means but is also rooted in real experience, in paint, in the material world with its divisions and structures. Physics is required for metaphysics to arise.

Notions

In the years decisive for the crystallisation of the painting project that Stefan Gierowski has pursued with his *Paintings*, he was associated with Krzywe Koło Gallery run from 1956 by Marian Bogusz, whom he met in 1955 through the painter Marek Włodarski. In the period follow-

ing the Arsenal Show, Krzywe Koło became Poland's leading laboratory of artistic experimentation. An important role was also played by the club affiliated with the gallery, Klub Krzywego Koła, which was a discussion forum for creative intellectuals representing various disciplines. Among other issues, its debates concerned the condition and future of art, abstraction, and the ontology of painting and artwork in general. Gierowski actively participated in developing that discourse.

In subsequent years, after Krzywe Koło's closure, Bogusz, a tireless organiser, gained recognition as the initiator of a series of events that heralded yet another shift in the artistic paradigm. Art events organised or co-organised by Bogusz, such as the Koszalin Retreat in Osieki (1963), the First Biennale of Spatial Forms in Elbląg (1965), and the Wrocław '70 Symposium, were veritable workshops where new conceptual, performative, and post-artistic art forms were hammered out. From these experiments the conceptual and neo-avant-garde movement would sprout, which gained strong traction in Poland during the 1970s.

Gierowski did not sign up for it. During that time, he followed his own path, one that

Stefan Gierowski
Painting DCCXVII, 1997
Oil on canvas
130 x 100 cm

did not fit into the distinction, borrowed from Jerzy Stajuda above, between a neo-avant-garde conceptual "left" and a "right" representing modernity construed more conservatively. The anti-artistic tradition revived in the neo-avant-garde was not so much unfamiliar to Gierowski as useless for the goals he had set out to achieve. But this does not mean that the conceptual aspect of the work does not play any role in his practice. Quite the opposite. It is impossible to fully understand Gierowski's work outside of a dialectic of its emotional and intellectual dimensions. Concept – a category fundamental for conceptual art – is also something important to Gierowski, although in his case it does not lead to a move beyond the artefact, traditional media, or painting itself. Gierowski notes that a basic element of this discipline, colour, is in itself not only a sensation, but also a concept. It was not by accident that at some point he took up an interest in Orthodox Christian art, the practice of icon painting, where every colour is strictly connected with a particular notion and metaphysical concept. "Colours have their conceptual consequences", Gierowski says. Like shape, every colour means something, although, unlike the order of liturgy, the tradition of old art, or synaesthetic systems, Gierowski's visual language has not been permanently codified, and the concepts it entails are subject to constant negotiation between the artist's intention and the viewer's sensibility. A meeting of colours on the canvas surface calls into being the concept of the interaction of things. The light of the picture evokes a concept of the absolute. And the creation itself of the picture establishes a distinction between the concepts of existence and nonexistence.

Beginning and End

Writing about Gierowski, the critic Barbara Majewska suggests that we should see him as a painter who asks the question, Is it possible to paint Nothing?[13] Is it possible, once the object has been eliminated from the pictorial field, to see that which is not? The concept of "nothing" could of course be reversed, and then we would see in Gierowski a painter who endeavours to paint "everything". It is impossible to paint everything, but this impossibility has never been an obstacle for him – rather, it has been one of the driving forces of his work. It has also been a driver of the history of modern art in general, a history that in its striving towards universality is, according to Gierowski, far from complete. Like every absolute category, universality is also an impossibility, but, as Gierowski says, it is precisely on the basis of the impossible that the most interesting constructions are often built.

Gierowski's painting happens therefore in a space with boundaries defined by absolute categories, darkness and light, black and white. A shrewd researcher of colour, Gierowski has devoted a lot of attention to these anti-colours. It is worth remembering here that the nature of black and white in painting is a reverse of their isness as understood in physical terms. Painterly white is the absence of pigments, whereas white light is the sum total of all its spectral colours. Physical black in turn is the absence of light, whereas black in painting contains all other colours. Black, as Gierowski says, seems to "kill" the picture, but that is just an appearance; we should rather speak of black devouring other colours and containing all their potentiality. White can be referred to the concept of death, to nonexistence – and yet it is also a figure of light, which is what makes it possible to notice the existence of being. "They are extreme", the artist says of black and white. "These are the first colours you perceive, and the last ones. Prehistoric painting began with black and white. In these colours is contained all that exists in painting. Black swallows up all colours, white emits them all: they are the mother and father of painting. We keep searching for a oneness of the world, its governing principle, including, or perhaps first of all, through art. And this universal principle does exist: it is contained in the distinction between black and white. They are the same quantity – they are unity."

1 Michel Gauthier, *Deep Impact: Stefan Gierowski and European avant-gardes in the 60s*, exh. cat., Stefan Gierowski Foundation, Warsaw, 14 September – 15 November 2019. Gauthier was the exhibition curator.
2 In Stalinist Poland and other Soviet-bloc countries, the Nazi-coined term "degenerate art" was not in use; instead, there was talk of "formalist deviation", "bourgeois deviation", or cosmopolitanism. These labels were similar in meaning to those the Third Reich employed to condemn modern art. Both totalitarian regimes, Nazi and Stalinist, recognised it as politically unacceptable.
3 Piotr Piotrowski, *Znaczenia modernizmu. W stronę historii sztuki polskiej po 1945 roku* [Meanings of modernism: Towards a history of Polish art after 1945] (Poznań: Rebis, 1999), p. 34.
4 Ibid., p. 12.
5 "Ściany już są. Ze Stefanem Gierowskim rozmawia Jan Michalski" [The walls are already there: Stefan Gierowski talks to Jan Michalski], in *Stefan Gierowski*, exh. cat., Muzeum Górnośląskie, Bytom, 16 April – 14 June 1998 (Bytom: Muzeum Górnośląskie, 1998).
6 Unless otherwise noted, statements by Stefan Gierowski are excerpts from the author's unpublished phone interview with him in August 2020.
7 See "Ściany już są".
8 Jerzy Stajuda, "Malarstwo i.e. malarstwo" [Painting i.e. painting], *Miesięcznik Literacki*, February 1968.
9 Maria Olejarnik, "Malarstwo Stefana Gierowskiego i jego związki z teorią sztuki Władysława Strzemińskiego" [The painting of Stefan Gierowski and its ties with Władysław Strzemiński's theory of art], *ARTykuły*, no. 5–6 (2012).
10 Stefan Gierowski in *Gierowski – linia – dążenie* [Gierowski – line – striving], exh. cat., Andzelm Gallery, Lublin, May 2005 (Ząbki: Apostolicum and Lublin: Andzelm Gallery, 2005), p. 3.
11 See "Ściany już są".
12 Władysław Strzemiński, "B=2", in *Pisma* [Writings], ed. Zofia Baranowicz (Wrocław: Zakład Narodowy im. Ossolińskich, 1975), p. 20.
13 Barbara Majewska, "Pustka Gierowskiego" [Gierowski's void], *Więź* 10 (2010): 120–21.

The Deep Field. Stefan Gierowski and the Colour-Space

Michel Gauthier

Stefan Gierowski
Painting CCLXXIII, 1971
Oil on canvas
67 x 67 cm

It was in 1968, during the preparation of the exhibition to be mounted in the Polish Pavilion at the 34th Venice Biennale,[1] that Stefan Gierowski's painting experienced an important shift that would be confirmed in the following decade. In the 1960s, his work focused on the dynamics of forms where the line, like a beam of light, was one of the main driving forces (a phase in his work to which the Zachęta National Gallery in Warsaw dedicated an exhibition in 1967). The painter was now interested by the ground, against which, in the previous paintings, the line followed its trajectory, or the forms metamorphosed into forces. The form thus tends to become a zone, and the beam of light is morphed into a halo. The circular arcs, some of which recall the cosmic landscapes of works such as *CLXXVI* (1963–64), *CXCIII* (1965) or *CCXXIII* (1967, p. 75), are now on the edges of the pictorial field or even already completely out of view, leaving the gaze to take in chromatic and luminous events only. Of course, the transition from one period to the next is never a clean break and here, the dynamics of forms and chromatic spatiality can indeed coexist. In 1969, Gierowski produced both a nebulous red canvas (*CCXLVI*) and a painting where a red and white curve anchored at the two upper corners, recalling works from a few years earlier, plunges into the gloomy depths of the pictorial field (*CCXLVII*). However, it is much more than an area of overlap between two styles, one fading away and the other emerging. The concomitance of the two approaches must not be interpreted as the sign of indecision: it proves instead that there is not a paradigmatic break in the artist's output, but rather a change in focus within the same paradigm. In 1977, the curve became a "V" and reappeared in *CCCLXXIX*.

Among the fascinating paintings of the transition, *CCXXVI* (p. 107), *CCXXXIII* (p. 81), *CCXXXV* (p. 84) (all 1968), *CCXXXIX* (p. 106) and *CCXLI* (both 1969) must be pointed out. These works give the impression of having enlarged a detail of a previous work. In *CCXXXIII*, the forms suggested by the curves have grown distant from one another, resisting the mutual attraction portrayed in some paintings of the mid-1960s. The segment of circle is so close to the edge of the picture that it can no longer sketch out a form, but rather serves to add tension to the ground. In *CCXXXV*, it is instead the instant of the dynamic encounter of the forms that the enlargement has captured, showing two vertical

Stefan Gierowski
Painting CDLXXV, 1982
Oil on canvas
200 x 135 cm

Stefan Gierowski
Painting CDLXV, 1981
Oil on canvas
100 x 100 cm

areas in different colours separated by a beam of light. With *CCXLV* (1969, p. 109), the transition is nearly complete: there is no longer any line nor any shape, but just the encounter of two zones, a green one in the upper section and a red one in the lower section. However, not all the dynamics have disappeared – the border between the two sections is curved and not flat, and the green area seems to pass beneath the red, scattering corpuscles that almost reach the bottom of the painting. *CCXLVI* (1969) proposes an even tighter framing: everything happens as if only the red zone of the previous canvas had been framed, so to allow a better observation of the play of light as well as the green particles around.

With this change in focus, on the threshold of the 1970s, Gierowski's painting deals with a pictorial field that is no longer a simple ground but a chromatic space in its own right, which, without any form(s) to inhabit it, has a value in itself. So, it is tempting for the art historian to relate this moment in Gierowski's output to the American current of Color Field Painting, as it developed from the work of Barnett Newman, Mark Rothko and Clyfford Still to that of Helen Frankenthaler, Sam Gilliam or Jules Olitski, passing through Morris Louis along the way. Indeed, this painting is characterised by two traits that also belong to the works of Gierowski in question: the tendency of the form to mutate into zone and, later, the questioning of the distinction between this form-become-zone and the ground. In the critical writings and the theories that he advanced about this movement, Clement Greenberg essentially insisted on its anti-illusionist nature. According to him, Color Field Painting embodied the age when painting, which since Manet had progressively freed itself of all conventions not necessary for its viability, came closest to its essence. This painting would consist of formal events that do not create an illusion of depth of the field, but rather exalt its two-dimensional nature. Nothing of the sort can be said about Gierowski, since his painting stands out for its nearly constant pursuit of an effect of depth. Among the many experiments that marked the painter's activity in this period, two main methods emerge: the "Pointillist nebulosity" and the "floating monochrome quadrangle".

Thus, it was as early as 1969, at the heart of the transition period, that the Pointillist solution came to light. As shown by *CCXLV* (p. 109)

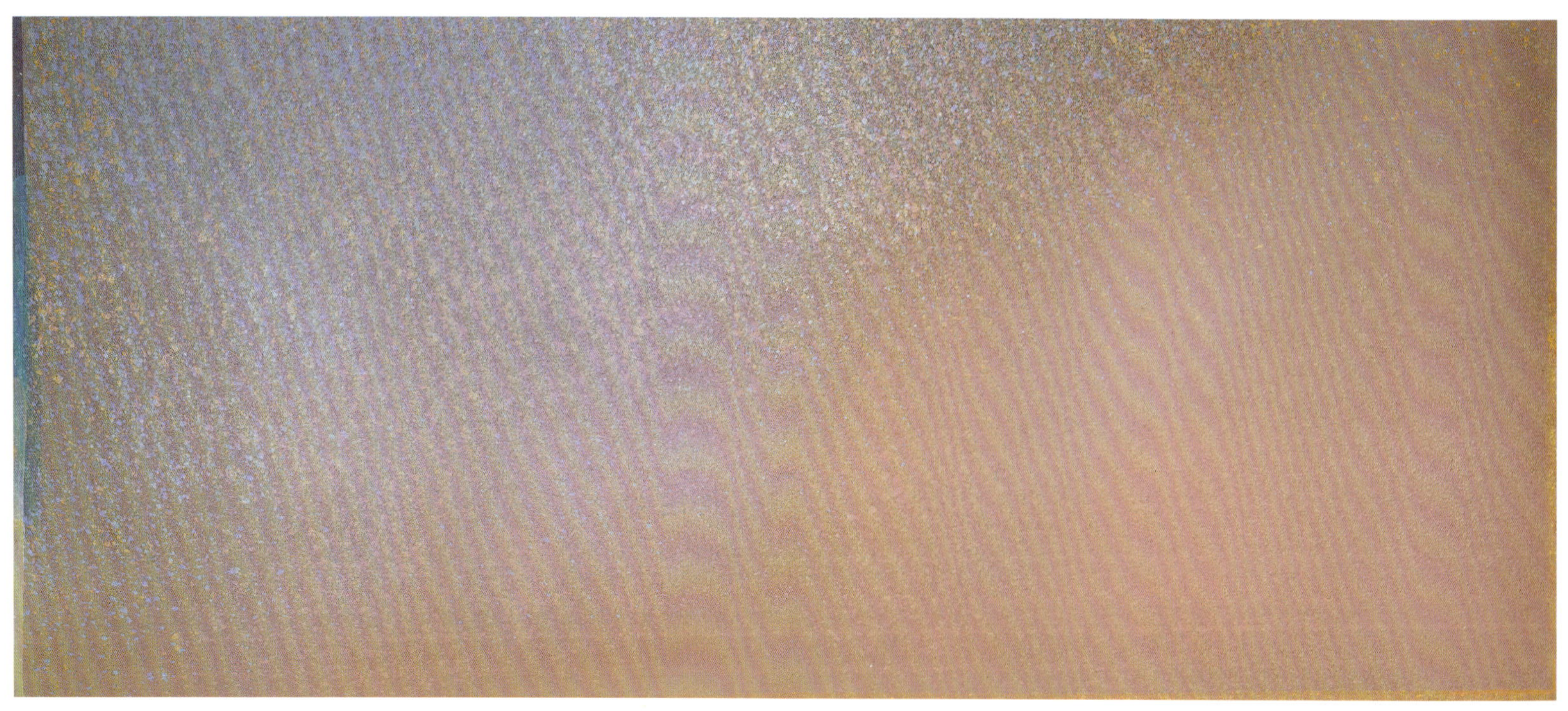

Jules Olitski
(Twice) Disarmed, 1968
Acrylic on canvas
233.7 x 539.9 cm
The Metropolitan Museum
of Art, New York. Gift of
Barbara and Eugene
Schwartz, 1986 (1986.364)

as well as *CCLX* (1970), *CCLXVII* (1971), *CCLIX* (1972), *CCLXXXVIII* and *CCC* (p. 120) (both 1973), the cloud of points is used to ensure the transition from one colour zone to another. Here, the Pointillism is akin to *sfumato*; this is to prevent the pictorial field from appearing as an arrangement of forms, even if they are just simple bands, and instead ensure it is perceived as a pure chromatic space.

Very soon, however, the Pointillist clouds are no longer confined to the border between two coloured bands but invade the entire canvas. This is the case with the blue painting *CCLXXVII* (1970) or the small yellow canvas *CCLXXIII* (1971, p. 23). The irregular density of the dots creates variations in the light and chromatic intensity. In these paintings, the pictorial field no longer functions as a surface, defined by the edges of the canvas. Instead, it appears as a space that, through a microscopic or telescopic lens, acquires the very depth of the light-color being diffused. These paintings should also be seen as a stance with respect to the monochrome. A descendant of the three small canvases that Alexander Rodchenko painted in 1921, the monochrome uniformly covered by a solid layer of paint did not interest Gierowski, since it was self-contained and inert, without the slight illusionism that makes a painted surface also an image. In Gierowski's monochromes – which

are not monochromes at all – the dots, either because of their diverse chromatic values, or because of the range of densities across the areas of the canvas, exclude any effect of flatness. Such paintings testify to a dream of depth that, however, should not be confused with the three-dimensional nature of the object. Rather, it emerges from the "dimensionless" depth of the sky, of the ether. It is, of course, possible to compare such works with the Pointillism that Kuno Gonschior had been practising since 1959,[2] although his paintings are less "atmospheric". This is why it would seem more legitimate to compare Gierowski's dots clouds with the thin layers of colour that Jules Olitski obtained with the spray gun.[3] Paintings such as *CCXLVI*, *CCXLIX* (both 1969), *CCLXXI* (1971), *CCCV* and *CCCXVI* (both 1973) are related to *Instant Loveland*, *(Twice) Disarmed* (both 1968) and *Irkusk IV* (1970).

Sometimes, the dots could be replaced by small bumps lending texture to the pictorial field. The white surface of *CDLXXV* (1982, p. 24) thus acquires relief, tiny plays of light and shade enlivening it. Rather than taking in the monochrome plane as a whole, the eye runs over the surface, skipping from one irregularity to another. This painting style provides proof, if proof were needed, that Gierowski's Pointillism was driven by spatial as well as chromatic

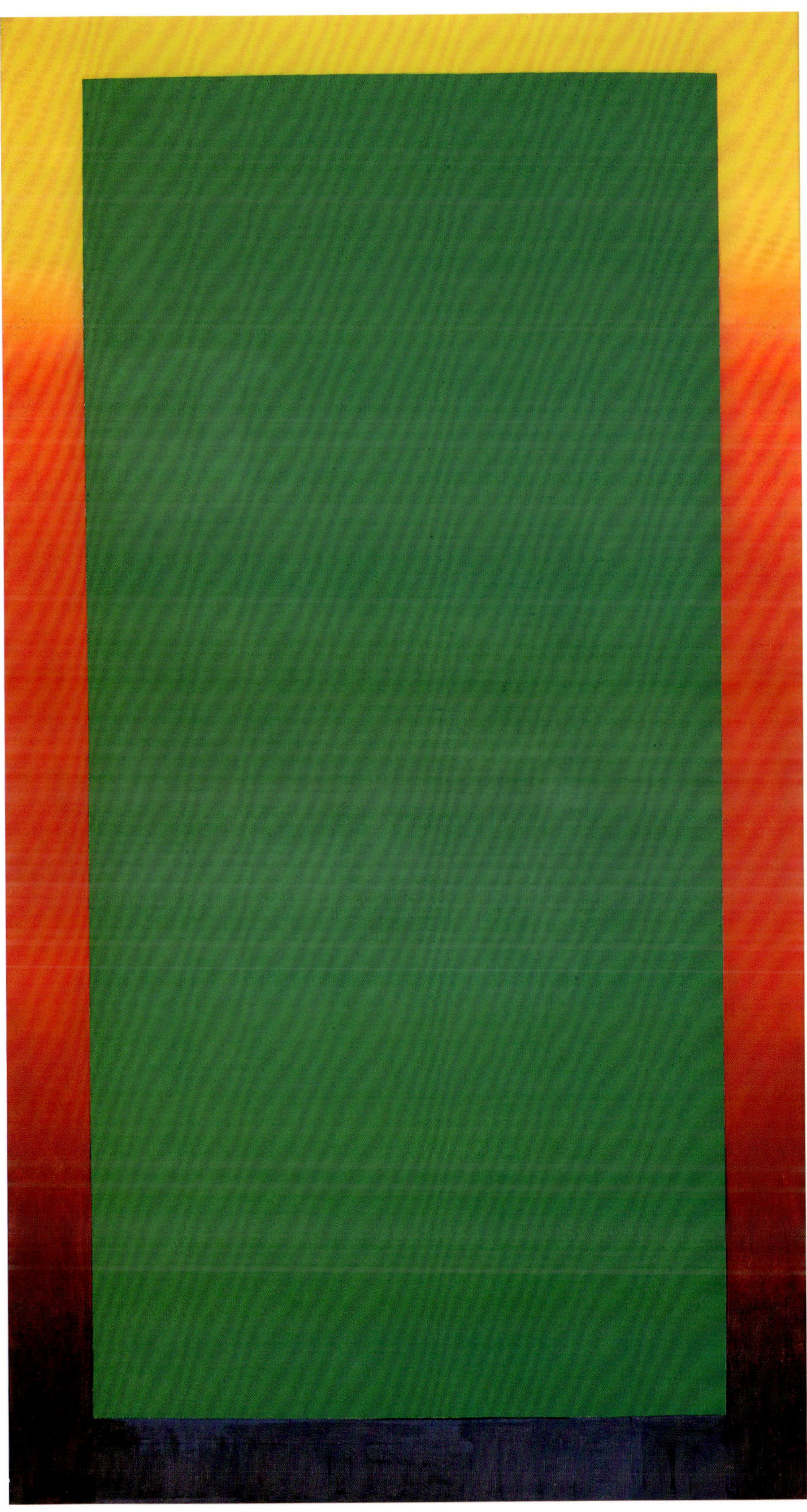

Stefan Gierowski
Painting CCCXLIV, 1975
Oil on canvas
139 x 76.5 cm

considerations. In *CDXI* (1977), the black field studded with white dots undoubtedly owes more to cosmic imagery than to the post-Impressionism of Georges Seurat or Paul Signac. In the rich history of Pointillism, ranging from Seurat to early-1930s Paul Klee, it is more on the side of Futurism: it is alongside a work like *Spherical Expansion of Light – Centripetal and Centrifugal* (1913–14) by Gino Severini, with its deep space luministic and chromatic vibration, that we should situate Gierowski's Pointillism. With some paintings, such as *CDLXIV* and *CDLXV* (p. 25), both 1981, the dots seem animated by a centrifugal force that at once hollows out the pictorial space in the centre and suggests movement beyond the painting's edges. Thus, there is a return to the dynamic dimension of the paintings of the 1960s.

In several "Pointillist" paintings, the dots exist alongside *à-plat* areas. In *CCLXVI* (1971, p. 108), the bands of colours – red, green, blue and yellow in sequence from the bottom up – disintegrate in the upper two thirds of the canvas into a cloud of dots of all four colours. In *CCCL* (1976), the *à-plat* bands frame the dots zone. The most striking success among these paintings based on the tension between *à-plat* areas and clouds of dots is unquestionably *CCCI* (1972): the centre of the canvas, where the angles of three polygons join up – a blue one, a red one and a yellow one – is the scene of a dots explosion: it is as though at the point of their convergence, the forms dissolved into myriads of particles.

The other main method that Gierowski uses to try to spatialise the chromatic phenomenon is that of the floating quadrangle. It was in 1973, with the small painting *CCCII*, that he first floated a coloured form over a chromatically unstable space. A red square with perfectly defined contours – in this, very different from the rectangles that had occupied the pictorial field of Rothko's paintings since the close of the 1940s[4] – stands out against a blue ground that is lent depth and openness by the variations of light intensity. The blue part of the canvas thus appears as an underlying space and not as a frame reproducing within the painting its limits. In the second half of the 1950s, Hans Hofmann started making paintings with precisely orthogonal monochrome quadrangles that stand out against a very painterly ground.[5] But it was not until the following decade that he was able to make these quadrangles float even more than they had before, thanks to the ground prepared

Stefan Gierowski
Painting CCCXIX, 1974
Oil on canvas
155 x 155 cm
The Wojtek Fibak
Collection

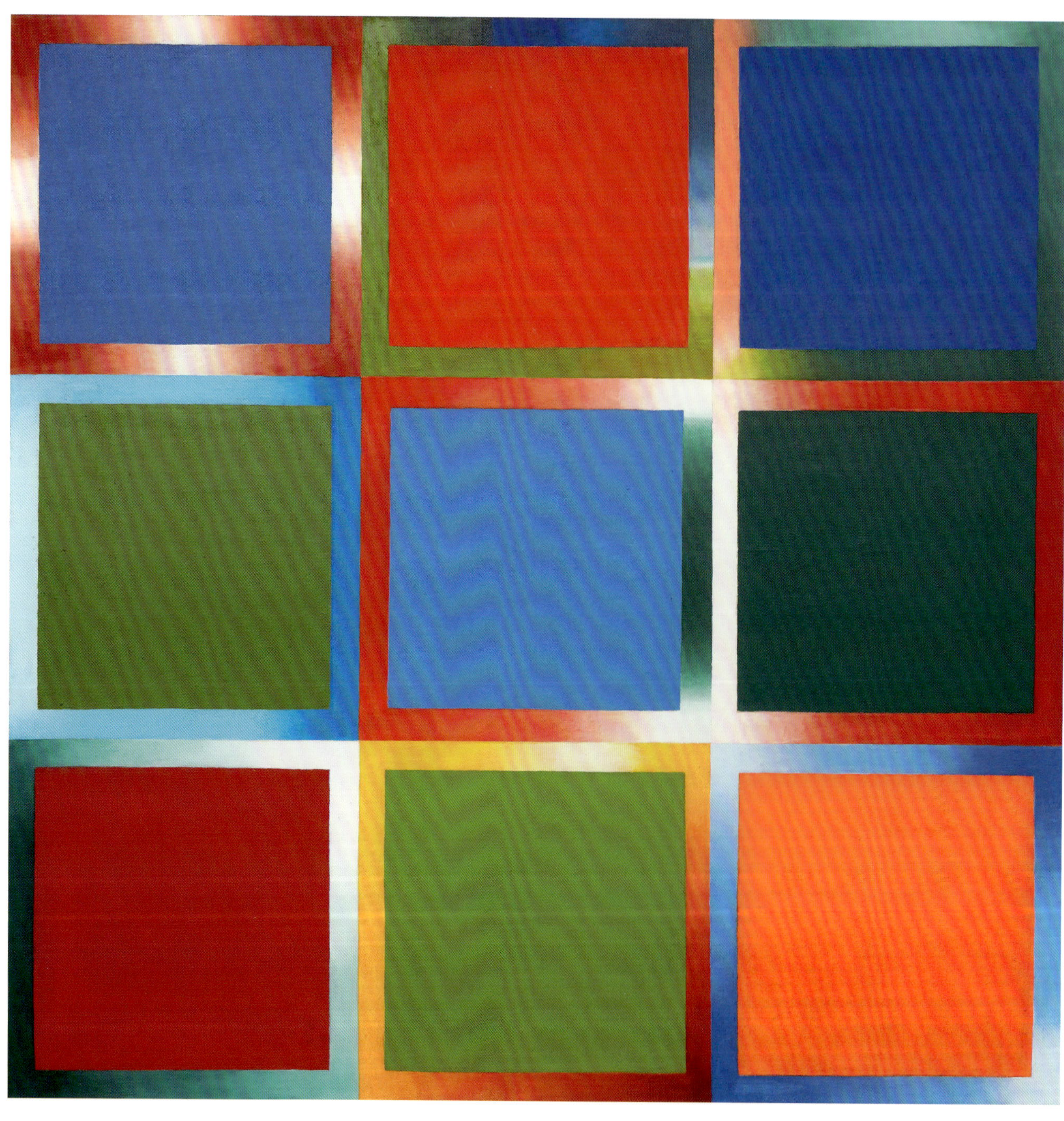

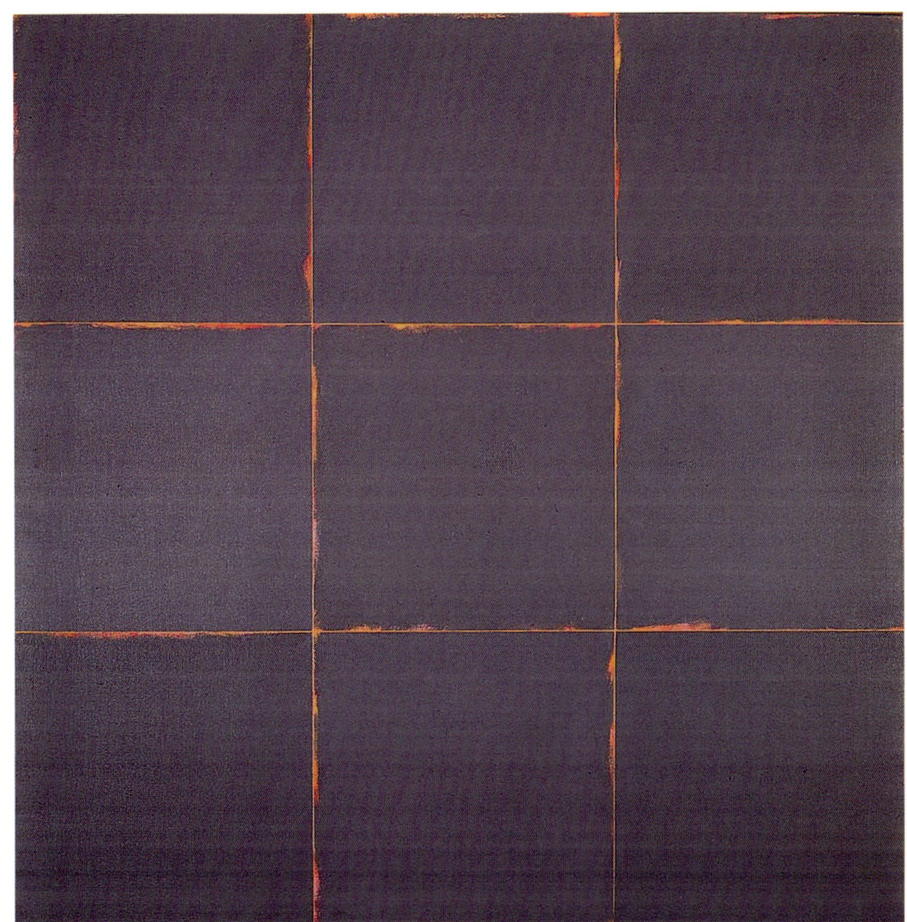

Claudio Verna
A 28, 1971
Acrylic on canvas
150 x 150 cm
Intesa Sanpaolo Gallerie
d'Italia Collection,
Piazza Scala, Milan

with a dilute acrylic paint (*Memoria in Aeternum*, 1962; *Polyhymnia*, 1963; *The Southwind*, 1964). With Hofmann, as with Gierowski, chromatic and spatial sensations go hand in hand. Like Hofmann's paintings, a 1974 painting by Gierowski features not one but many quadrangles – in fact, there are nine squares of different colours, arranged in three rows of three, levitating over as many slightly nebulous square spaces that seem to come straight from canvases from the middle of the previous decade. Rosalind Krauss's analysis of the role of the grid in modern painting is worth recalling here: "In the flatness that results from its coordinates, the grid is the means of crowding out the dimensions of the real and replacing them with the lateral spread of a single surface".[6] It would be very difficult to speak of the grid of *CCCXIX* (p. 28) in this way. Here, in the grid – which Modernism had seen as an ideal tool for exalting the flatness of painting – the different boxes acquire spatial depth. *CCCXIX* can be compared with the canvas entitled *A 28* (1971), produced around the same time by Claudio Verna, one of the leading exponents of the Italian Analytic Painting movement.[7] In it, the spaces between nine purple squares also arranged in rows of three reveal pictorial touches that bear witness to a painting style that is in no way monochromatic. The similarity of two contemporary canvases painted by artists belonging to at the time very different geopolitical universes is a fine example of historic medium specificity.

The floating monochrome quadrangle finds its canonical form in such paintings as *CCCXXVI* (1974), *CCCXLIV* (1975, p. 27), *CCCLXXI* (1976), *CCCLXXXIV* (1977, p. 185) and *CDLIII* (1979): a vertical rectangle suspended over a field with a colour gradient running from top to bottom. The colour of the rectangle either contrasts with those of the gradient or is very close to one of them. For example, this is the case with *CDXXVI* (1978, p. 30): a red shape floats over an equally red ground, treated in a gradient of three shades, going from the darkest one at the top to the lightest at the bottom. In contemporary painting, James Bishop is one of the few who created such convincing examples of abstract *chiaroscuro* (see, for instance, *Slate*, 1972).[8]

Among the variants of this model, one is particularly effective, proposed in *CDXXXVII* (1979): three vertical green bands, running from one edge of the canvas to the other, replace the quadrangle, each one enclosed by two bands

Stefan Gierowski
Painting CDXXVI, 1978
Oil on canvas
200 x 145 cm

James Bishop
State, 1972
Oil on canvas
182.9 x 183.2 cm
Courtesy David Zwirner

of the same width showing inverted gradients, ranging from blue to green. Here, Gierowski's painting almost flirts with Op Art, like those of Jef Verheyen who, at the same time, also sought to use nebulous gradients to lend spatial depth to the colour field.[9]

Certainly, Gierowski's output during the period from the late 1960s to the early 1980s was not limited to the two great ensembles we have just examined. In his own way, the painter explored different methods for achieving the spatial effects that Hofmann invoked in his "push and pull" theories (contrasting coloured forms that advance or recede in an abstract space). However, the Pointillist nebulosity and the monochrome floating quadrangle stand out as Gierowski's most important contributions to the painting of this period, after the lumino-dynamism of the 1960s. Henceforth, art history, as it develops in publications or in exhibitions, should no longer overlook these works when considering the course of the pictorial avant-gardes in the 1970s.

1 Two artists, stylistically very divergent, displayed their work in the Polish Pavilion in 1968: Stefan Gierowski and Jerzy Tchórzewski.
2 The German painter Kuno Gonschior (1933–2010) was a classmate of Gotthard Graubner's in Karl Otto Götz's Art Informel painting course. His Pointillism derives directly from Josef Albers's theories on colour.
3 Jules Olitski was born in the Ukraine in 1922 but grew up from an early age in the United States. He returned to Europe to study in Paris in 1949 and 1950. One of the greatest exponents of Abstract Expressionism, he was still influenced by European Art Informel.
4 The painting by Gierowski that comes closest to Rothko's work, during this period, is *CCCIV* (1973), which combines floating quadrangle and Pointillism.
5 Hans Hofmann was born in Bavaria in 1880. After an intense activity in the European avant-gardes, he emigrated to the United States in 1930. He became a pioneer of Abstract Expressionism as well as one of the greatest teachers of his time. He died in New York in 1966.
6 Rosalind E. Krauss, *The Originality of the Avant-Garde and Other Modernist Myths* (Cambridge MA: The MIT Press, 1985), p. 10.
7 Claudio Verna was born in 1937. He has lived and worked in Rome since 1961.
8 James Bishop, born in 1927 in Missouri, studied at Black Mountain College before settling in France in 1959, where he died in 2021.
9 The Belgian artist Jef Verheyen (1932–1984) was one of the most active members of the international Zero movement. When it comes to nebulous gradients, we think in particular of paintings such as *Apollo I* (1979) or *Megaron* (1981–82).

A Periodic Table

David Anfam

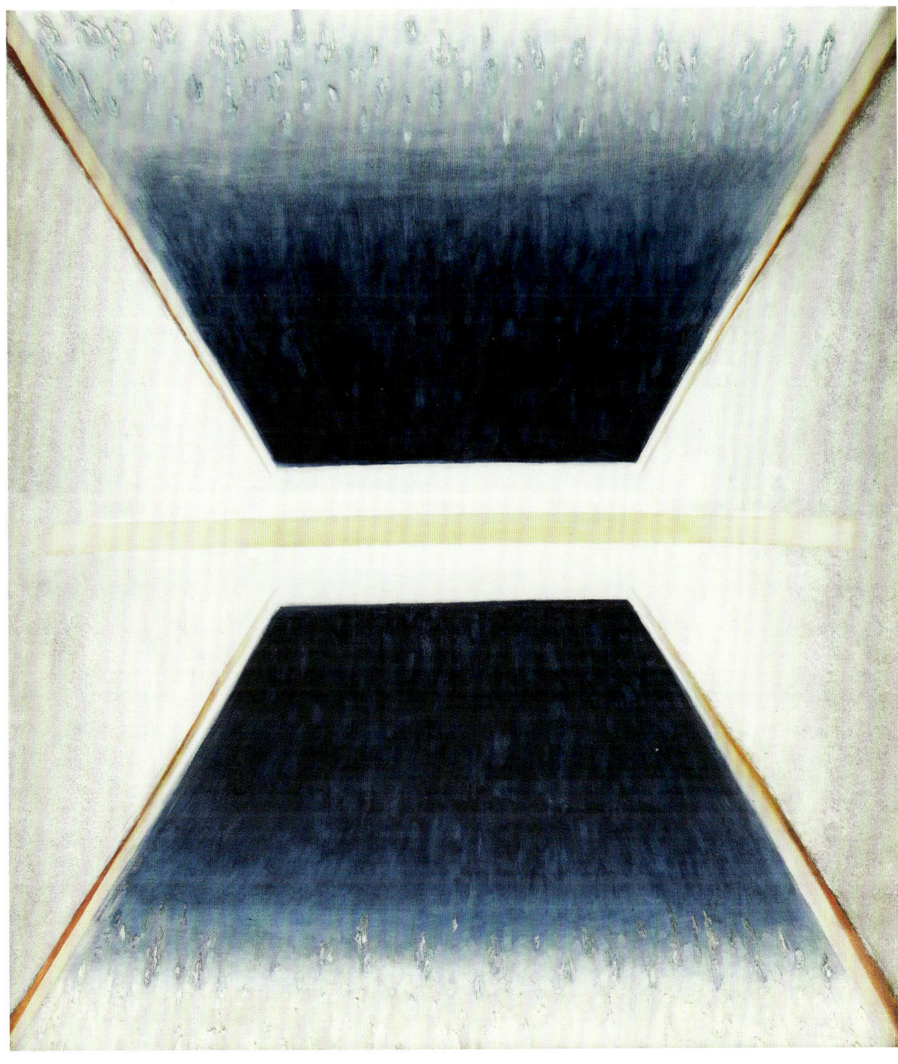

Stefan Gierowski
Painting CCXXV, 1968
Oil on canvas
130 x 114 cm

Towards the middle of the twentieth century, two artists unknown to each other, in different continents and separated by more than four thousand miles (though with a shared homeland) nevertheless reached similar verdicts about where they stood in the face of recent events. Recollecting that moment a quarter of a century later, one of them confessed, "Painting was dead in the sense that the situation, the world situation, was such that the whole enterprise as it was being practised by myself and by my friends and colleagues seemed to be a dead enterprise. . . . I felt that there was nothing in painting that was a source that I could use. . . . And that's what I mean by beginning from scratch. We couldn't build on anything. The world was going to pot. It was worse than that".[1] In 1949, the second wrote, poignantly: "The question, so much discussed now, of what art is to be like, does not exist. The question here is whether there is any need for art. It is very sad that practically a vast majority of the public would say no though in theory they would probably say yes".[2] The two names at issue were respectively those of Barnett Newman and Stefan Gierowski.

Of course, Gierowski is Polish; and Newman's parents had emigrated to the United States from that country. Both reckoned with what one might call – to echo the message of the Italian director Roberto Rossellini's bleak 1948 neo-realist film that captured the zeitgeist – their "zero years". To all intents and purposes, a *tabula rasa*.[3] The concept of "zero" itself is a risky premise because it can go in any direction, from everything to nothing.[4] Newman's and Gierowski's futures courted the same uncertainty. They could have sunk to creative despair amid the post-war ruins (in Gierowski's case literally the ravaged cities of Kraków and Warsaw) or risen, Phoenix-like, from the ashes of global conflict, to renew themselves and forge ahead. Fortunately for the story of abstract art since 1945 they made the right choice. In a nutshell, to start from scratch.

By now, Newman is a canonical figure. Less so Gierowski. Why? The answer is obvious. America's new-won power and prestige – the stark opposite to an exhausted Europe – dominated the second half of the twentieth century. Art's fortunes and its concomitant historical narratives followed suit. Over the past few decades, the balance has progressively shifted. Once-prominent European artists and movements have fast regained their proper standing.[5] Together with influx from South America, the

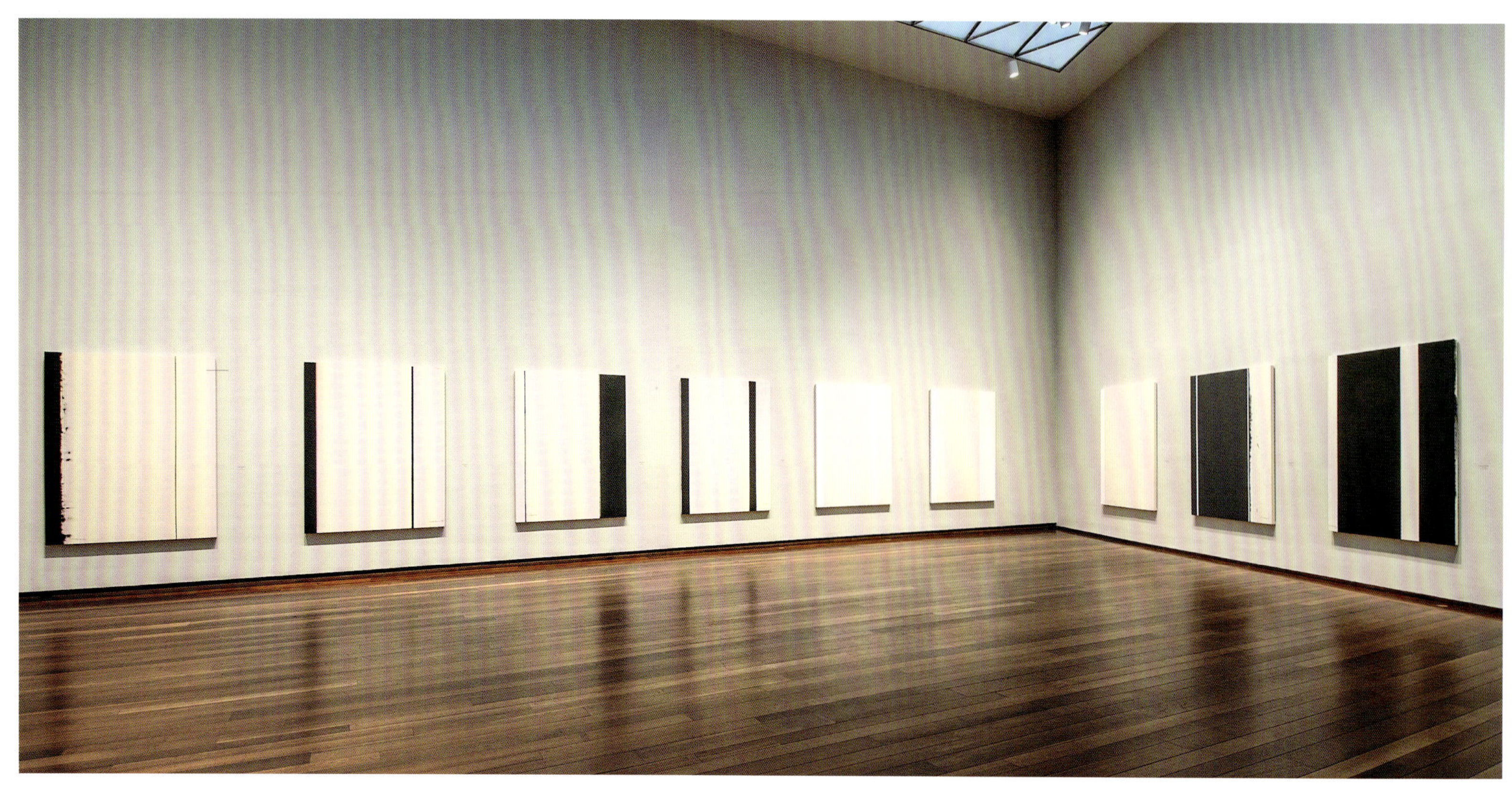

Barnett Newman
Stations of the Cross,
1958–66
National Gallery of Art,
Washington, DC

Middle and Far East, Africa and other regions, this revision has lent a fresh multiculturalism to the evolving critical discourse, museum programmes and galleries both local and international. To cite a topical example, the exhibition *Abstract Expressionism Behind the Iron Curtain* held at the Pollock-Krasner House and Study Center on Long Island, New York in 2017 demonstrated that the titular movement (I prefer to characterise it as a "phenomenon") was more widespread and fecund in former Communist countries than previously thought.[6] If New York "stole the idea of modern art" from Paris during the Cold War – as a popular though problematic academic study of the period's politics has argued[7] – its resurgent booty soon spread forcefully and far enough to penetrate even the Iron Curtain, albeit often with the CIA's support. For example, the *International Conference of Twentieth Century Music* held in Warsaw in 1954 saw a surprising prevalence of atonal compositions,[8] just as the Arsenal Show of young painters the following year – in which Gierowski participated – pointed away from dour Socialist Realism.

Nonetheless, Gierowski's Kielce, Kraków and Warsaw are not London, Berlin or New York. Nor will they probably ever enjoy such an influential, cosmopolitan status.[9] Furthermore, Poland's national fortunes have been chequered. In addition to the devastation that Nazism wreaked on its neighbour, the nation then lingered under Stalinism's intermittent sway (which waned during Władysław Gomułka's "thaw") and thereafter has experienced the ongoing turbulence and reactionary tendencies that have ensued in the wake of the Soviet Union's breakup. That Gierowski has not only withstood these challenges but also triumphed over them attests to a profound resilience, a faith in art as almost a surrogate theology that has sustained him well into his nineties. Indeed, his output in the present century is splendiferous and diverse, as though change within unity were its sole constant. Light and vitality pulse through his canvases, watercolours and drawings on paper (no wonder he titled a 1955 picture *I Love Life*, p. 12). As such, despite the steadfast non-objectivity, Gierowski's project overall retains an existential edge, not to mention that he designed sets for Jean-Paul Sartre's *La Putaine respecteuse* (1946). To invoke Newman's most catchy title,[10] his stylistic panache evinces a subtle daring. The inexhaustible palette and geometries seem

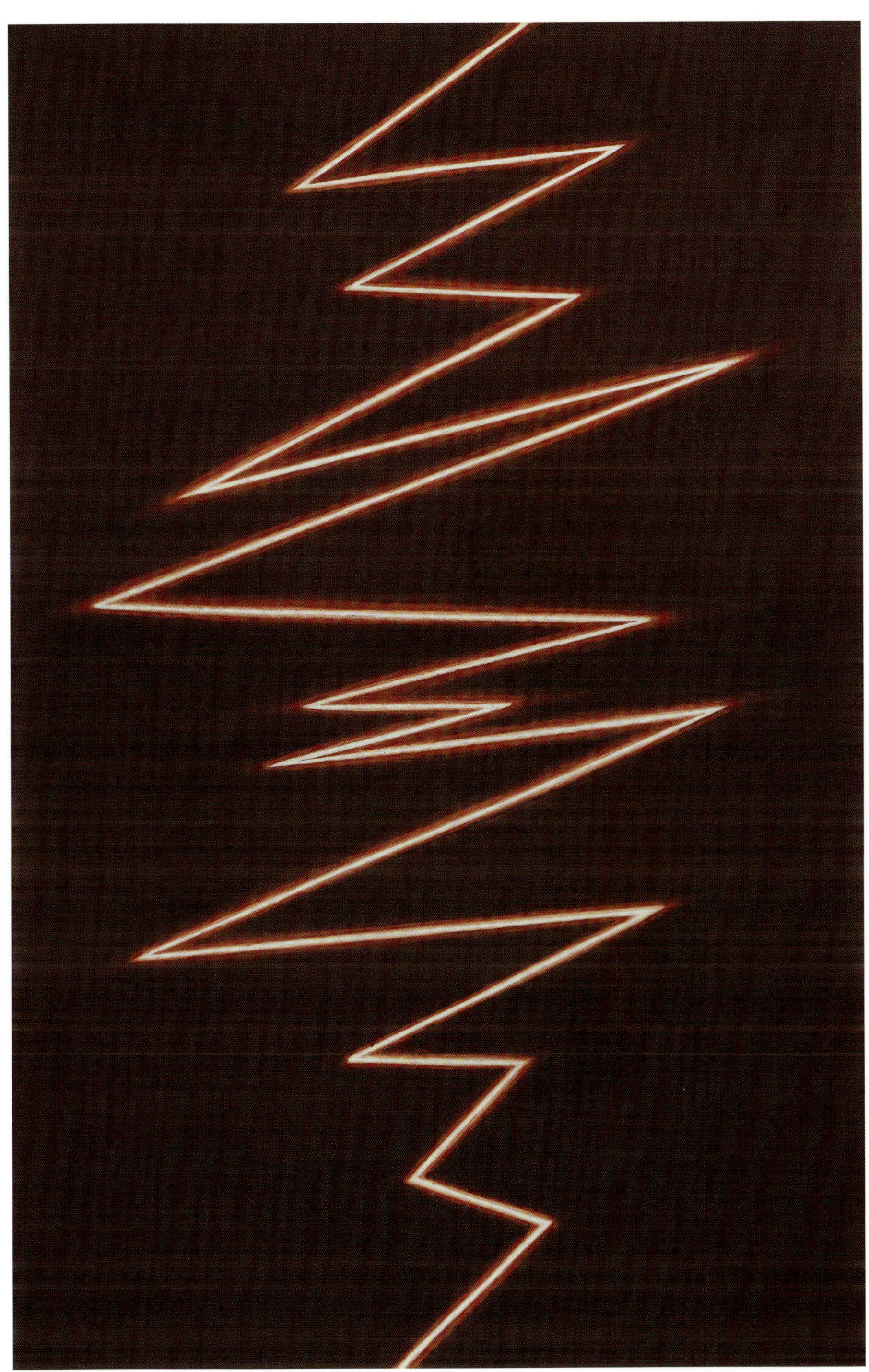

Stefan Gierowski
Painting DLXXVI
(Thou shalt not take
the name of the Lord
thy God in vain), 1987
Oil on canvas
200 x 130 cm

to quiz the viewer's perceptual faculties. Who's afraid of colour, composition and infinities? Not Gierowski for sure.

In a 1947 watercolour, *Sketch for Set Design*, pyramidal steps amassed in a tabular fashion lead upwards from a tenebrous lowermost crowd into supernal circles on high. Its symbolism doubles as a sketch for things to come. The tacit utopianism may cast an implicit backward glance to the great wave of European abstraction around the time of the First World War and especially Olga Rozanova (or even earlier, if we count the Swedish female mystic Hilma af Klint's precedent). But the ascent from figuration to geometric enlightenment, a veritable Jacob's Ladder, addresses the future. Exactly a decade later, Gierowski broke with his representational past and began to designate his production with Roman numerals. Counting is inseparable from time and time inseparable from motion. The move into abstraction, which Gierowski has mined to the present day, begs the question of where to situate his vision.

Newman already offers a contextual clue. Firstly, consider the trust in abstraction as, for want of a better term, a spiritual language. Newman executed his fourteen *Stations of the Cross* between 1958 and 1966. They constituted the artist's most overt religious statement, although Talmudic references abound throughout his oeuvre.[11] As Newman frankly declared, quoting the opening Aramaic words of Psalm 22, "*Lema Sabachthani* . . . This is the Passion. The outcry of Jesus. Not the terrible walk up the Via Dolorosa, but the question that has no answer . . . world without end".[12] On one level, Gierowski's *Painting the Ten Commandments* cycle (1986–87, p. 177) was inspired by the anonymous fifteenth-century Gdańsk Master's *Ten Commandments* (c. 1485) in that city's Basilica of the Assumption of the Blessed Virgin Mary. On another, it also belongs to a specific phase in modern Polish art – namely, the rise in the 1980s of *sacrum* ("sanctity", a transcendental sphere of meeting between the deity and the believer) promulgated by the Polish critic, gallerist and art historian, Janusz Bogucki.[13] Apart from Gierowski, two other painters in this vein were Jerzy Tchórzewski and Jerzy Bereś. (There was even a cinematic counterpart in Krzysztof Kieślowski's ten hour-long films, *Dekalog: The Ten Commandments*.)[14]

Alongside Newman, Mark Rothko's fourteen murals for the chapel in Houston bearing

Stefan Gierowski
Painting DCCCIV, 2005
Oil on canvas
100 x 73 cm

Stefan Gierowski
Painting DCCXXVIII, 1998
Oil on canvas
200 x 135 cm

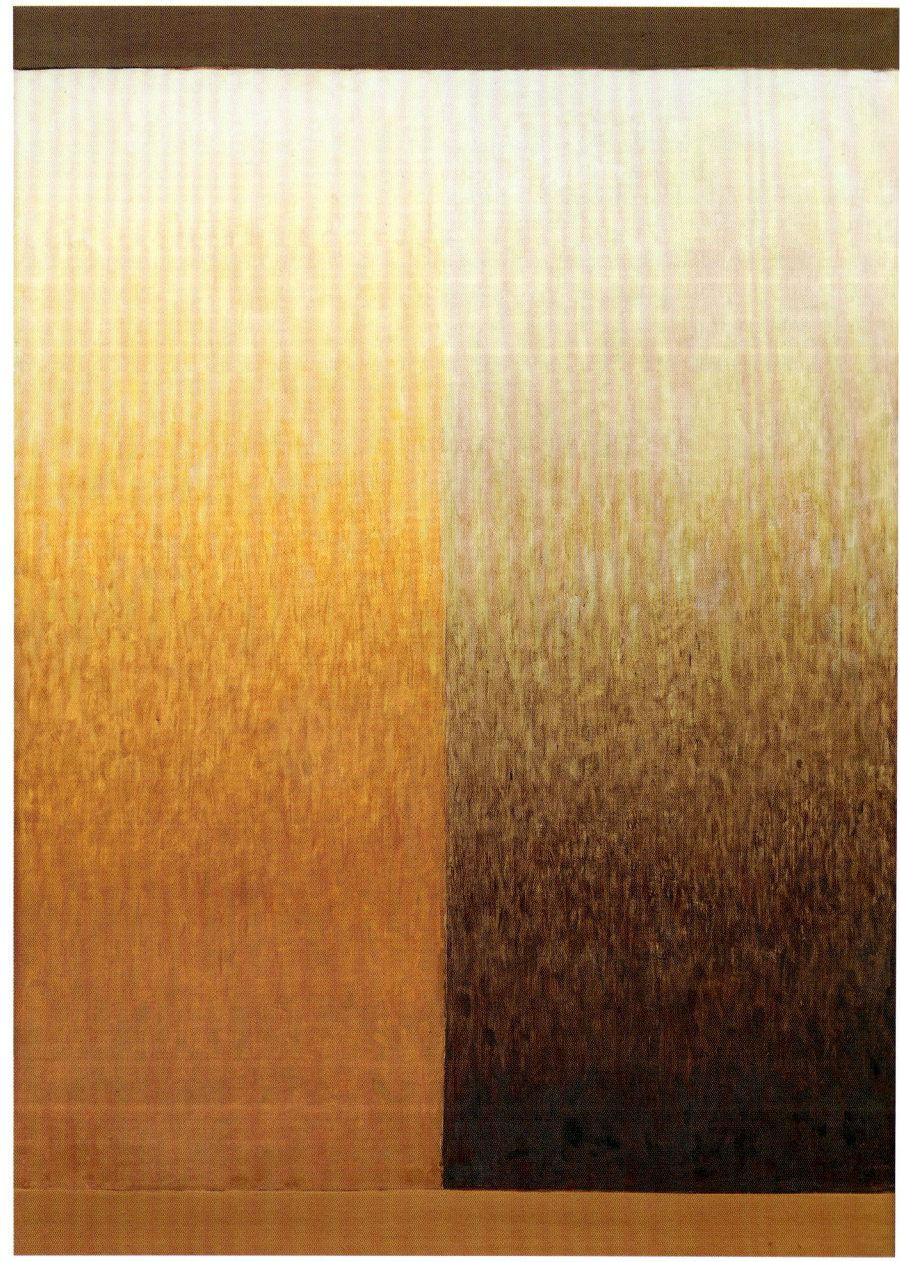

his name (dedicated in 1971) also exemplify a non-representational approach to the idea of the holy. Nor is there any incongruity between the sacred and the effaced/aniconic, since the notion that divinity is veiled or in some way lies beyond mimetic representation has venerable foundations, notably in the Old Testament itself.[15] Why else does Yahweh communicate through such means as fire, the whirlwind and light, while the storied "Veil of the Temple" speaks for itself?[16] *Mutatis mutandis*, hence perhaps the analogous burning intensity to some of Gierowski's reds, the vortex-like or abyssal flux exemplified by *DXLVI* (1985) and *DCCXCV* (2002, p. 125),[17] as well as the ubiquitous luminescence that sometimes softens into hazes (again a little reminiscent of Rozanova). Often we appear to behold perceptual wonders hovering somewhere between contemporary science's macro- or microcosmic revelations[18] and far more ancient cosmologies.

In the modern age, the theologian Rudolf Otto codified the equation between the supernatural and the sacred with his concepts of "numen" and "numinous". According to Otto, the Latin word and its English derivative (which he coined) encapsulate feelings of near-irrational, uncanny awe and mystery involving urgency and energy.[19] This state approximates a theological equivalent to the ancient aesthetic category of "the sublime" that was revived in the Romantic era, just as Otto's phrase "ideograms for the unique content of feeling" could well apply to Gierowski's painterly force fields.[20] For Otto, "silence", "darkness" and "empty distances" are further dimensions in play. The self-same agencies, communing with bright hues, drive Gierowski's path from around 1960 to the present. Witness the quiescence to the muted misty space in evocations such as the penumbral *DCCCIV* (2005) and the evanescent *DCCCLXV* (2009), the quintessential central black in *DLVI* (1986, p. 163) and the frequent aura of voided plenitude. Monochrome articulates the void, the dappled brushstrokes convey fullness. Here we hardly need also remember that it was Newman who in a 1948 essay title famously declared that "The Sublime is Now".[21] In turn, to mention "energy" highlights again a key element common to Newman's and Gierowski's art. Radiance.

By restricting himself to monochrome in the *Stations*, Newman had sought not only to convey his subject matter's gravitas but also to extract luminosity from the interaction between

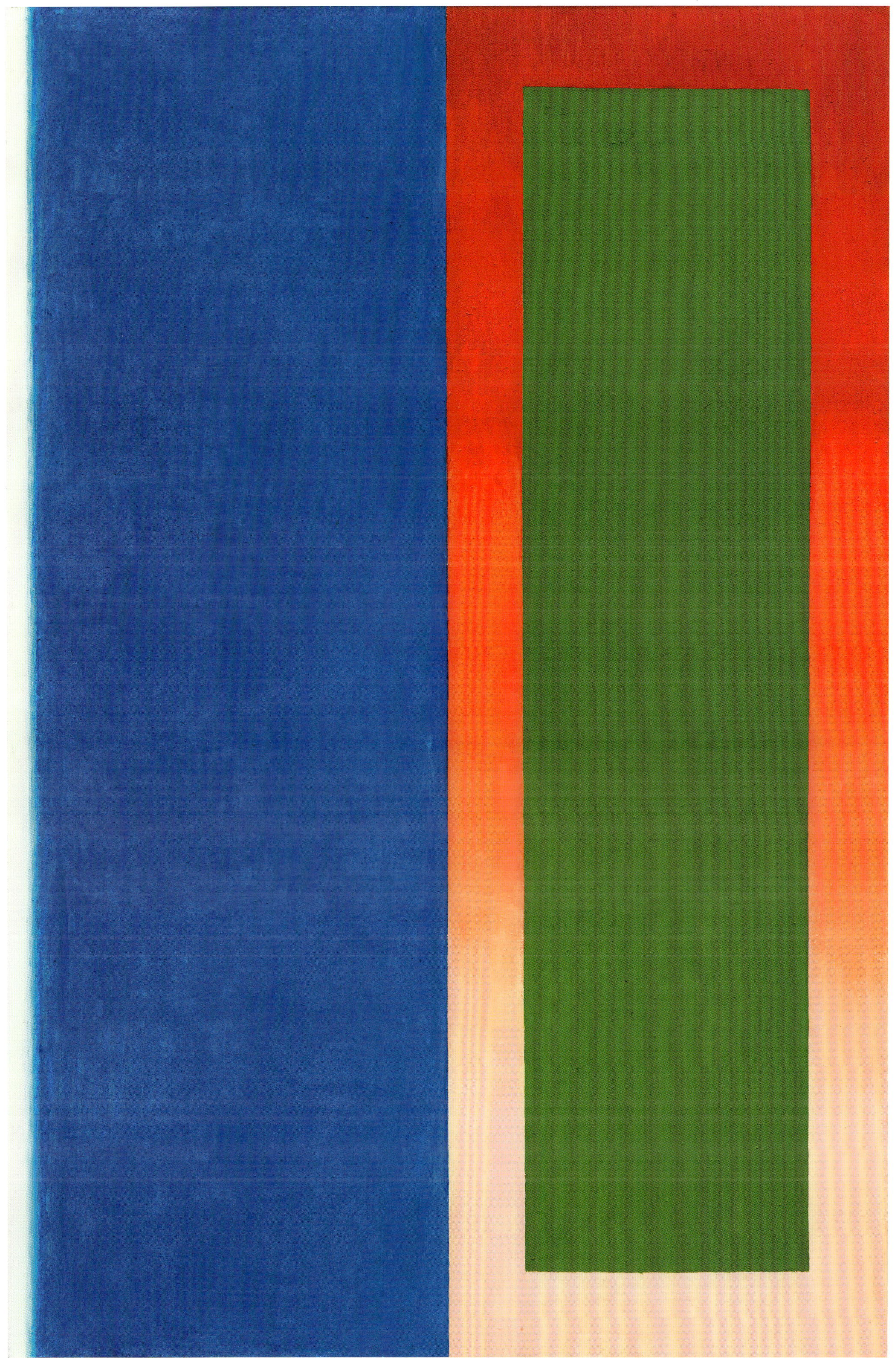

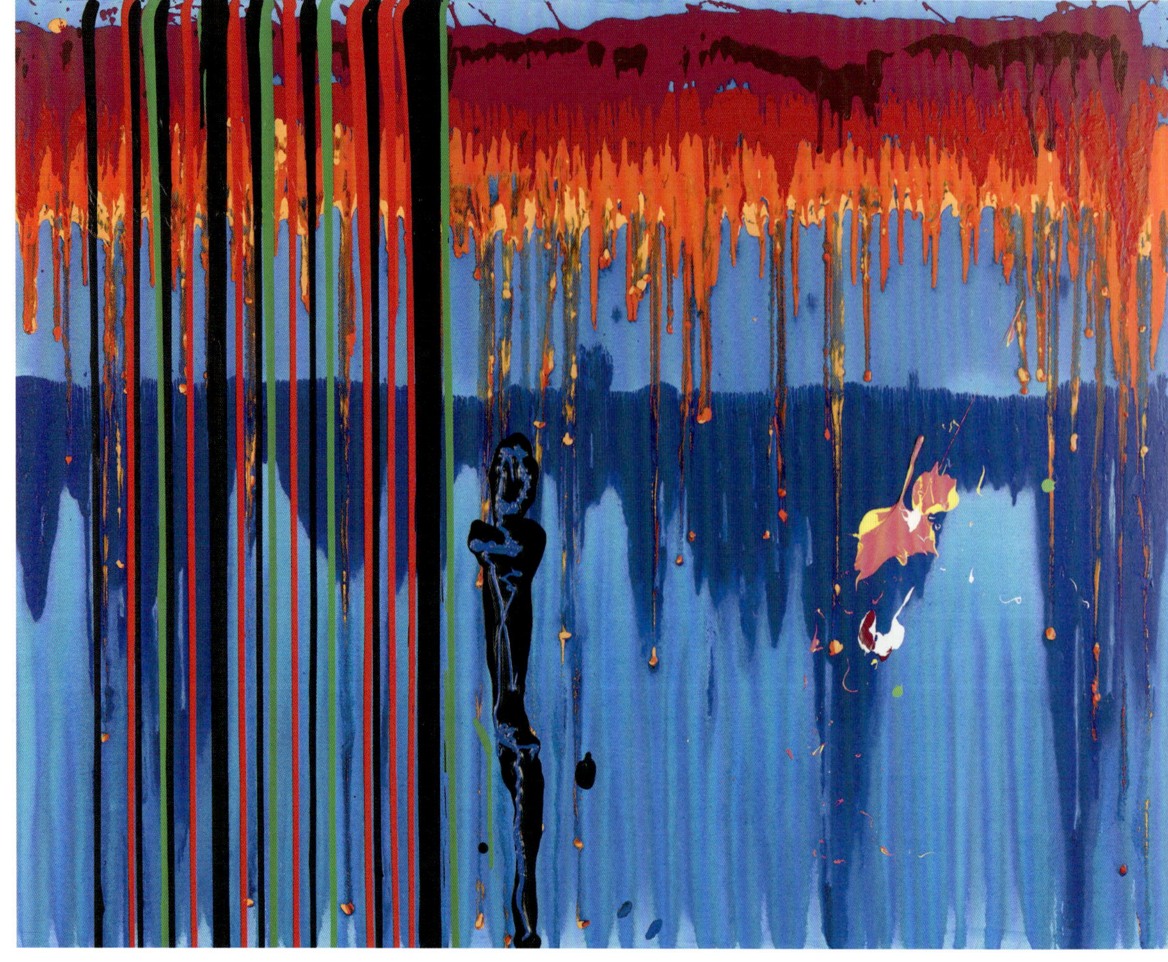

black (paint) and white (canvas). In contrast, Gierowski's "Decalogue" uses colorism at its fiercest. That seeking equivalents proves tricky and tends to veer towards artists otherwise alien to Gierowski's temperament probably gives a measure of his singularity. For instance, the sheer intensity to the hues allied to the gridded or rectangular motifs in two of the *Commandments* at first might call to mind Peter Halley's razzle-dazzle effects. Then again, the American's Neo-Conceptualism, his recourse to the additive Roll-a-Tex and, critically, the fluorescent Day-Glo paints sound a warning note that this is a mismatch. Unlike Halley's three crafty tricks that bespeak ironical distance or alienation, Gierowski's technique evinces respectively materialist authenticity, manual dexterity and brightness generated by chromatic values and dissonances rather than chemicals in the pigment. Halley deems his "conduits" to be post-modern prisons, whereas Gierowski's rectangles and other geometries are closer to limens and prisms. Being old-fashioned has its own virtues and valency.

Somewhat more apt are parallels between Gierowski's shimmering atmospheres – as in the opalescent, indefinable optical textures informing the lilac-tinted *DCCCLXIX* and the roseate *DCCCLXXIII* (p. 134) (both 2010) – and those of the Polish-born Julian Stańczak (1928–2017). Both create scintillating surfaces resonant with a semi-transparent air (and therefore matrices for potentially illimitable distances beyond) that approach Op Art yet jettison its often gimmicky demands on the gaze.[22] From another angle, Gierowski can ratchet more solid colour planes to a full-throttle pitch – for instance, the sky blue, orange and red *DCCCV* (2003–04, p. 39) together with several of the *Ten Commandments*, typified by the criss-crossing blue, yellow, purples and so forth in *Thou shalt not commit adultery* (p. 175) – that has scant parallels except for the British colour painter John Hoyland's late output. Hoyland's extravagant, almost mind-boggling brilliance possesses, as does Gierowski's, cosmic overtones.[23] Such fantastical refulgence returns us to Newman for a second and last time.

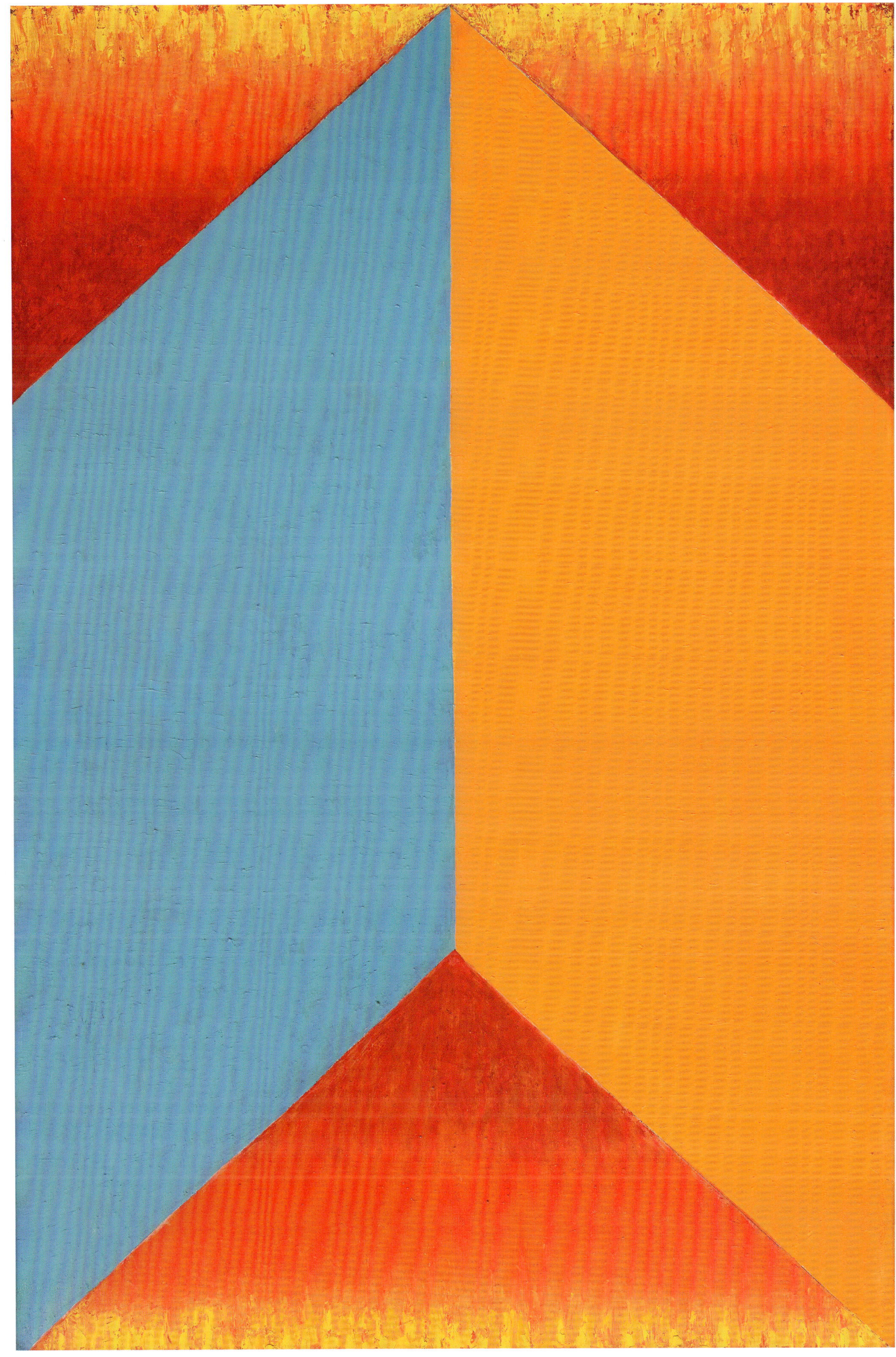

Stefan Gierowski
Painting DCCXCVII, 2002
Oil on canvas
100 x 140 cm

Newman's preoccupation with light was inseparable from his verticals, which became known as "zips". As he explained, "Now the thing I would like to say about that is that I did not decide, either in '48 or '47 or whatever it was, 'I'm going to paint stripes.' I did not make an arbitrary abstract decision. Now, I suppose I thought of them as streaks of light".[24] Indeed, streaks of light are what illuminate Gierowski's initial abstractions from the late 1950s. Consequently, in the process they bear a co-incidental resemblance to Rothko's so-called "multiforms" done exactly a decade earlier, in which the spreading pigment marks assume a fuzzy phosphorescent appearance. The orange and blue *XXXIII* (1958, p. 103) is quintessential. Both Rothko and Gierowski dissolved their figurative remnants in this lambent continuum so as to render the composition a totality rather than the sum of discrete parts. Likewise, akin to how Newman's "zips" are not autonomous shapes – that is, objects – but instead function as almost organic measures fusing with or amplifying the chromatic fields, Gierowski regards line in a similar way. In conversation with David Sylvester, Newman described his lineations in terms of "a field that brings life to the other fields, just as the other fields bring life to this so-called line", adding on another occasion that a painting should move as a "totality . . . The beginning and the end are there at once".[25] In Gierowski's words, "The line divides and connects space and time. The line has hidden energy. . . . A line like a living organism".[26] When his lines curve (as Newman's never do), their vitalism increases, suggesting magnetism or Albert Einstein's discovery that gravity bends light rays. Alternatively, in *Thou shalt not take the name of the Lord thy God in vain* (1987, p. 35) the zigzag gash resembles a lightning bolt, fault or streaking blitz – shades of the Abstract Expressionist Clyfford Still's electrifying "lifelines". By comparison, in the next of the *Ten Commandments*, *Remember the Sabbath Day, to keep it holy*, the line splinters and stiffens into ramrod straight uprights that melt into whiteness above. Line, so to speak, as probity (the Latin *probitas* means "uprightness"). Line as fragility (diverse late drawings waft upon the paper like gentle thought clouds suspended in the aether). Line as trajectory (the pale vectors cutting through darkness in *CDLXXIX*, 1982, p. 88 and *CDXCVIII*, 1983, p. 87). Line, we might almost say, as destiny. Far-fetched? Perhaps

not, because these slices soar and plunge, stop in a trice and speed away to infinity. In *DCCXCVII* (2003) they become a tight phalanx like massed spears. Yet in *DCCCVIII* (2004) mild equilibrium rules as two simple diagonals meet harmoniously amid serene paleness.

All these scenarios may belong to pure abstraction's dominion, absolutes. Nevertheless, it is difficult to resist also seeing them as seasons of the soul – by turns ardent, violent, contemplative, dynamic, ordered, in flux, and more. In the last analysis, Gierowski's draftsmanship in paint and pencil always reminds the viewer of the old adage that line is a point in motion. An observation by a historian of the subject is pertinent: "Indeed the line, like life, has no end. As in life, what matters is not the final destination, but all the interesting things that occur along the way. *For wherever you are, there is somewhere further you can go*".[27] Again, the faint but distinct undertow beneath the strict forms has an experiential tinge. Gierowski's fundamental humanism will not admit the total erasure of inwardness: the self's sentience must register, regardless of how subliminally it might do so. He avows as much: "What I do is to seek in the matter of painting the means by which to convey what I have observed, what I have felt".[28] Thereby Gierowski tempers objectivity with observation. This is not the Bauhaus's design mechanisms redivivus nor Piet Mondrian's Swiss watch-like pictorial mechanisms. Emotions ripple through these spectrums, signs, cadences and strokes.

Finally, "fulness" triangulates Gierowski, Newman and Rothko. Newman once declared, "The *fullness thereof* is what I am involved in".[29] Rothko prized the same quality. Gierowski mentions "how time is filled in terms of seeing".[30] In other words, pleroma in the present.[31] And Newman clinched the latter's tying the temporal with materiality: "I insist on my experiences of sensations in time – not the *sense* of time but the physical *sensation* of time".[32] What emphasises the fact that Gierowski's images fill time – remember the philosopher Martin Heidegger's insight that we live time – is how they are in constant motion, kinetic traces of Gierowski's touch and, ergo, his mind.[33] Beware, though, of reducing them to dry mental constructs. On the contrary, they emanate an auratic presence and immediacy. Colour is their content while not their ultimate intent. When Gierowski wrote in 1962 that "Colour has made a remarkable career", he took care to add that "artists have found a vast potential for emotional expression".[34] Furthermore, he summoned an implicit trinity: "In the beginning is light. Only later does one think about space, and lastly about matter".[35] Rothko, the perennial radiance-meister, put a similar sentiment another way. In doing so he rendered overt what Gierowski tended to keep covert: "The people who weep before my pictures are having the same religious experience I had when I painted them. And if you, as you say, are moved only by their color relationships, then you miss the point".[36] A wry rejoinder to Rothko's emotionalism is simple. To quote a contemporary physicist, "it is ourselves whom we study in studying light".[37]

However, the last thing I want is to portray Gierowski as a latter-day Central or Eastern European "Abstract Expressionist" (that role better fell to, say, Tadeusz Kantor and the Yugoslav Edo Murtić), still less a "religious" painter per se despite his affinities with both areas.[38] As he remarks: "To be 'religious' does not mean to practice, but rather, to search for values".[39] Instead, Gierowski strikes me as a seeker who has skirted many artistic trends prevalent during his career while squarely belonging to none. As such, Poland's comparative provincialism, an artistic outlier rather than an international capital, has preserved him from being co-opted into the mainstream. Had his life's endeavour unfolded in London, Berlin or New York it might have been otherwise. As it stands, he has kept the even tenor of a self-sufficient way across two centuries, appearing over and again to spark associations with diverse foreign artists and movements while remaining true to himself.

Thus Michel Gauthier has rightly compared Gierowski to the Zero group – but he never belonged to it on account of Poland's relative remoteness and other strictures.[40] The frequent recourse to monochrome and rectangular configurations has precursors in Kazimir Malevich's Suprematism – in particular his dictum, "Any painting surface is more alive than any face" would find favour with Gierowski[41] – and Alexander Rodchenko's most radical monochromes from the early 1920s. Yet it simultaneously rubs shoulders with a passing roster of contemporaries that range from Ad Reinhardt and Milton Resnick to Yves Klein, Lucio Fontana, Simon Hantaï, Joseph Marioni, Christopher Le Brun and many other possible contenders besides.[42] Notwithstanding, the most plausible catalyst for Gierowski's lengthy

romance with monochromatism was Władysław Strzemiński's Unism, its ethos the artwork's organic wholeness.[43] The extraordinary spectacle when Gierowski atomizes light into a myriad dots and speckles – Divisionism unbound to expand *ad infinitum* – invites comparisons with Piero Dorazio and Jules Olitski.[44] But early pictures such as *Boat-Races* and *Falling Down* (p. 7) (both 1948) indicate that he attained these particulate expanses independently and, if anything, partly by way of Rayonism and Analytical Cubism's dappled facture.[45] The same proviso applies to any resemblances with French Tachisme.

Elsewhere parallels lurk with Hard Edge or Colour Field Painting and their exponents such as Gene Davis, Patrick Heron, John Golding, Kenneth Noland and Frank Stella. Again, direct influence is improbable. The corpuscular motifs in paintings like *DCCCLVIII* may have a precedent in the earlier Sam Francis. Still, it is just a precedent, no more. Ditto the alignment between *DCCXCV* (p. 125) and Morris Louis's lush "Florals". Sometimes I even see links to the Korean artist Yun Hyong-keun, notably due to the mutual preoccupation with light and shadow, monochrome, duration, amplitude, vacancy and a lurking spirituality.[46] Yet it would be hard to envisage two countries as distant from each other in essence as Poland and South Korea (the sole commonality being that both were once "Communist" or, more accurately, totalitarian regimes). The sightlines could continue indefinitely. To labour them would be a pointless exercise in a game of art historical tag-and-touch, of pseudomorphosis – the accidental occurrence of similar forms in works of an otherwise very different kind.[47] I prefer another conclusion, mindful of a detail: while the Ten Commandments were inscribed on Tablets of Stone, we do well to keep in mind the operative word, the gerund, in Gierowski's title *Painting the Ten Commandments*. Painting, to him, means thinking.[48]

The Oxford English Dictionary defines "tabular" as "having the form of a 'table', tablet or slab". Needless to say, no tables (understood as furniture) occur in Gierowski's iconography. Think again, though. Tablets and slabs abound, as does a *genius loci*, the *tabula rasa*. The work *DCCXXVII* (p. 90) aggrandizes a zero motif. In *CCXXV* (1968, p. 33) two stacked dark Prussian blue slabs – an uncanny harbinger of the enigmatic monolith that may symbolize the universe's mystery in Stanley Kubrick's film *2001:*

A Space Odyssey (1968) – recede towards a vanishing point. Chroma marries an endless vista. Oblong horizontal slabs feature prominently in several compositions from 1962–64. Later they metamorphose and become entire rectangular planes (*DCXIX*, 1991); solid black blocks that counter rainbow-tinted cascades (*DCLXXVIII*, 1993); gestalts such as the leaf green, sky blue and red-fading-to-white vertical tablets that comprise *DCCXXVIII* (1998, p. 37); smaller, equal-sized columnar tables (*DCCXLVI*, 1999); and finally their diverse progeny – encompassing diagonals, blanks outlined with colourful margins, more curved variants or simpler rectangles, and so forth – that proliferate into the twenty-first century without any sign of stopping their mingled transformations and fixity. The module *in excelsis*.

Special instances arise when the tablets split or shear, as with the prismatic *DCCCV* (2003–04, p. 39) and *DCCCVI* (2004), or grow attenuated like the intersecting clustered "sticks" of *DCCCXXXVII* (2007, p. 94). Here the OED helps again by further defining "tabular": "flat and (usually) comparatively thin; consisting of, or tending to split into, pieces of this form, as a rock; of a short prismatic form with flat base and top, as a crystal". No wonder that for his

1965 show at the Galerie Lacloche in Paris the artist assigned dynamic, lapidary titles like "cut light", "cut surface" and "shard of white".[49] Metaphorically, Gierowski hones tinted, variegated and saturated facets until they glint and glow. The history of light is also the history of space.[50]

Dispelling the ghosts of Josef Albers's squares and Hans Hofmann's late sharp-edge, palette-knifed masses amid loose painterliness, what is Gierowski up to overall? Simply stated, he tabulates colour. In the process he counts and calculates what it can do and express. This suggests a rationale for the titular Roman numerals – counting captures and therefore shapes time[51] – appropriately for someone who began his artistic odyssey from zero, the classical system has no notation for that "place-holder" conundrum, thus substituting presence for absence. There is an order, perhaps even almost a structuring by templates, yet nothing is iron-clad or flypapered to theory – which anyway would be at odds with Gierowski's humanist ideology. Instead, he aims to lend colour's inherent numinous power its intervals, sequential alignments and periodicity. A painter's periodic table intuitively parses and therefore makes sensible what Donald Judd rightly saw as colour's crux: fathomless mystery and potential. Now, Judd merits quoting at length: "Color will always be interpreted in a new way, so that I hardly think my use is final. In fact, I think it is a beginning. Infinite change may be its constant nature. . . . Color, like material, is what art is made from … After a few decades the discussion of color is so unknown that it would have to begin with a spot. . . . The contrasting pairs are just as well known: red and blue, red and green, red and yellow, blue and green, blue and yellow. Some are not: red and orange, yellow and orange. This list is finite, since it is of primaries and secondaries. The other possible pairs are infinite, as is color".[52] Without any personal or intellectual interaction between the two, Judd's thoughts invite us to ponder Gierowski's contrast-filled universe. Here the plot thickens to demand a short, sharp dénouement.

Science has tabulated the universe's building blocks with the arrangement known as the periodic table. As it happens, in chemistry Roman numerals have often been used to denote the groups of this serial formation. Like Gierowski's art, it involves columns and rows, colours and counting, elements ranging from extreme density to uttermost lightness. In 1967, Gierowski also tabulated his world into a list of sixteen facts:

- The war
- A-bomb
- Socialism
- Stalin
- Khrushchev
- October 1956
- Space flights
- Cybernetics
- The artificial lung-and-heart apparatus
- The laser
- John XXIII
- Kennedy
- Mao Zedong
- The Skoplje earthquake
- The Florence flood
- The drought and famine in India

and continued, "I believe that doubt and hope connected with the human being and the point of existence are as difficult to explain as painting".[53] The periodic table enables science to attend to life as the most basic matter, another of the artist's longstanding concerns. Yet is there any conceivable interface between the human condition to which Gierowski alludes in his count (coupling it to art's imponderables) and science's essential objectivity (allowing it to overcome human frailty)? Oddly enough, yes – one that brings sufficient resolution to the irreconcilable extremes at stake.

In 1984 Primo Levi published *The Periodic Table*, a book hard to label just like, in an altogether different realm, chameleonic colour itself. By training a chemist, Levi's chronicle conforms to its title, a numerical construct that organizes and measures matter's atomicity and valency. Each chapter bears the name of an element. However, each successive element's relation to Levi's changeful life is mercurial – just as atomic valency is about variables, combinations that cause transformations – akin to Gierowski's very view of reality.[54] When the Nazis occupied Italy, Levi's existence hung in the balance after they sent him to Auschwitz. Gierowski determined to be a painter during the Nazi occupation of Poland.[55] The chemist shared with the artist (for whom physics is a crucial science)[56] an implicit conviction, "Matter is matter, neither noble nor vile, infinitely transformable".[57] It can go either way, to the good or the bad, the dark or the light. Near the narrative's end, Levi envisions the odyssey of an atom of carbon, from calcium carbonate to carbon dioxide and, through photosynthesis[58] – "the flashing form of a packet of solar light" – to leaf tissue, to glucose and ultimately to "energy", the pulse that "guides this hand of mine to impress on the paper this dot, this one".[59] The one and the many, the dot and the tablet, emotions within and reality outside: these are some of the factors that guide Gierowski's own questing hand through colour's time and spaces.[60]

My thanks to Stefan Gierowski and Łukasz Dybalski for their patience and input and to Prof. Steven Mansbach for his scholarly advice.

1 Barnett Newman (1970) in John P. O'Neill, ed., *Barnett Newman: Selected Writings and Interviews* (New York: Alfred A. Knopf, 1990), pp. 302–04.
2 Janusz Zagrodzki, *Stefan Gierowski* (Warsaw: Galeria Prezydencka, 2005), p. 7.
3 The Rossellini film's title was *Germany Year Zero*.
4 Charles Seife, *Zero: The Biography of a Dangerous Idea* (London: Souvenir Press, 2000).
5 To cite two among many possible examples, Pierre Soulages (as a centenarian, so far biographically outdoing even Gierowski), once sidelined compared to the Abstract Expressionists, now enjoys a high international reputation. Likewise the Ghanaian sculptor El Anatsui: thirty years ago such an African art star would have been unheard of.
6 Joana Grevers and Helen A. Harrison, *Abstract Expressionism Behind the Iron Curtain*, exh. cat. (East Hampton: Pollock-Krasner House and Study Center, 2017).
7 Serge Guilbaut, *How New York Stole the Idea of Modern Art. Abstract Expressionism, Freedom, and the Cold War* trans. Arthur Goldhammer (Chicago and London: Univer-

sity of Chicago Press, 1983). The book's core problem is a monolithic thesis that lacks theoretical suppleness.

8 Charlotta Kotik, "Painting and Politics", in Grevers and Harrison, *Abstract Expressionism*, p. 13. Note, though, that this event had covert CIA support: see Shannon E. Pahl, *The Congress for Cultural Freedom, La Musica nel XX secolo, and Aesthetic "Othering": An Archival Investigation* (M.A. diss., University of Wisconsin, Milwaukee, 2012).

9 However, in 1961 Peter Selz included Gierowski in *15 Polish Painters* at the Museum of Modern Art, New York.

10 The series of four paintings that Newman designated as *Who's Afraid of Red, Yellow and Blue* (1966–70).

11 See David Anfam, "'The Field Is No Longer Simple', Barnett Newman, Mark Rothko and Color-Field Painting", in *Reflections on the Collection of the Stedelijk Museum, Amsterdam* (Amsterdam: Stedelijk Museum and NAi0101 Publishers, 2012), pp. 345–54.

12 Barnett Newman (1966) in O'Neill, *Barnett Newman*, p. 188.

13 Agnieszka Gralinska-Toborek, "The idea of Sacrum in Polish art of the 1980s", *Inferno: Journal of Art History* 7 (2003): 1–7.

14 For a seminal account, see also Jacek Sempoliński, Aleksander Wojciechowski, Janusz Zagrodzki et al., *Malowanie Dziesięciorga Przykazań 1986–1987* (Warsaw: Stefan Gierowski Foundation, 2014).

15 David Anfam, "To See, or Not To See", in K. C. Eynatten, Kate Hutchins and Don Quaintance, eds., *Image of the Not-Seen: Search for Understanding. The Rothko Chapel Art Series* (Houston: The Rothko Chapel, 1998), pp. 64–77. Also, Paul Hills, *Veiled Presence: Body and Drapery from Giotto to Titian* (New Haven and London: Yale University Press, 2019).

16 Beneath the Veil stood the Ark of the Covenant that according to Hebrew Scripture held the Ten Commandments.

17 For concision's sake, all Roman numerical titles elide Gierowski's use of the word *Obraz* (Painting) preceding said numbers.

18 Michel Gauthier, *Deep Impact: Stefan Gierowski and European Avant-Gardes in the 60s*, exh. cat. (Warsaw: Stefan Gierowski Foundation, 2019), pp. 39 ff., notes the similarities with scientific imagery. The American photographer Barbara Morgan's striated *Light Waves* (1945) strongly resembles some of Gierowski's motifs.

19 Rudolf Otto, *The Idea of the Holy. An Inquiry into the non-rational factor in the idea of the divine and its relation to the rational* [1917], trans. John W. Harvey (Oxford and New York: Oxford University Press, 1958), pp. 5–30.

20 Ibid., p. 60.

21 Barnett Newman (1948) in O'Neill, *Barnett Newman*, pp. 170–73.

22 David Anfam, *Julian Stańczak. The Life of the Surface: Paintings 1970–1975* (New York: Mitchell-Innes & Nash, 2017). Gierowski concluded that Op Art's technical strategies could not supplant "painting pure and simple".

23 See David Anfam, "Out of this World", in ibid. and Natalie Adamson, Matthew Collings and Mel Gooding, *John Hoyland: The Last Paintings* (London: Ridinghouse, 2021), pp. 28–39. *DCCXCIII* (2003), *DCCCXLVII* (2008) and similar compositions most nearly approach Hoyland.

24 Barnett Newman (1970) in O'Neill, *Barnett Newman*, pp. 305–06.

25 Barnett Newman (1965 and 1970) in O'Neill, *Barnett Newman*, pp. 256 and 306.

26 Stefan Gierowski (2018) in *Stefan Gierowski. Overview of works related to the line in the care of the Foundation* (Warsaw: Stefan Gierowski Foundation, 2018), http://fundacjagierowskiego.pl/stefan-gierowski/wystawa/stefan-gierowski-przeglad-prac-zwiazanych-z-linia-bedacych-pod-opieka-fundacji/.

27 Tim Ingold, *Lines: A Brief History* (Abingdon and New York: Routledge, 2007), p. 170. What Ingold terms his "anthropology of the line" chimes with Gierowski's multifarious views about it.

28 Stefan Gierowski (1992) in Zagrodzki, *Stefan Gierowski*, p. 150.

29 Barnett Newman (1962) in O'Neill, *Barnett Newman*, p. 248.

30 Stefan Gierowski (2020) in *Stefan Gierowski. Drawn thoughts not fully seen. Drawings from 2018–2020* (Warsaw: Stefan Gierowski Foundation, 2020), http://fundacjagierowskiego.pl/stefan-gierowski/wystawa/stefan-gierowski-mysli-rysowane-nie-w-pelni-zobaczone-rysunki-z-lat-2018-2020/.

31 The Latin word "pleroma" is Biblical in origin, occurring seventeen times in the New Testament.

32 Barnett Newman (1949) in O'Neill, *Barnett Newman*, p. 175.

33 Rightly stressed by Gauthier, *Deep Impact*, passim.

34 Gierowski (1962) in Zagrodzki, *Stefan Gierowski*, p. 76.

35 Ibid.

36 Mark Rothko in Selden Rodman, *Conversations with Artists* (New York: Devin-Adair Co., 1957), p. 94.

37 Arthur Zajonc, *Catching the Light. The Entwined History of Light and Mind* (Oxford and New York: Oxford University Press, 1993), p. 329.

38 In 1983 Gierowski participated in the art historian Janusz Bogucki's exhibition *Sign of the Cross* held in the half-rebuilt Church of Divine Mercy in Warsaw as an explicit platform for the Catholic faith. See Maja and Reuben Fowkes, *Central and Eastern European Art Since 1950* (London and New York: Thames & Hudson, 2020), p. 105. Nevertheless, this move towards devout officialdom was arguably more an exception than the rule for Gierowski, although he has led a distinguished career as a teacher in academe.

39 Communication to the author, 7 December 2020. All subsequent references are to this date.

40 Gauthier, *Deep Impact*, pp. 9–10.

41 Kazimir Malevich (1915) in John Golding, *Paths to the Absolute. Mondrian, Malevich, Kandinsky, Pollock, Newman, Rothko and Still* (London: Thames & Hudson, 2000), p. 62.

42 Barbara Rose, *Monochrome: From Malevich to the Present* (Berkeley, Los Angeles and London: University of California Press, 2006), remains the standard text on this sprawling subject.

43 See Meghan Forbes, "Władysław Strzemiński's Theory of Vision", *Post: Notes on Art in a Global Context*, 30 May 2018, https://post.moma.org/wladyslaw-strzeminskis-theory-of-vision/.

44 See Serge Lemoine, "Piero Dorazio: A Master of Forms, A Genius of Colours", in *Piero Dorazio* (Paris: Tornabuoni Art, 2016), p. 21: "The unity and homogeneity of [Dorazio's] work strongly evoke the one of Polish artist Władysław Strzemiński and his Unism theory at the end of the 1920s". Dorazio's work remains outside Gierowski's purview (communication to the author).

45 An apposite survey for Gierowski's ceaselessly shifting attitude to colour is *Farbe im Fluss | Color in Flux* (Bielefeld: Kerber Verlag, 2011).

46 See David Anfam, "Timeless in Korea", in Kim Inhye and Daniela Ferretti, eds., *Yun Hyong-Keun* (Berlin: Hatje Cantz Verlag, 2019), pp. 36–41.

47 Erwin Panofsky, *Tomb Sculpture: Its Changing Aspects from Ancient Egypt to Bernini* (New York and London: Thames & Hudson, 1964), pp. 25–26.

48 Communication to the author.

49 Gauthier, *Deep Impact*, p. 38.

50 Zajonc, *Catching the Light*, p. 97.

51 On numerology as existential and keyed to beginnings/ends – that is, zeros – see Frank Kermode, *The Sense of an Ending. Studies in the Theory of Fiction* (Oxford and New York: Oxford University Press, 1967), Ch. 1, "The End".

52 Donald Judd (1993) in Nicholas Serota, ed., *Donald Judd* (London: Tate Publishing, 2004), pp. 157–58.

53 Zagrodzki, *Stefan Gierowski*, pp. 98, 100. An interesting parallel obtains here with Ad Reinhardt's chronologies that also list historical facts interwoven with biographical ones. Nor may it be happenstance that Reinhardt held staunch left-wing views, while his stress on repetition is another variant of numerology.

54 "I refuse to see reality as a set of purely external facts. It contains events hard to define": Gierowski in "Matter Also Means Light: Zbigniew Taranienko talks with Stefan Gierowski", *Literary Monthly* 3 (1983): 65.

55 Zagrodzki, *Stefan Gierowski*, p. 20.

56 Gierowski (1981) in "Matter Also Means Light", p. 69.

57 Primo Levi, *The Periodic Table* [1975], trans. Raymond Rosenthal (New York and London: Alfred A. Knopf, 1995), p. 188.

58 Tim Radford, "In his element: looking back on Primo Levi's *The Periodic Table*", *Nature*, 28 January 2019, https://www.nature.com/articles/d41586-019-00288-6. Photosynthesis of course converts matter into energy, deadness into vitality.

59 Levi, *The Periodic Table*, pp. 235, 241.

60 Gierowski (2013) in "Bzik Kulturalny – Stefan Gierowski", YouTube (7 June 2013): "Not only the intelligence which conceives and shapes the abstract painting is important, but also what is inside of me, the physical movement of my hand". See https://www.youtube.com/watch?v=QlVGyFYdmX4&fbclid=IwAR05QdGhl6CLu33gsNoNd2CGQwkFz5D6Th9UuPHwXMvALkrQTvgUgqCEPFw.

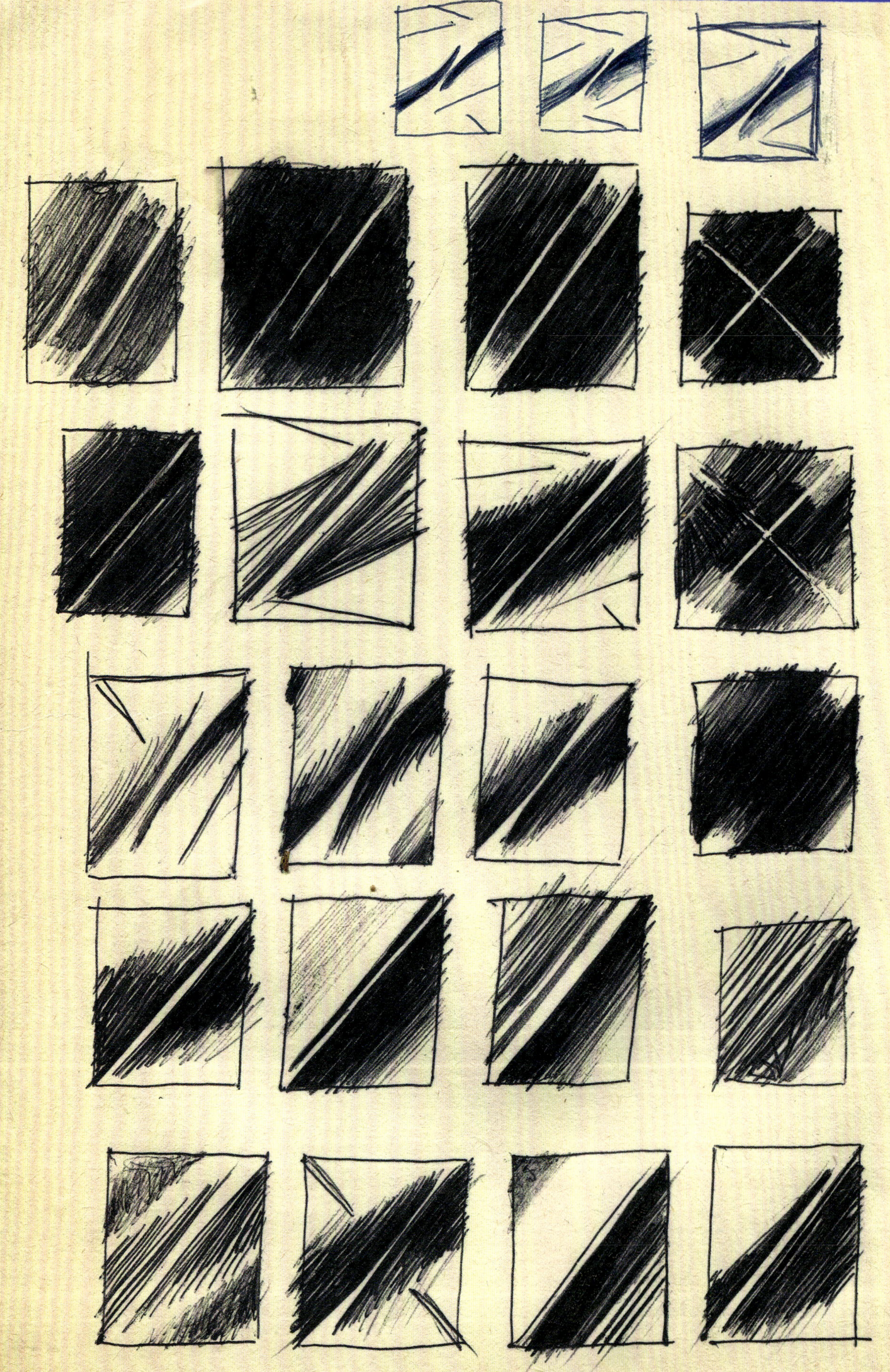

An endless space opened up. The common understanding of the Universe changed. A painted line without an end moved from imagination to reality. From a closed line to a dynamic opening-out to the Infinite. A great curiosity was born to plumb the active depths of space.

The simpler the way a line acts, the greater the energy in the reality outside the painting.

A change in line width adds extra space and creates new qualities and new gestural weight. In painting terms, what happens in a wide line revokes the power of sweeping movement and instead furnishes the weight of a particular object, and defines it.

Stefan Gierowski

Painting III, 1957
Oil on canvas
46.5 x 60.5 cm

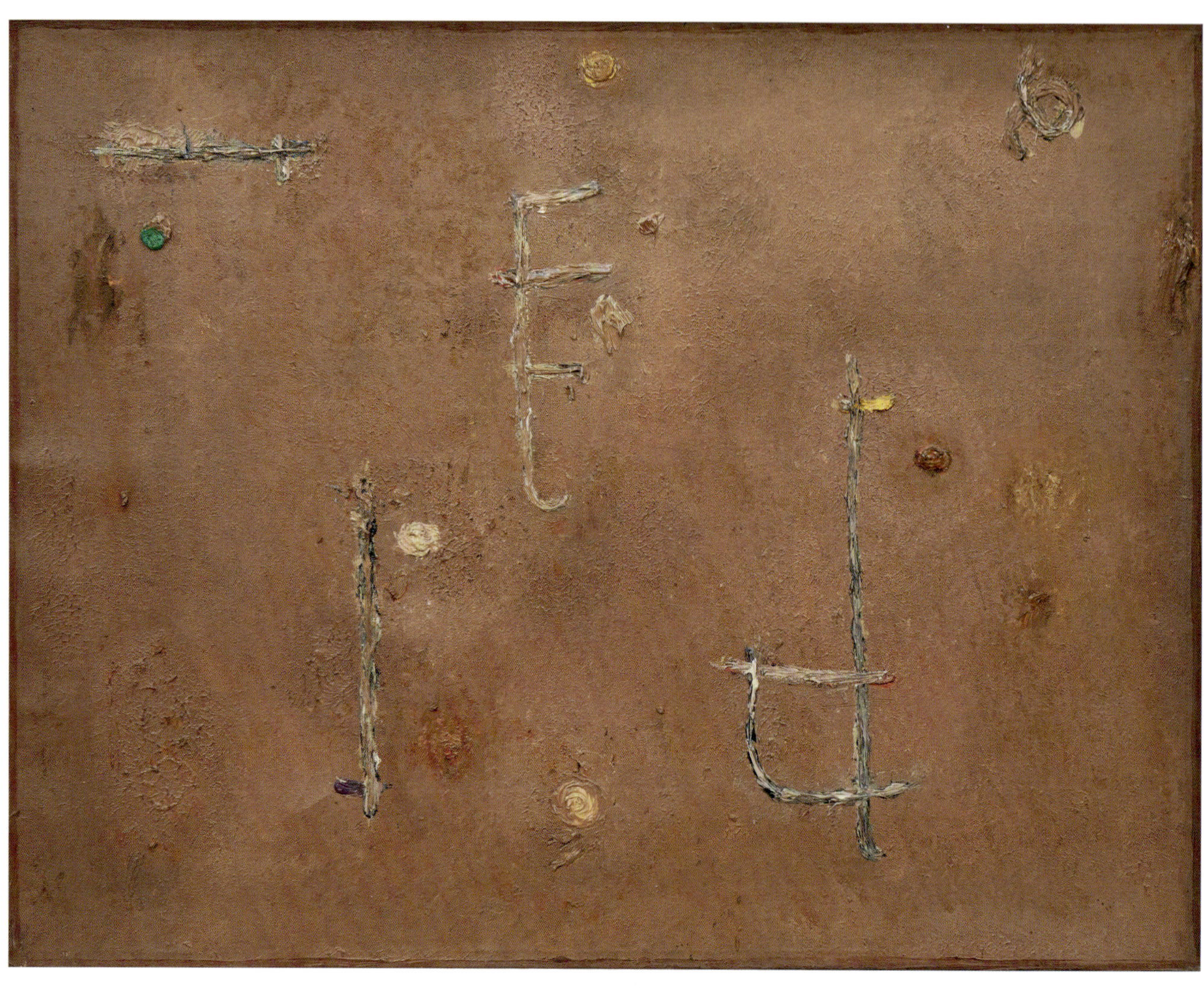

Painting V, 1957
Oil on canvas
60 x 45 cm

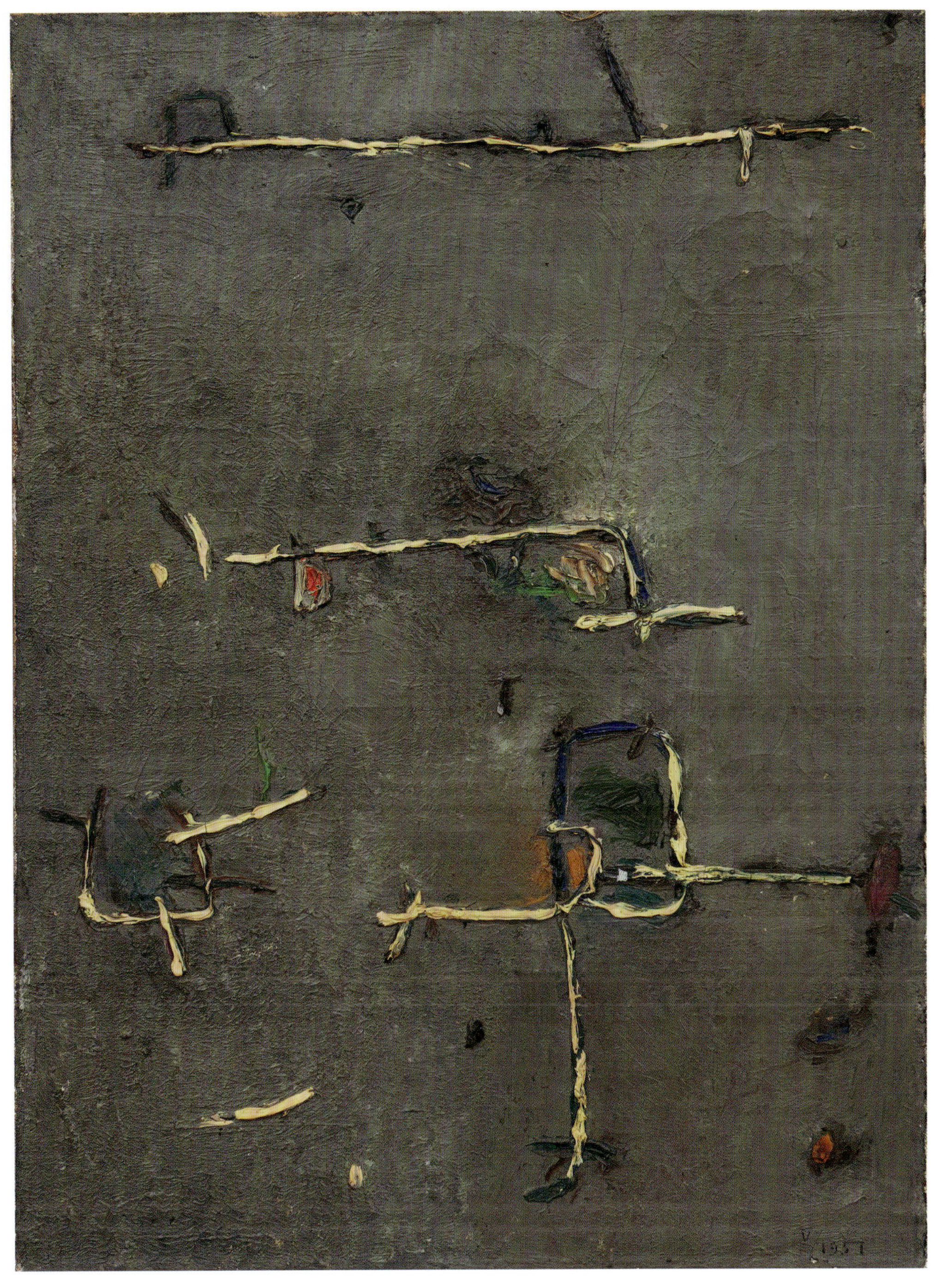

Painting CXVII, 1962
Oil on canvas
80 x 99 cm

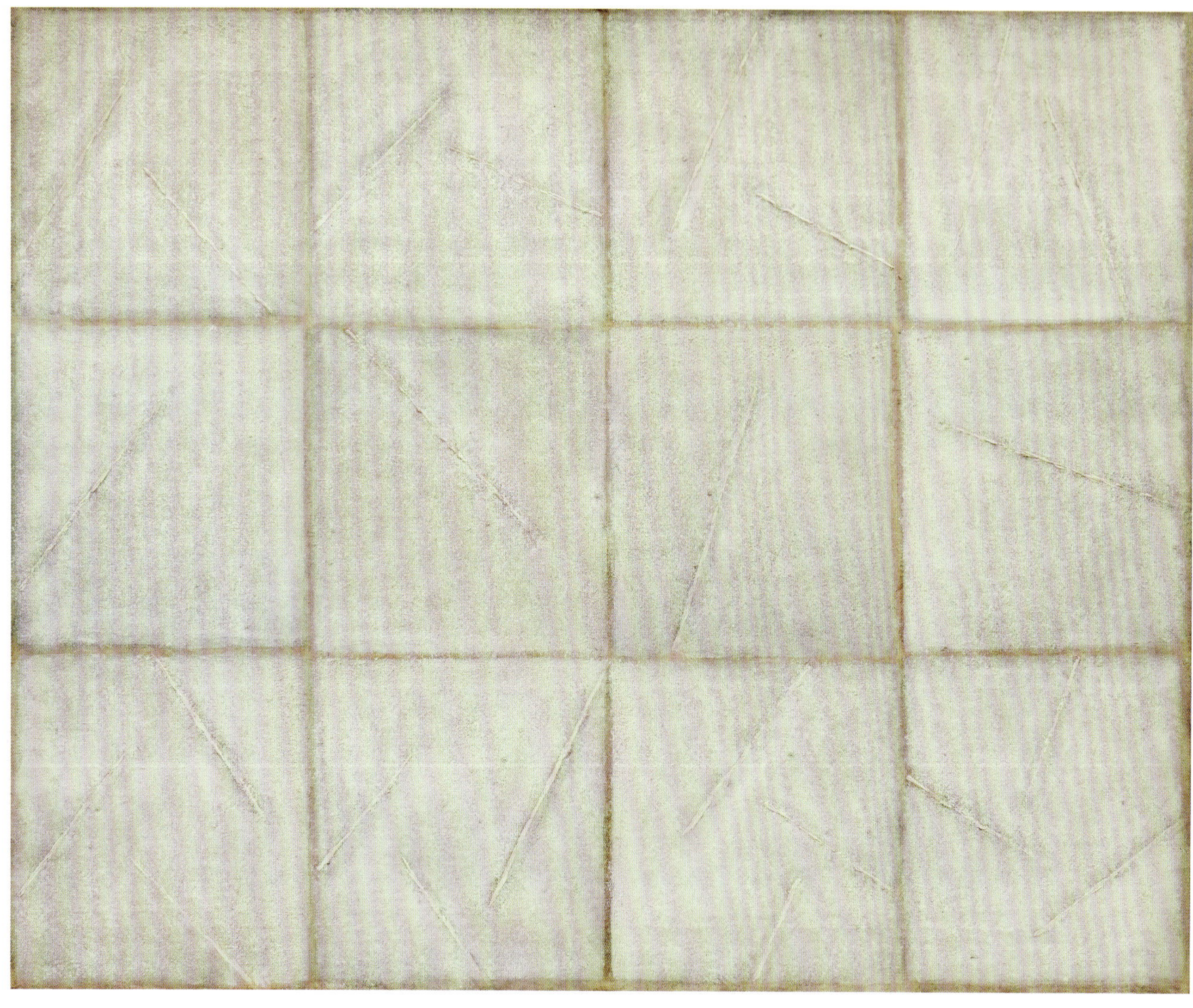

Painting CVI, 1961
Oil on canvas
60 x 80 cm

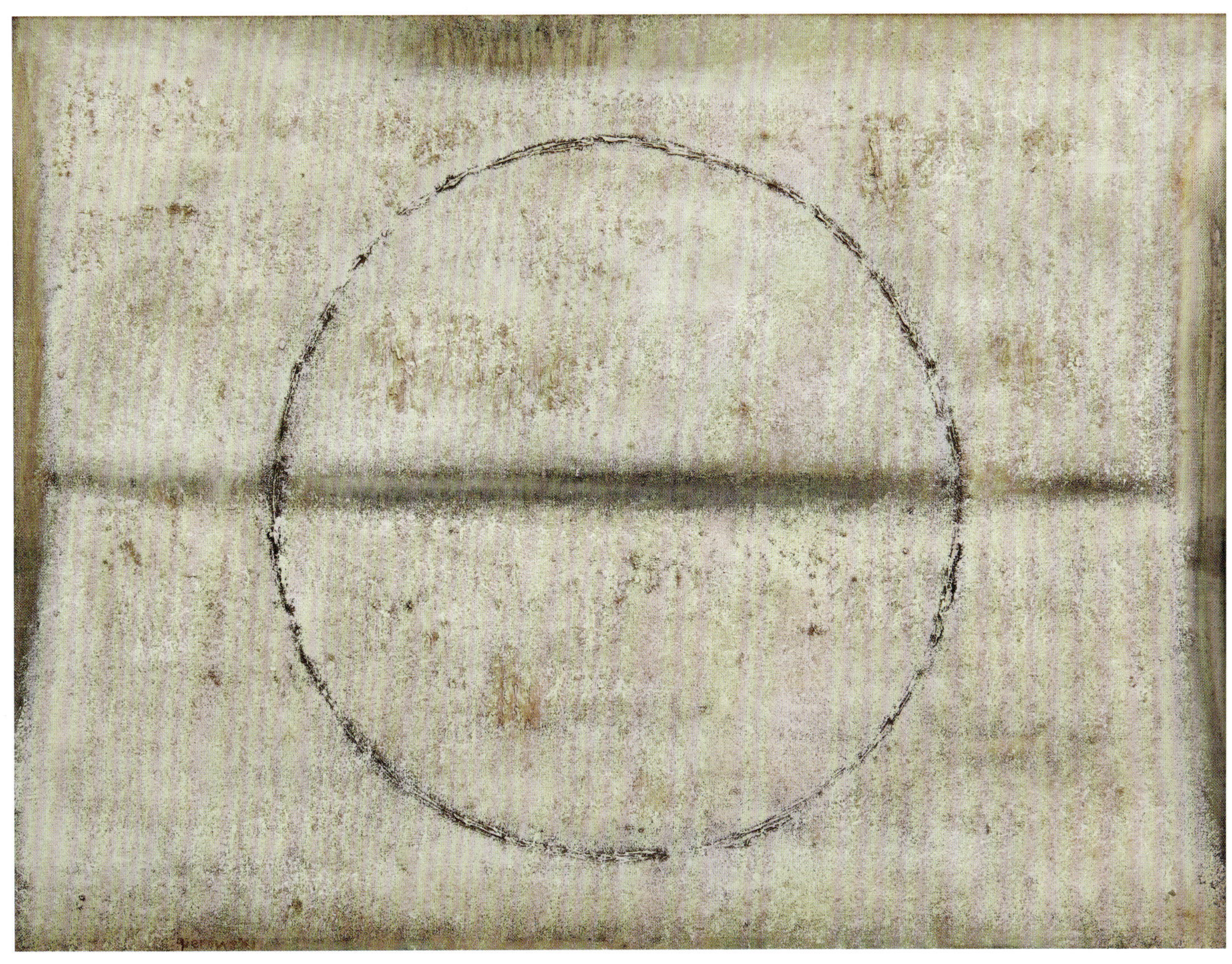

Painting XCVII, 1960
Oil on canvas
135 x 100 cm

Painting CXI, 1961
Oil on canvas
135 x 136 cm

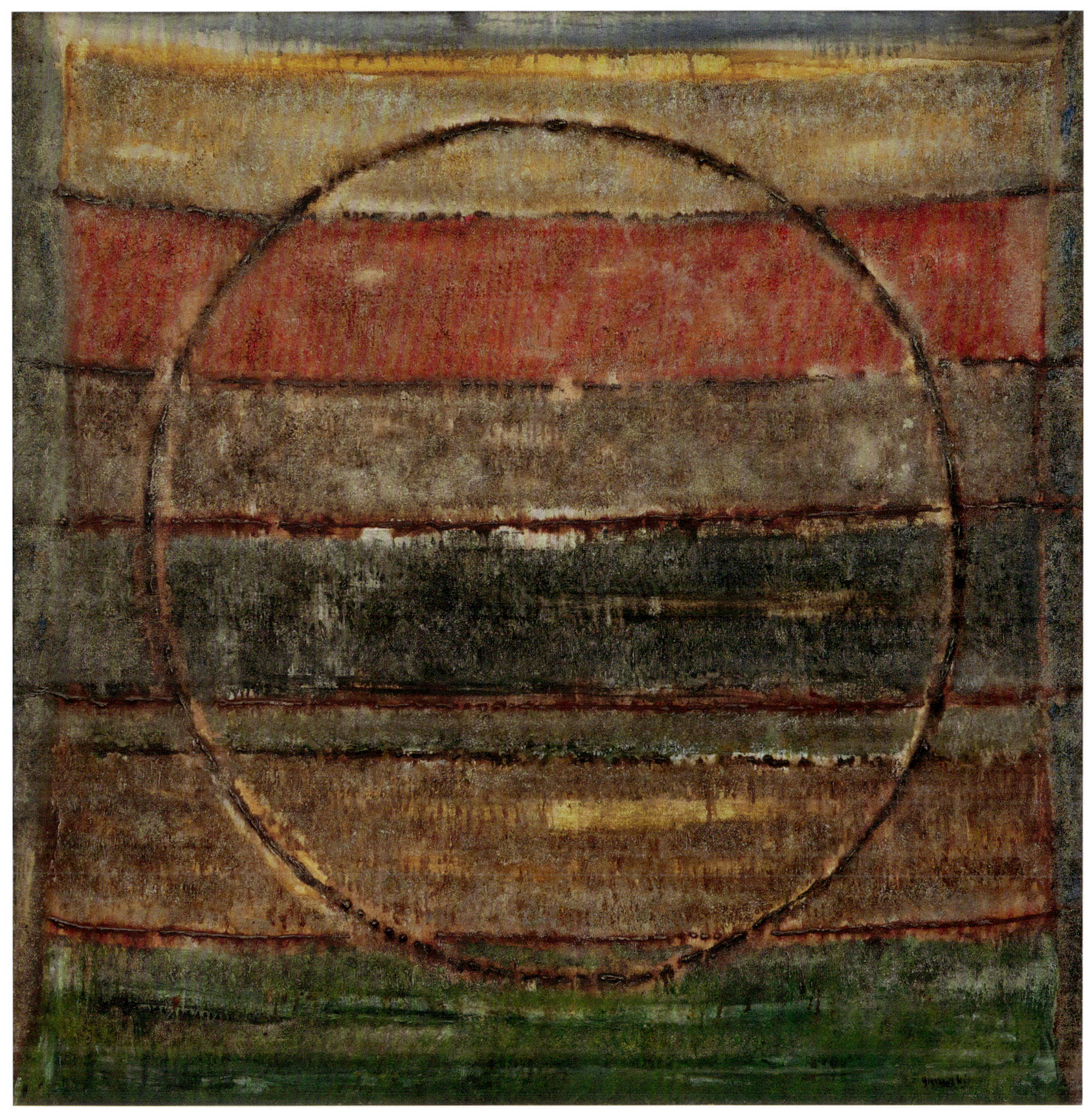

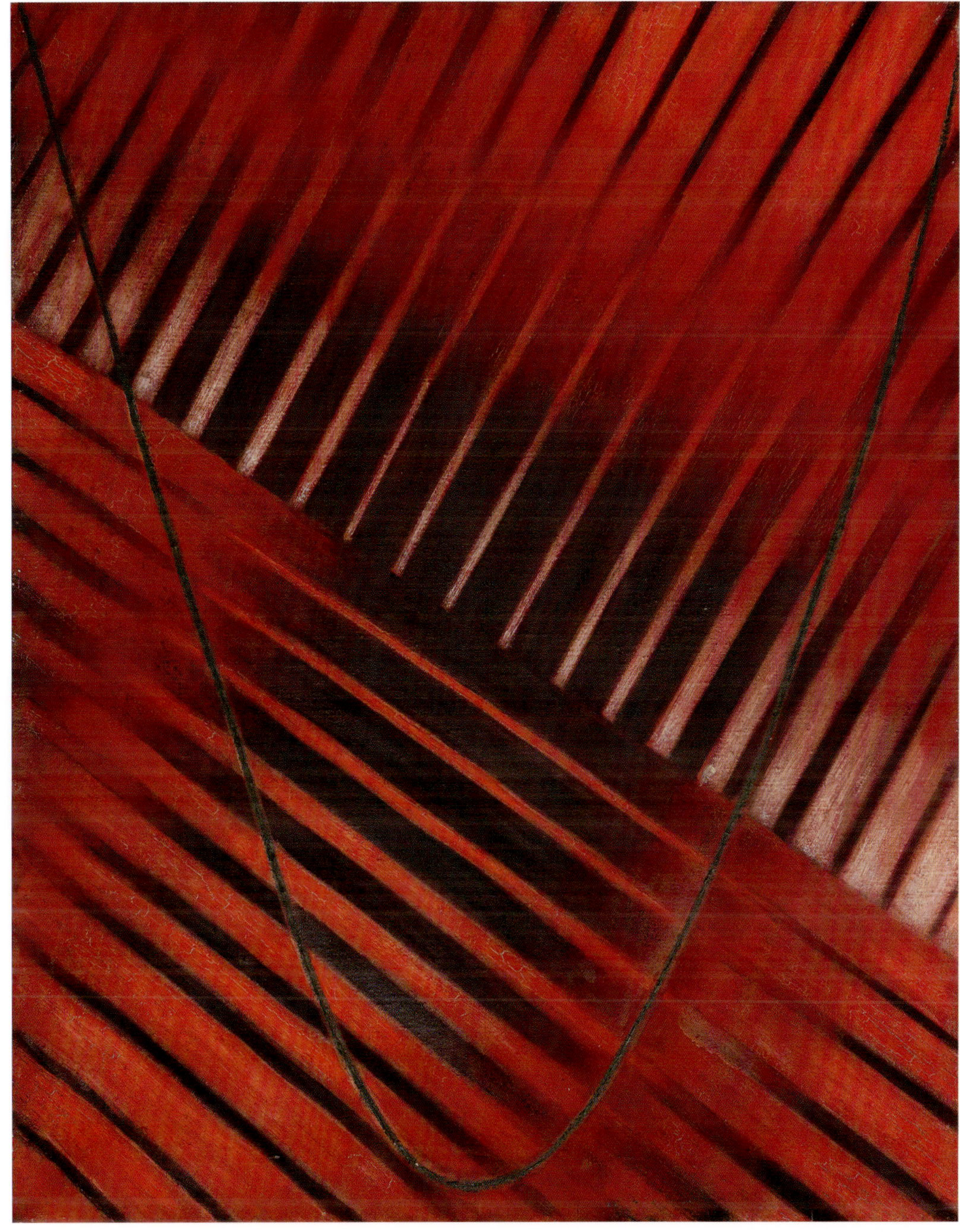

Painting CXLIX, 1963–64
Oil on canvas
135 x 100 cm
National Museum in Poznań

Painting CCXII, 1967
Oil on canvas
100 x 80 cm
The Wojtek Fibak
Collection

Painting CXXIX (*Bicolour Space*), 1962
Oil on canvas
203 x 200 cm
National Museum in Poznań

Painting CXLIII, 1963
Oil on canvas
200 x 136 cm
National Museum in Wrocław

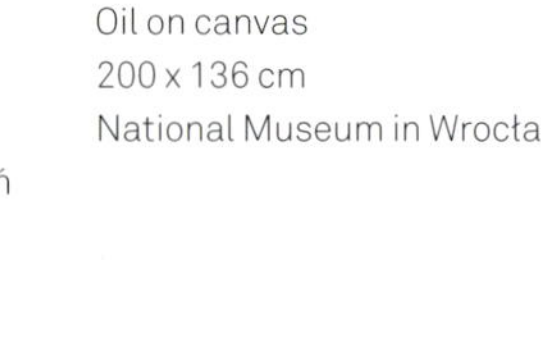

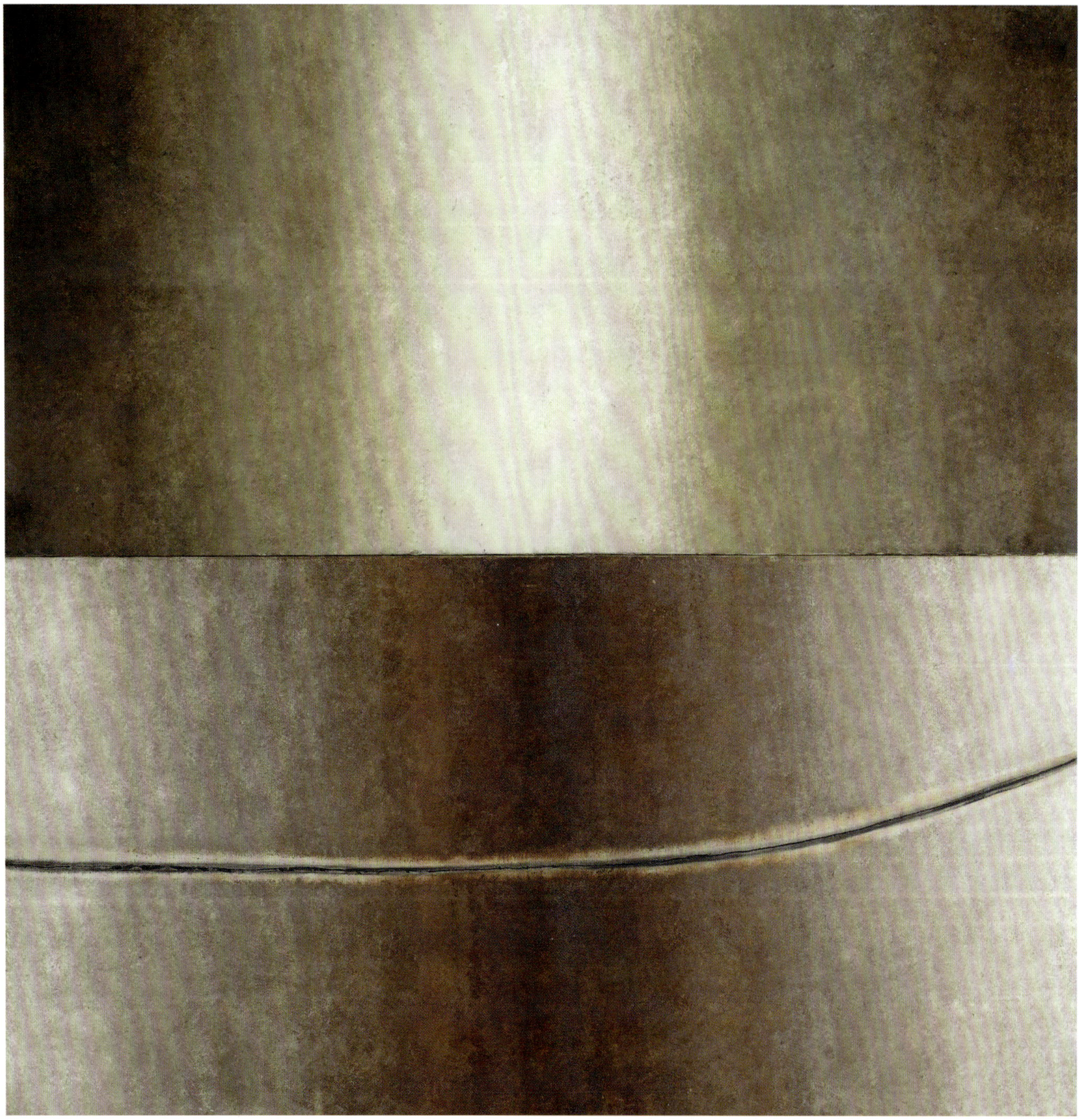

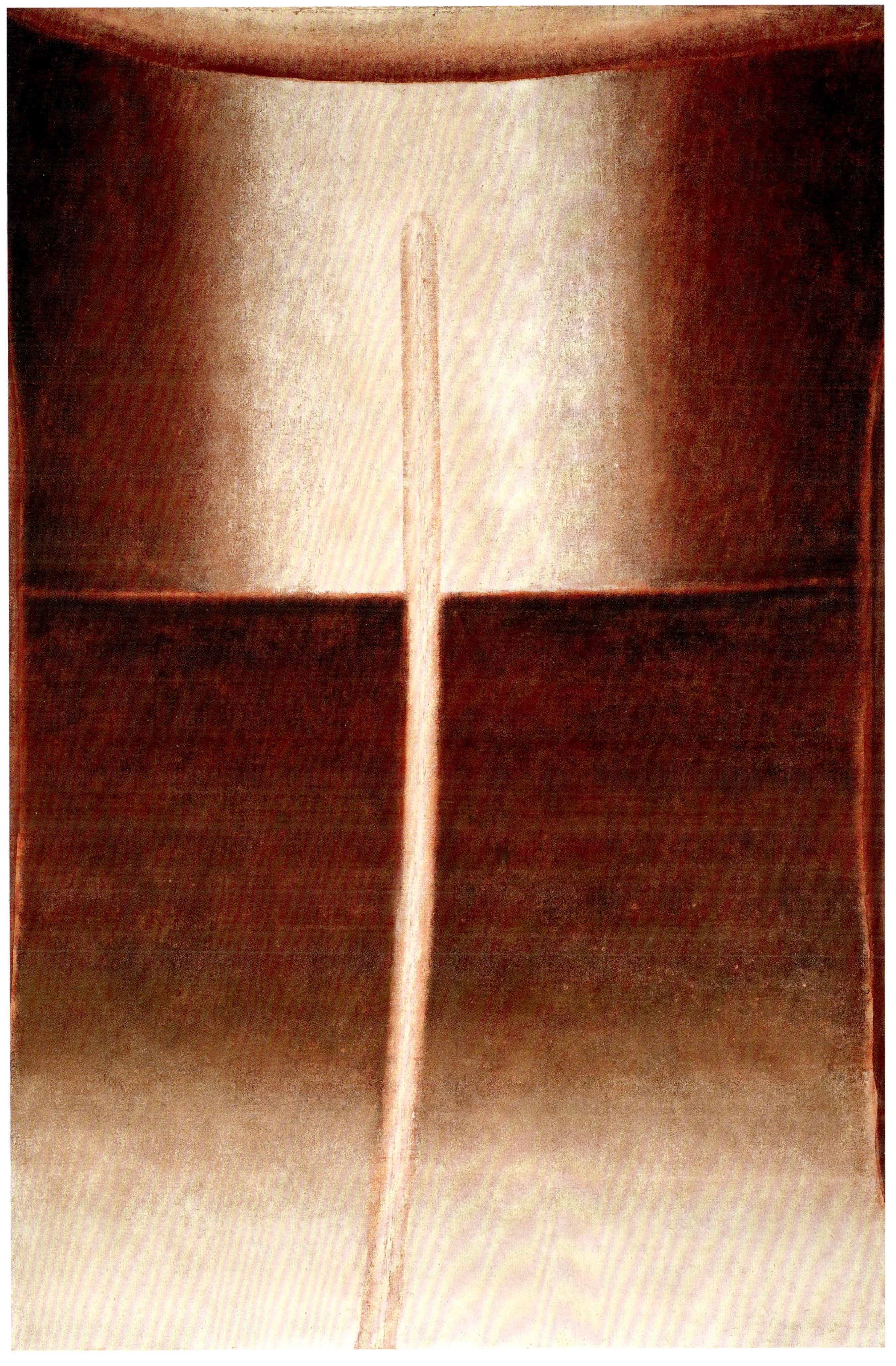

Painting CXCVII, 1966
Oil on canvas
100.5 x 134.5 cm

Painting CXCI, 1965
Oil on canvas
200 x 150 cm
Museum of Art in Łódź

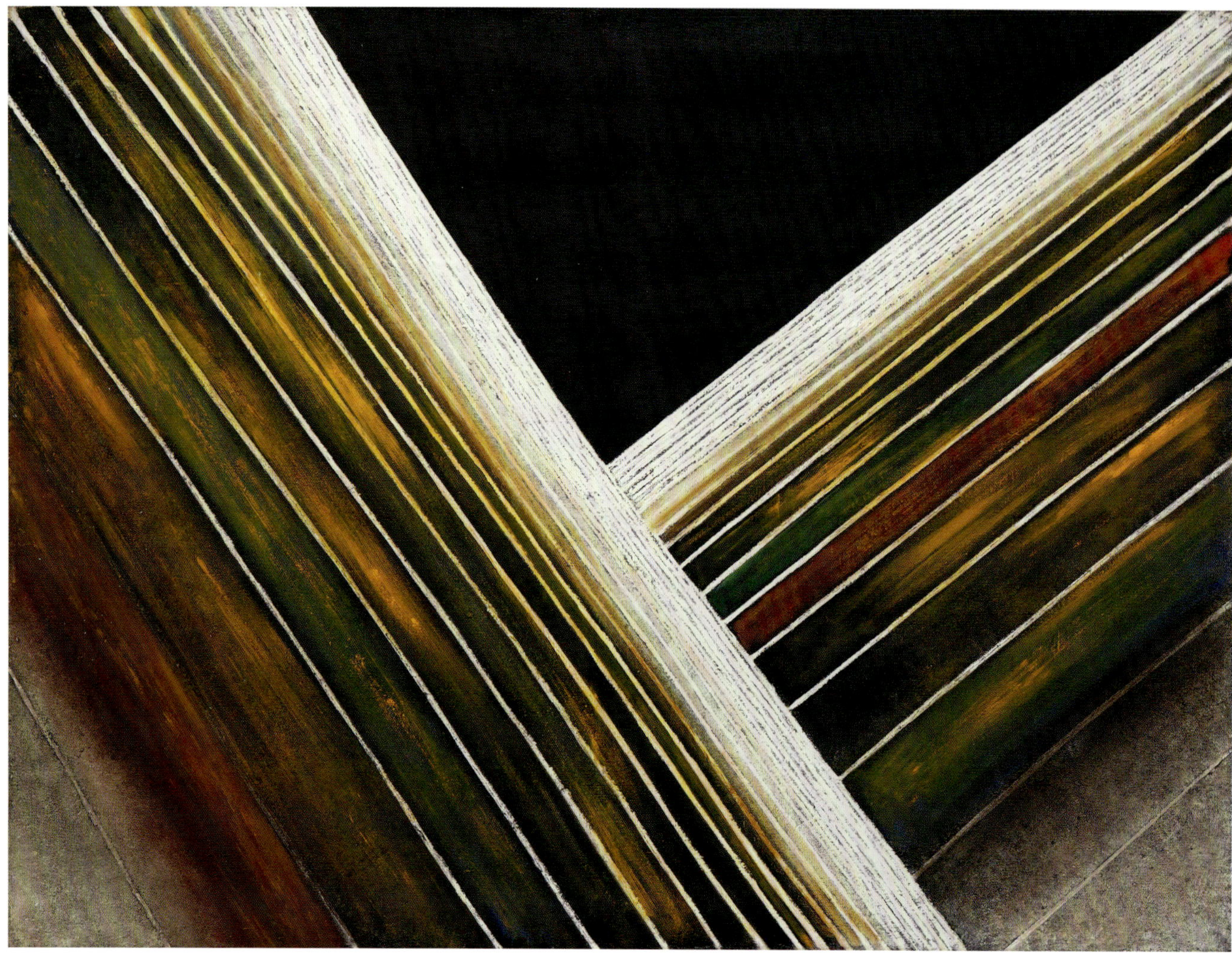

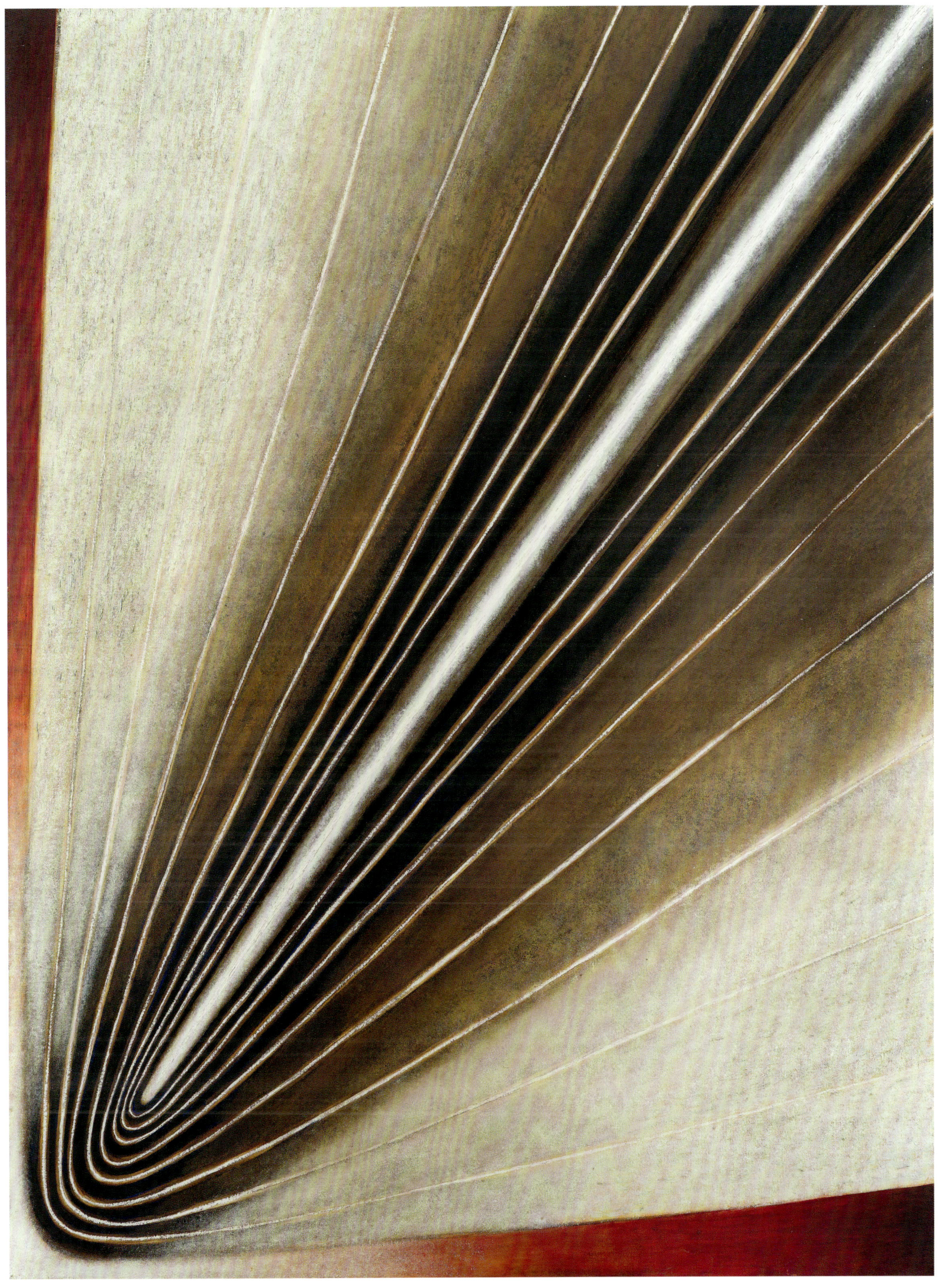

Painting CXCVIII, 1966
Oil on canvas
150 x 200 cm
National Museum in Poznań

Painting DXXI, 1984
Oil on canvas
200 x 130 cm

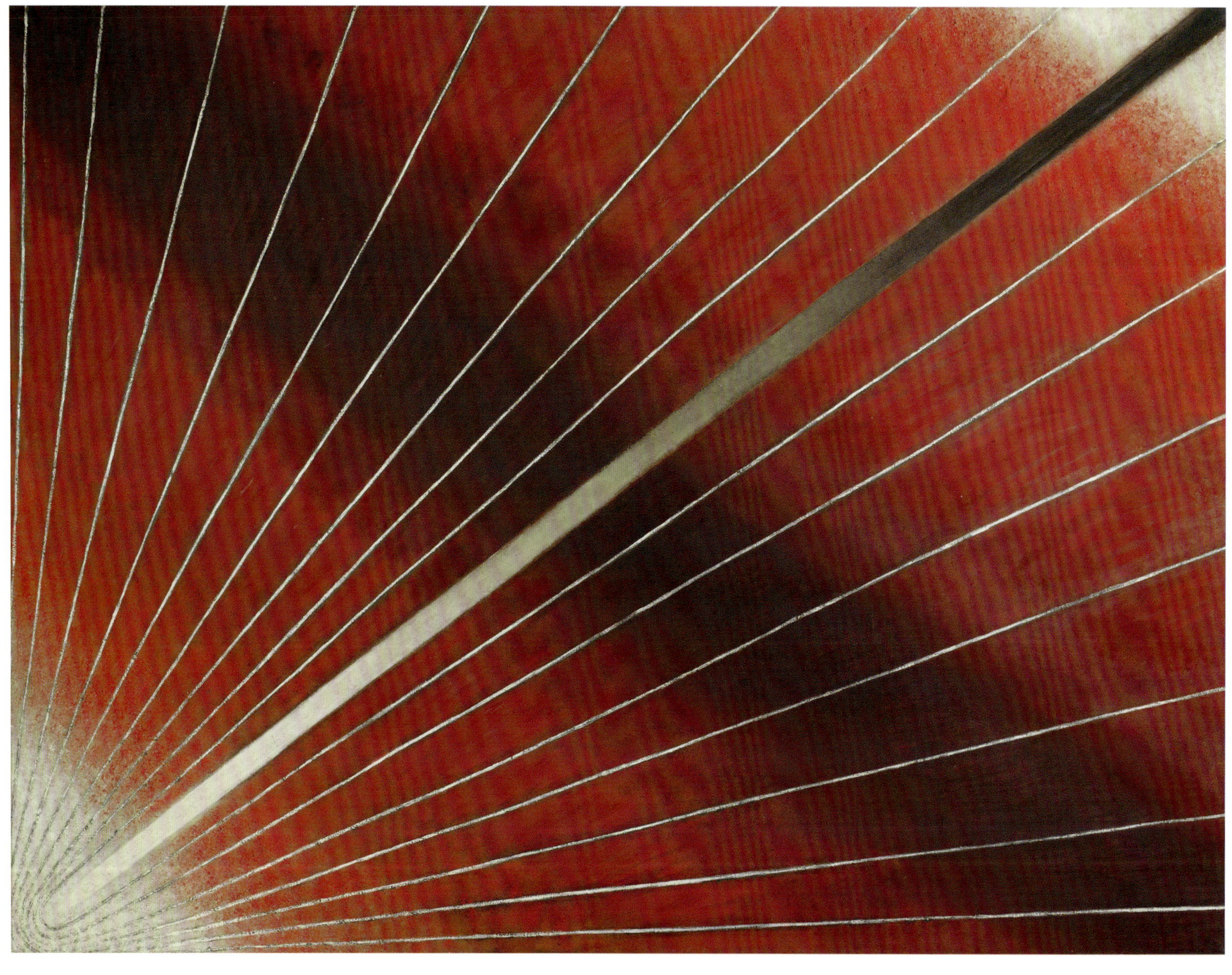

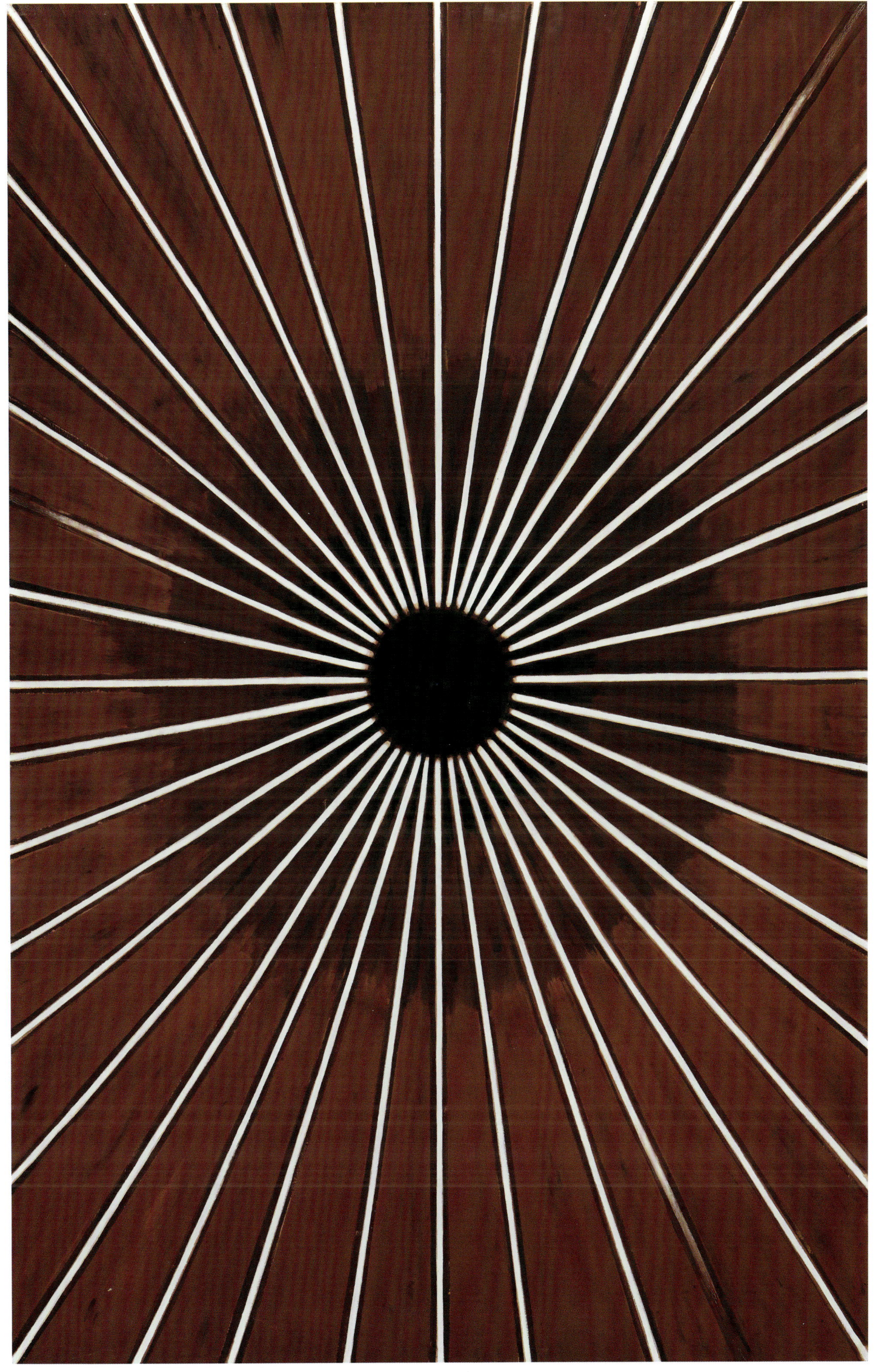

Painting CXC, 1965
Oil on canvas
150 x 150 cm
Museum of Art in Łódź

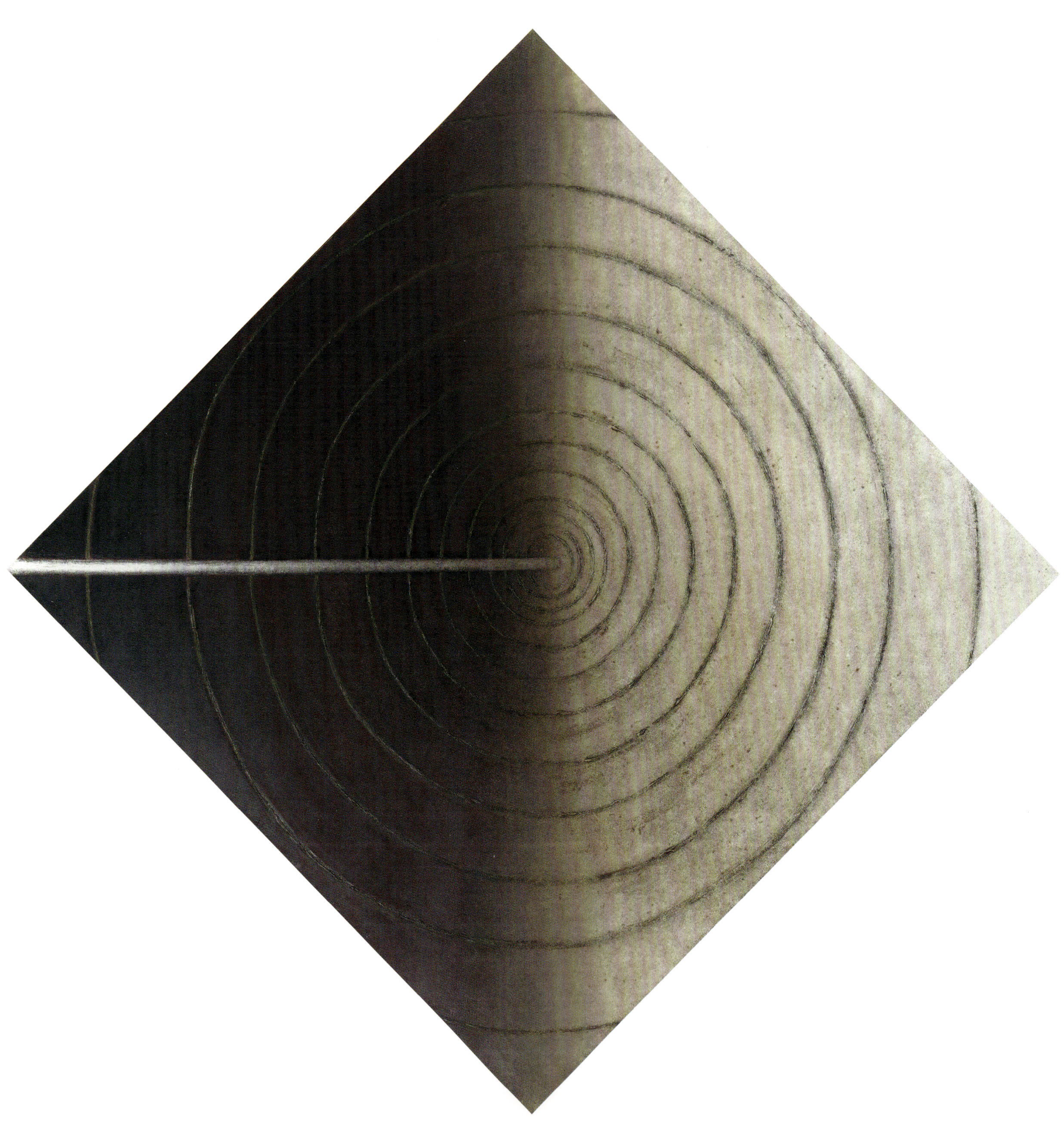

Painting CLXXXIX, 1965
Oil on canvas
100 x 135 cm
Museum of Art in Łódź

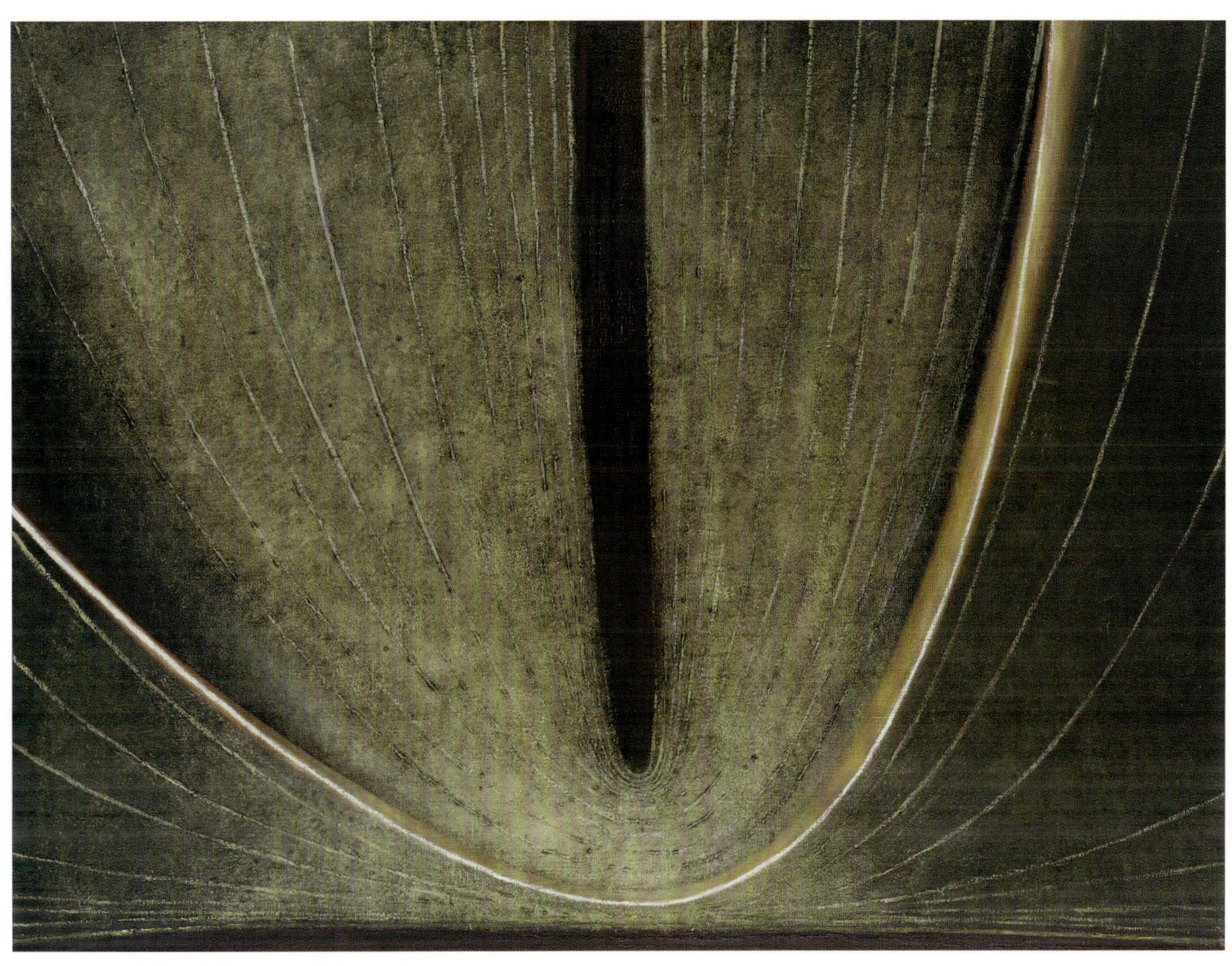

Painting CLXXX
(6 of 12 parts), 1964
Oil on canvas
100 x 100 cm each

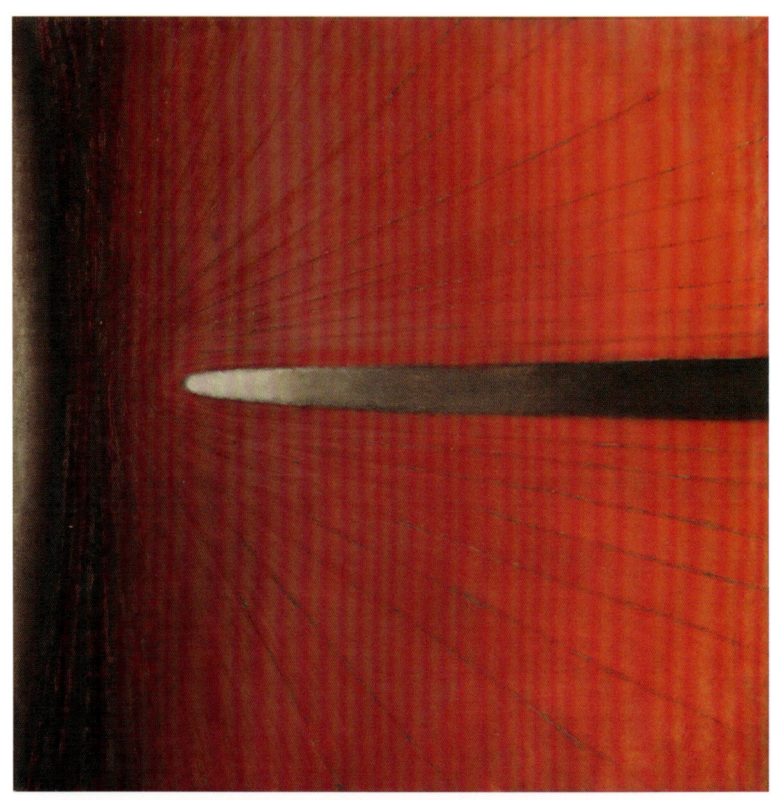

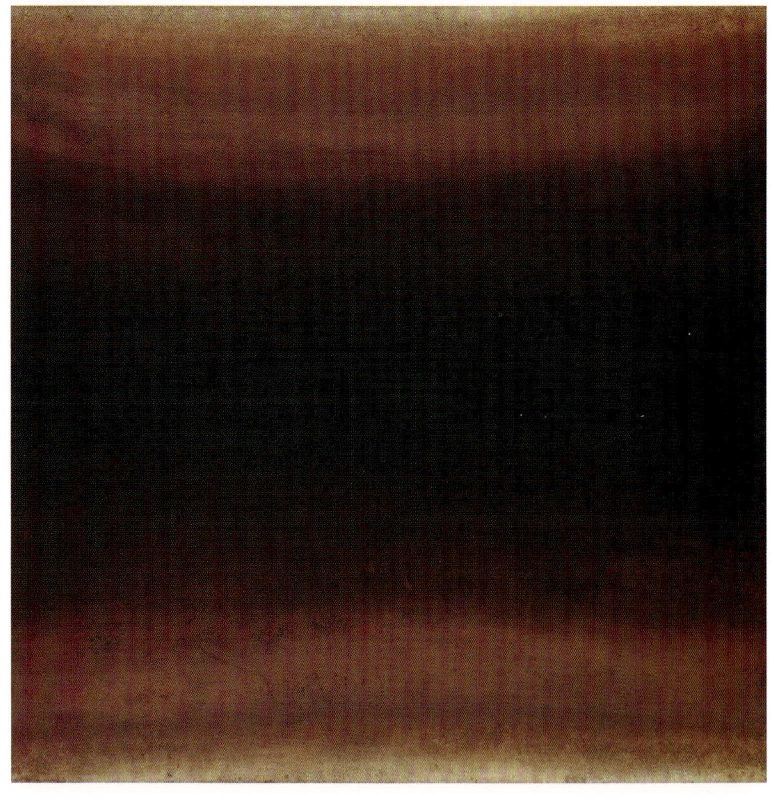

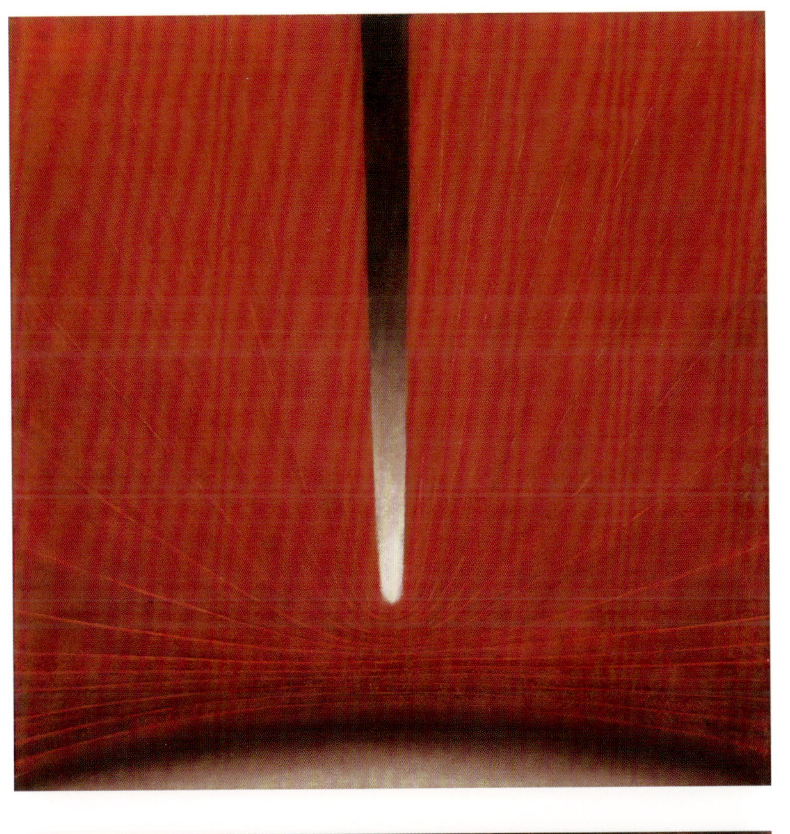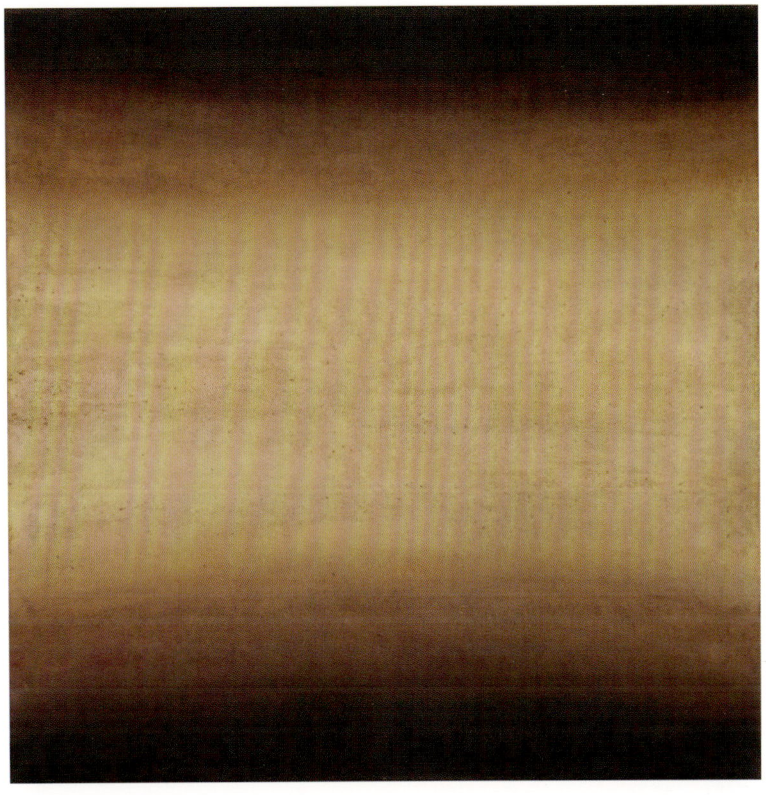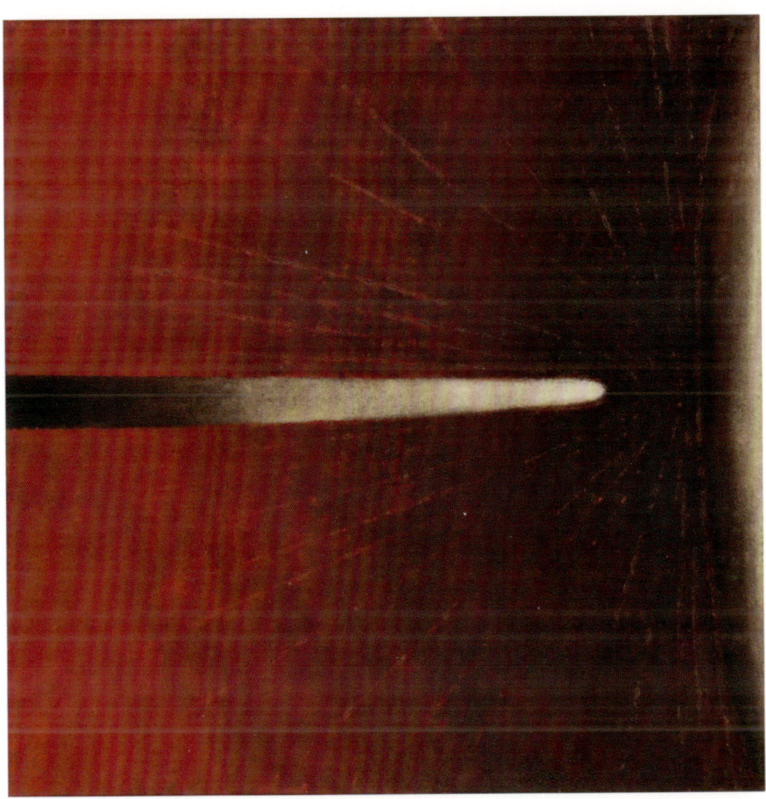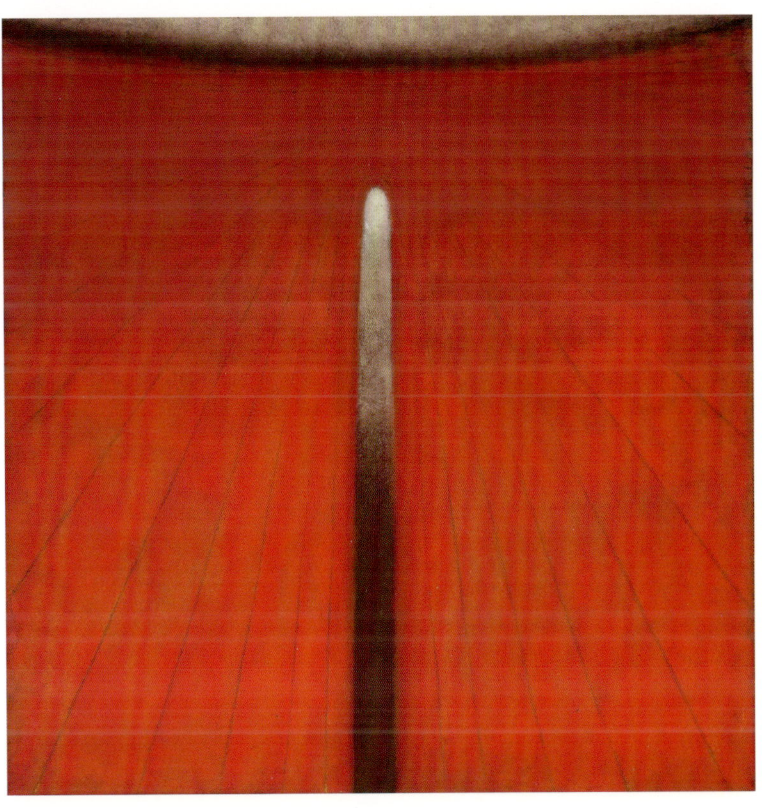

Painting CLXXX
(6 of 12 parts), 1964
Oil on canvas
100 x 100 cm each

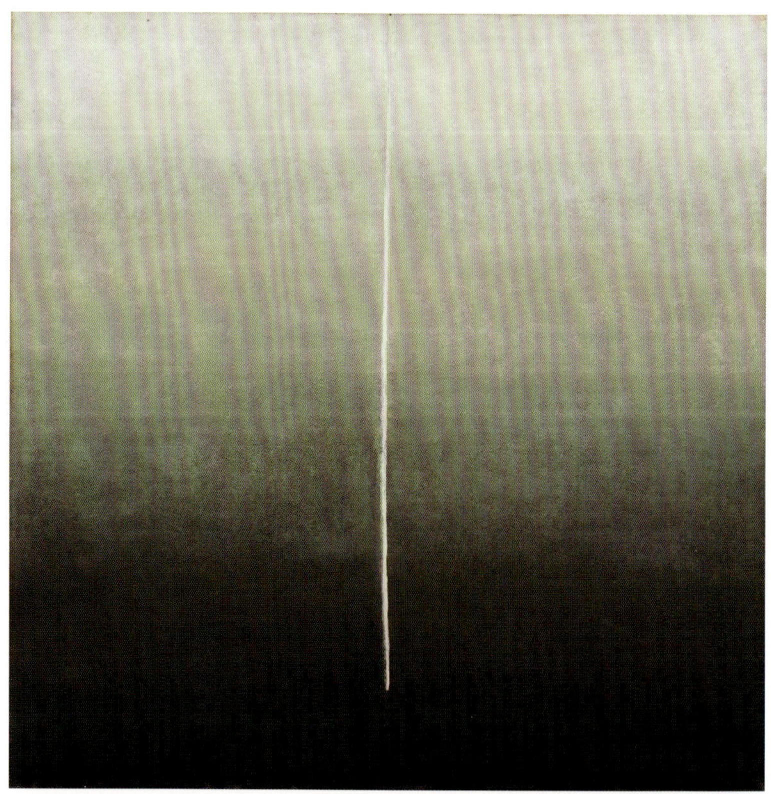

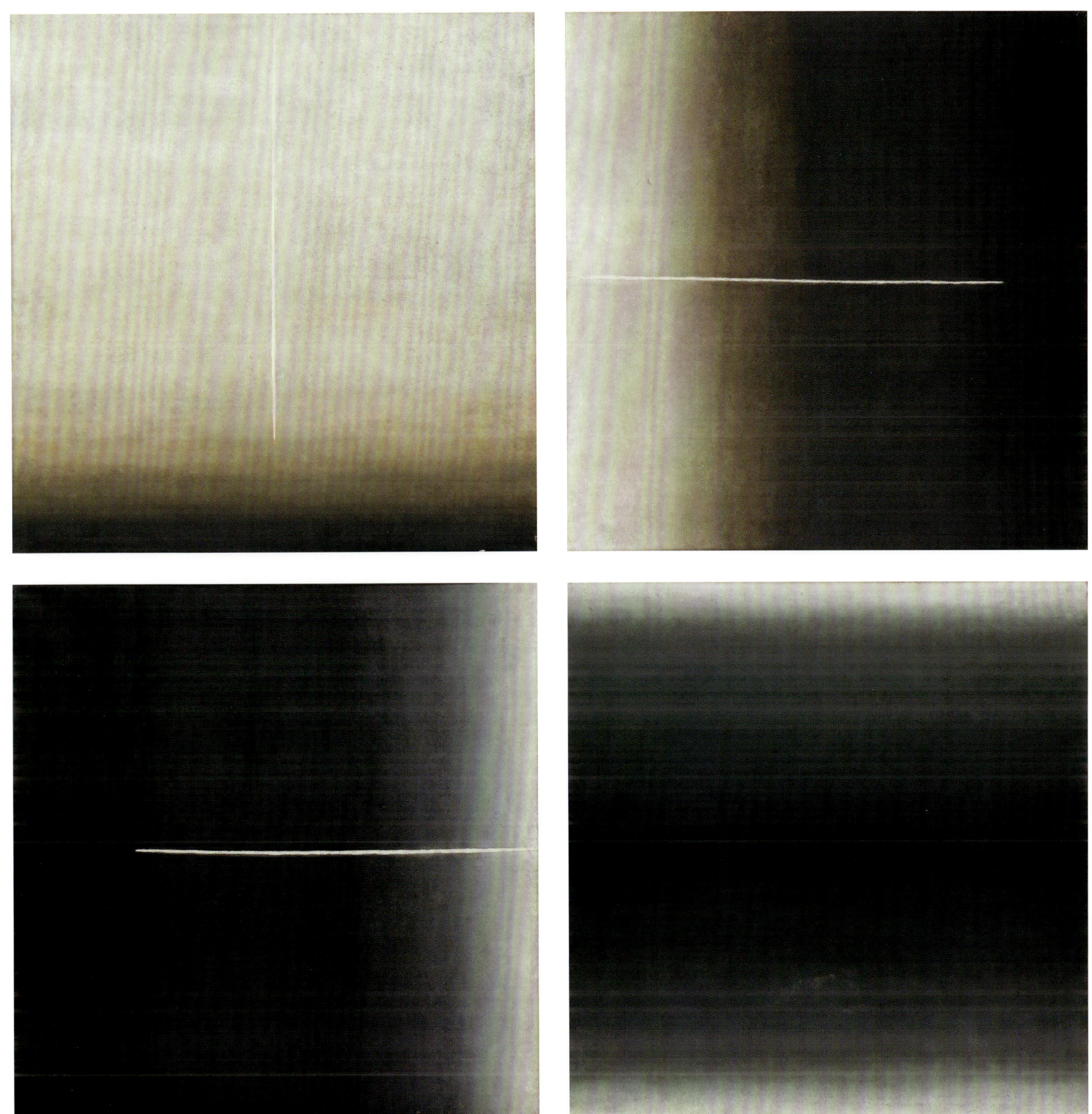

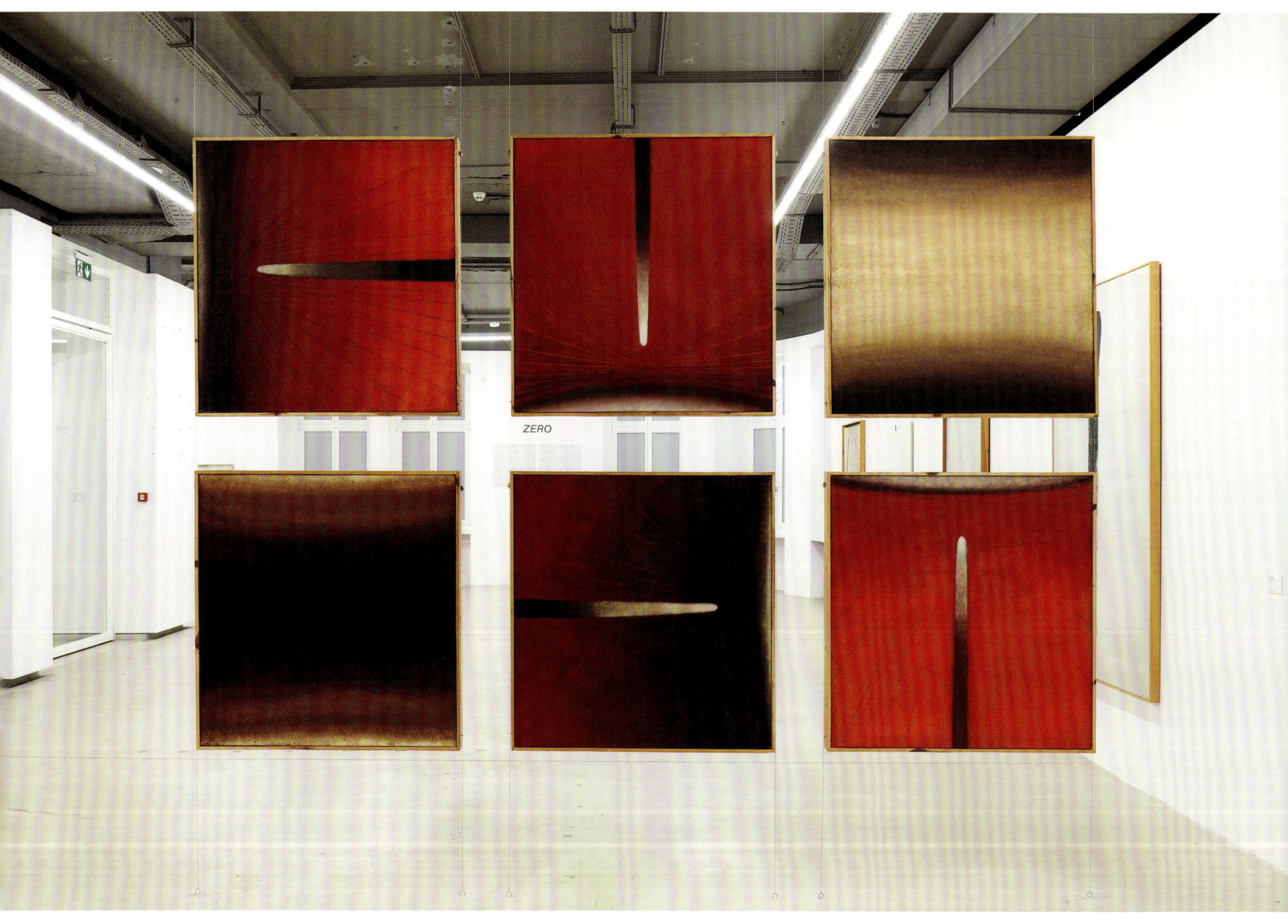

Painting CLXXX, 1964
*Deep Impact: Stefan Gierowski
and European Avant-Gardes
in the 60s*, exhibition view,
Stefan Gierowski Foundation,
Warsaw, 2019

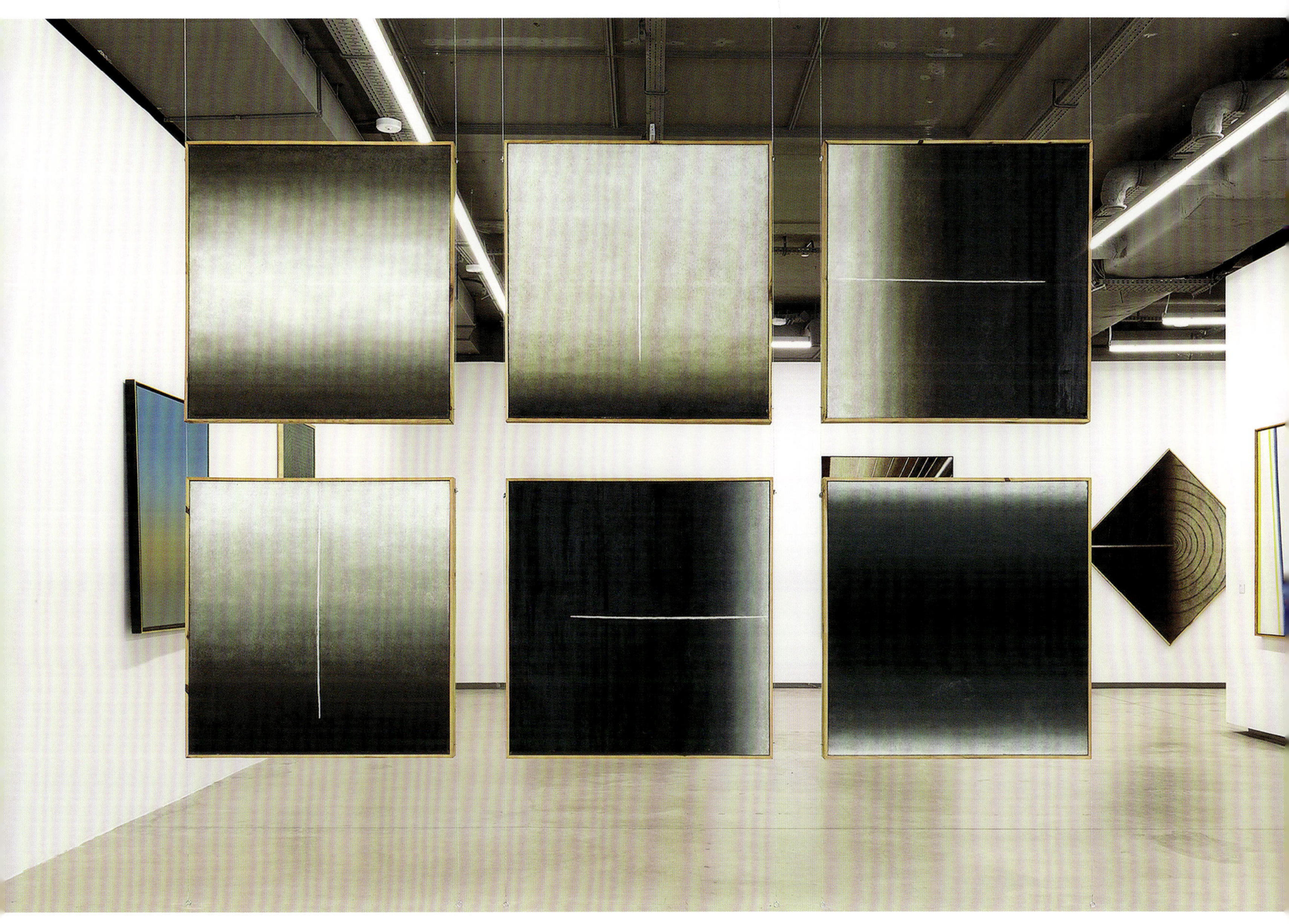

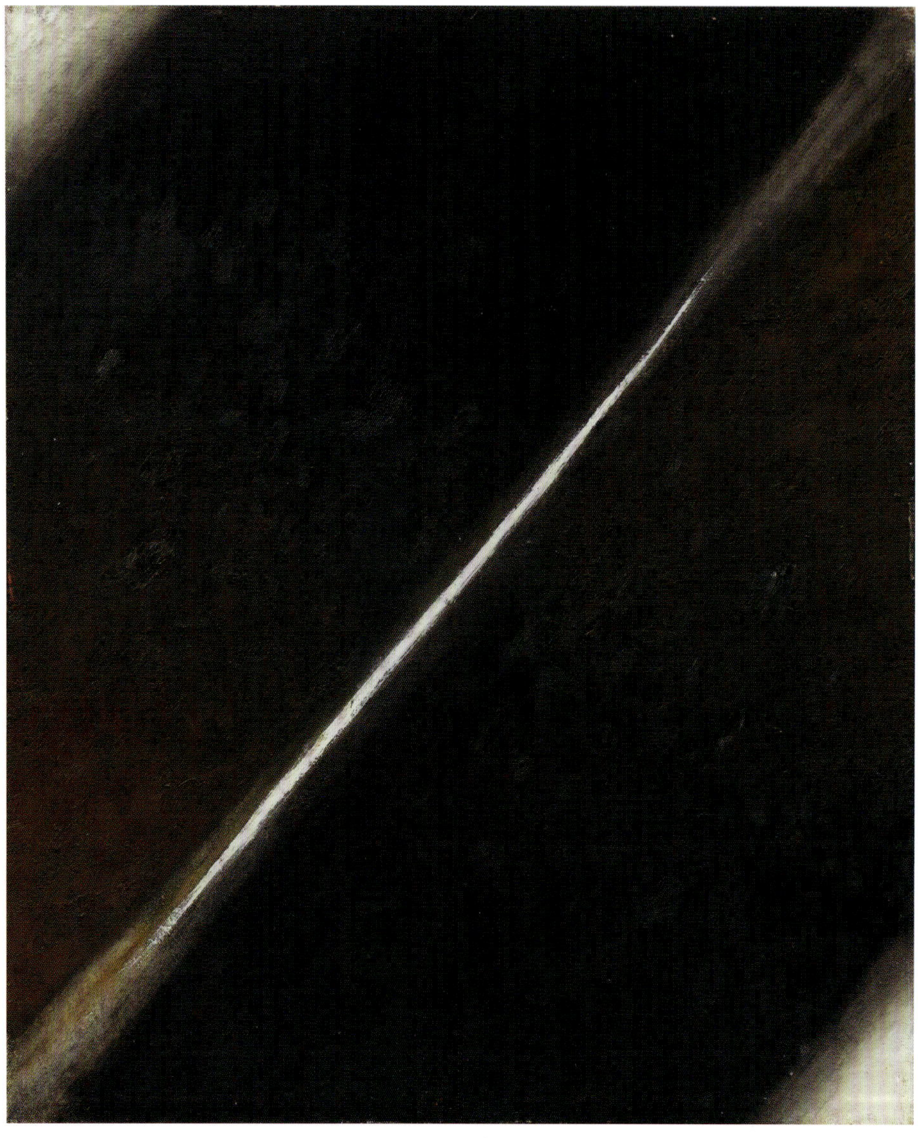

Painting CLXVII, c. 1962
Oil on canvas
59.5 x 50 cm

Painting CLV (*Strike*), 1964
Oil on canvas
199.5 x 180.5 cm
National Museum in Warsaw

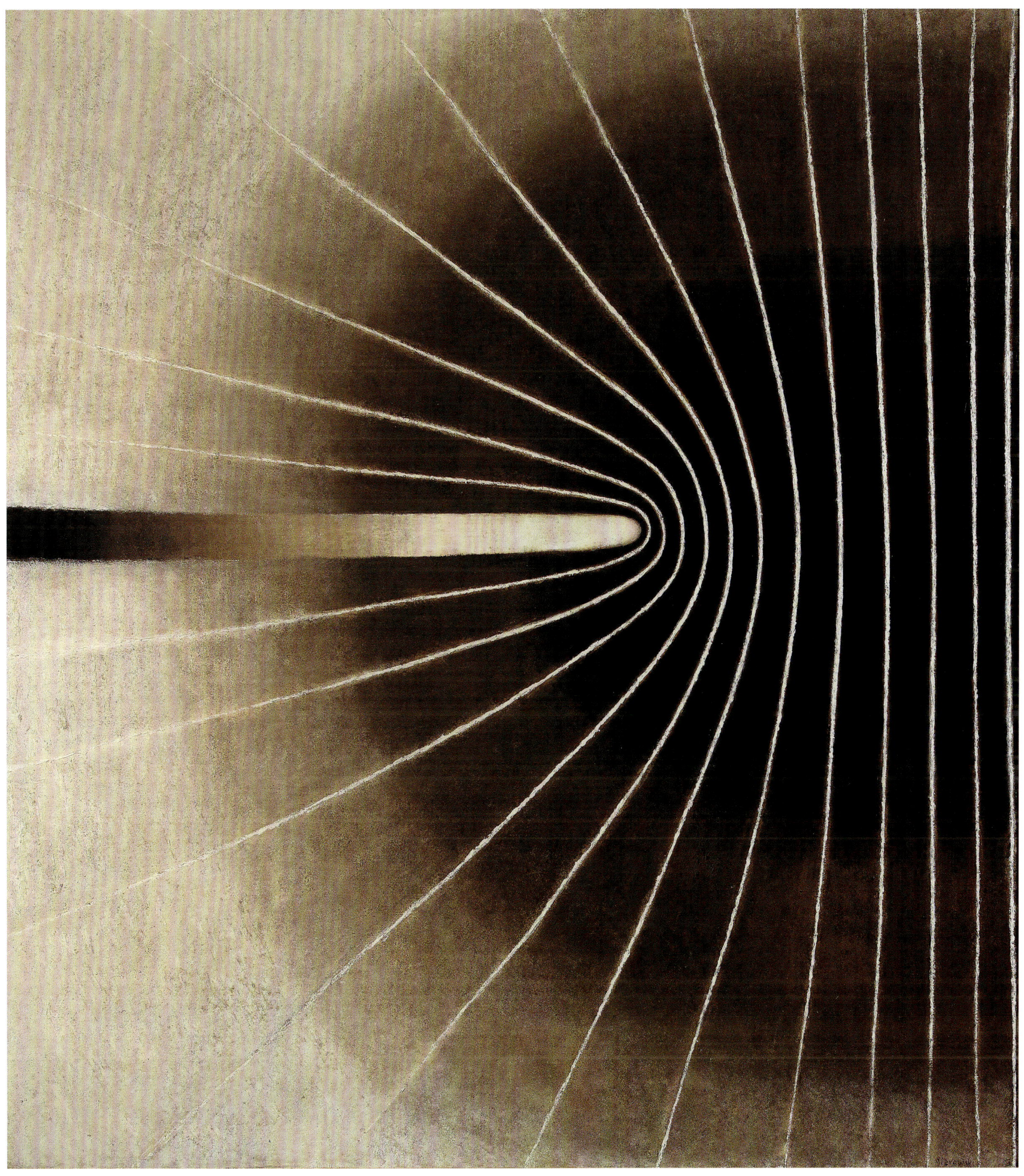

Painting CCXXI, 1968
Oil on canvas
120 x 80 cm

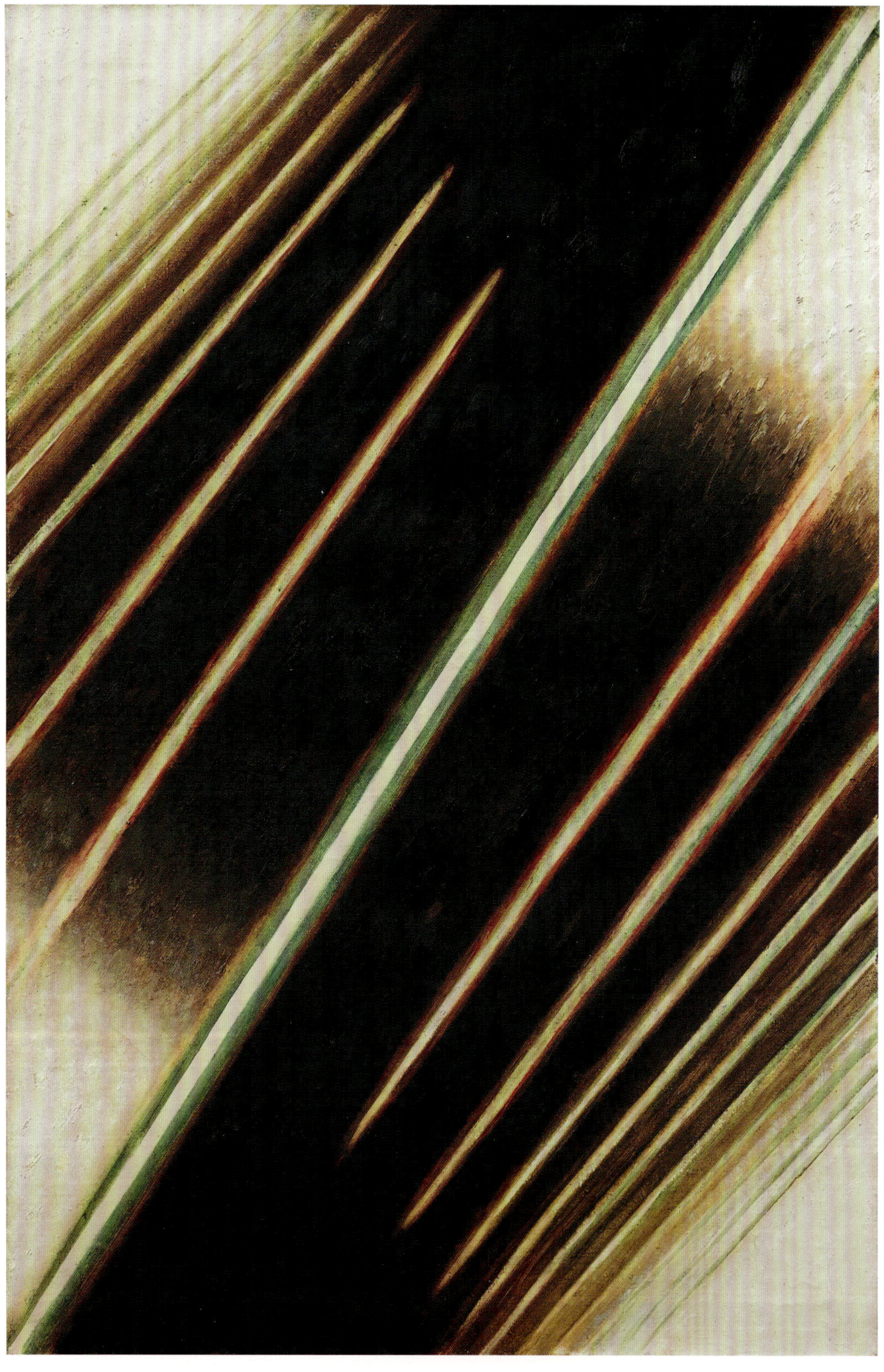

Painting CC (*Music*), 1966
Oil on canvas
134 x 100 cm
National Museum in Warsaw

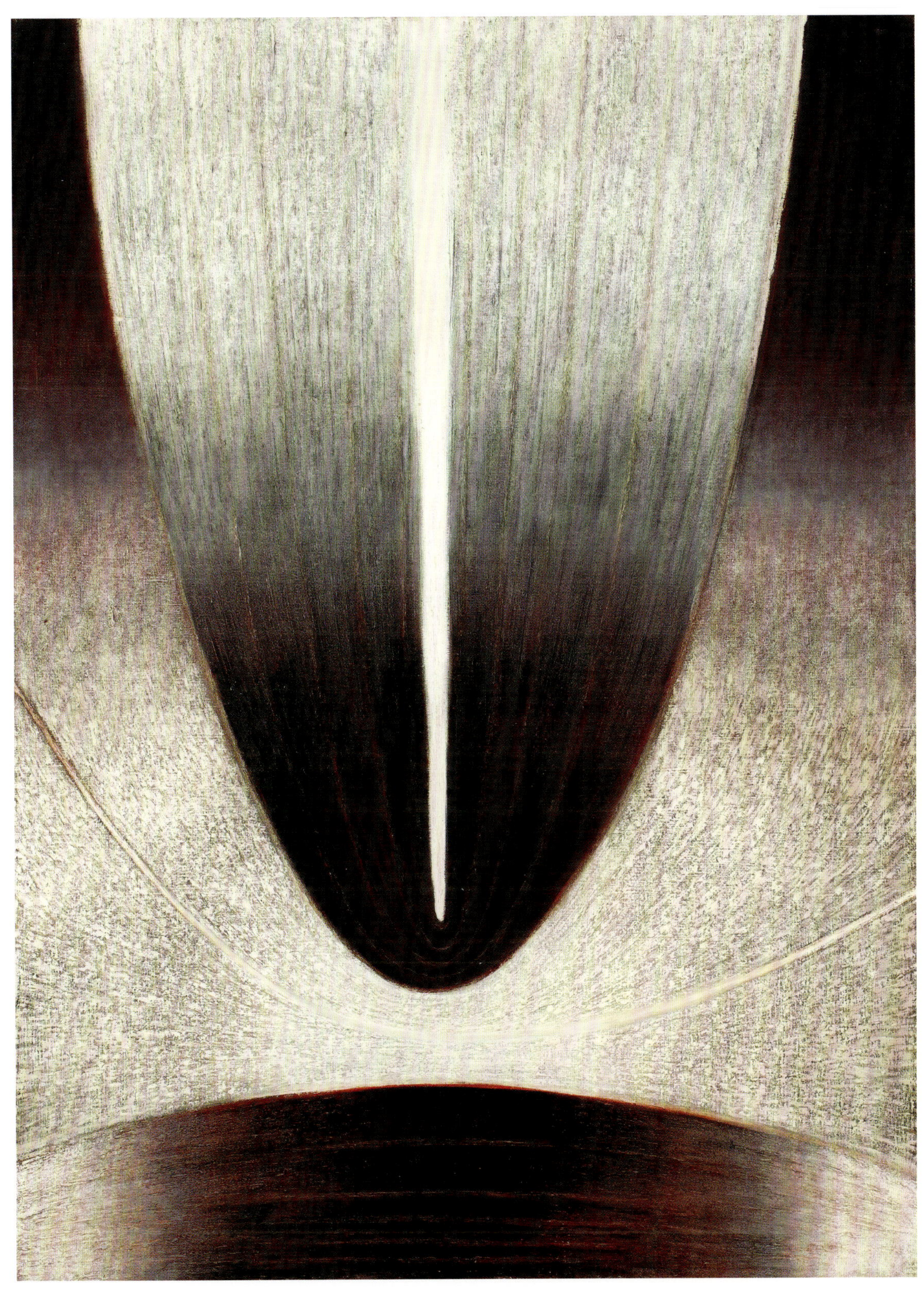

Painting CLXXXIV, 1964
Oil on canvas
65 x 50.6 cm

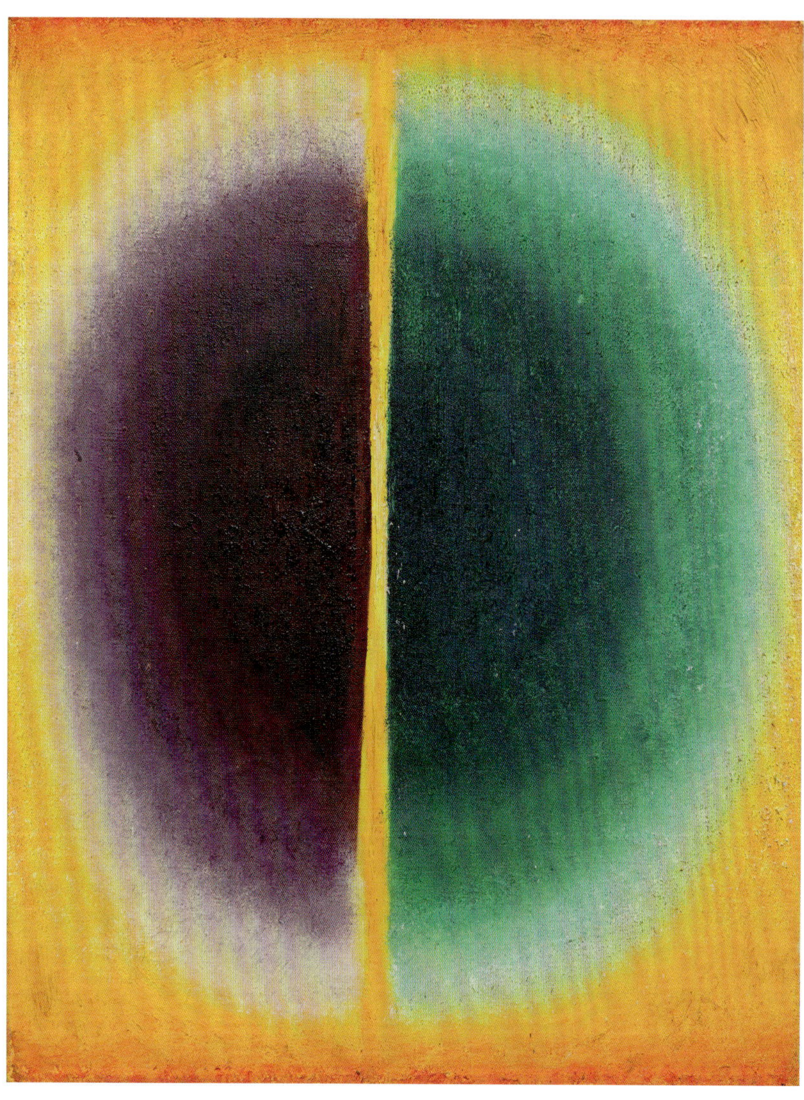

Painting CCXXIII, 1967
Oil on canvas
120 x 180 cm
Centre Pompidou, Musée
national d'art moderne, Paris

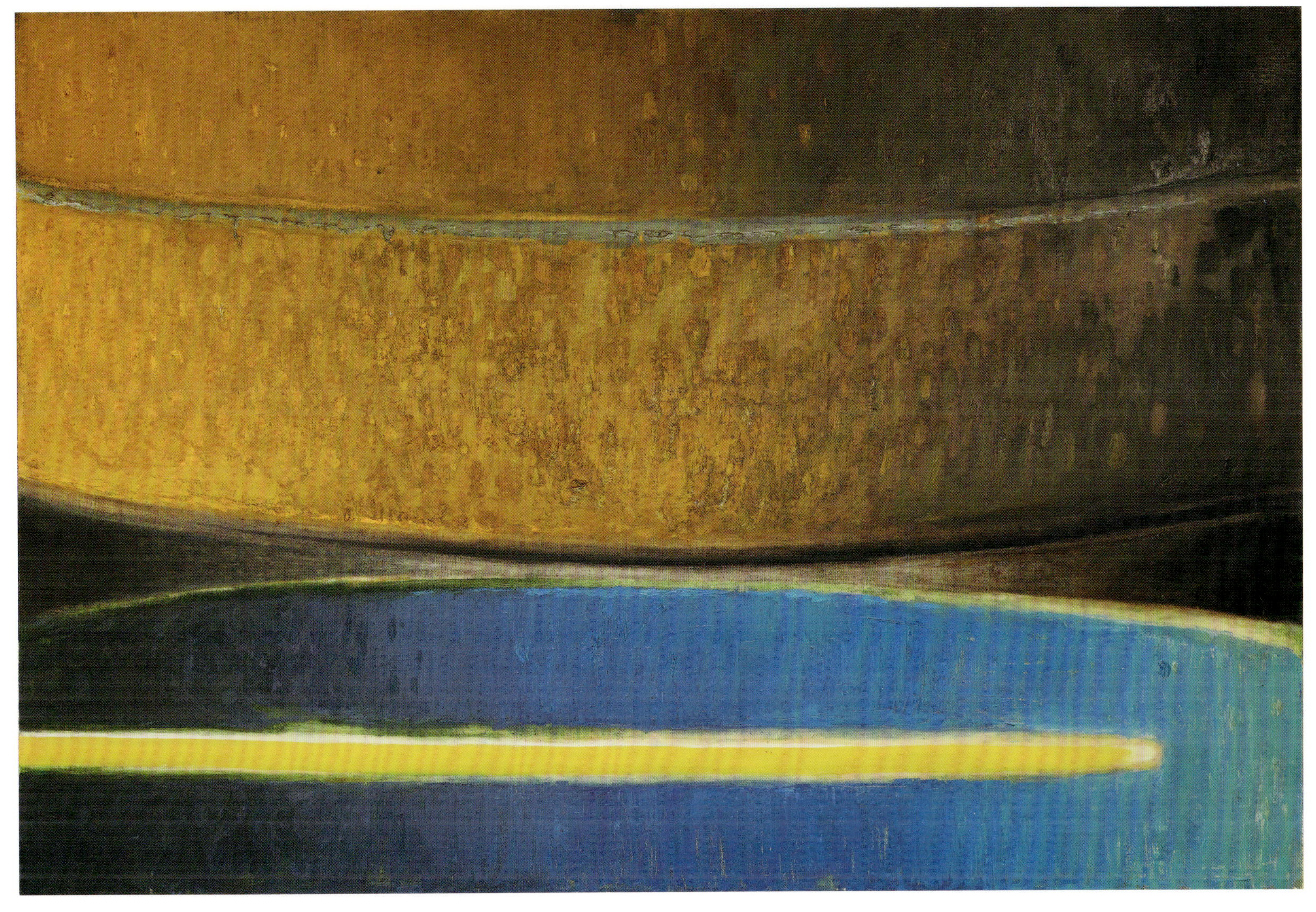

Painting CLX, 1964
Oil on canvas
135 x 90 cm
Jan Dekert Lubuskie Museum
in Gorzów Wielkopolski

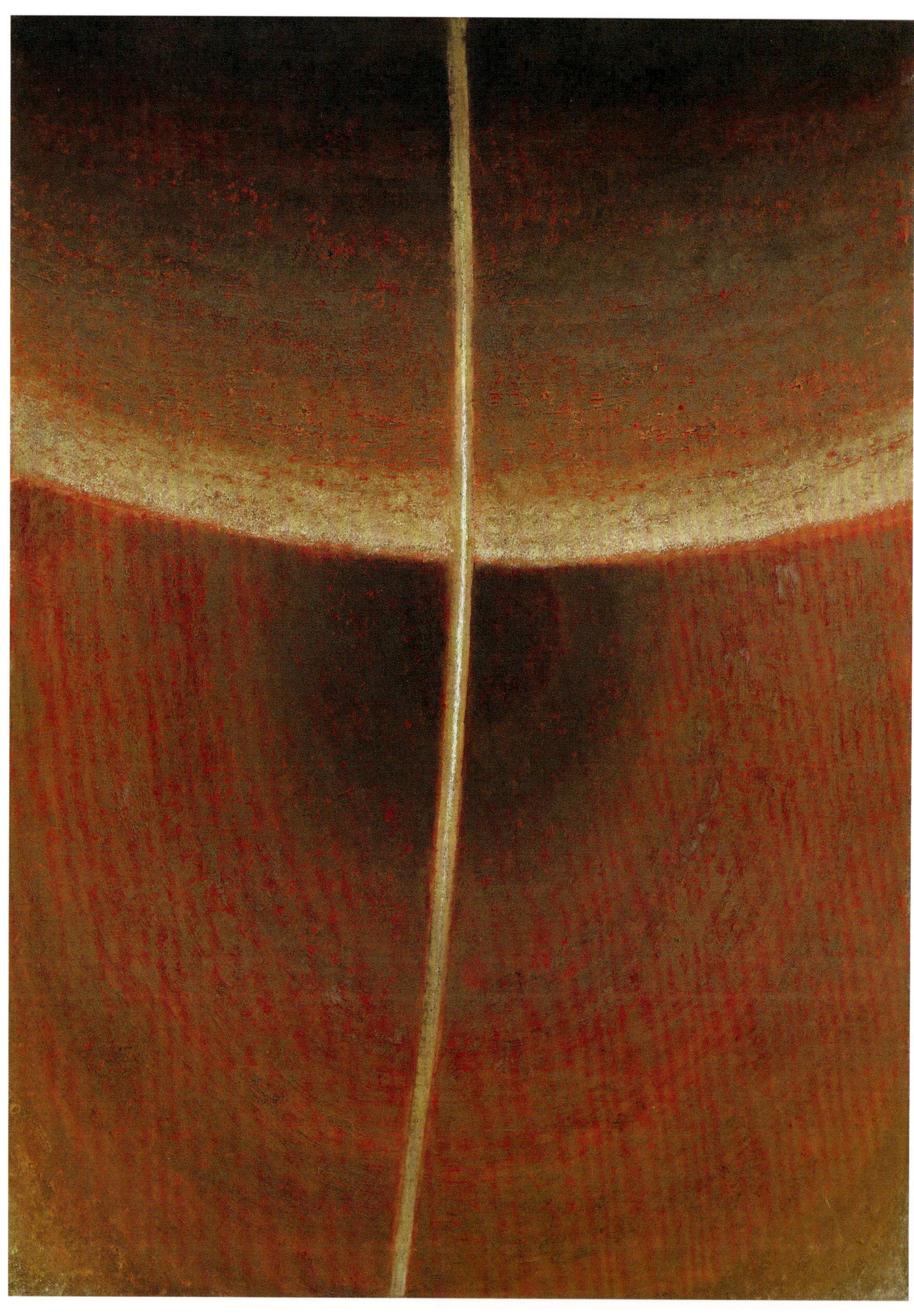

Painting CXXVII (Two Vertical Directions), 1962
Oil on canvas
134 x 101 cm
National Museum in Warsaw

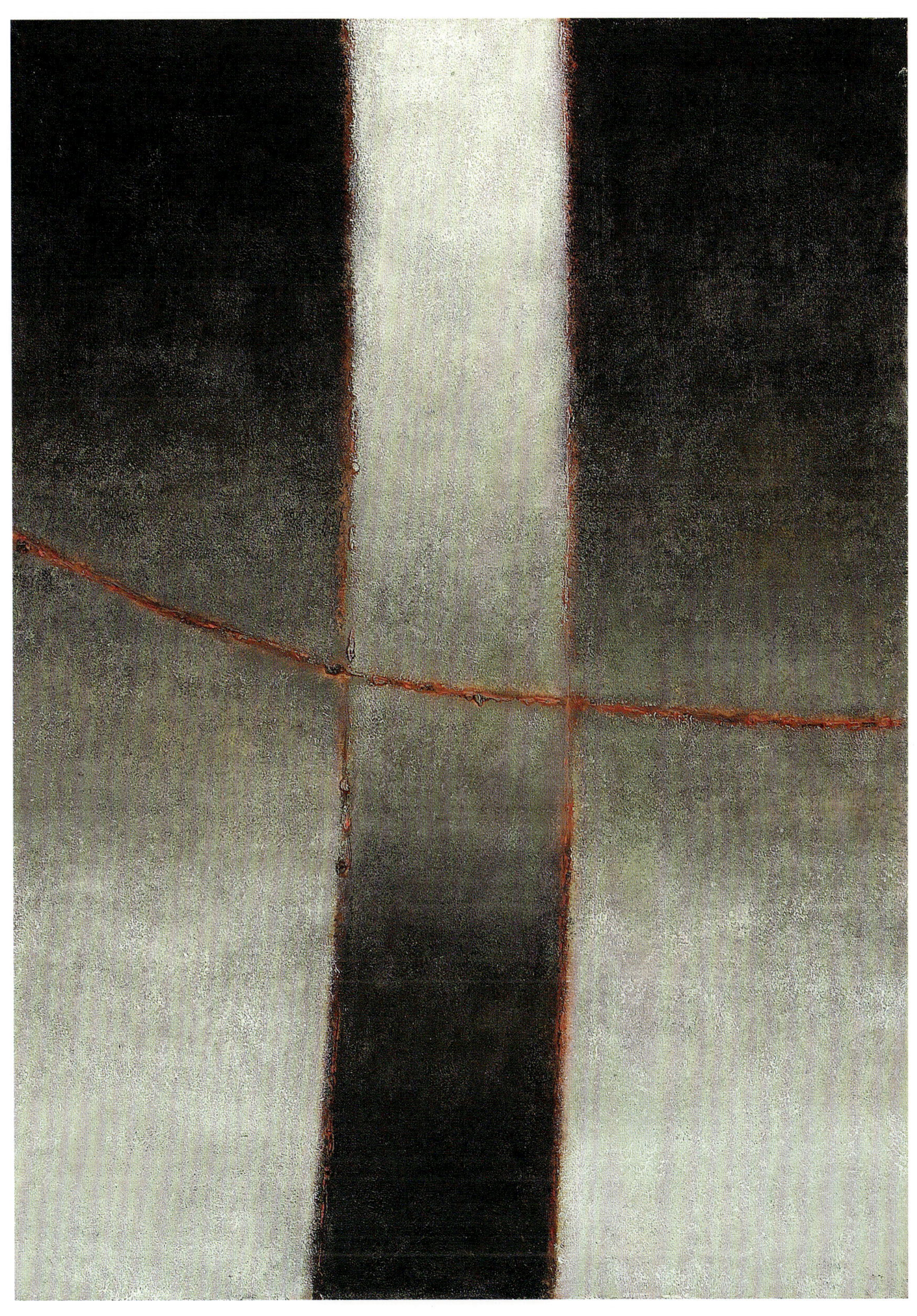

Painting CCIV, 1966
Oil on canvas
80 x 100 cm
Courtesy of Aleksander
Wojciechowski's family

Painting DCCCXXXVI, 2007
Oil on canvas
146 x 114 cm

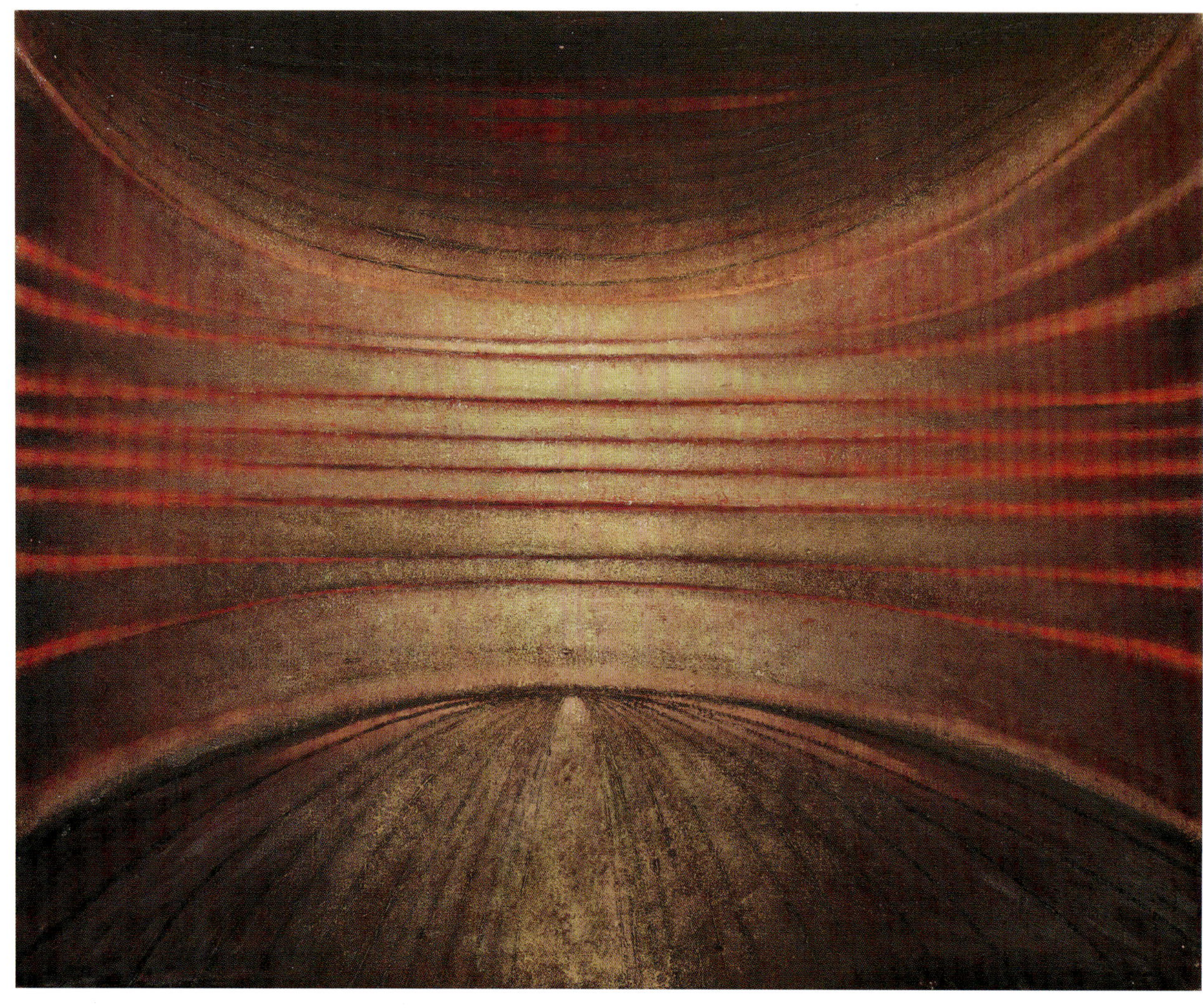

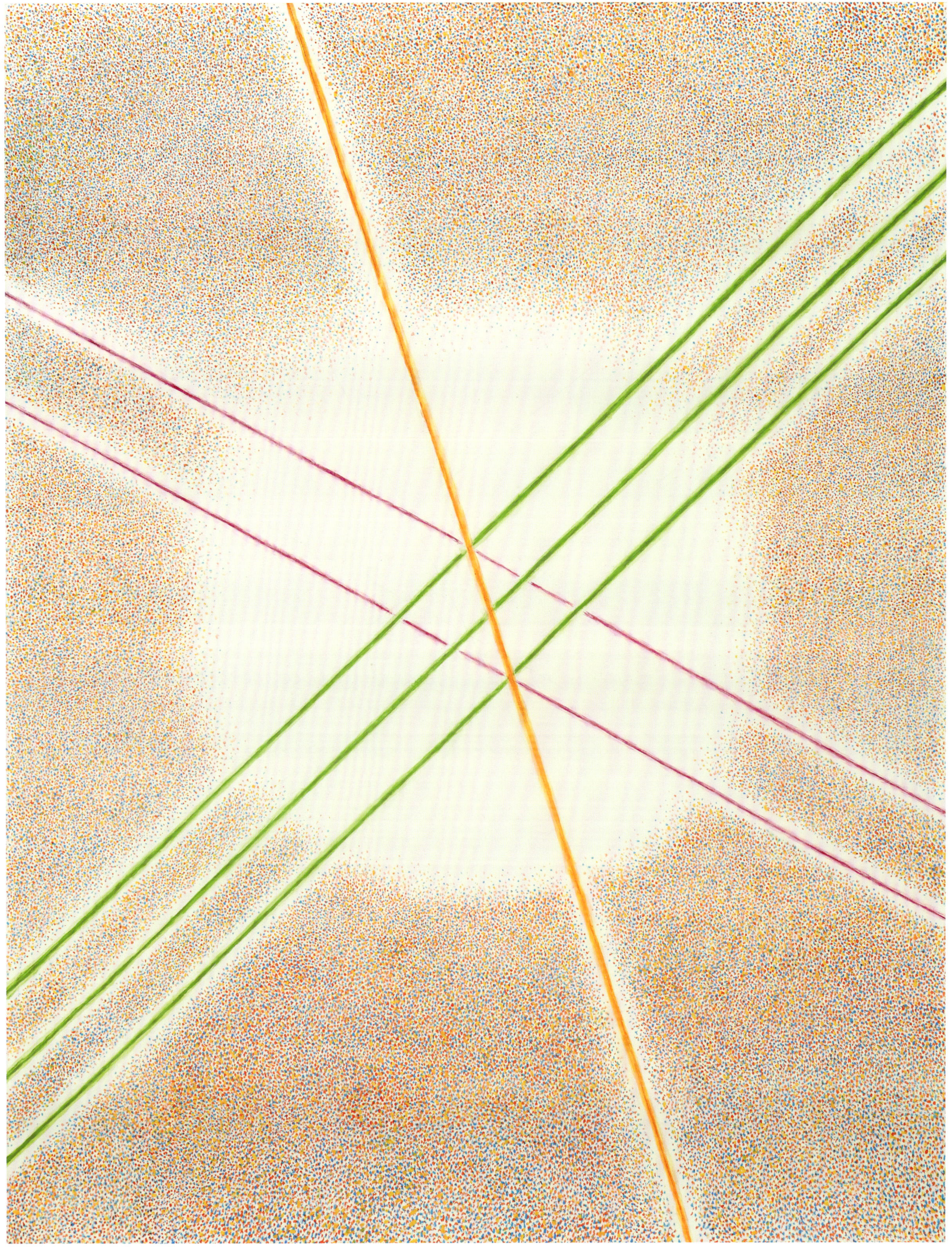

Painting CCXLIV, 1968–69
Oil on canvas
134 x 200 cm
National Museum in Wrocław

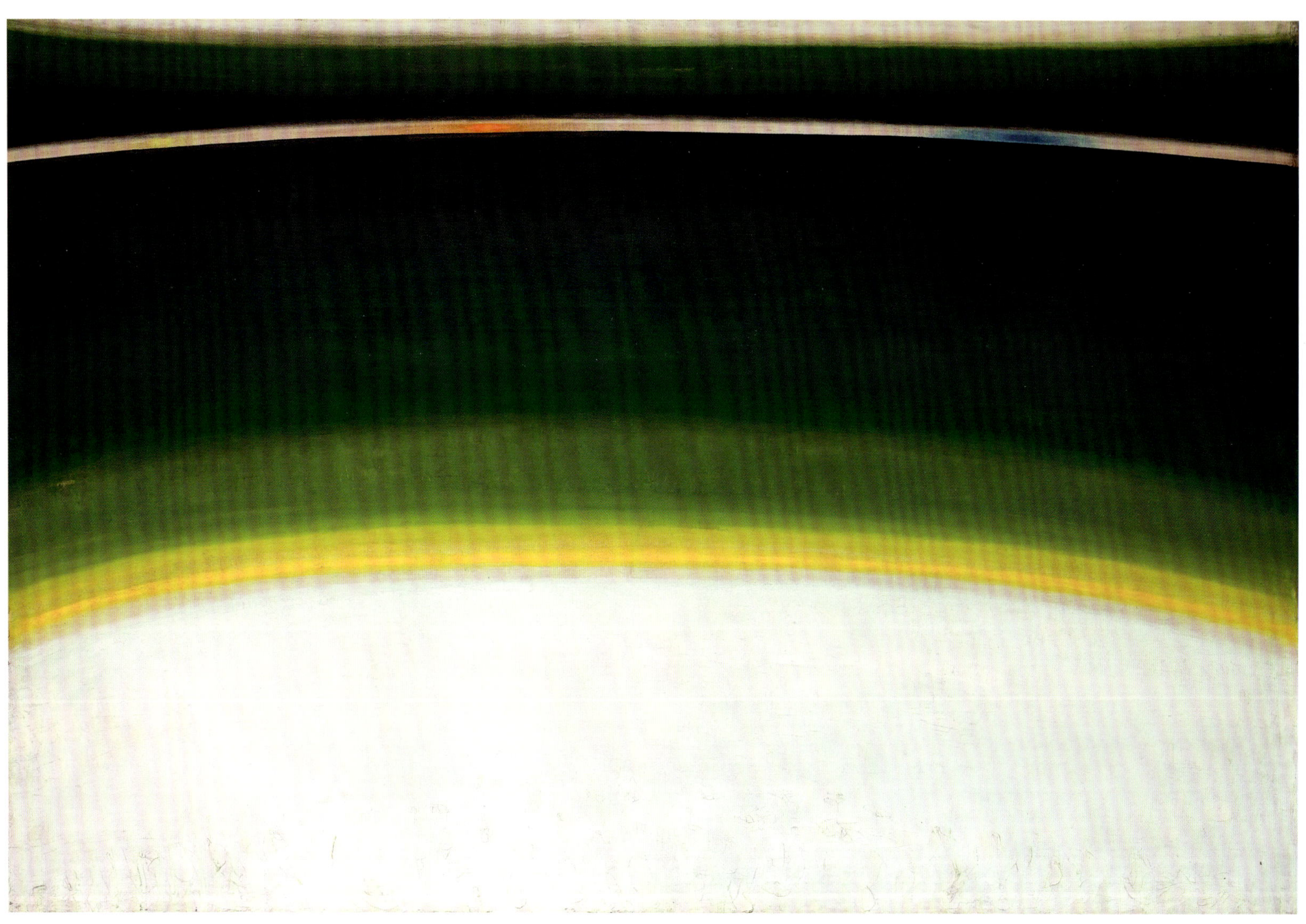

Painting CCXXXIII, 1968
Oil on canvas
133.5 x 98.5 cm

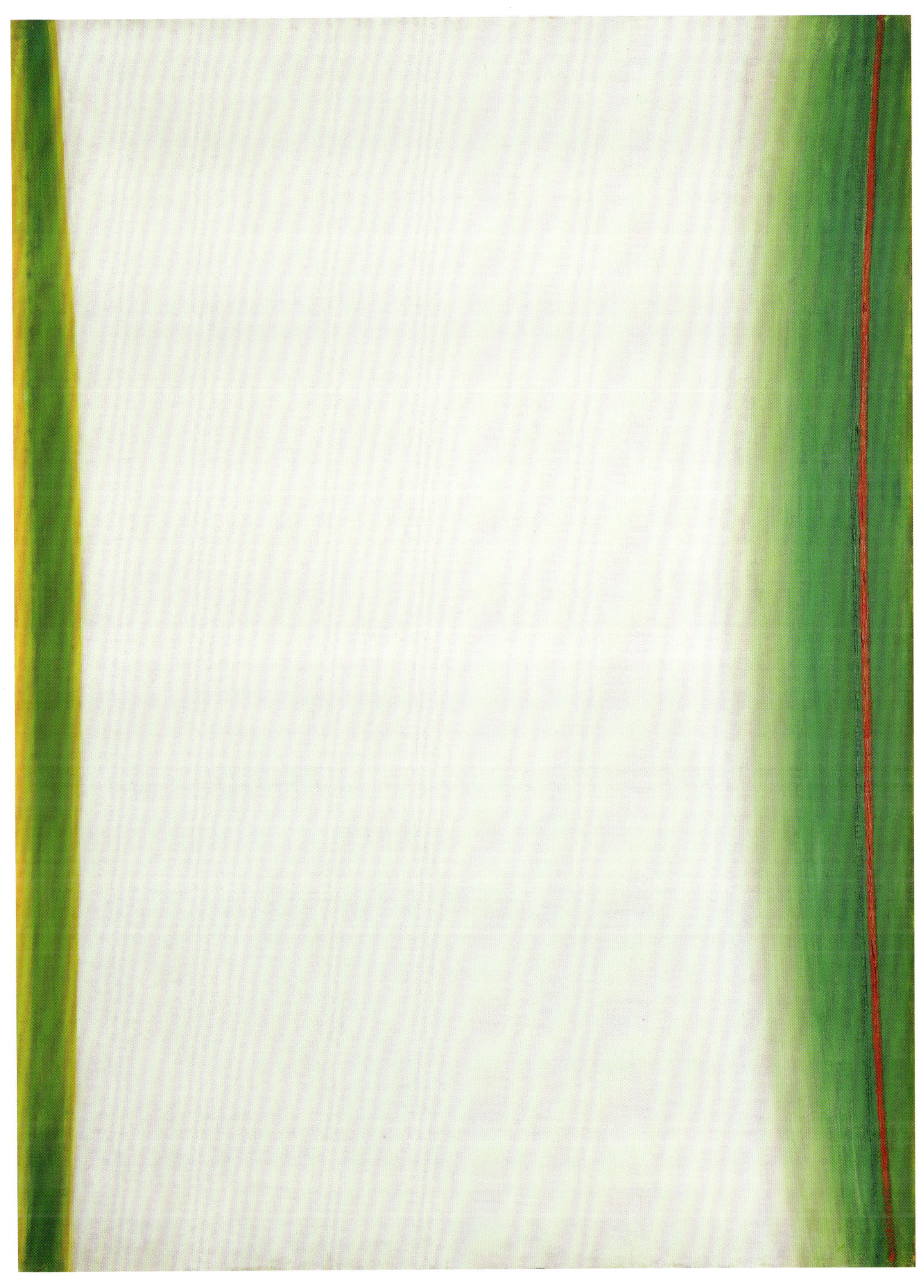

Painting CCXXVII, 1968
Oil on canvas
65 x 50 cm

Painting CCXXXVII, 1969
Oil on canvas
150 x 100 cm

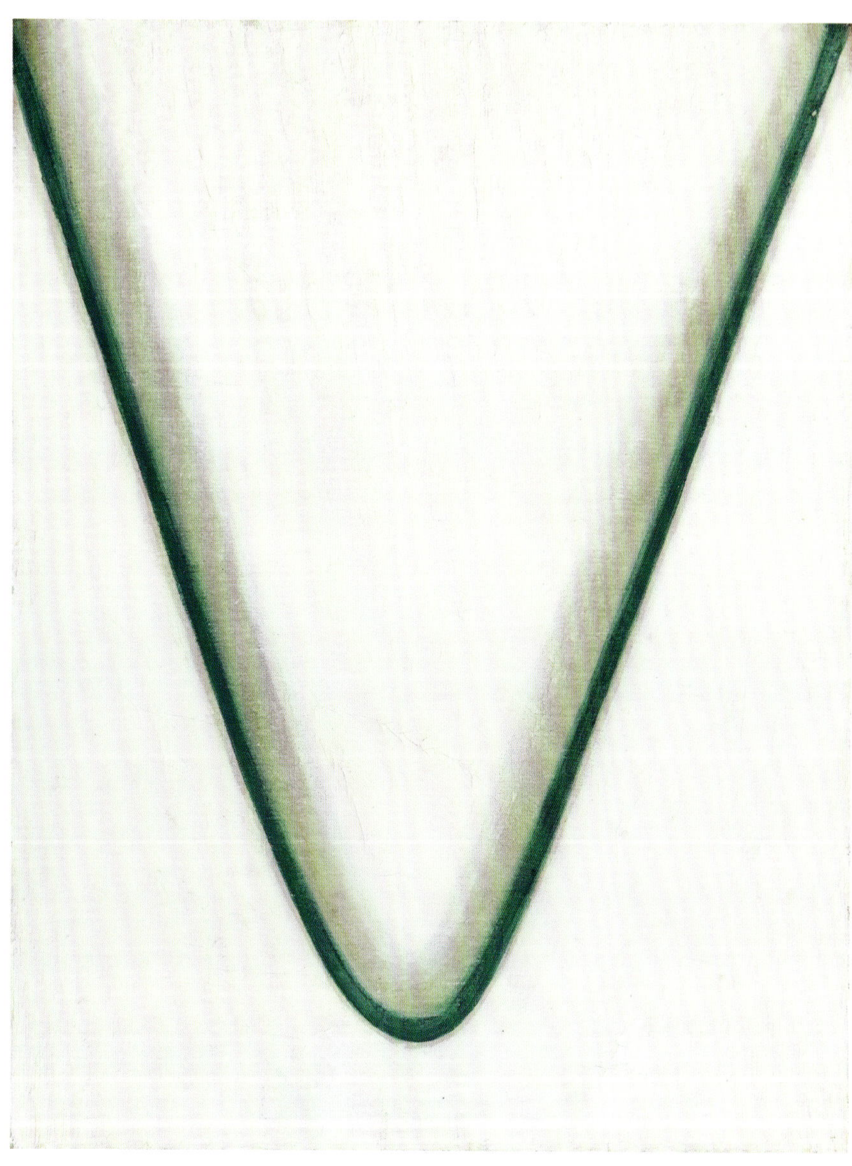

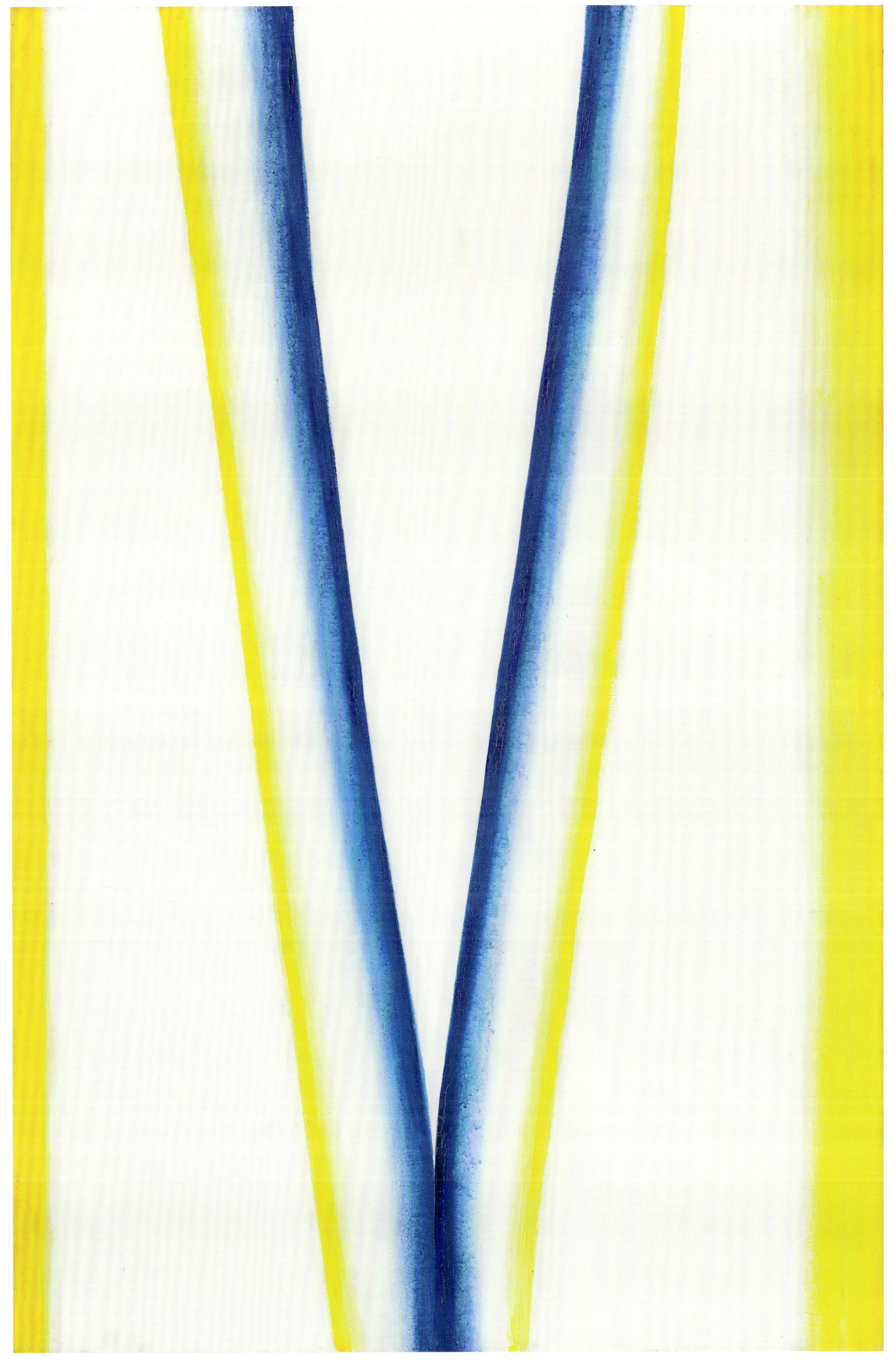

Painting CCXXXV, 1968
Oil on canvas
146 x 97 cm

Painting CCCXLIII, 1975
Oil on canvas
200 x 130 cm

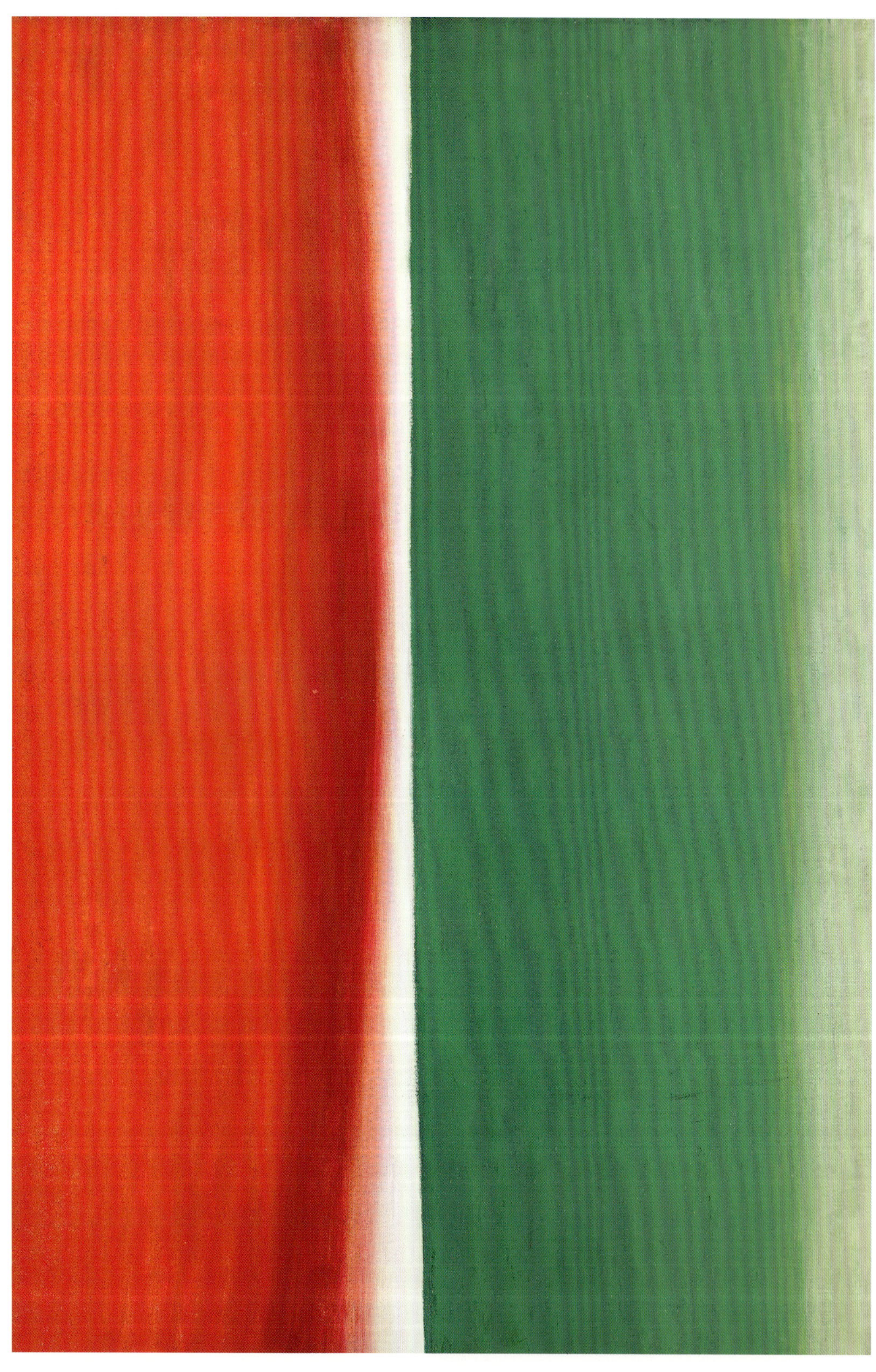

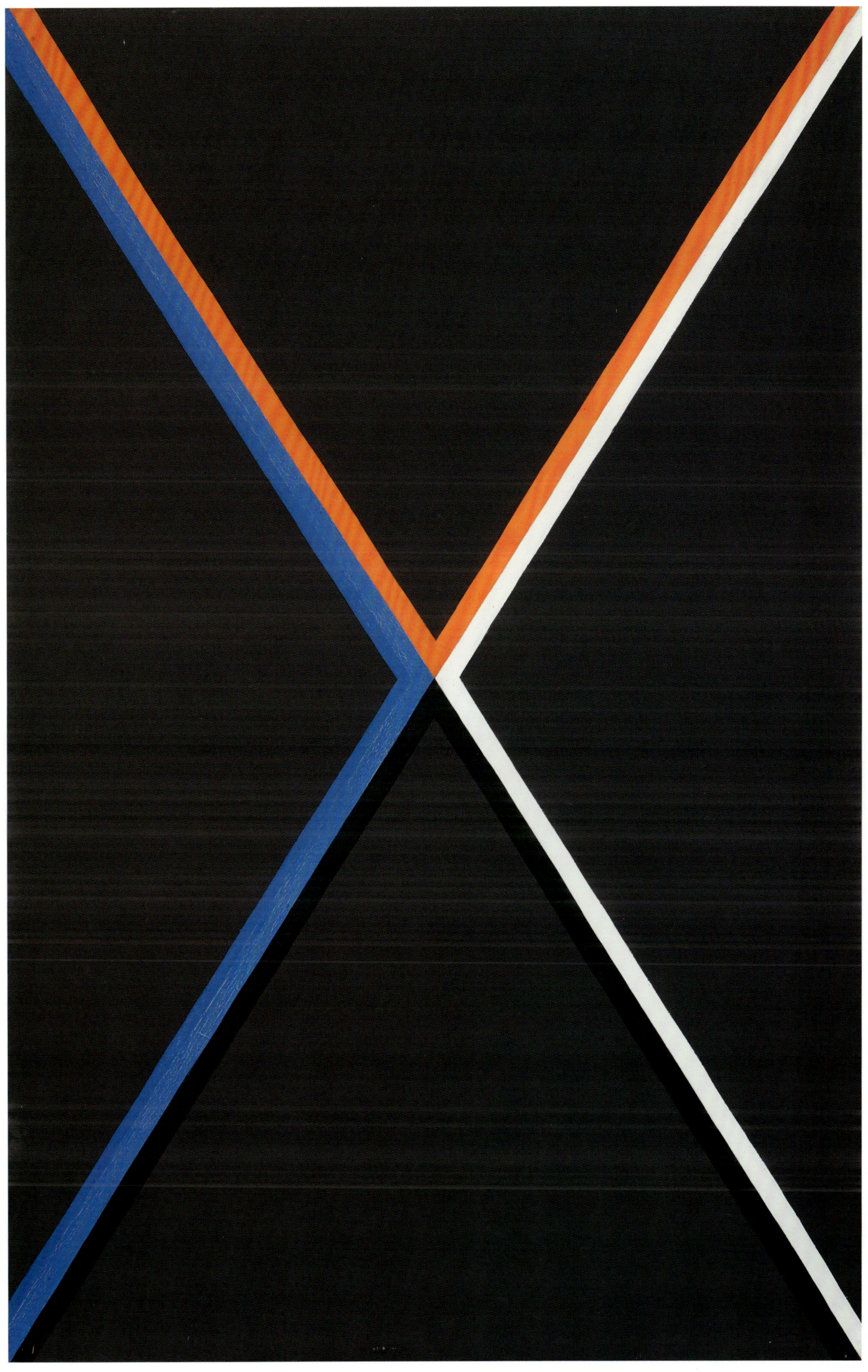

Painting DCCCXXXVIII, 2007
Oil on canvas
150 x 180 cm

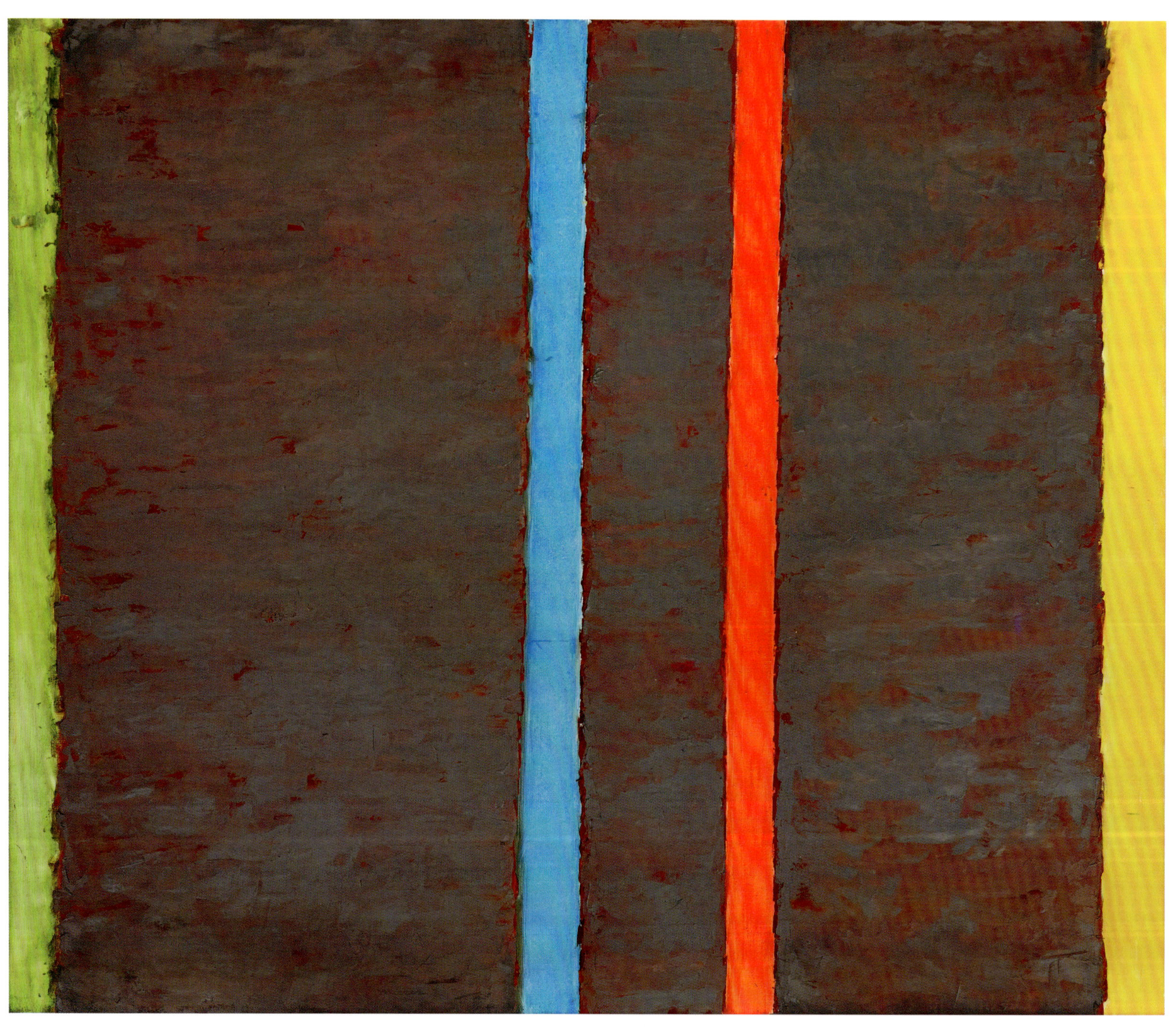

Painting CDXCVIII, 1983
Oil on canvas
100 x 70 cm

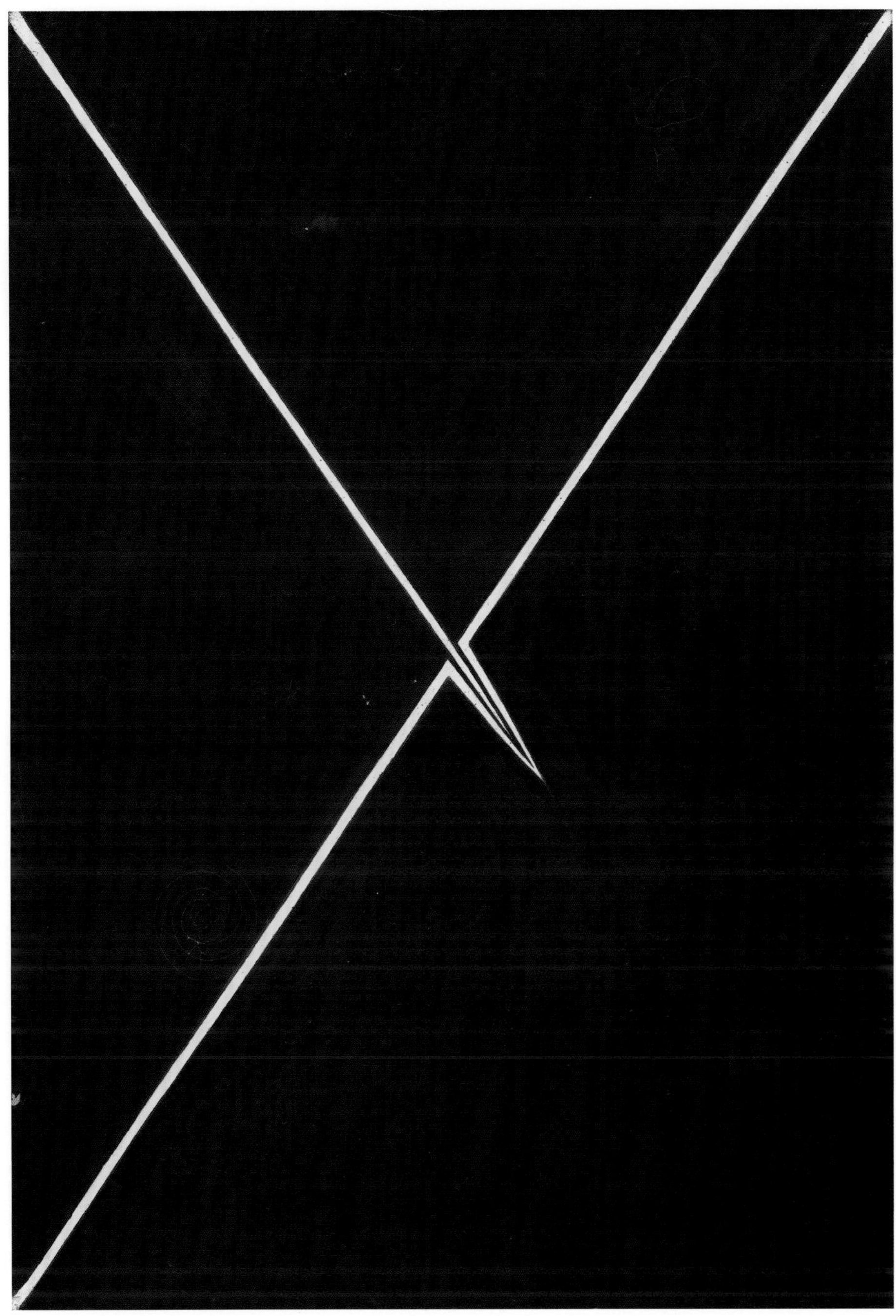

Painting CDLXXIX, 1982
Oil on canvas
100 x 79 cm

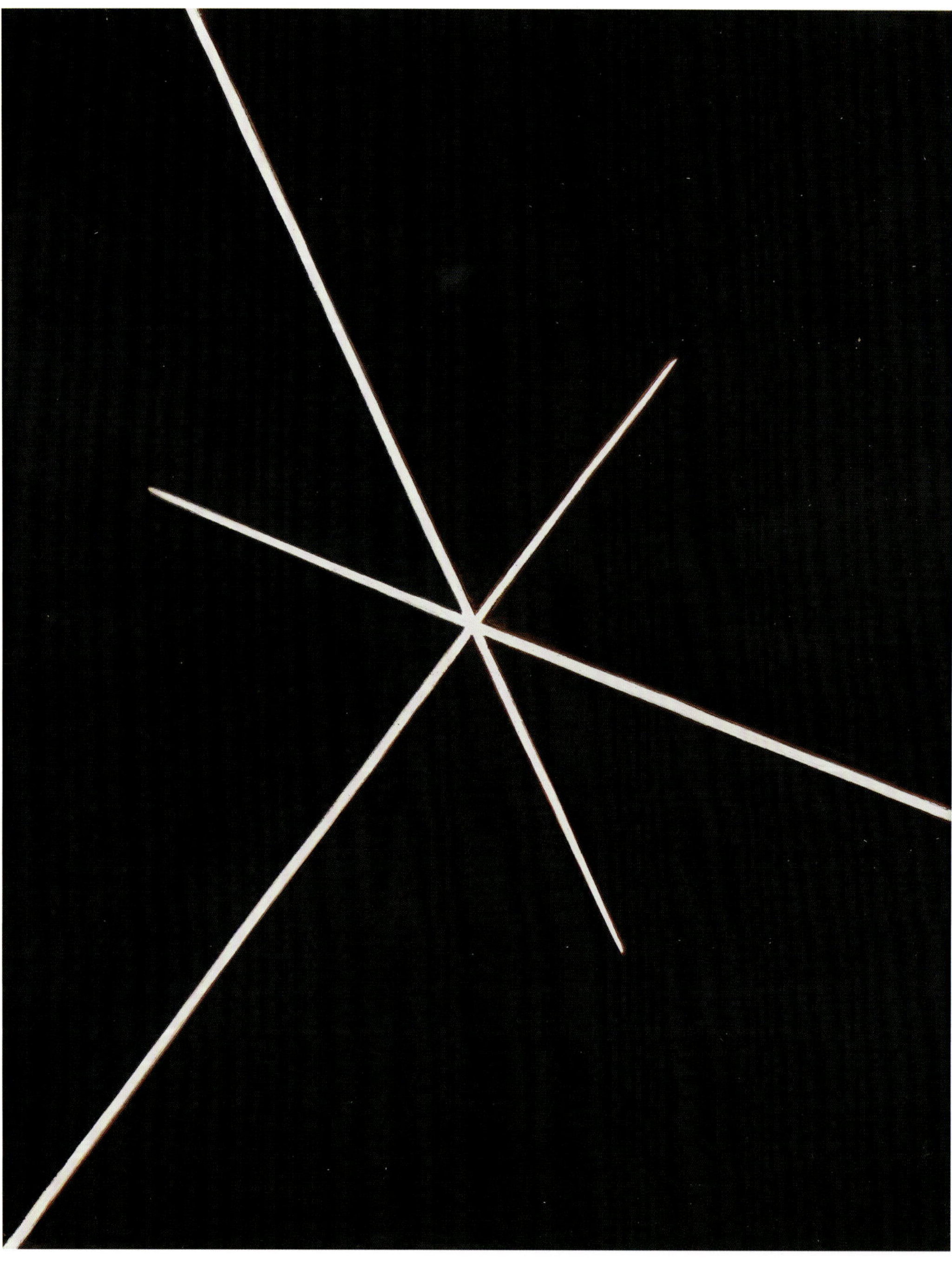

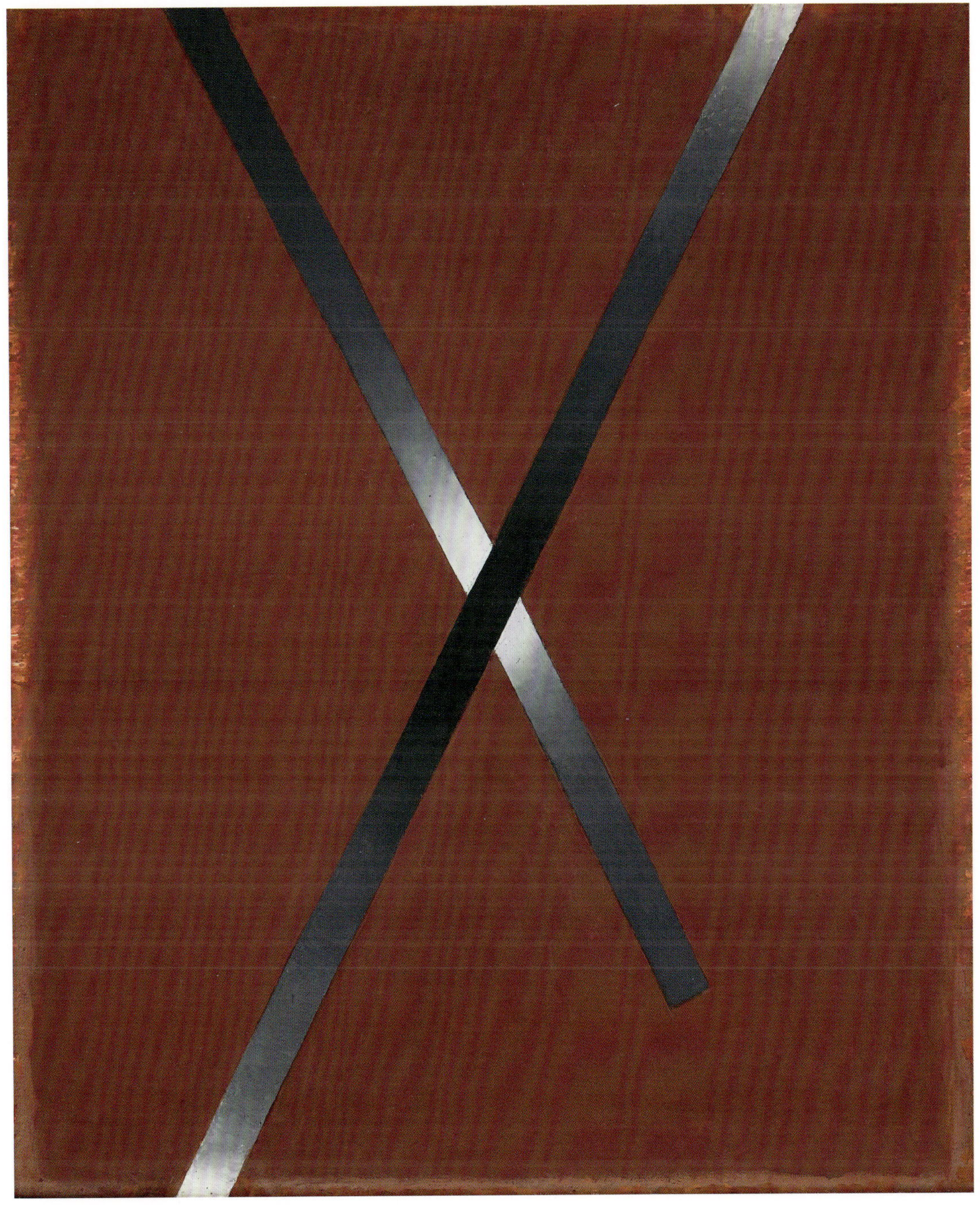

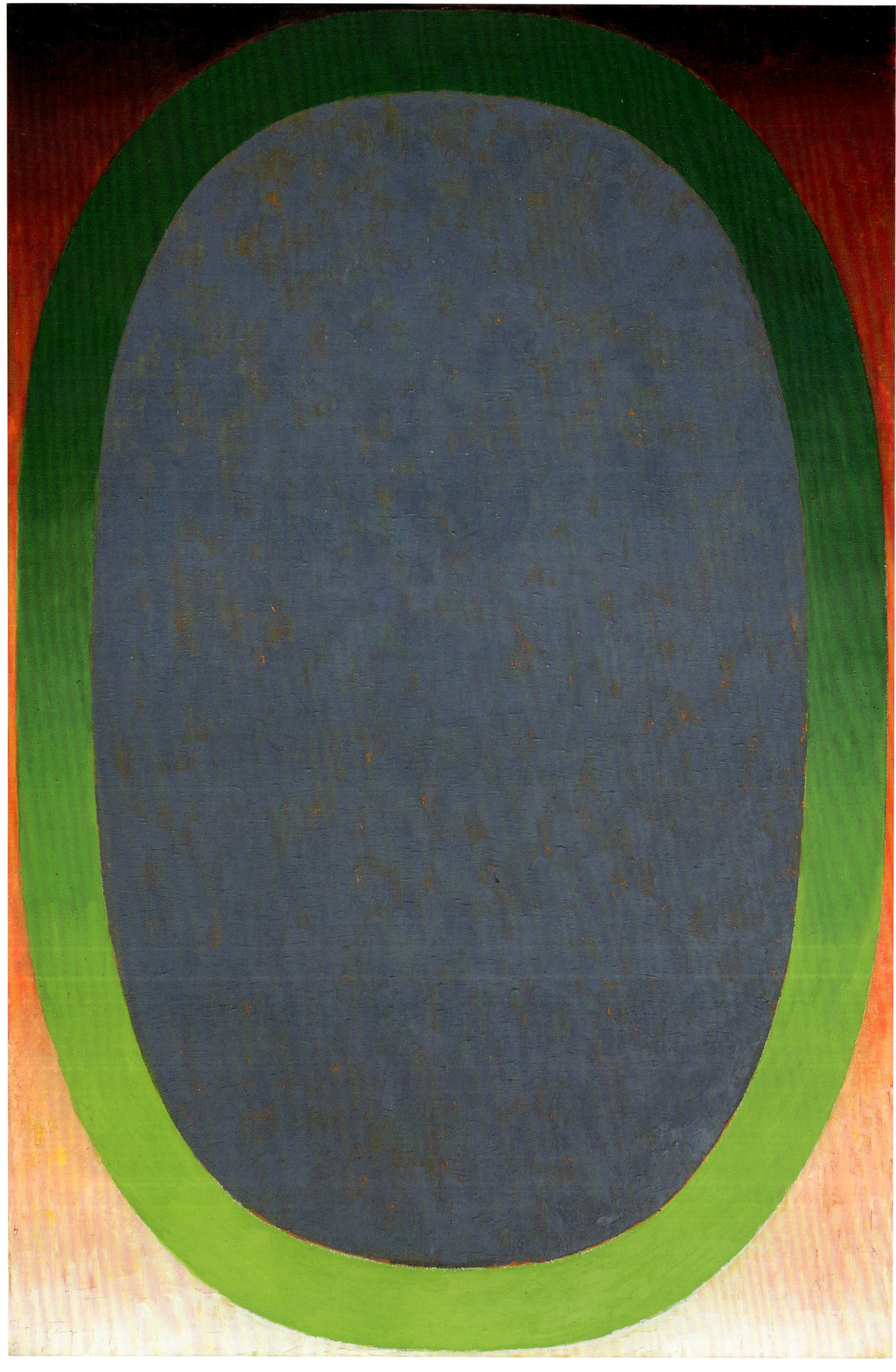

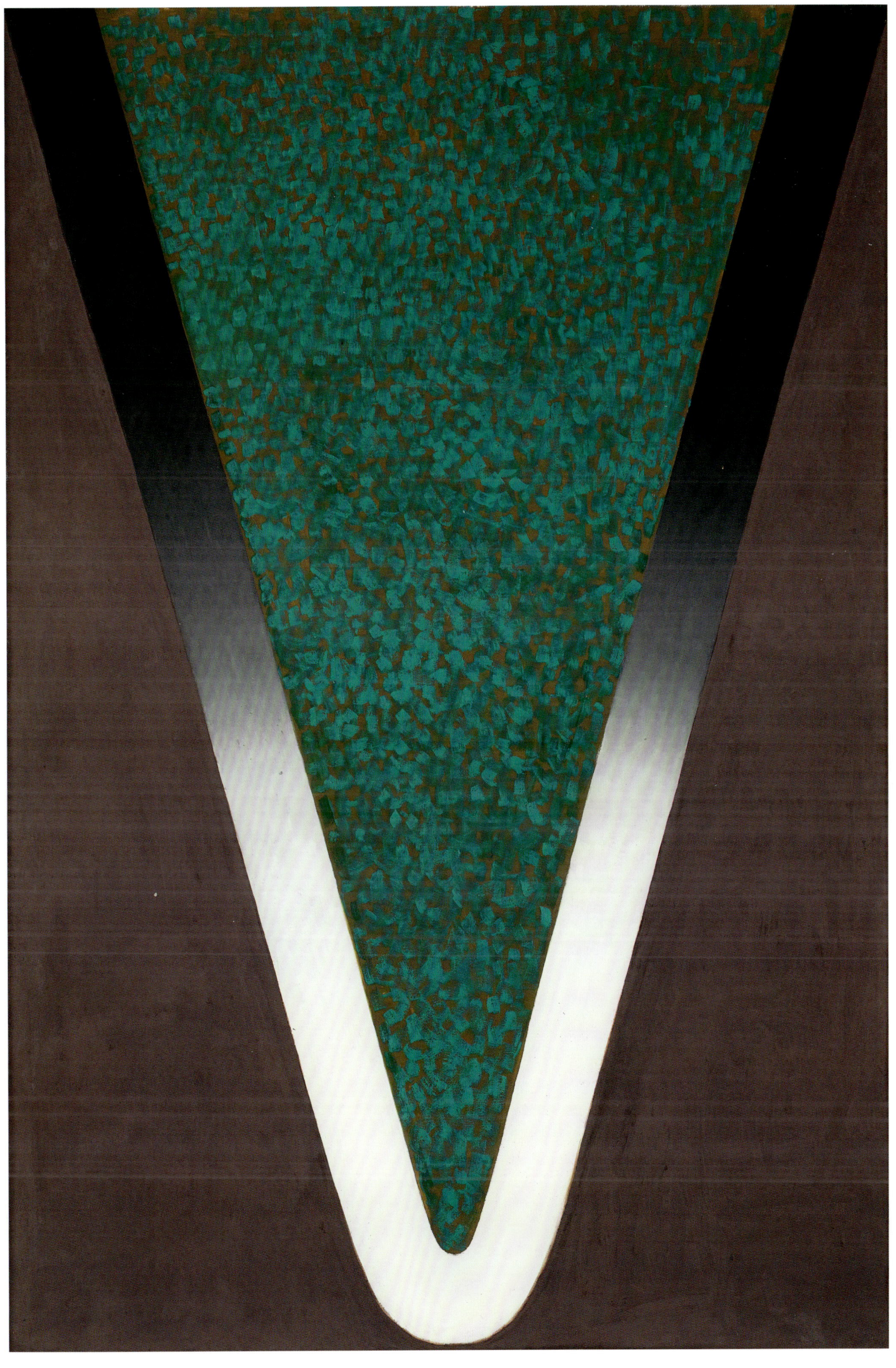

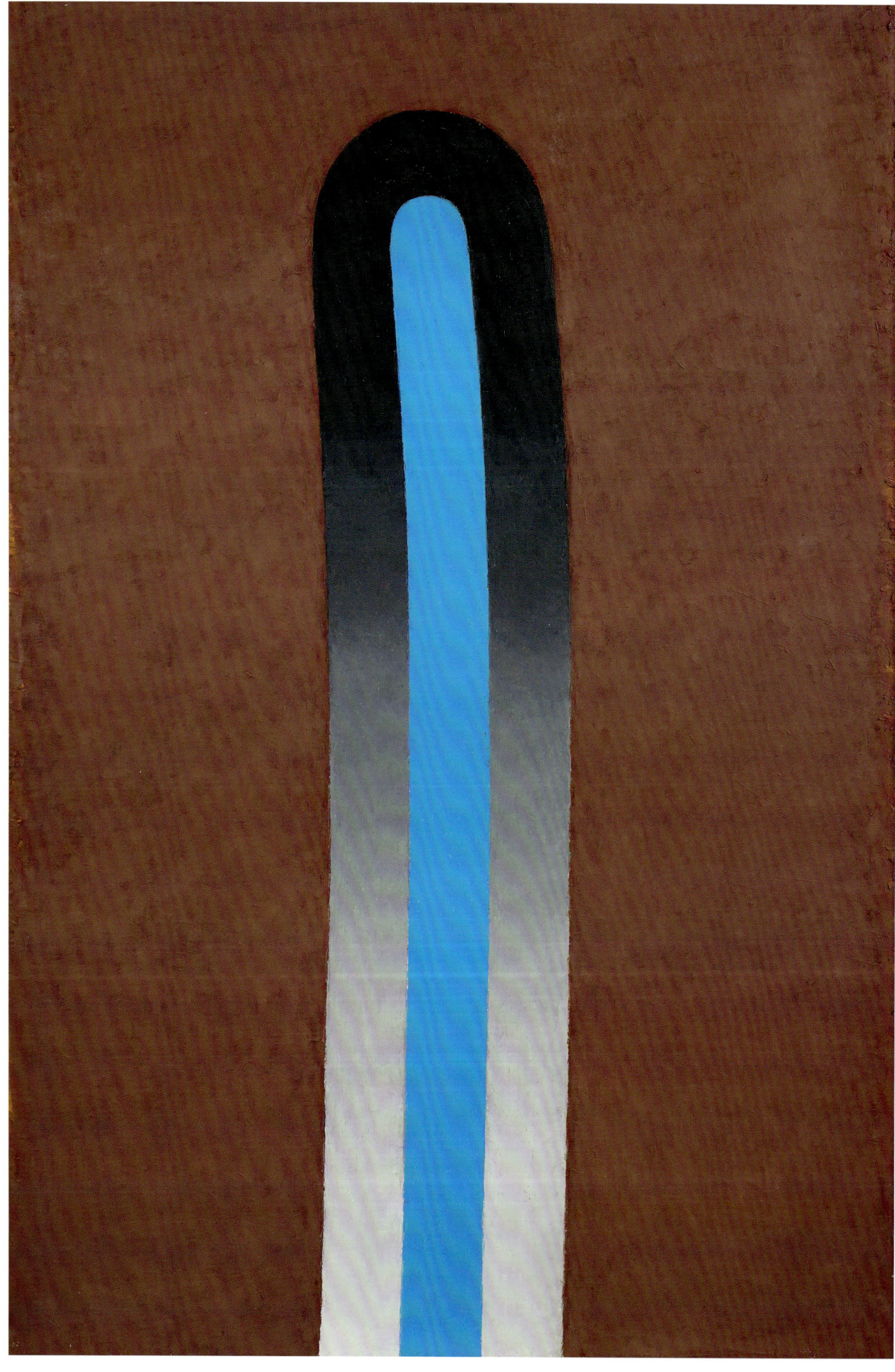

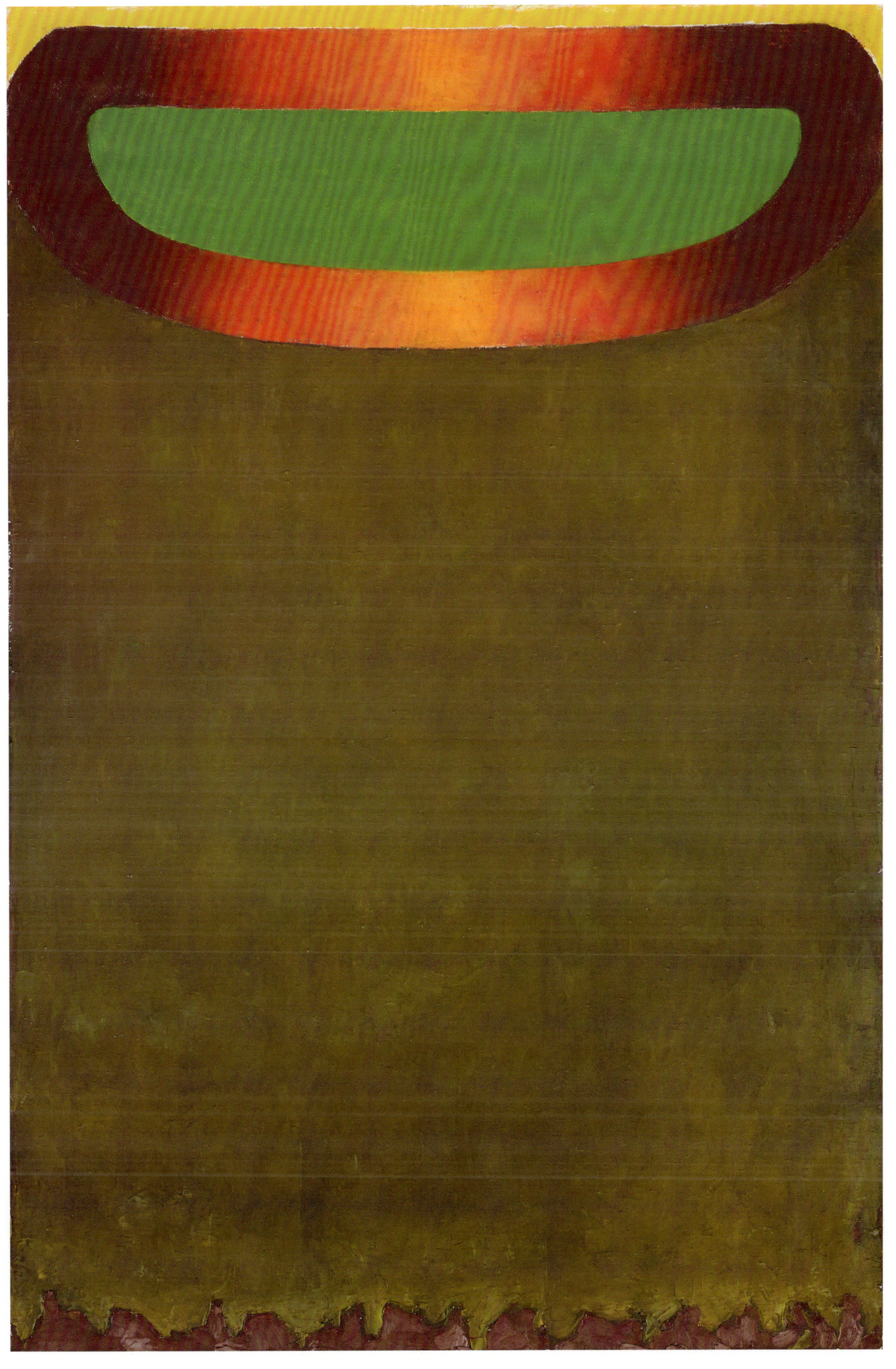

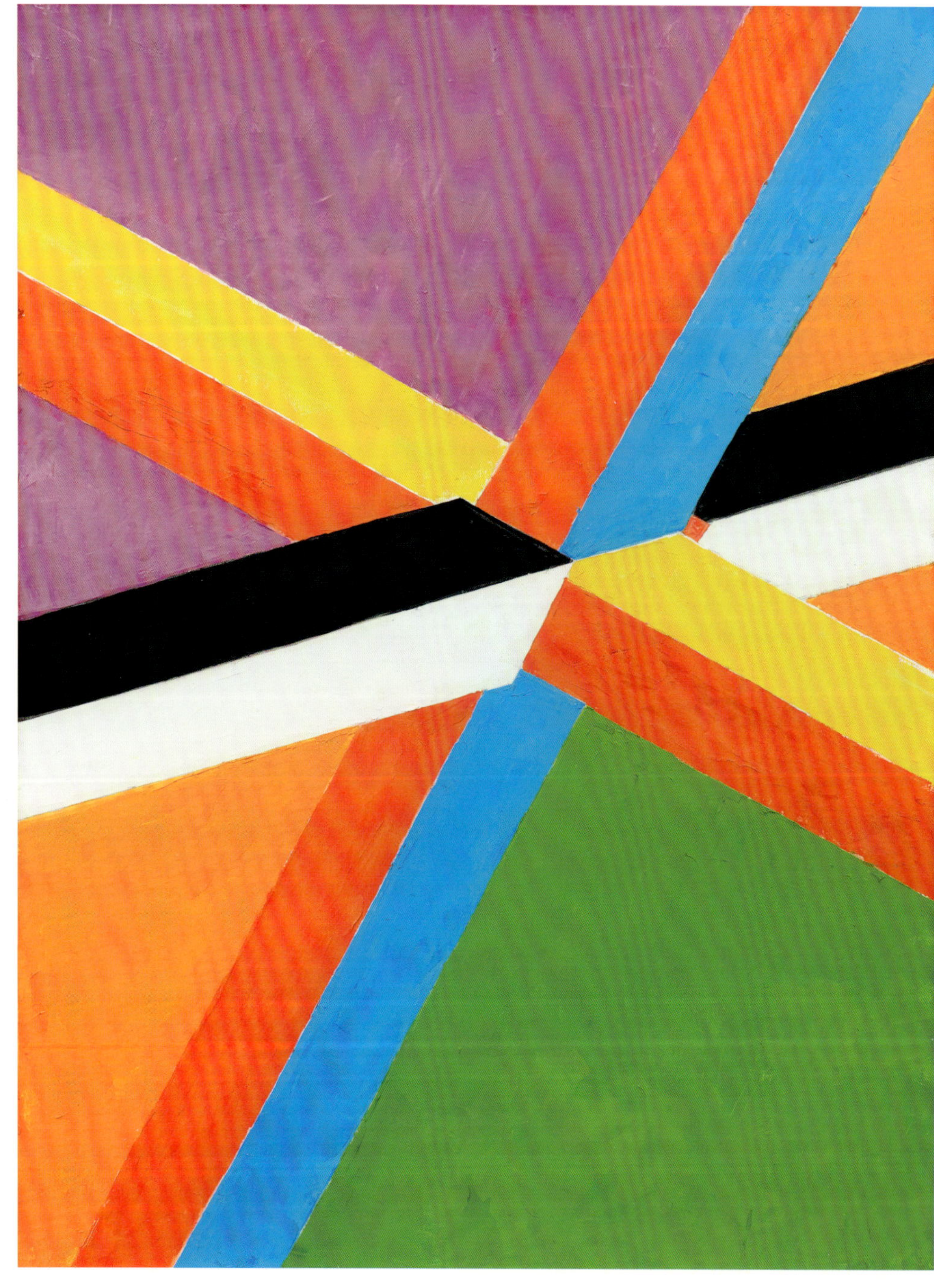

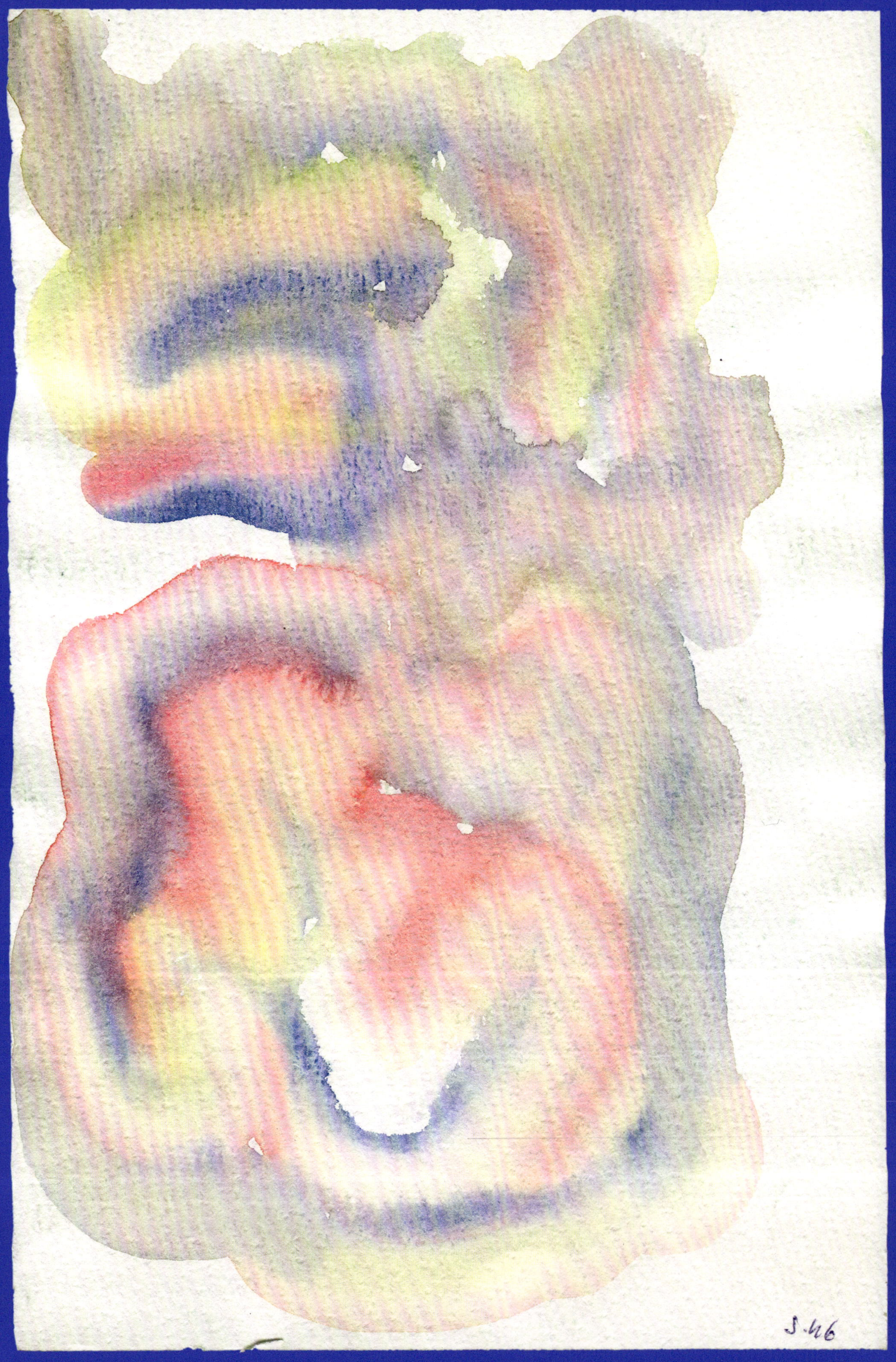
J.46

The mystery of light has probably accompanied painting as long as it has existed. An explanation was sought in the quality of the material, but it really exists through a special instance. Light can be present in dark colours as well as bright ones. The colour scale, whether of six or eight colours, does not matter here. What matters is knowledge of the psychophysical effect of colours, reactions to optical afterimages and colour saturation. It is worth exploring the different ways colours impinge on us, for they are the source of the mystery hidden in matter.

Curiosity – what happens when I juxtapose colours in a particular way?
Curiosity – how to achieve luminosity?

Stefan Gierowski

Painting XIII, 1957
Oil on canvas
135 x 99 cm
National Museum in Wrocław

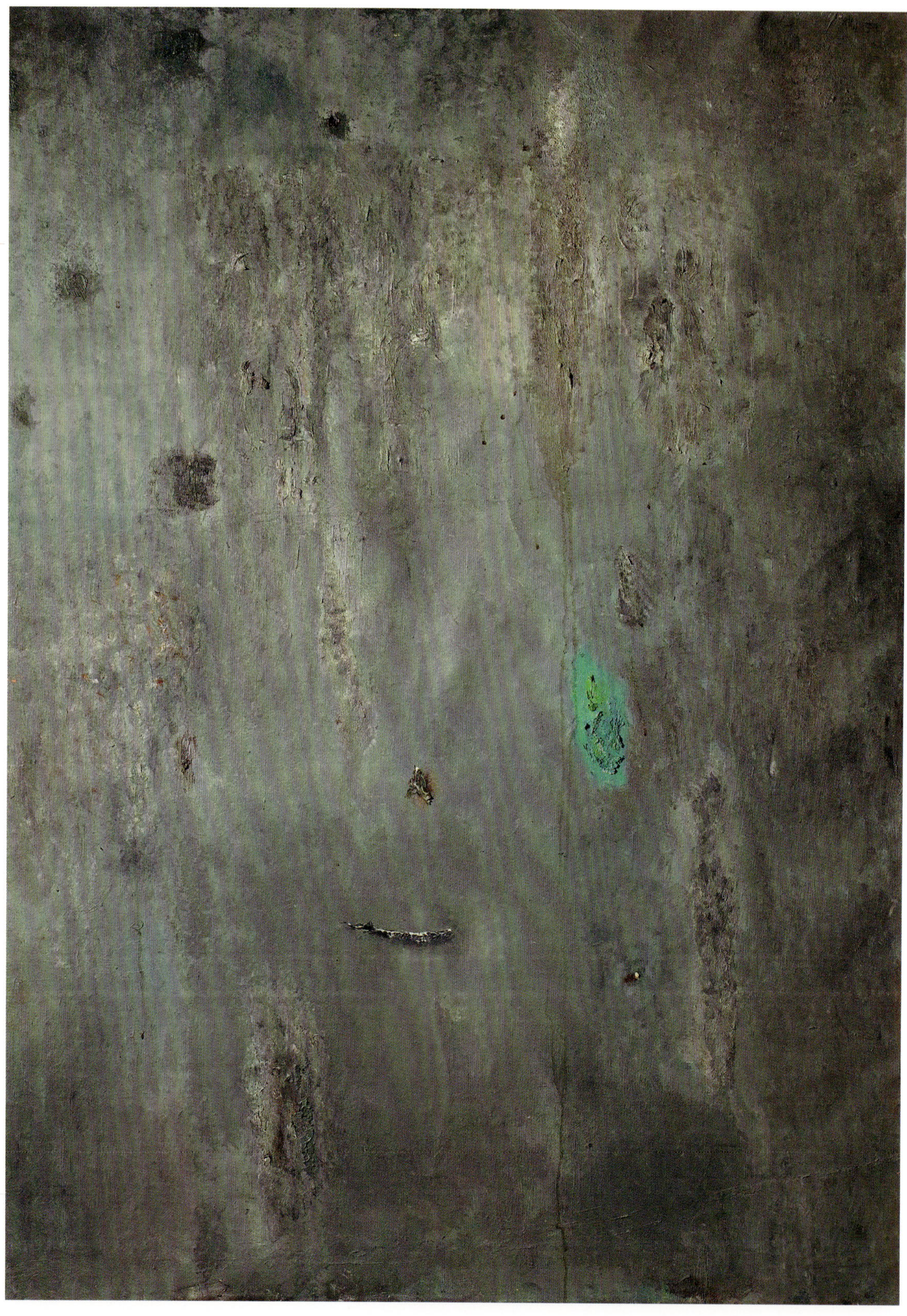

Painting XLIX, 1958
Oil on canvas
133 x 97 cm
National Museum in Warsaw

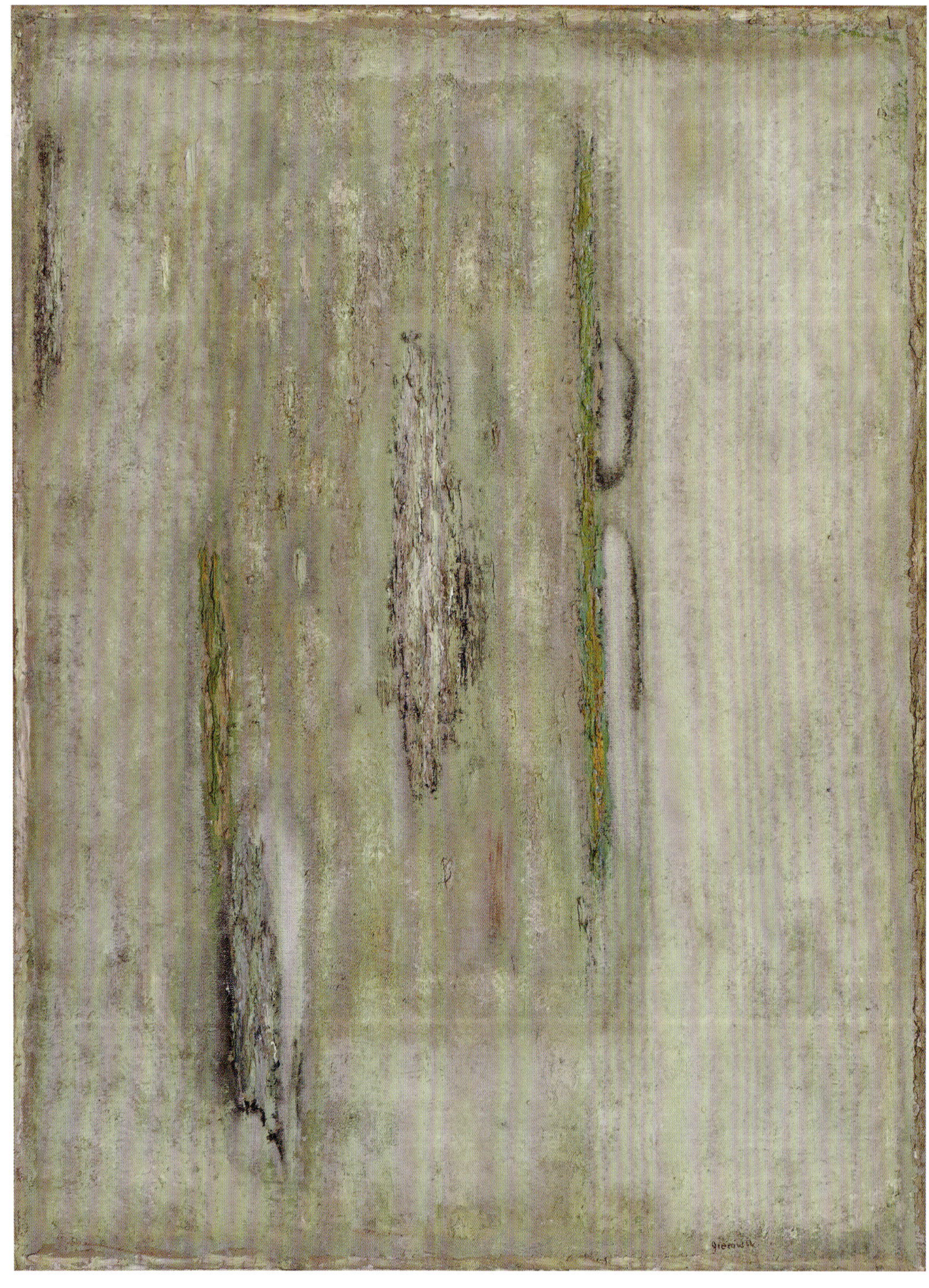

Painting LXXIII, 1959
Oil on canvas
100 x 70 cm

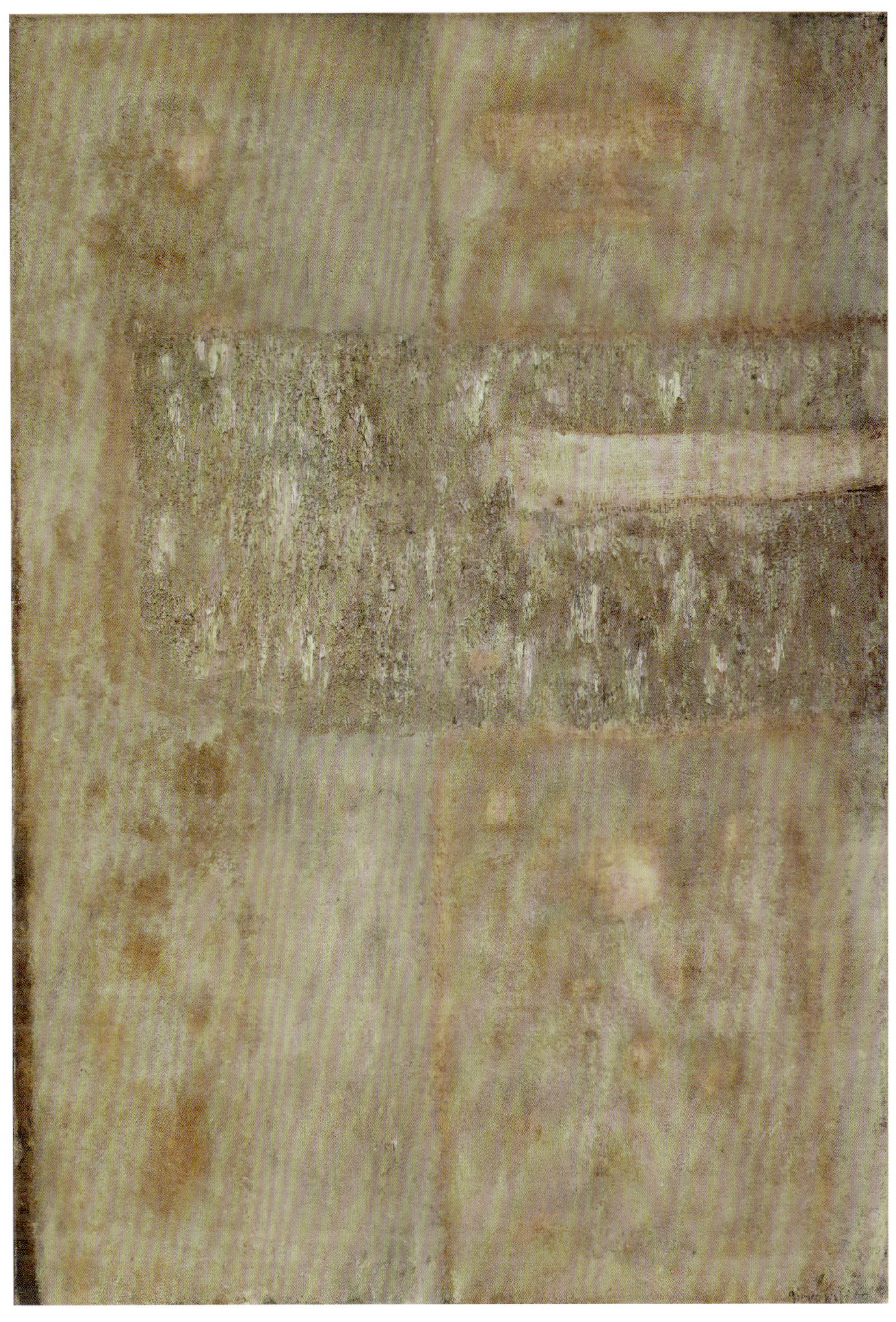

Painting XXXV, 1958
Oil on canvas
105 x 73 cm

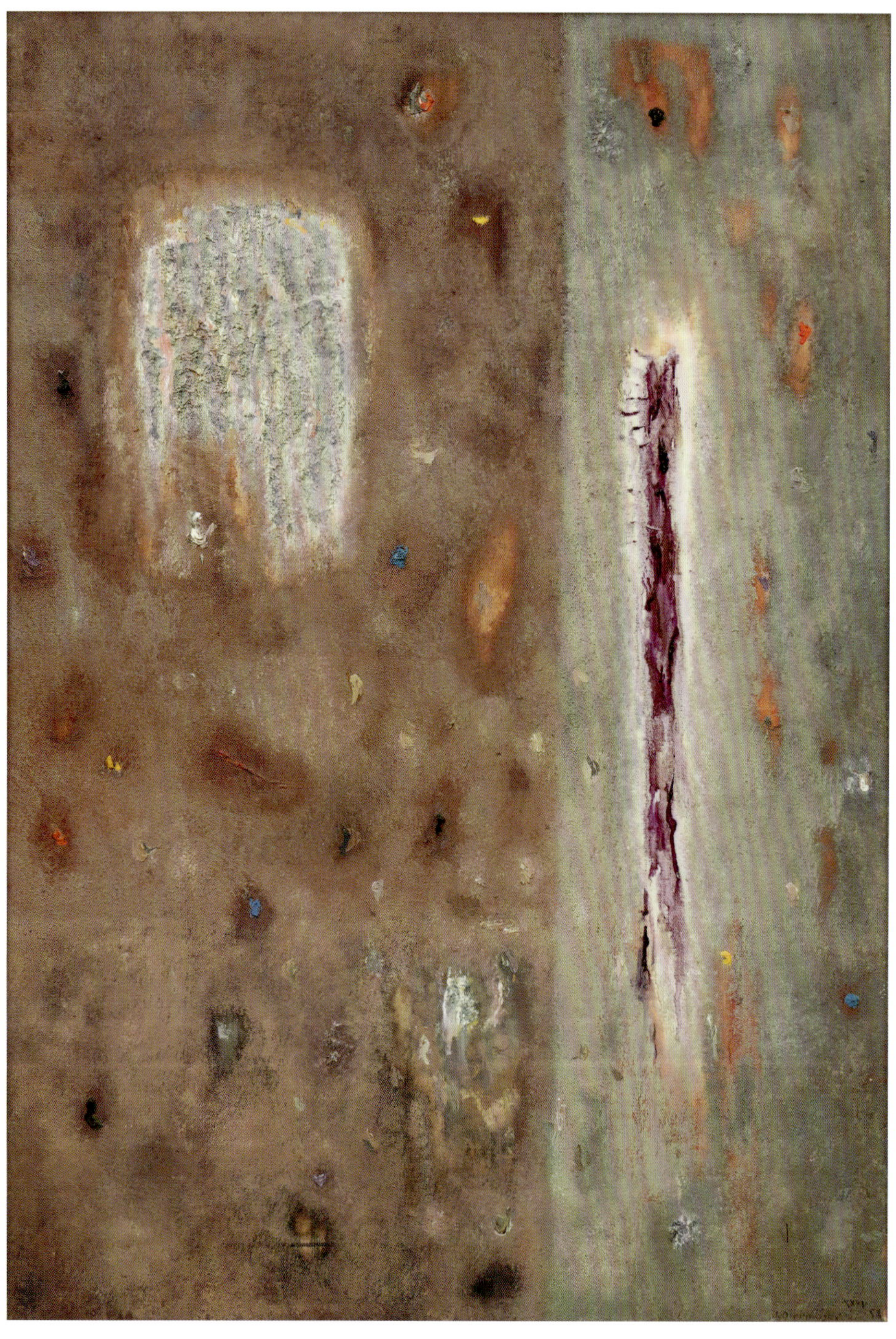

Painting XXXIII, 1958
Oil on canvas
104 x 73 cm

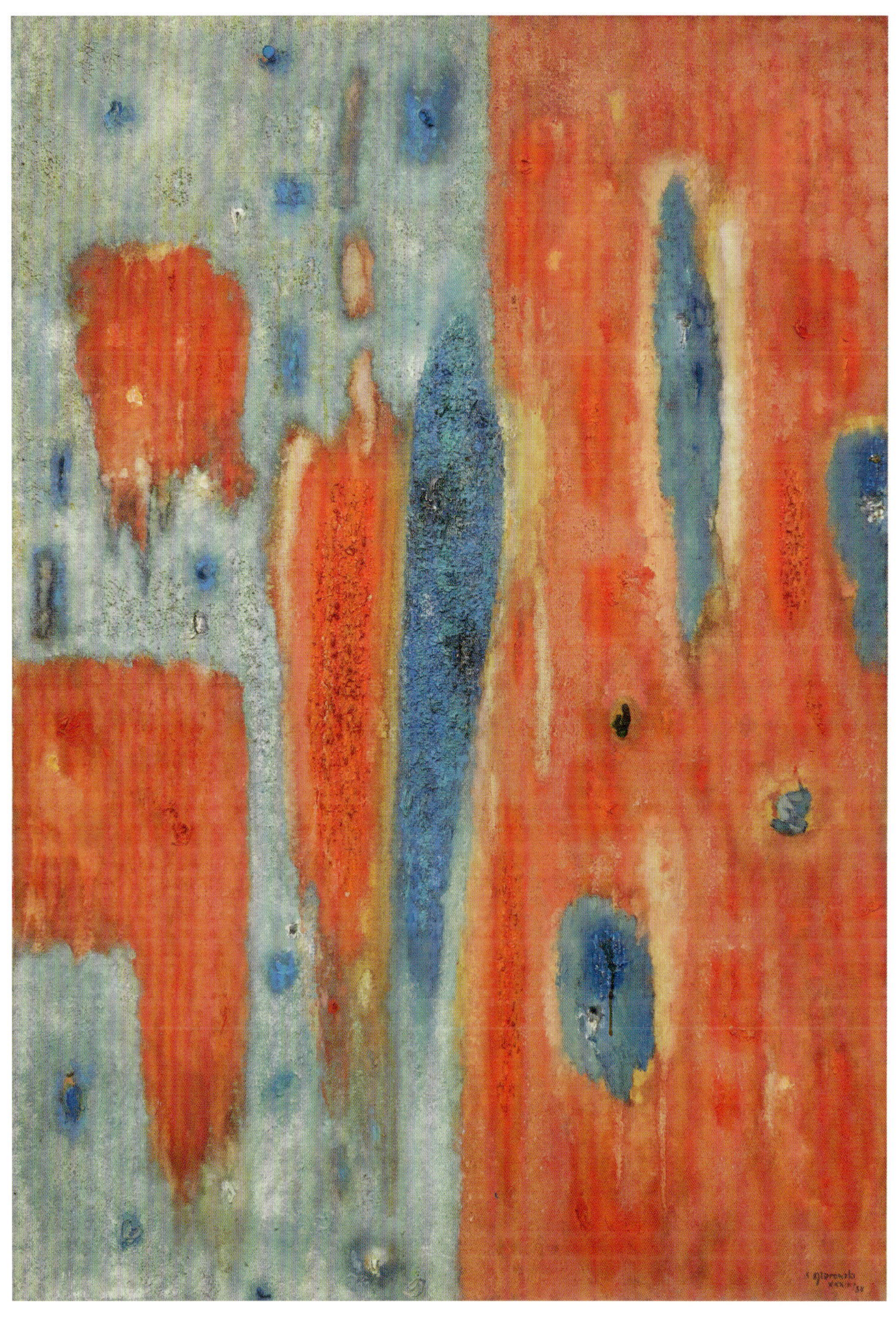

Painting CXIII (Two Directions
of Red), 1962
Oil on canvas
135 x 250 cm
National Museum in Warsaw

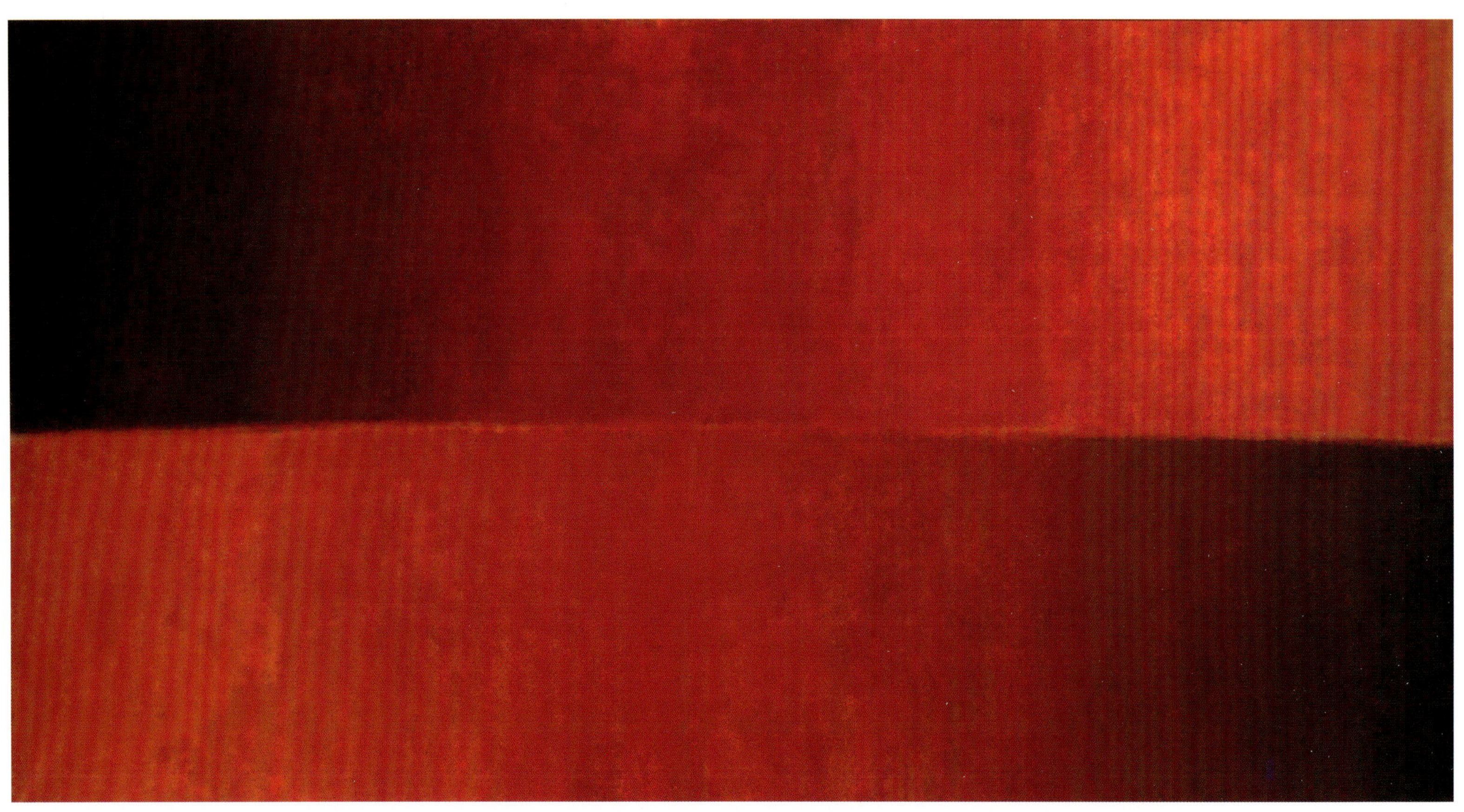

Painting CCCXXIV, 1974
Oil on canvas
100 x 69.5 cm

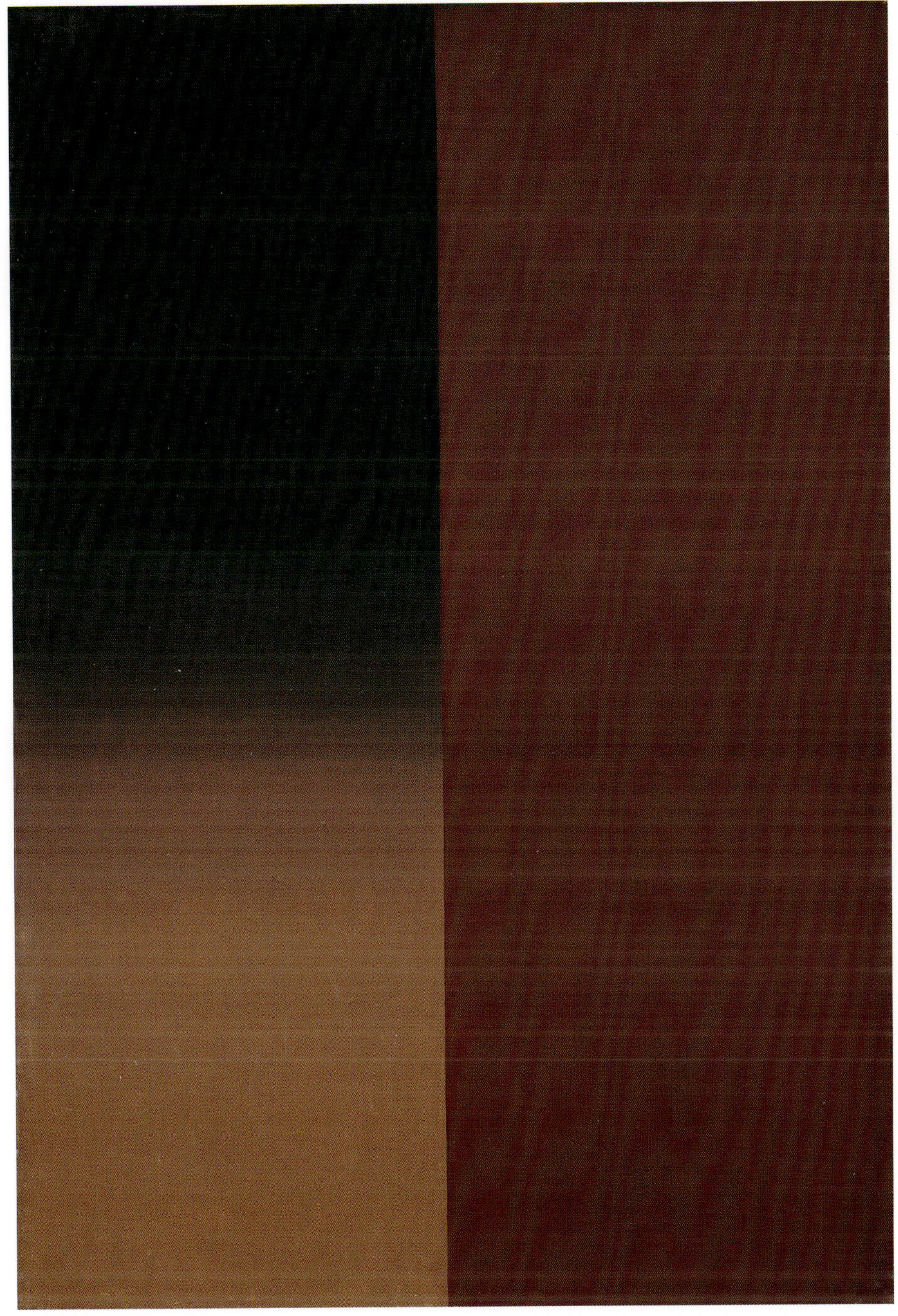

Painting CCXXXIX, 1969
Oil on canvas
145 x 200 cm

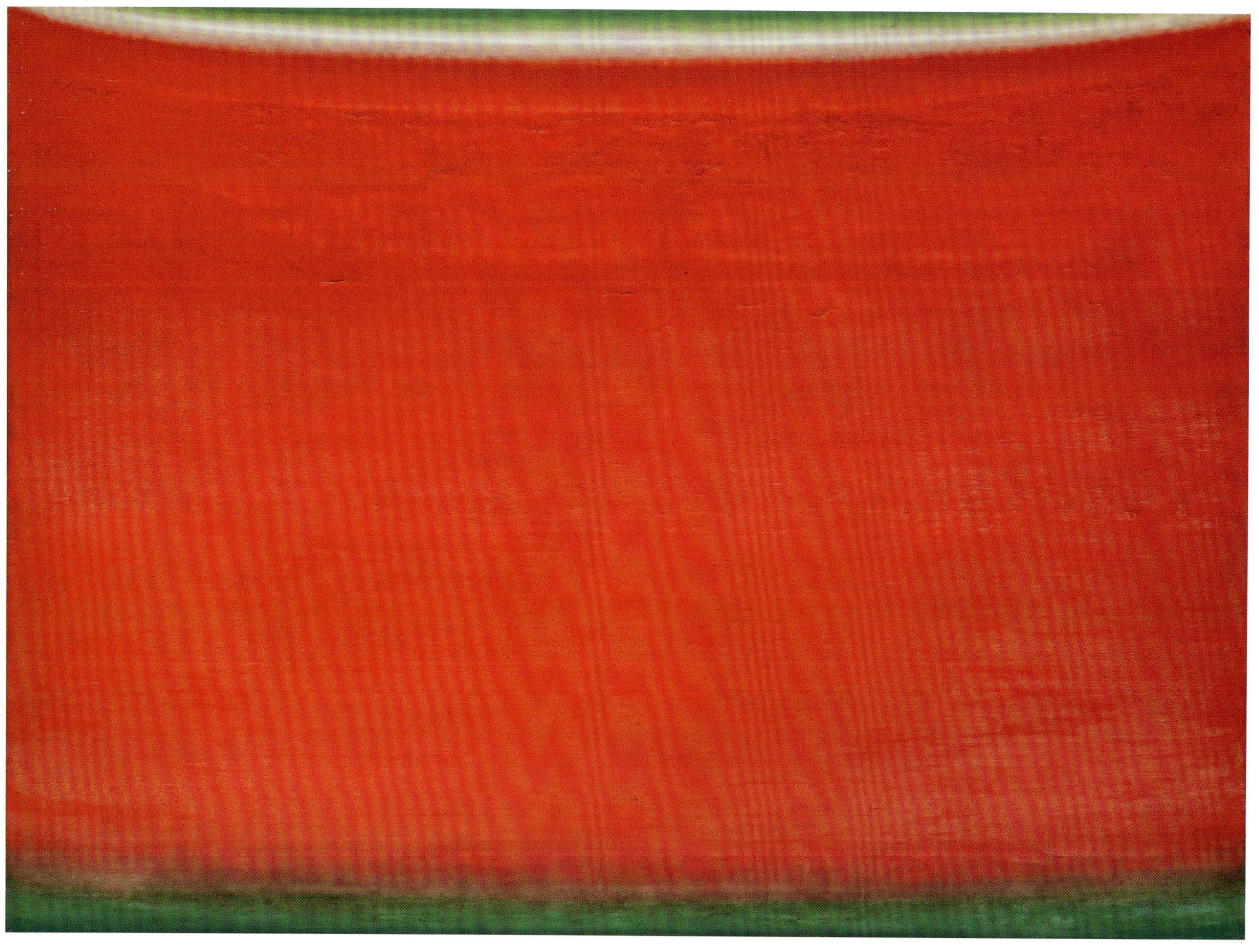

Painting CCXXVI, 1968
Oil on canvas
130 x 113 cm

Painting CCLXVI, 1971
Oil on canvas
100 x 74.5 cm

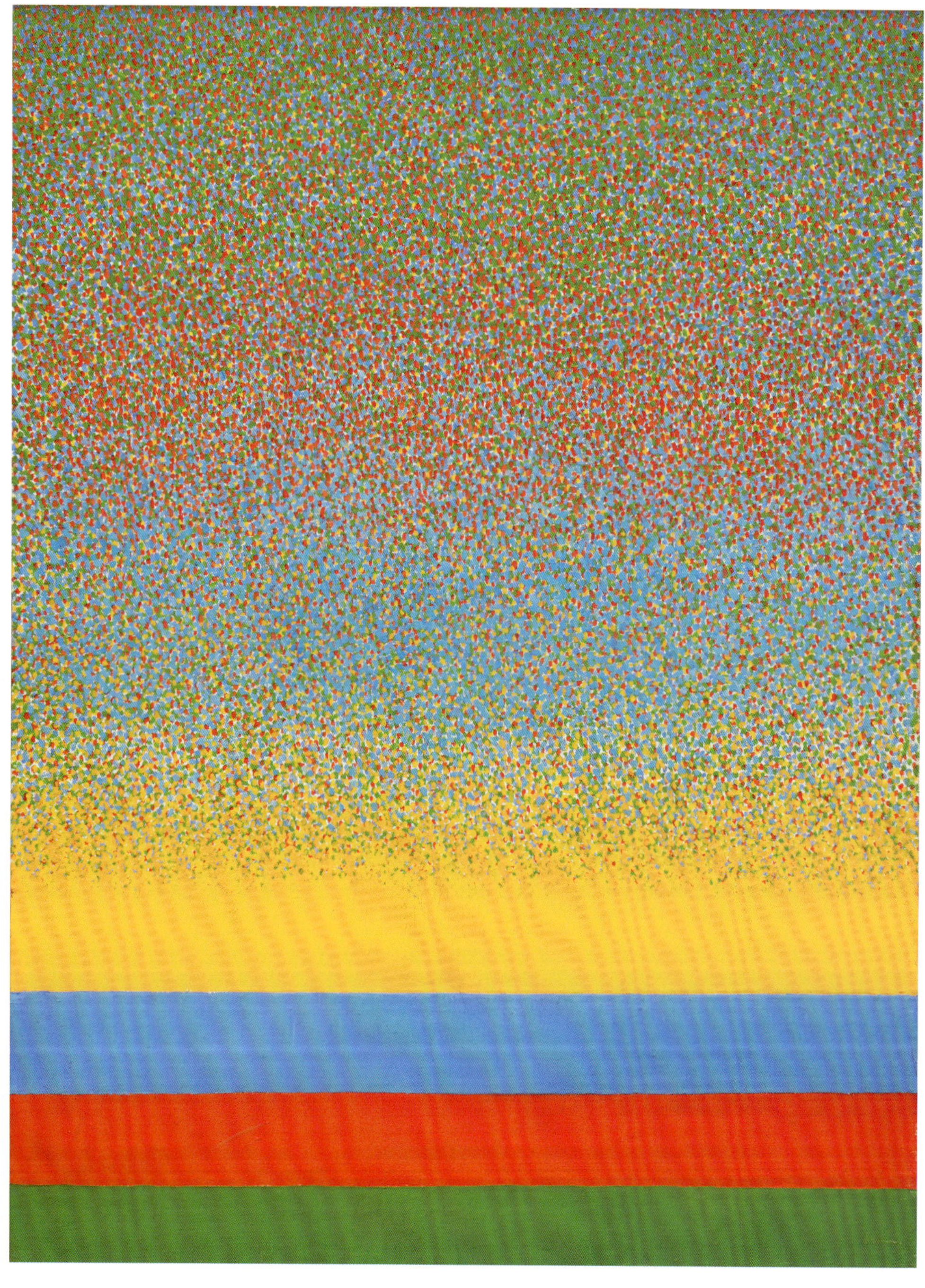

Painting CCXLV, 1969
Oil on canvas
91 x 72 cm

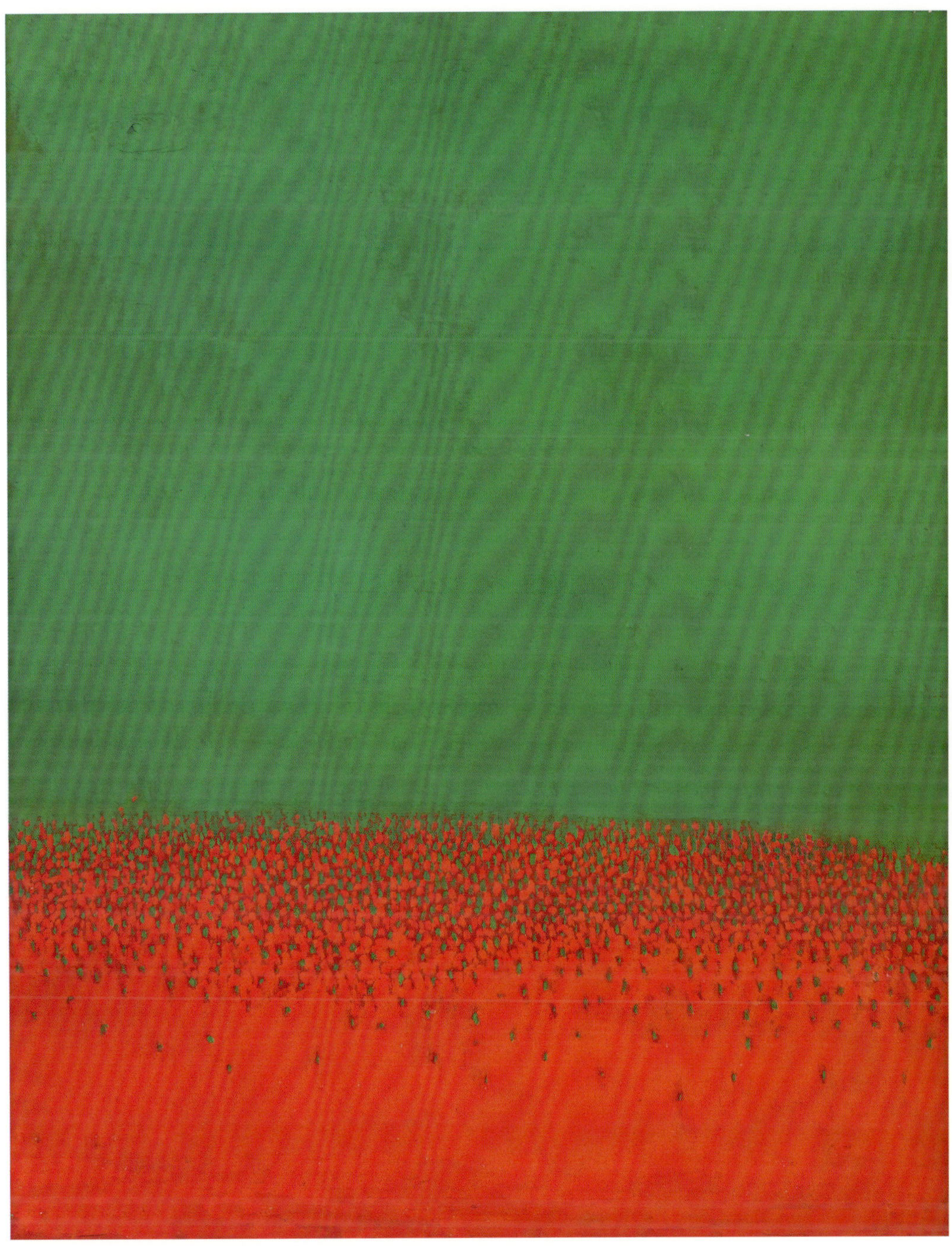

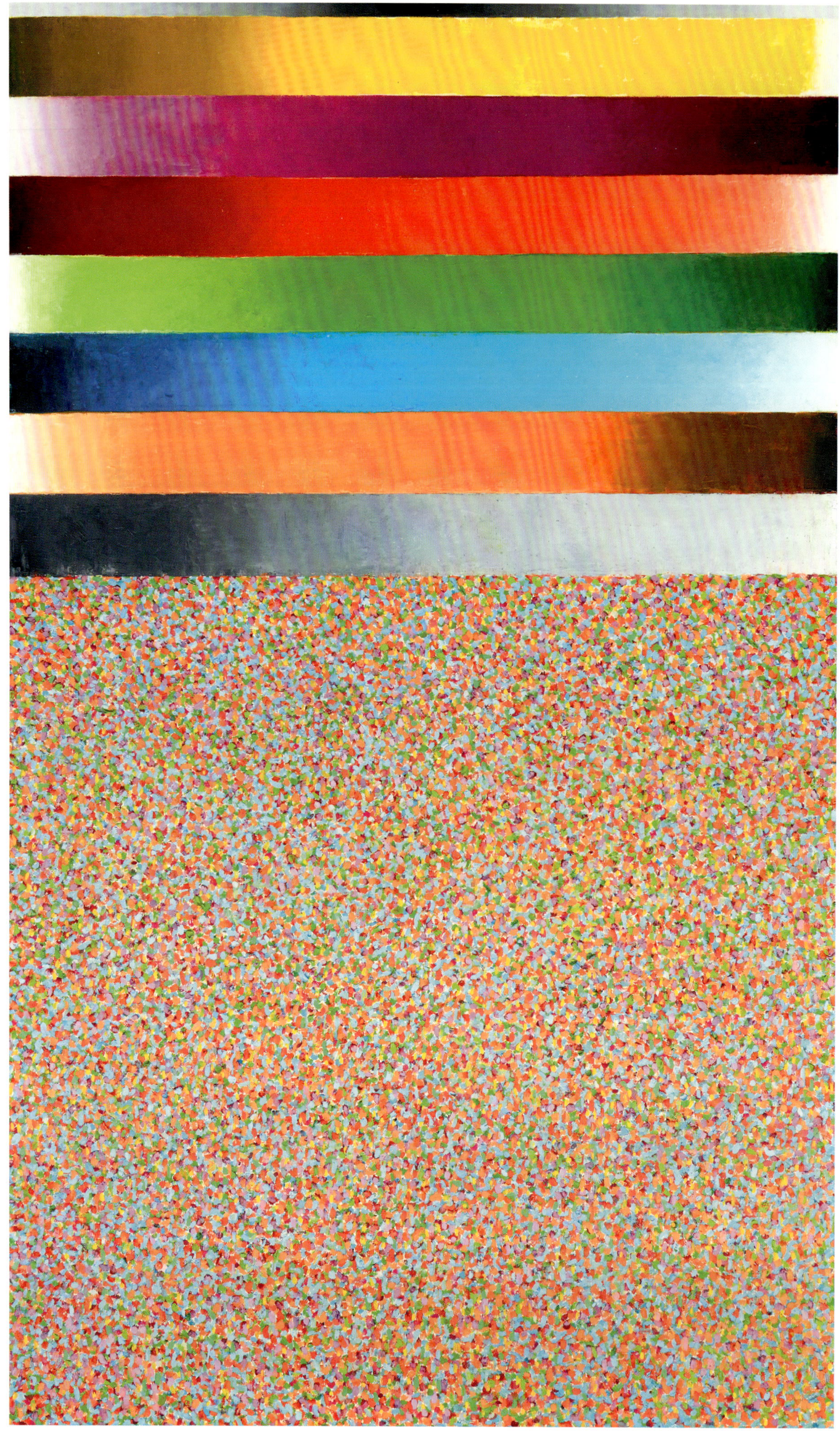

Painting DCCXXXVIII, 1999
Oil on canvas
250 x 150 cm

Painting CCCXLVII, 1975
Oil on canvas
110 x 110 cm

Painting CDXXXIV, 1979
Oil on canvas
92 x 65 cm

Painting CCCLXIII, 1976
Oil on canvas
80 x 65 cm

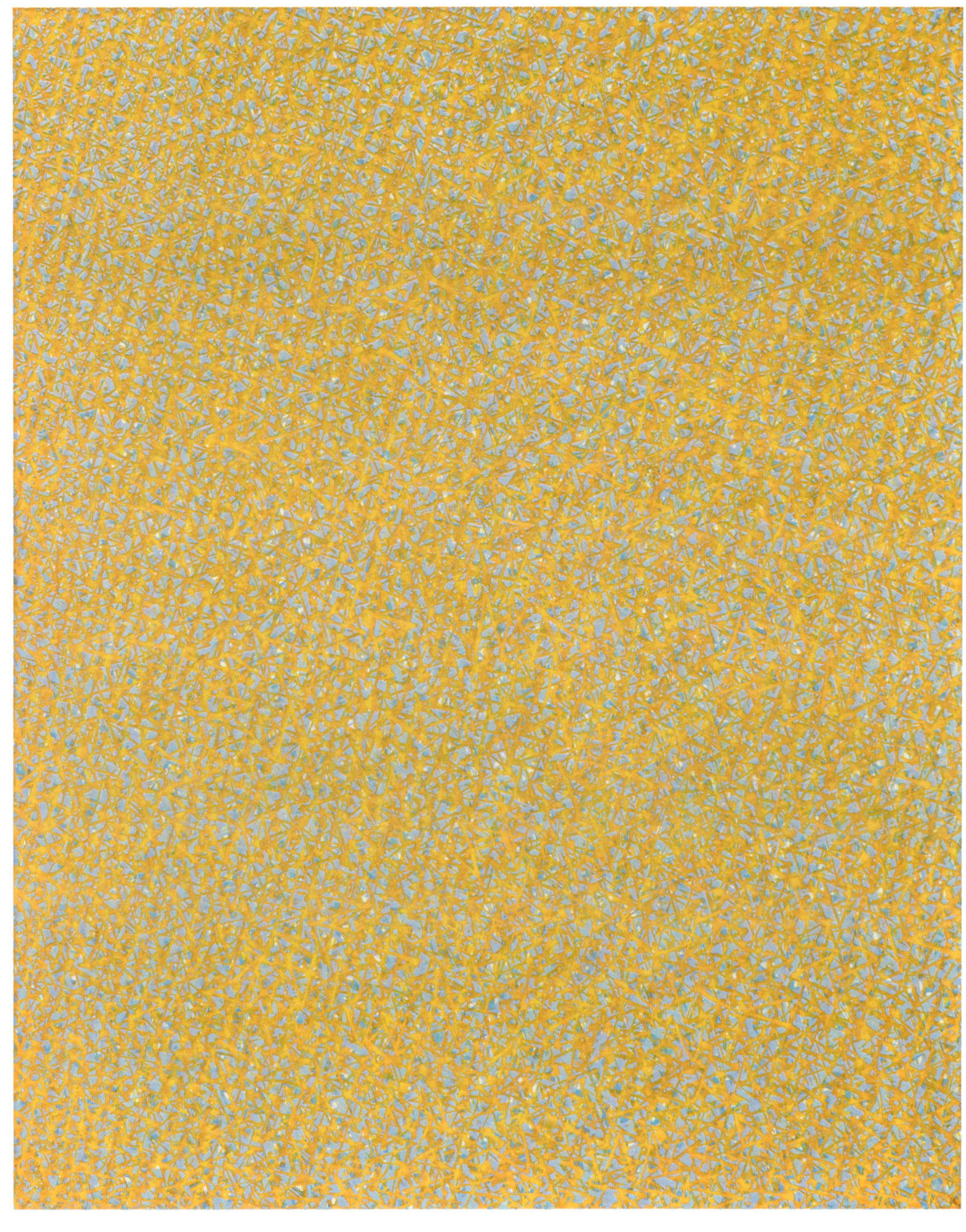

Painting CCLXXVI, 1971
Oil on canvas
100 x 80 cm

Painting CCLXXX, 1972
Oil on canvas
200 x 135 cm
Courtesy of Olomouc
Museum of Art

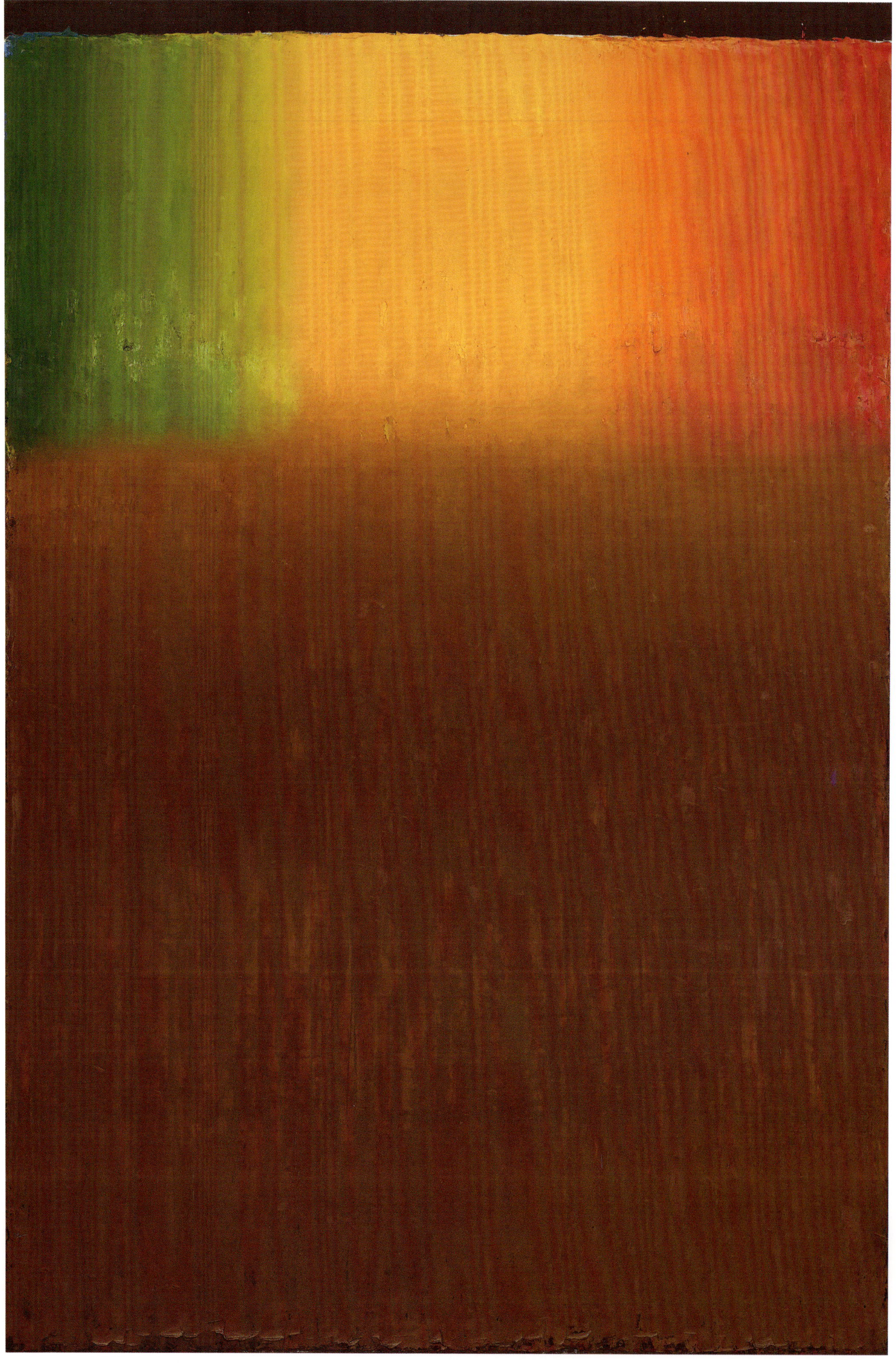

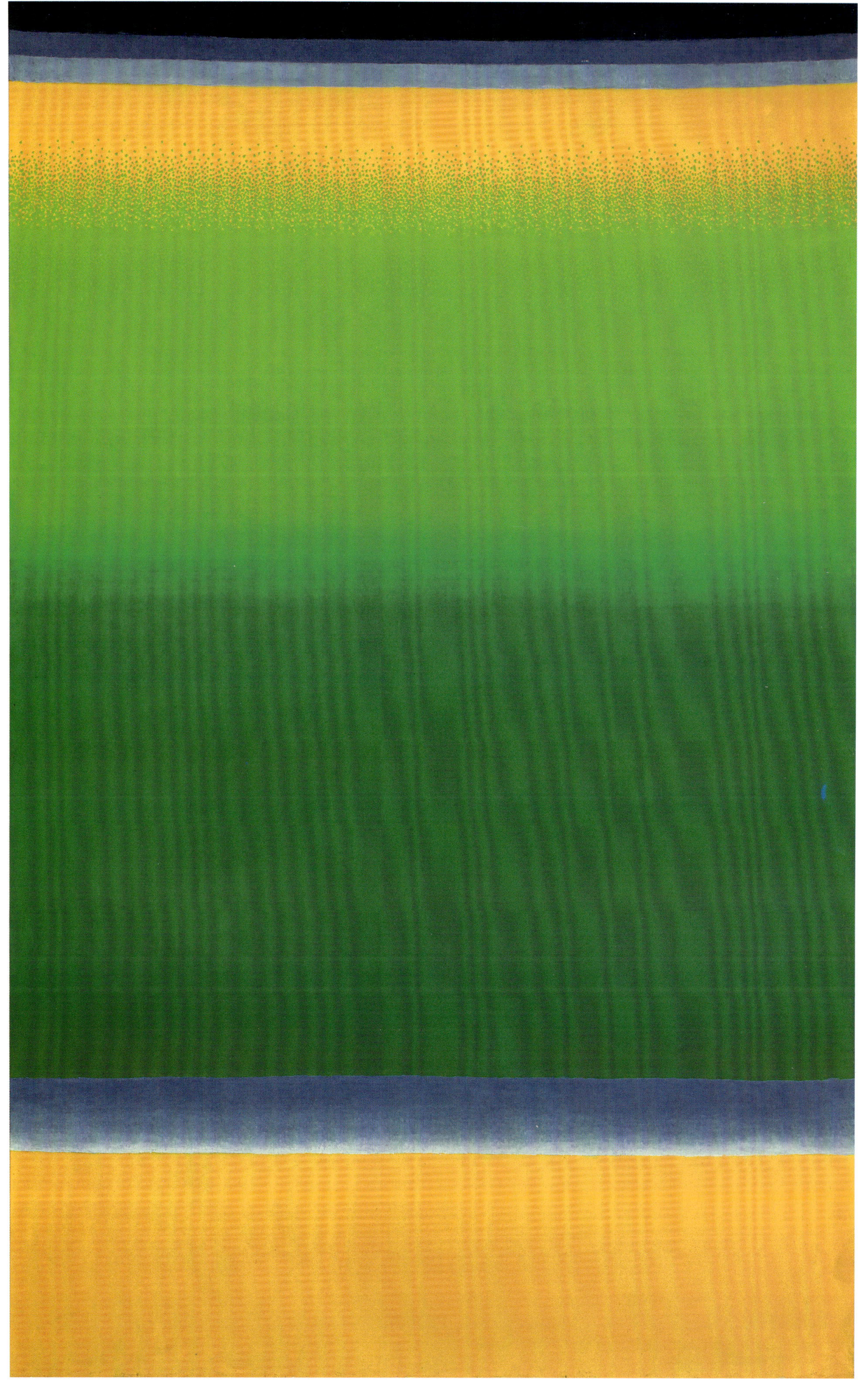

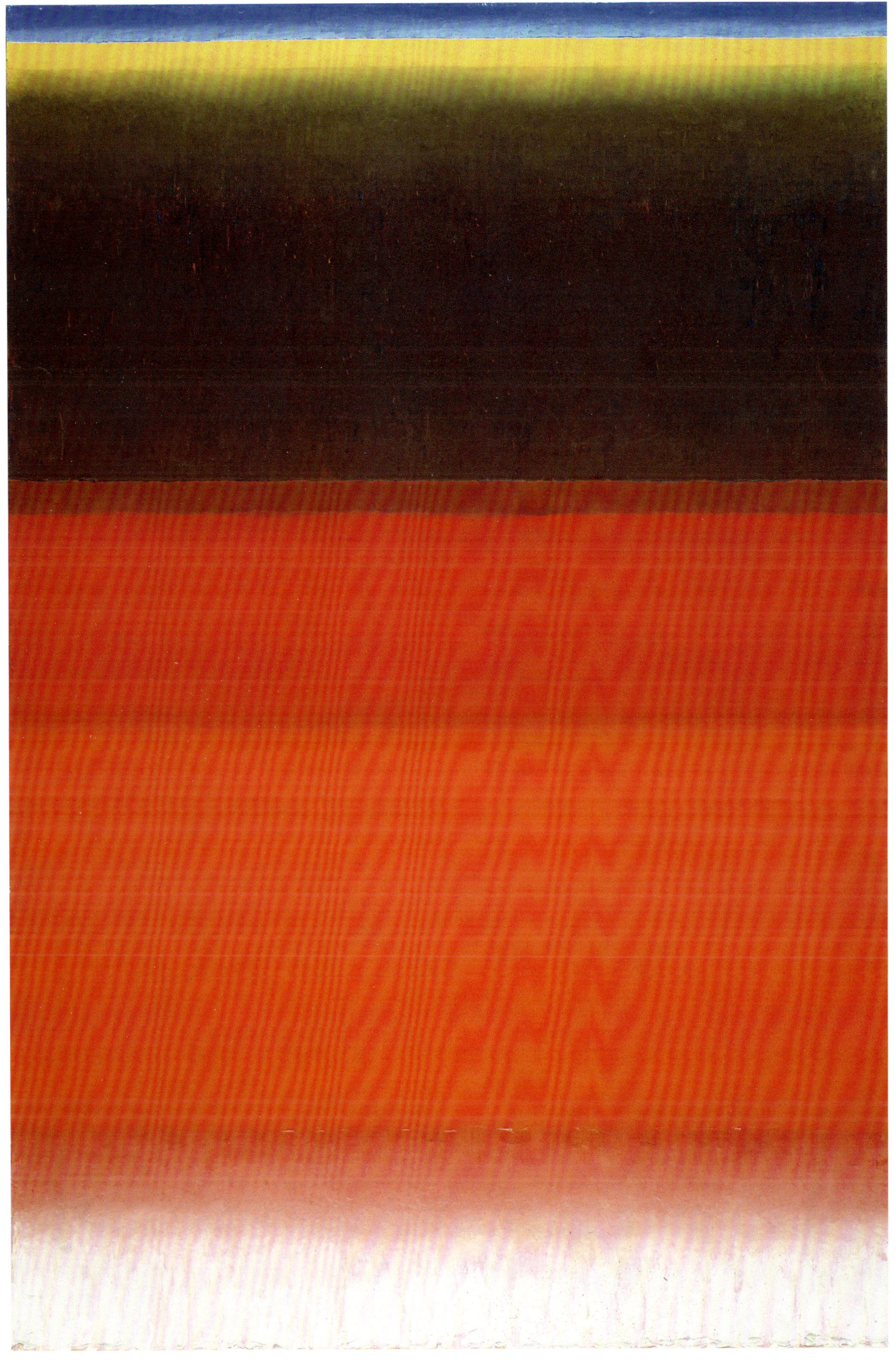

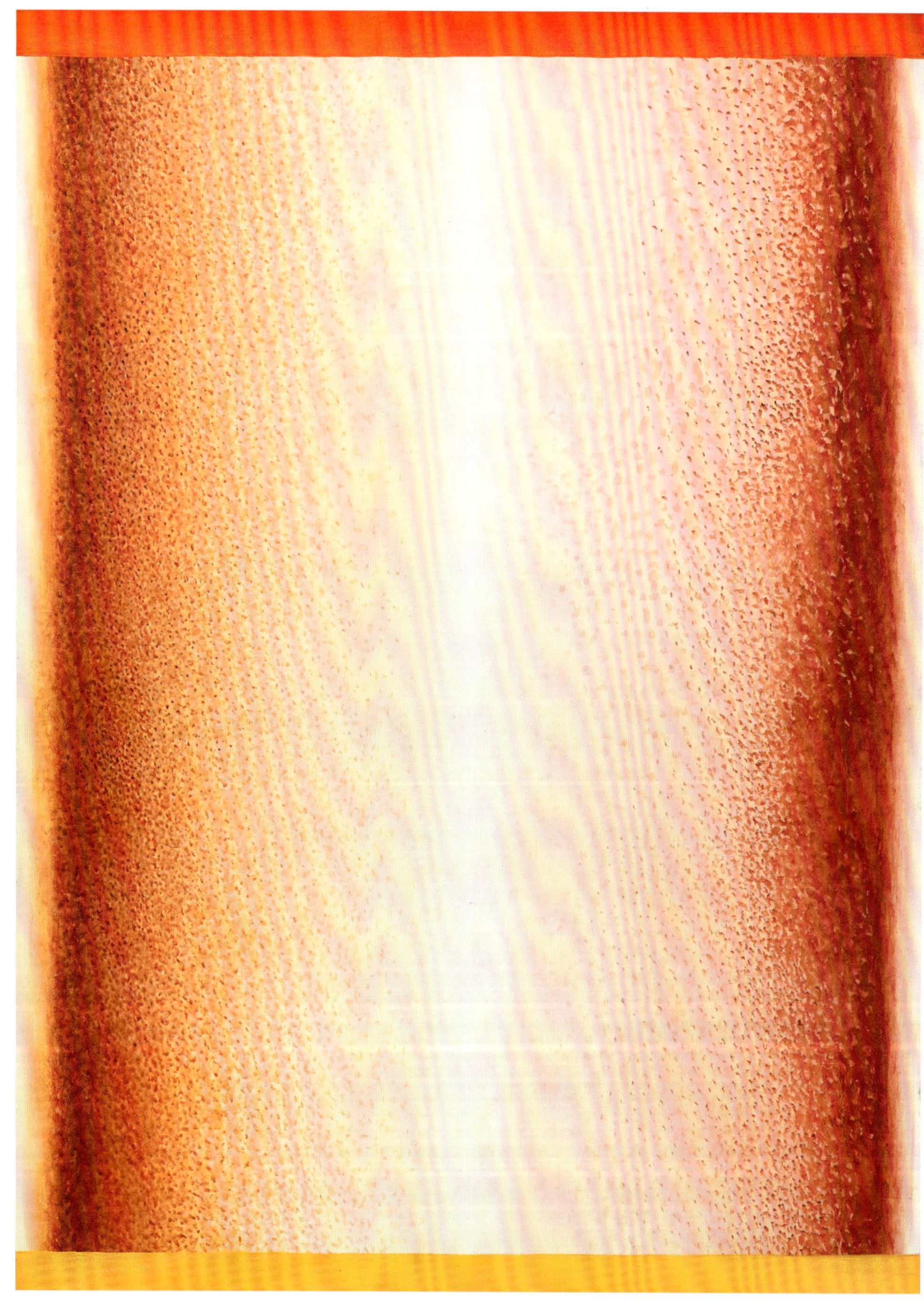

Painting DCCCXVI, 2005
Oil on canvas
100 x 73 cm

Painting DCCCXII, 2004–05
Oil on canvas
200 x 135 cm

p. 124
Painting DCCXXXVI, 1999
Oil on canvas
200 x 150 cm

p. 125
Painting DCCCXCV, 2002
Oil on canvas
200 x 135 cm

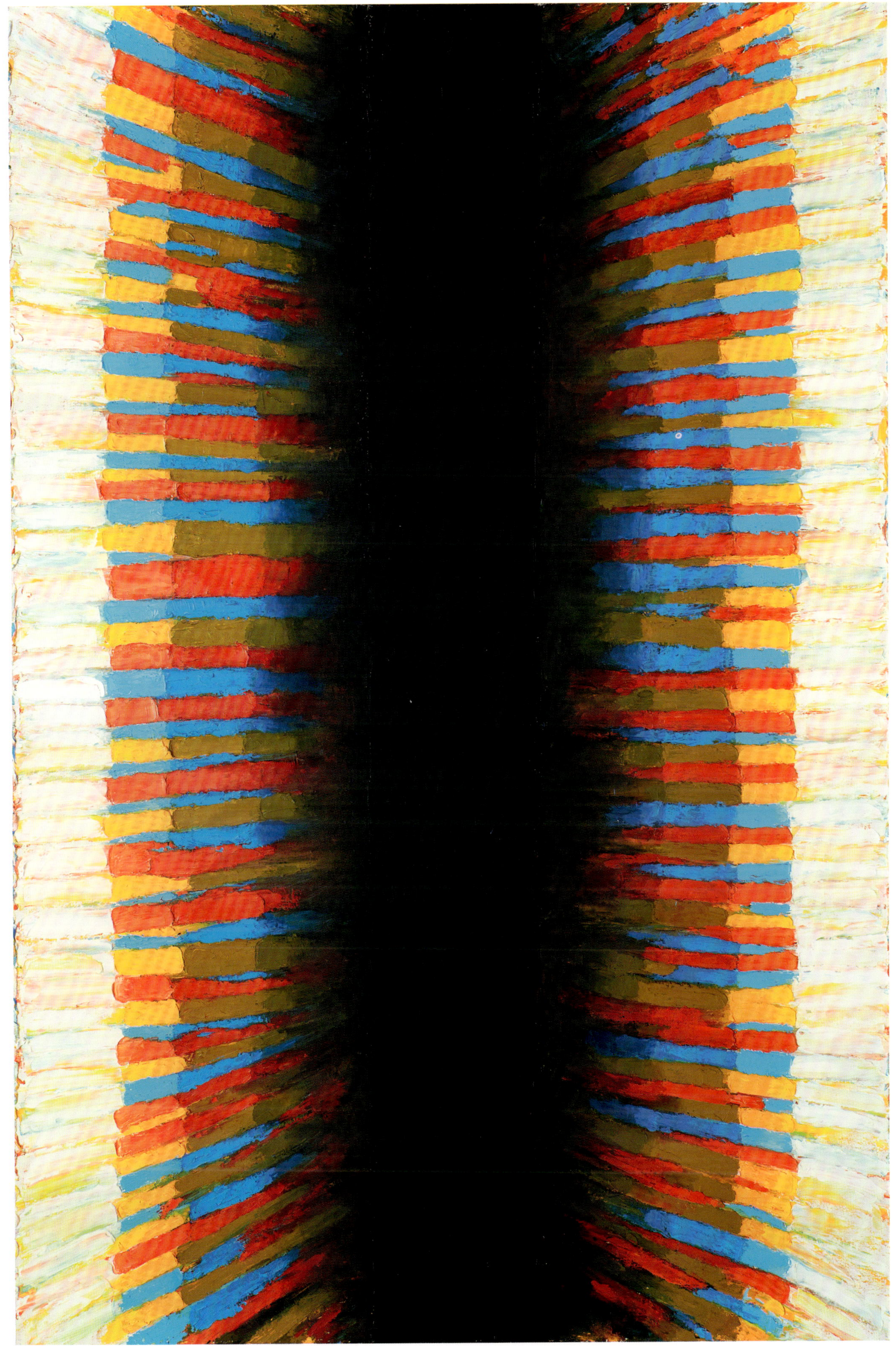

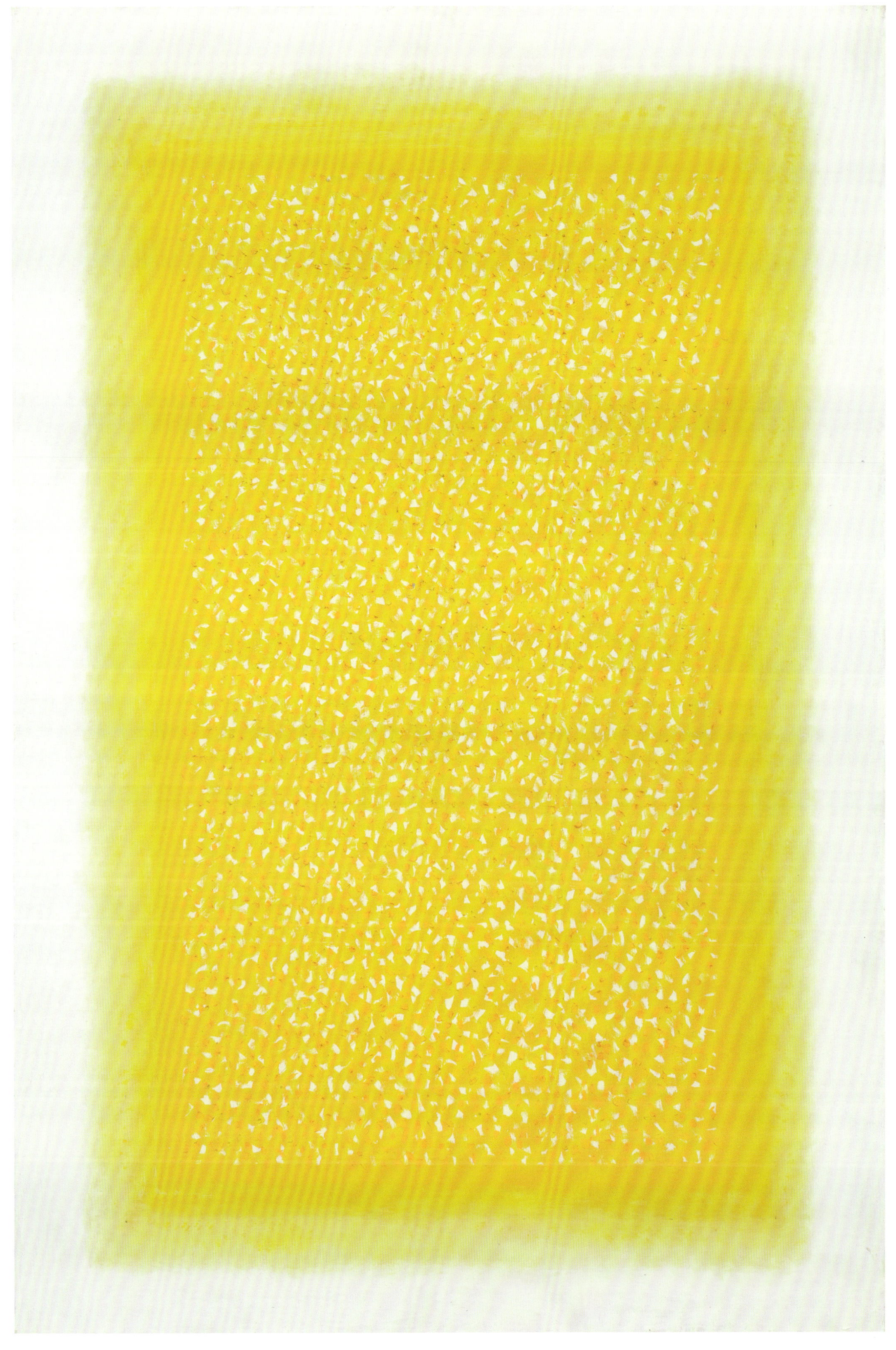

p. 126
Painting DCCIX, 1997
Oil on canvas
200 x 135 cm

p. 127
Painting DCC, 1996
Oil on canvas
200 x 135 cm

Painting DCCCXLI, 2007
Oil on canvas
190 x 190 cm

Painting DCXX, 1991
Oil on canvas
200 x 135 cm

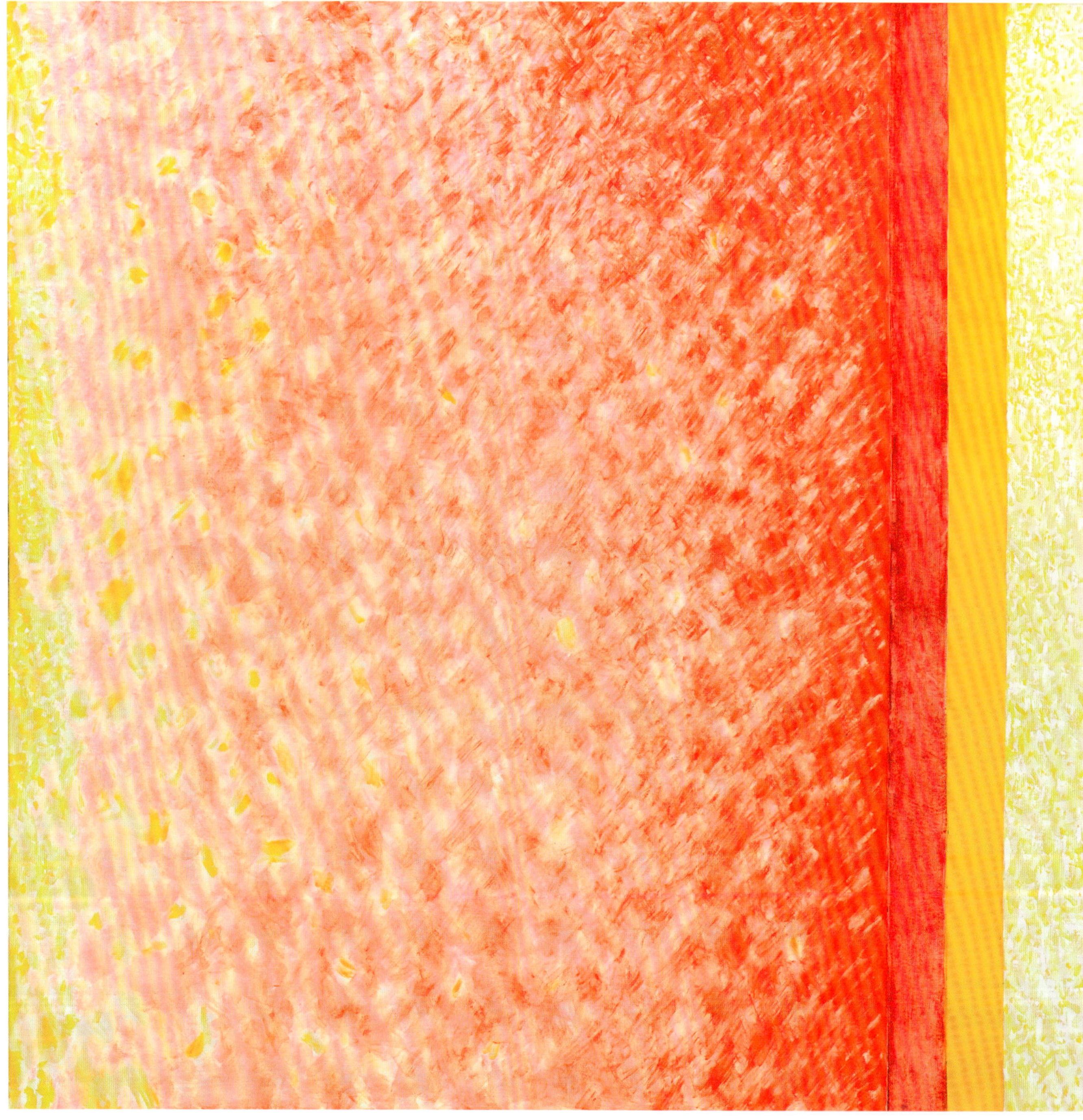

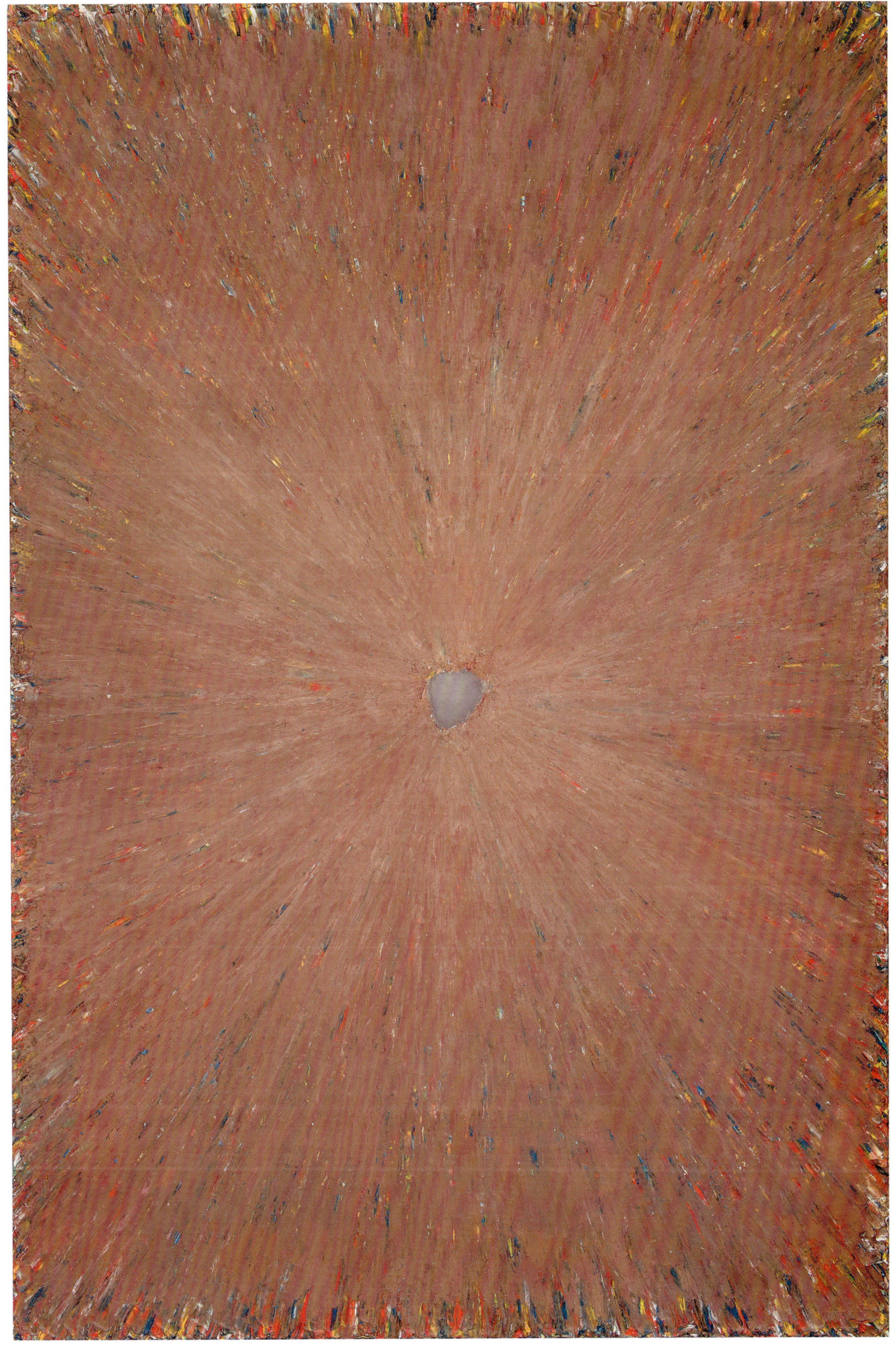

Painting DCCCLXI, 2009
Oil on canvas
150 x 120 cm

Painting DCCCLII, 2008
Oil on canvas
200 x 140 cm
Collection of Krzysztof Musiał,
deposited at the Museum
of the Academy of Fine Arts
in Warsaw

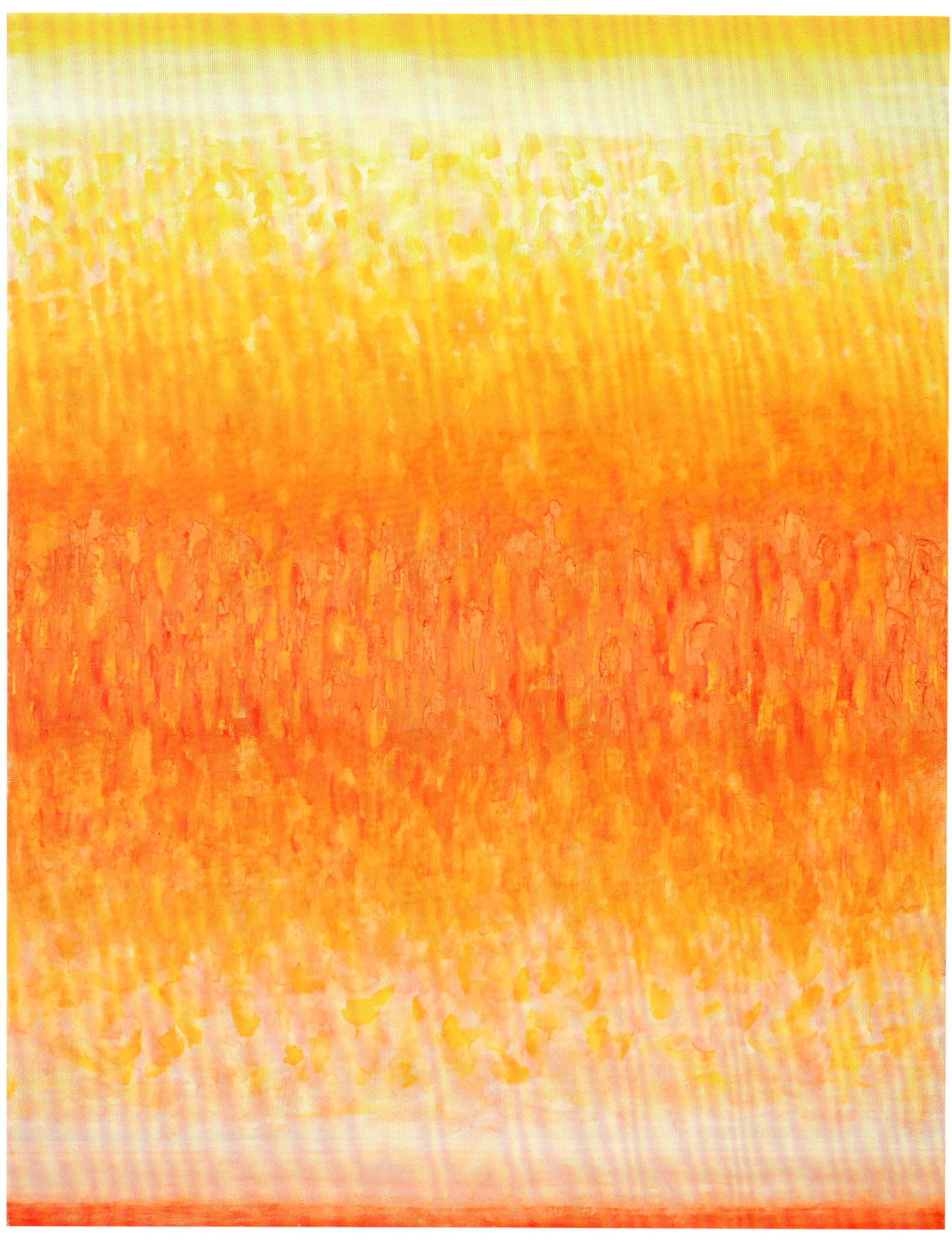

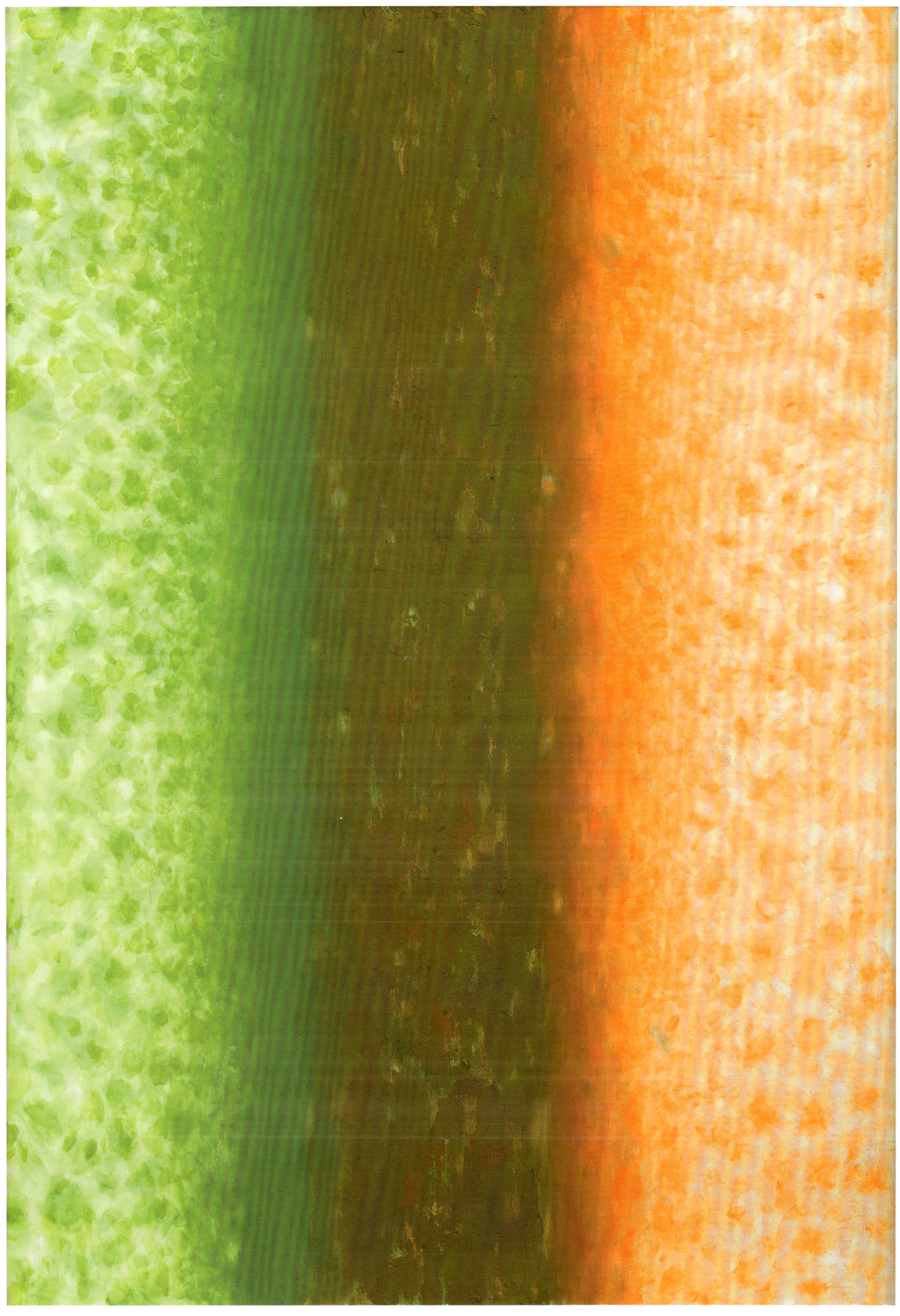

Painting DCCCLXXI, 2010
Oil on canvas
100 x 92 cm

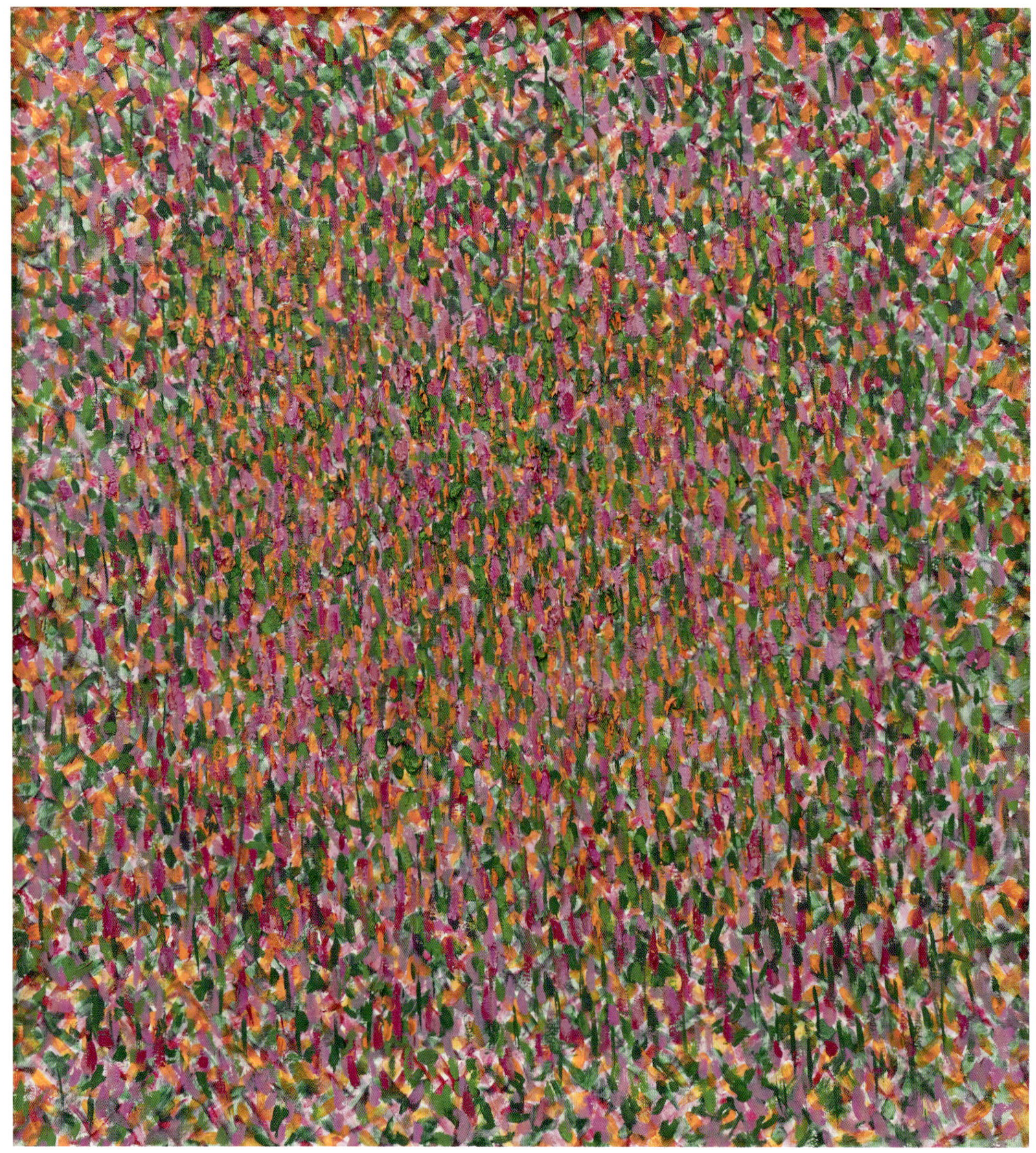

Painting DCCCLXIV, 2009
Oil on canvas
146 x 114 cm

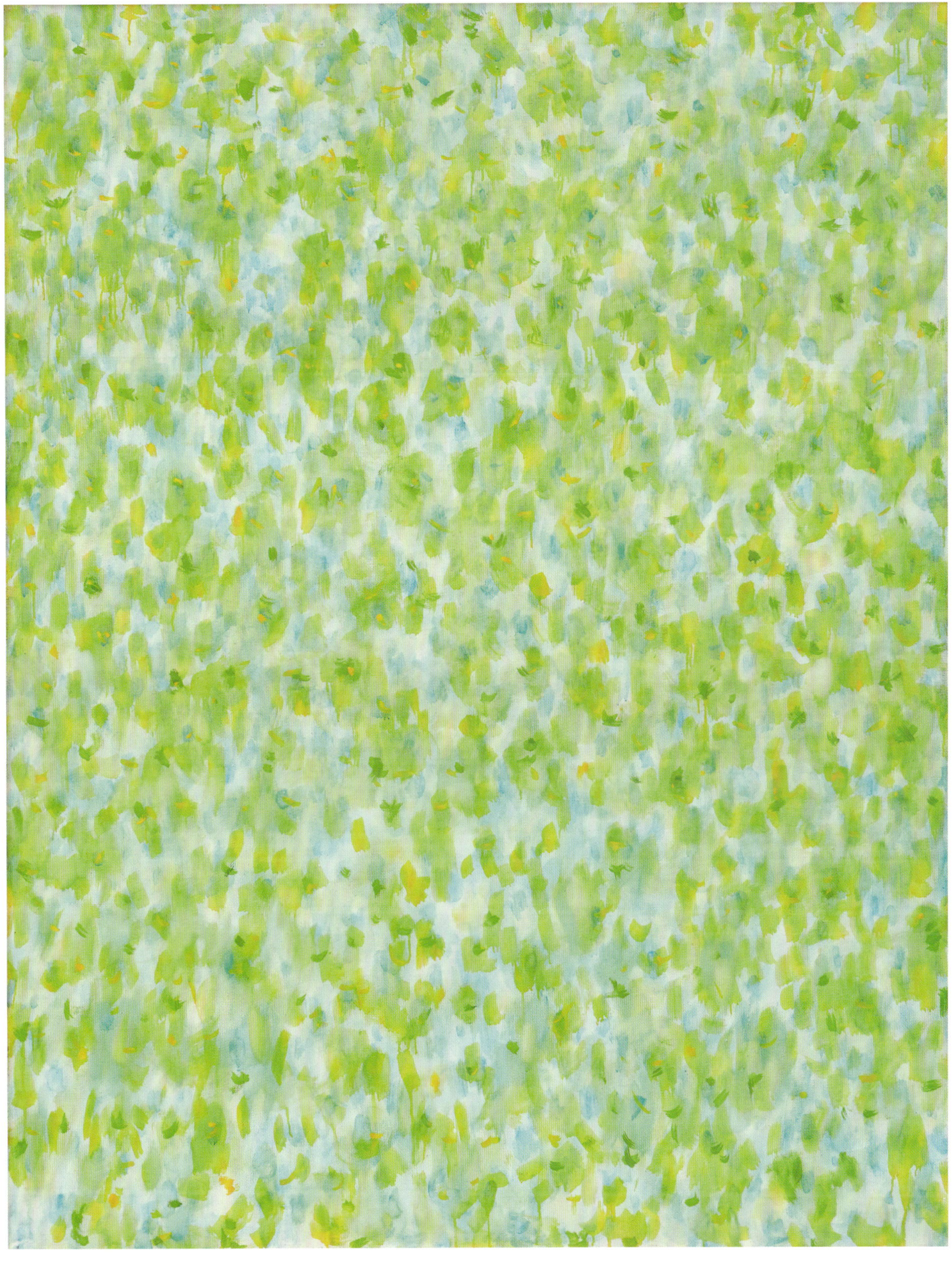

Painting DCCCLXXIII, 2010
Oil on canvas
150 x 120 cm

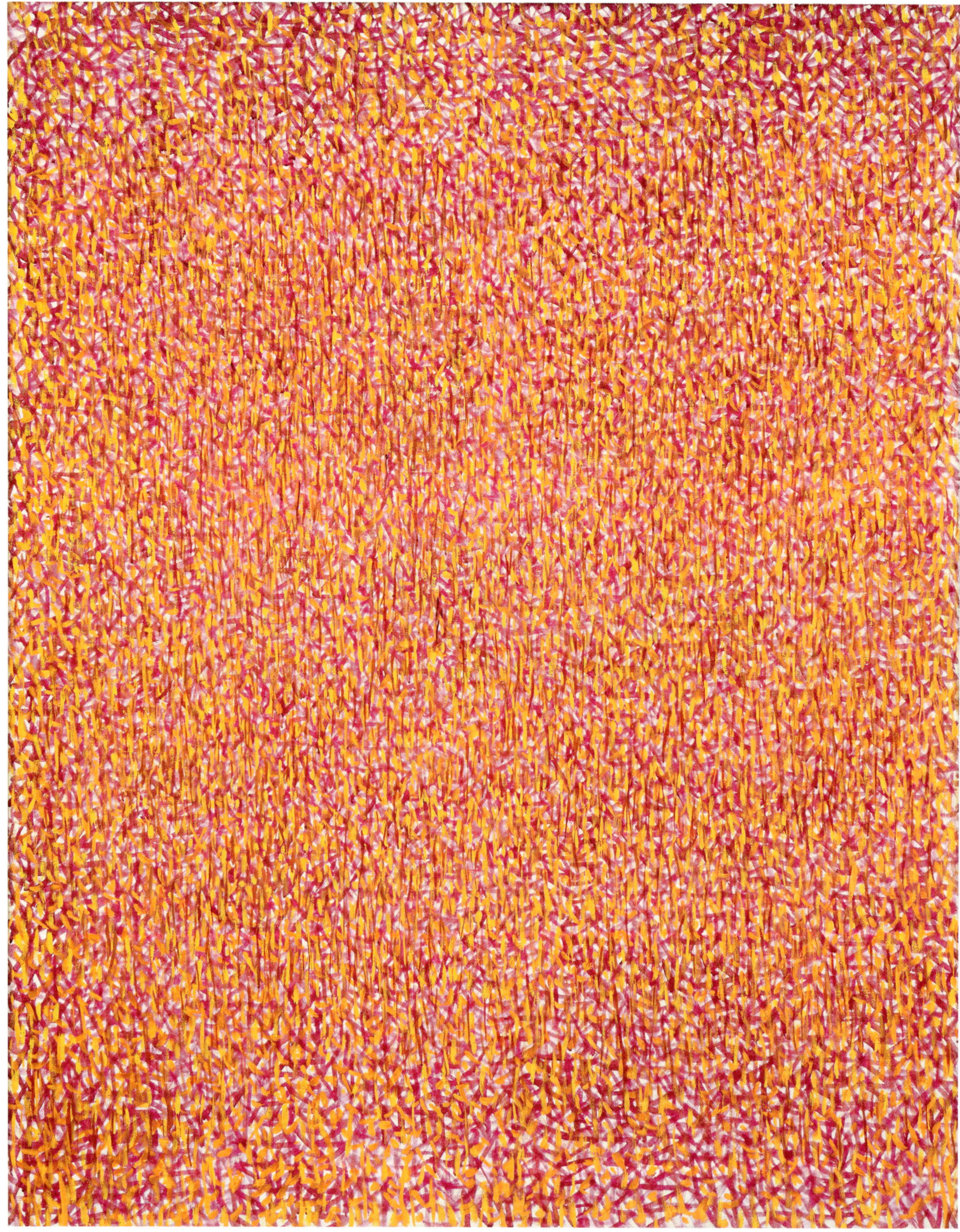

Painting DCCCLXXV, 2010
Oil on canvas
100 x 73 cm

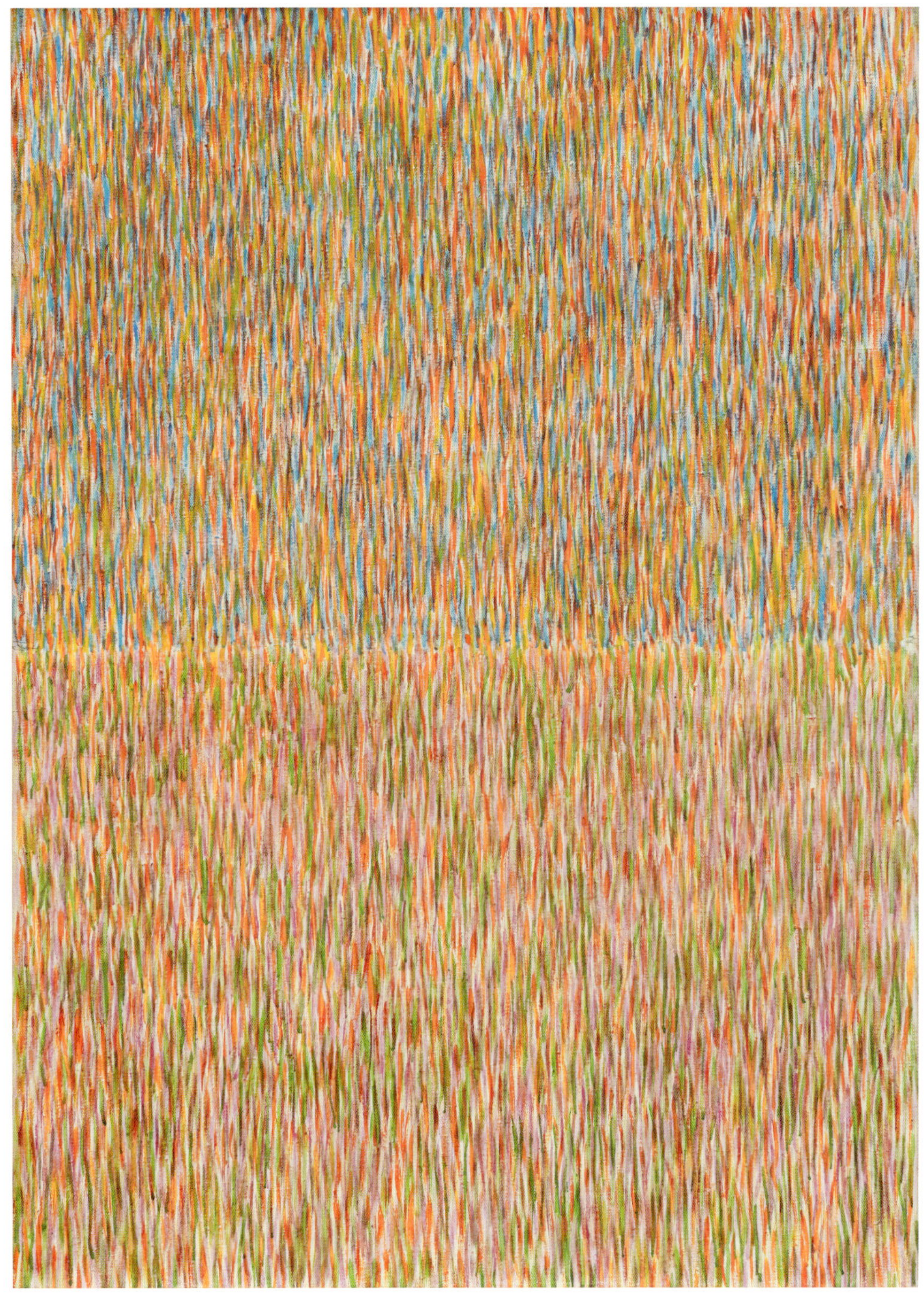

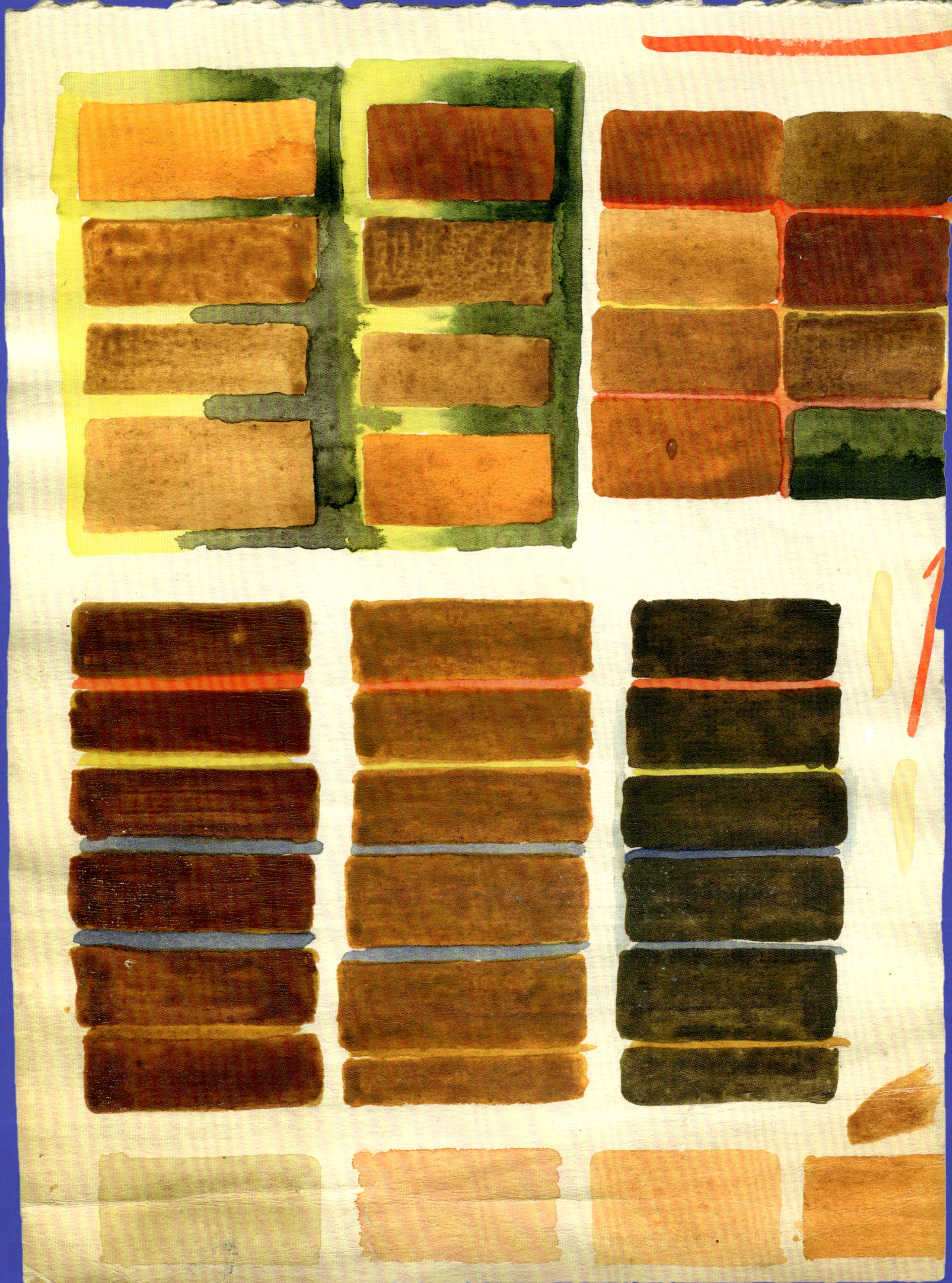

Sketch, 1980s
Gouache on cardboard
26.6 x 20.4 cm

Earth: Divisions

The rolling hills of the Holy Cross Mountains are
covered by compositions of fields of different colours.
This has remained engraved in memory, like the glow
of whiteness before a storm or the sheets of torrential
rain. This land and the impressions associated
with abstract thinking developed on a structure of closed
divisions of the logic of reality. Where is abstraction
and where is concreteness? That is the question
which presents itself to those who seek the truth of painting.
And above all is the canvas, the paints. Why does this
path unfold? I love life.

Stefan Gierowski

Painting CCCXCVI, 1977
Oil on canvas
150 x 119 cm

Painting CCCLXXXVII, 1977
Oil on canvas
200 x 124 cm

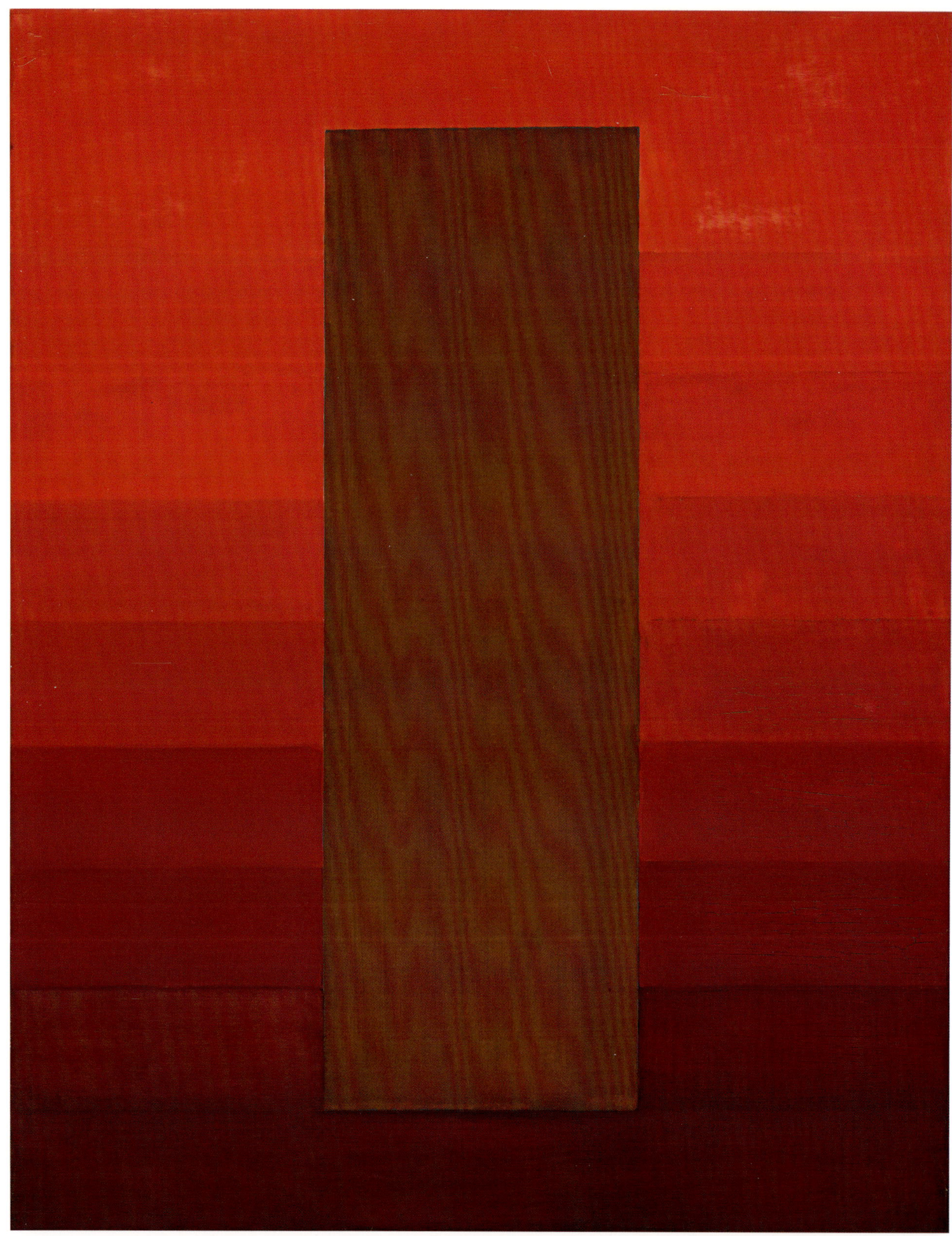

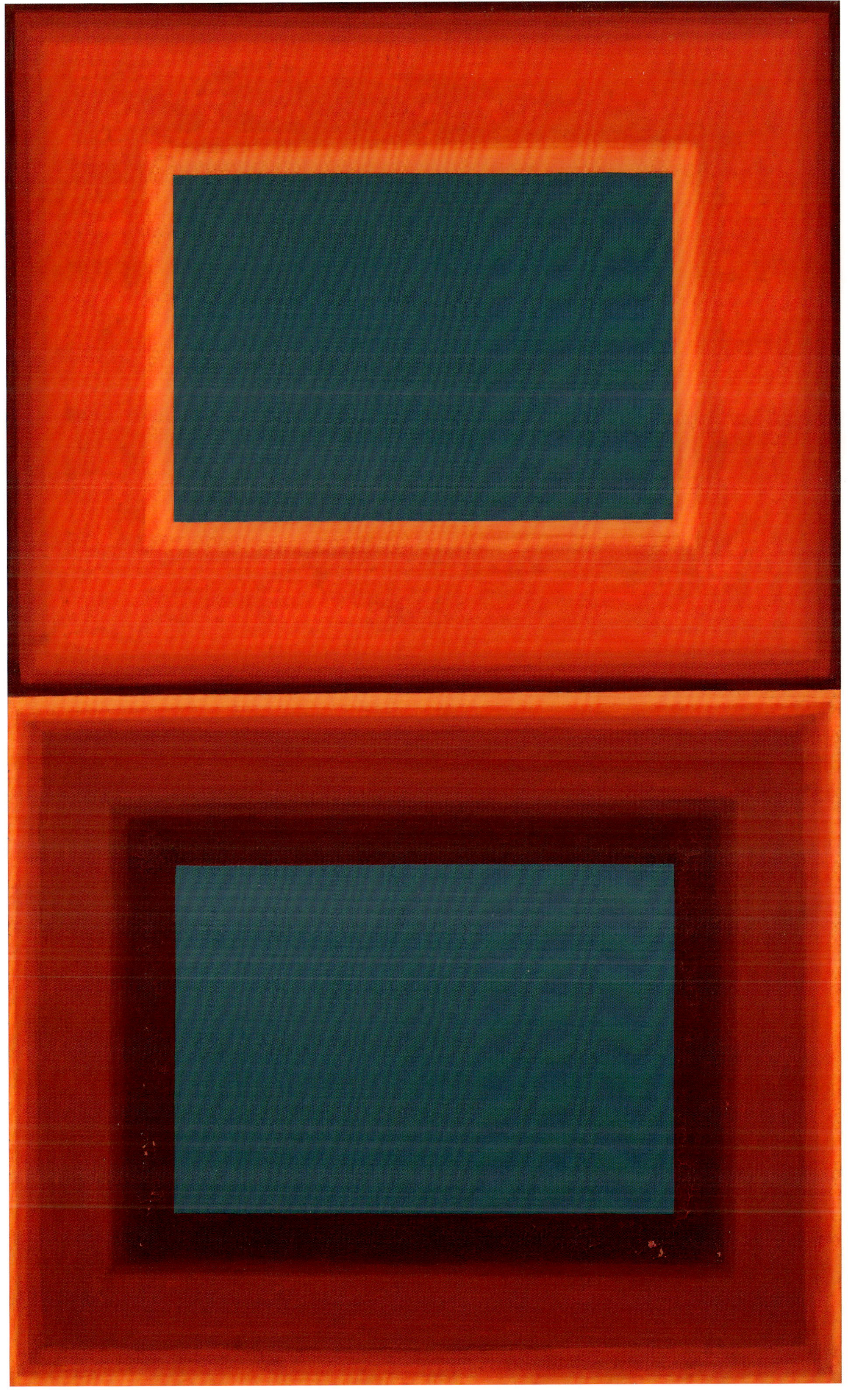

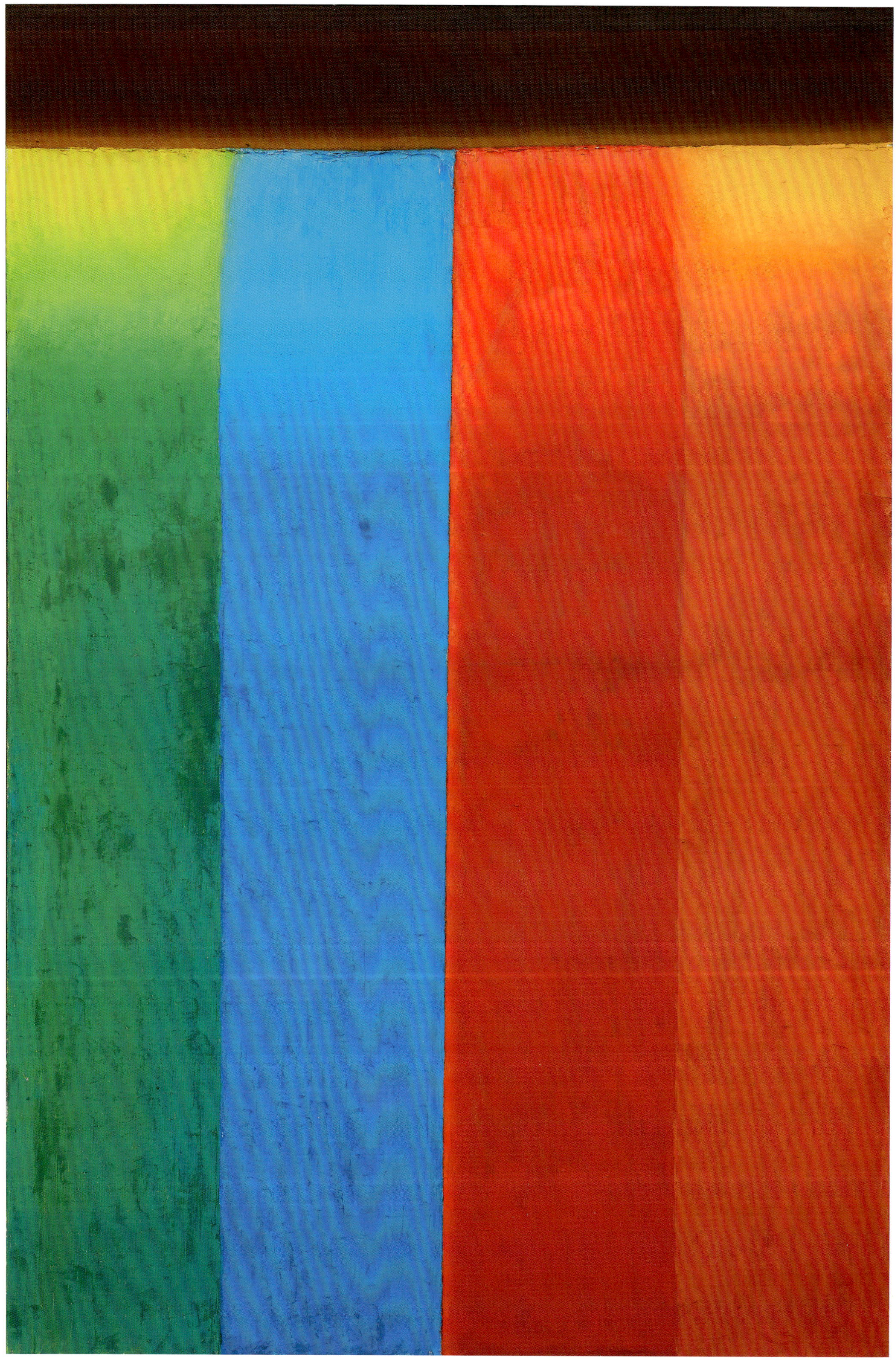

Painting DCV, 1990
Oil on canvas
200 x 135 cm

Painting DCCCIII, 2003–04
Oil on canvas
140 x 100 cm

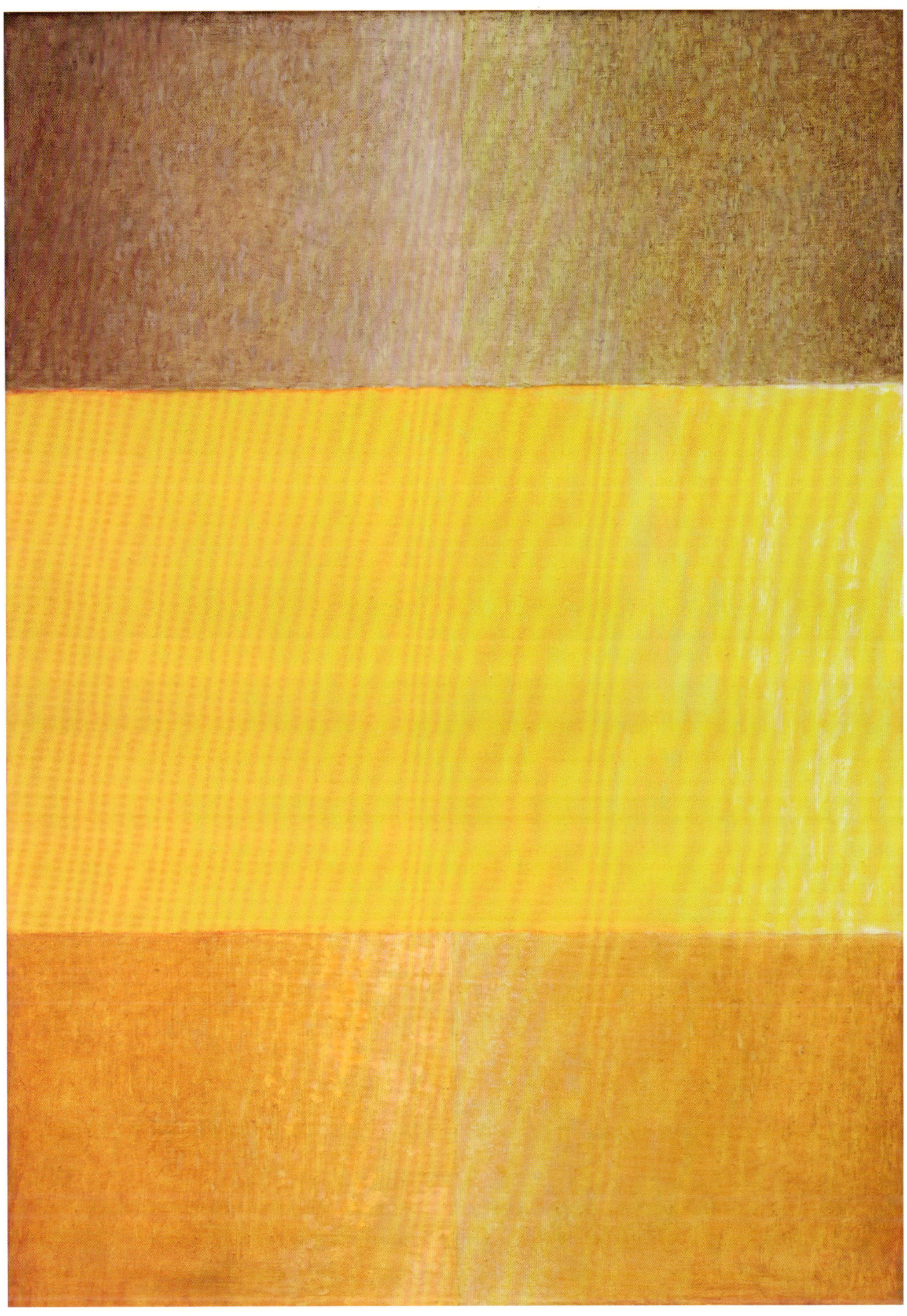

Painting CCCXCVIII, 1977
Oil on canvas
120 x 100 cm

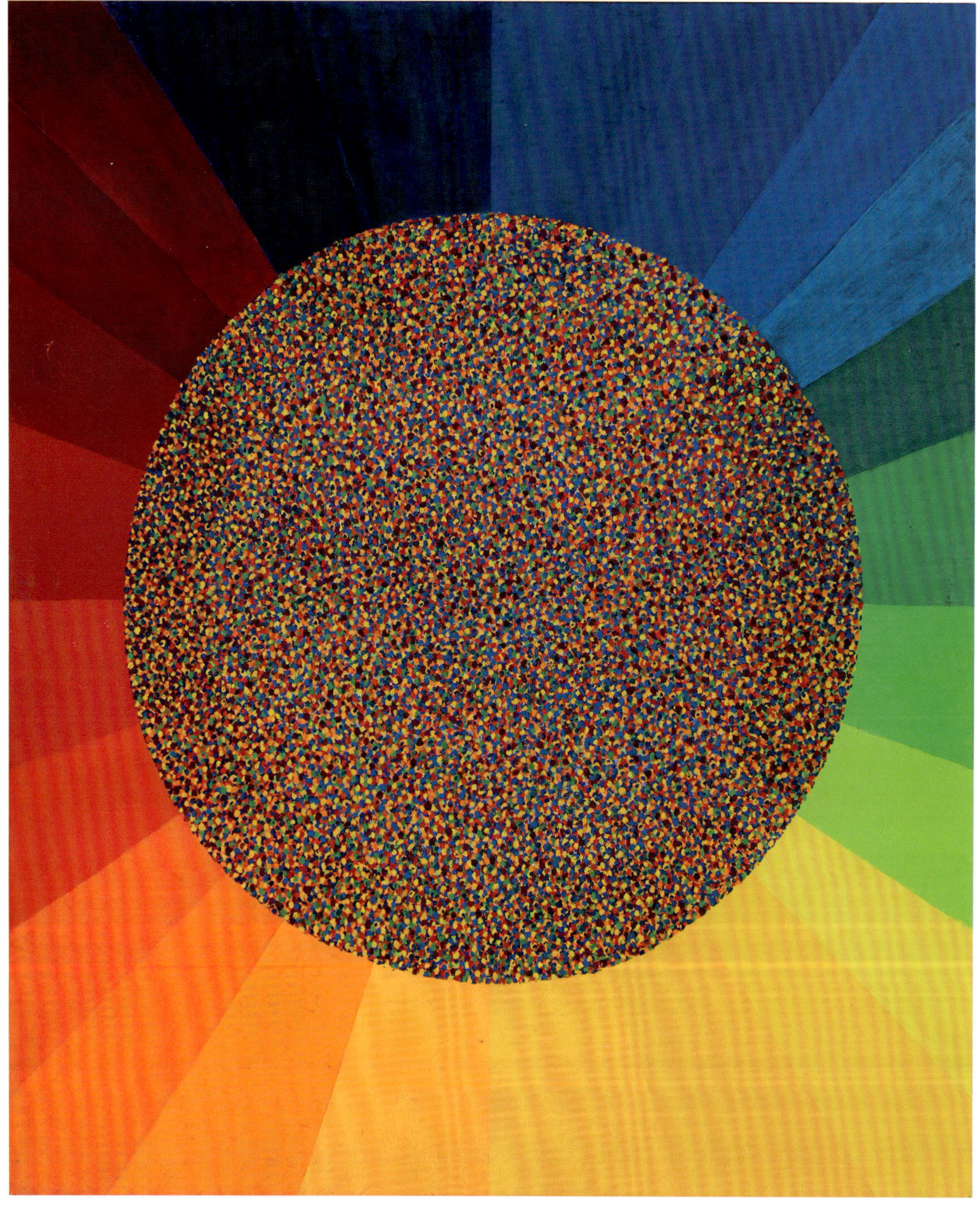

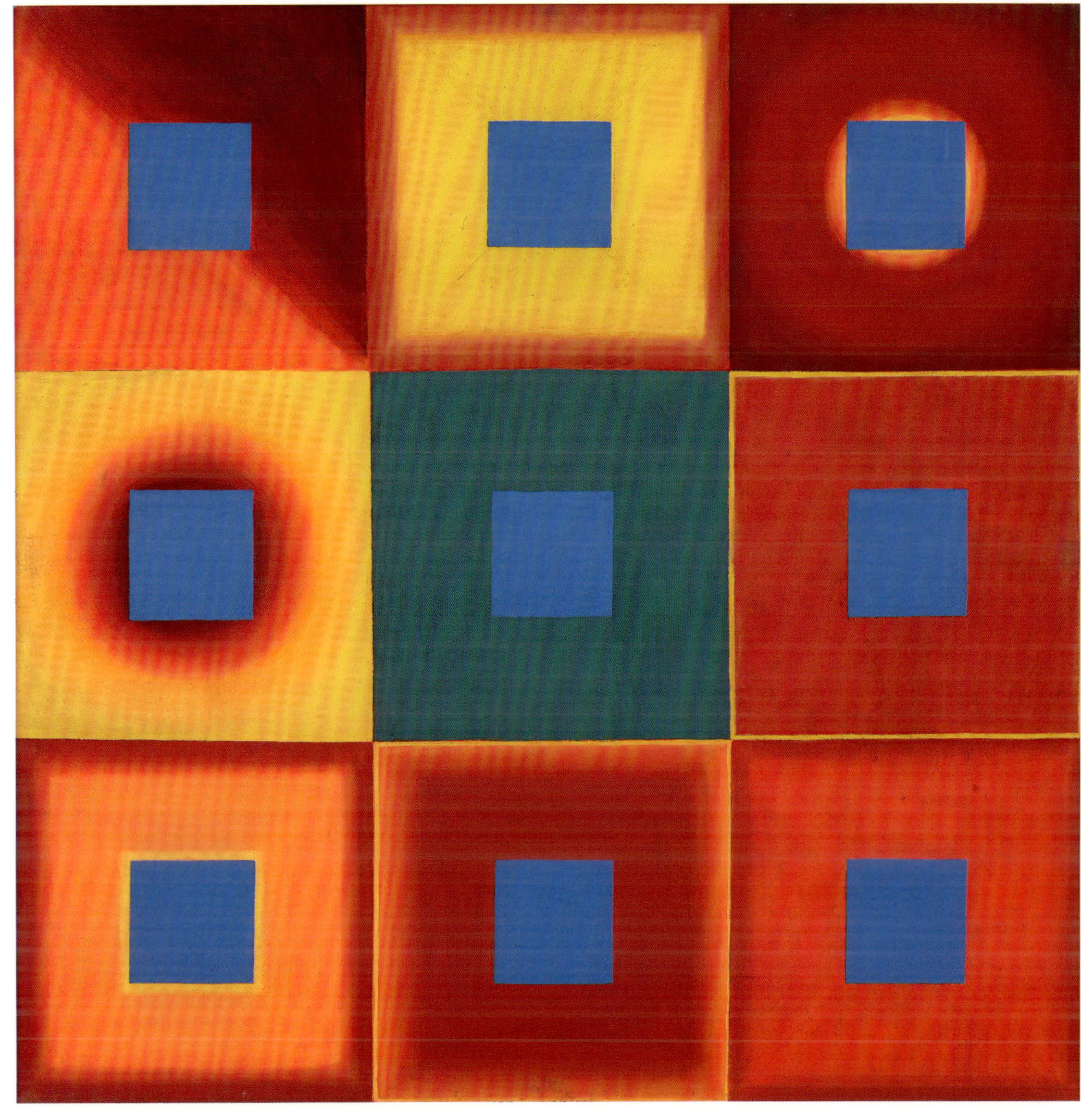

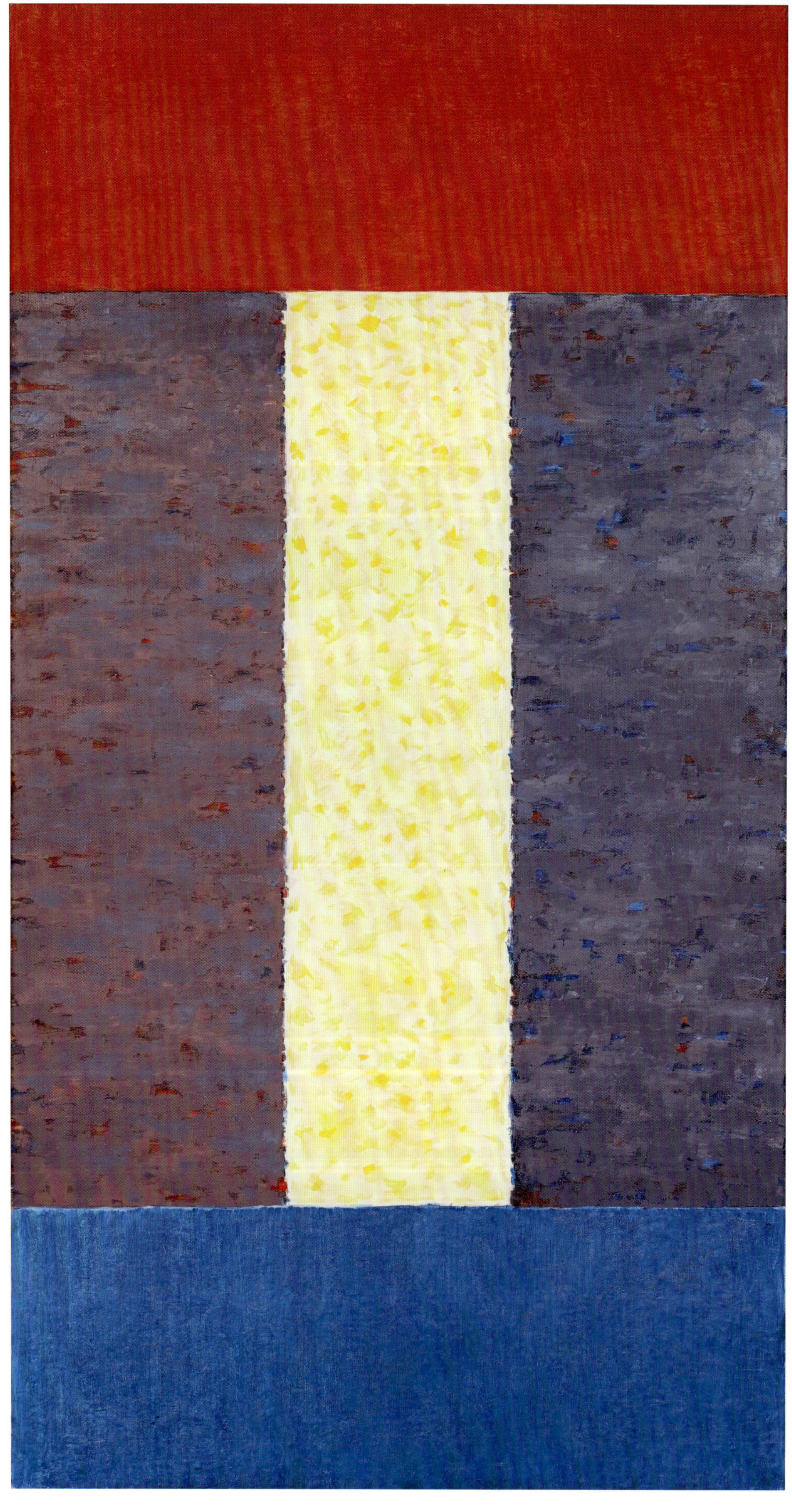

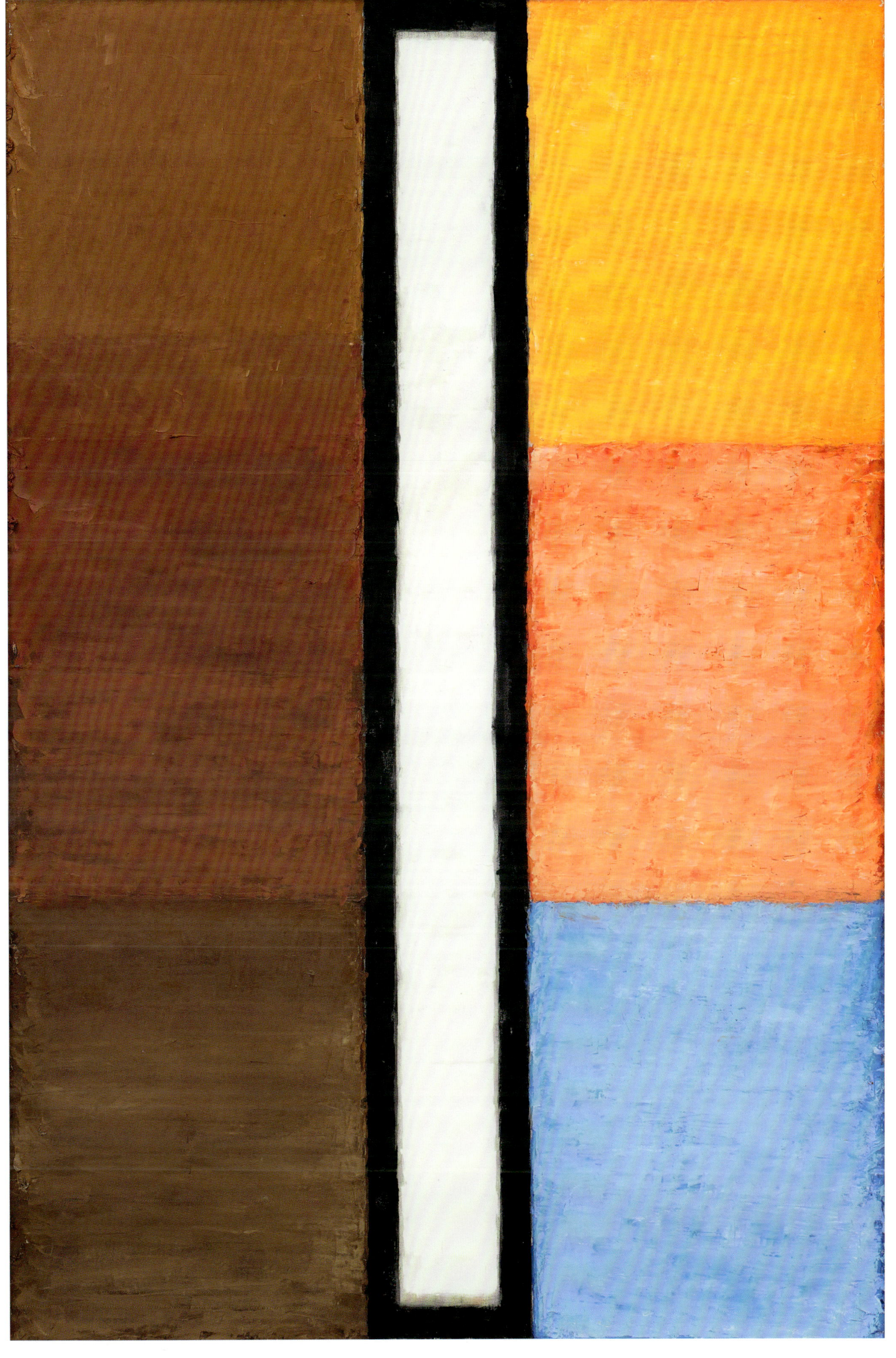

Painting DCCCXXXII, 2006
Oil on canvas
146 x 114 cm

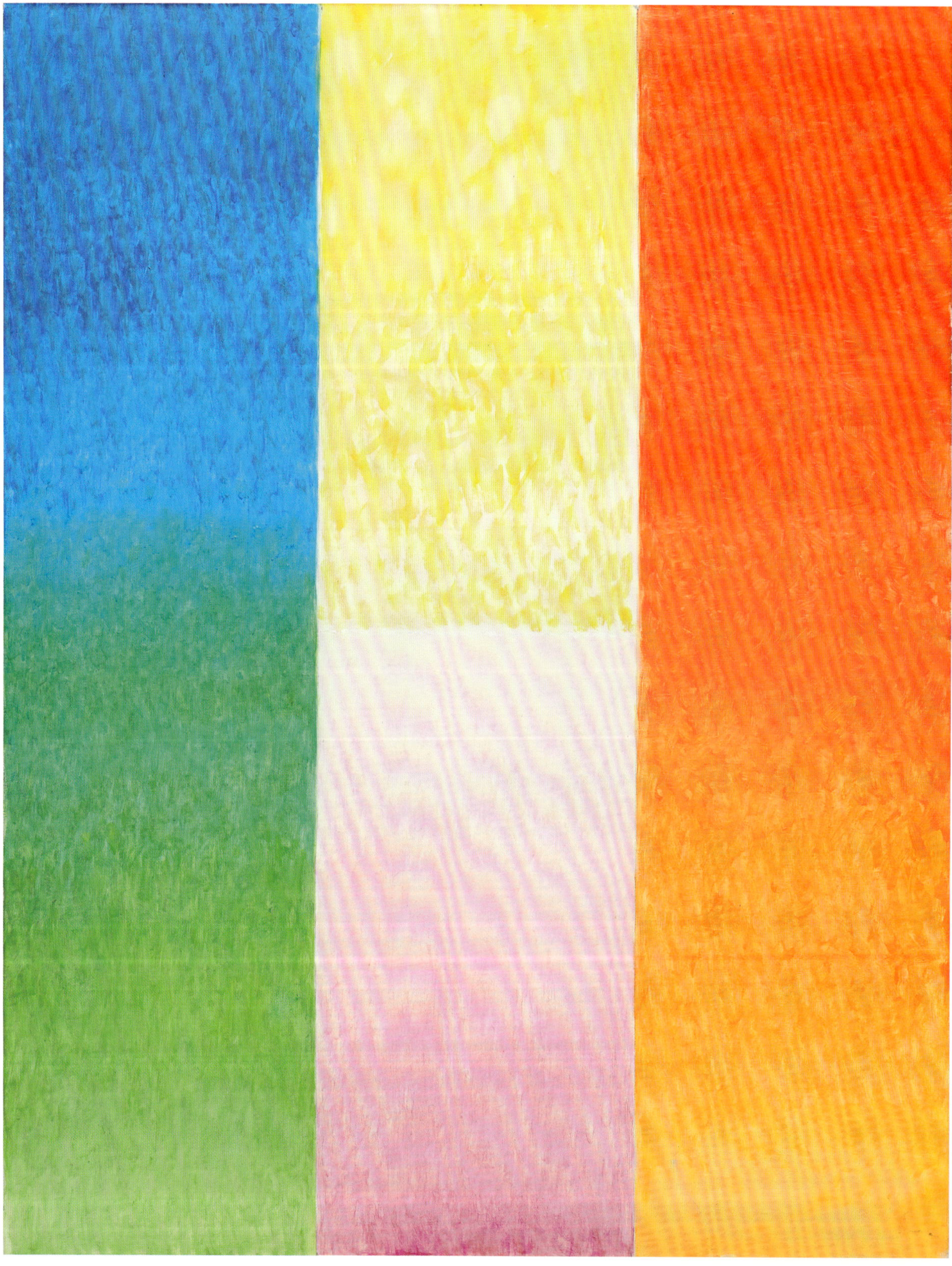

Painting DCCCXXVIII, 2005
Oil on canvas
140 x 100 cm

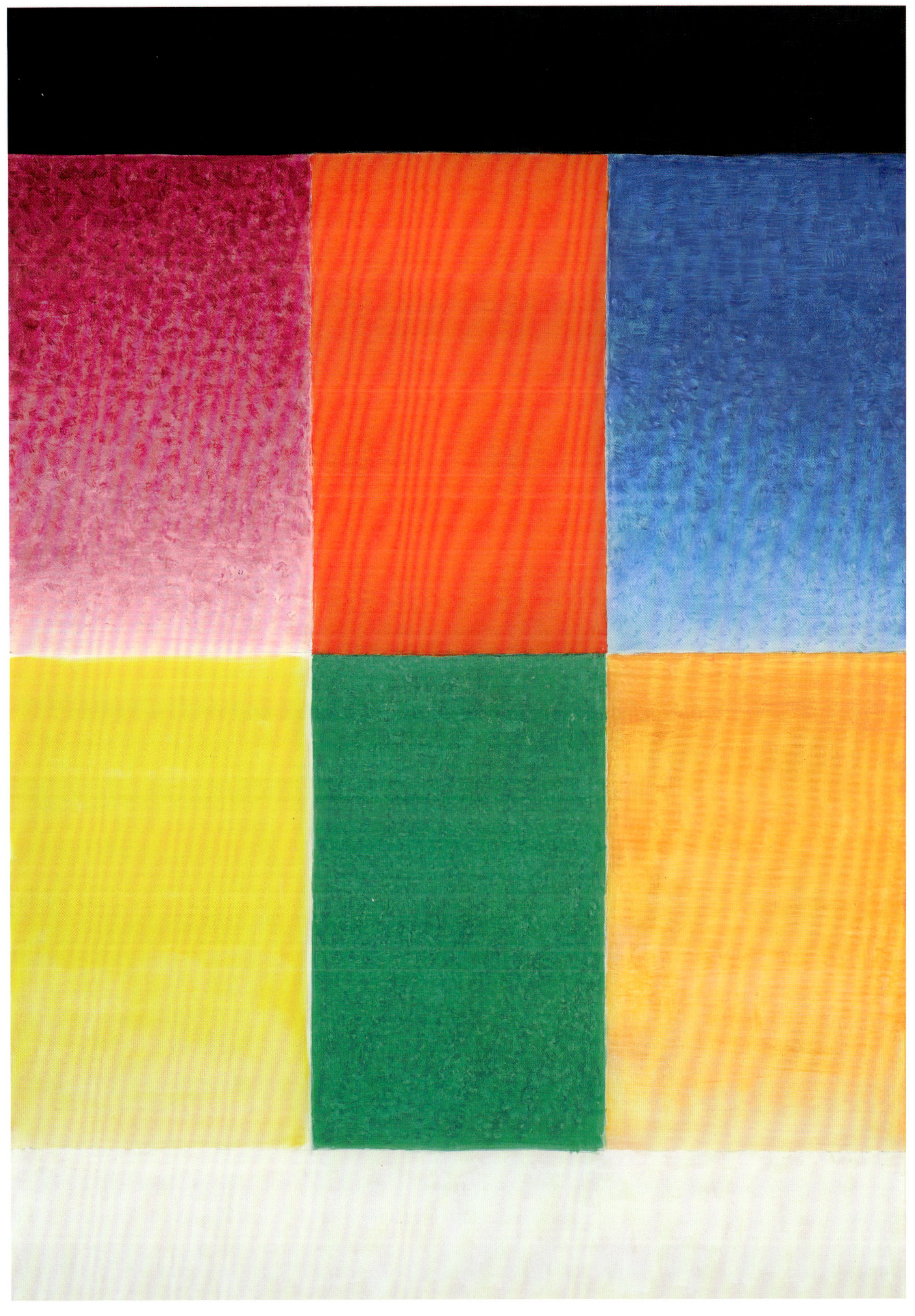

Painting DCCXC, 2002
Oil on canvas
130 x 100 cm

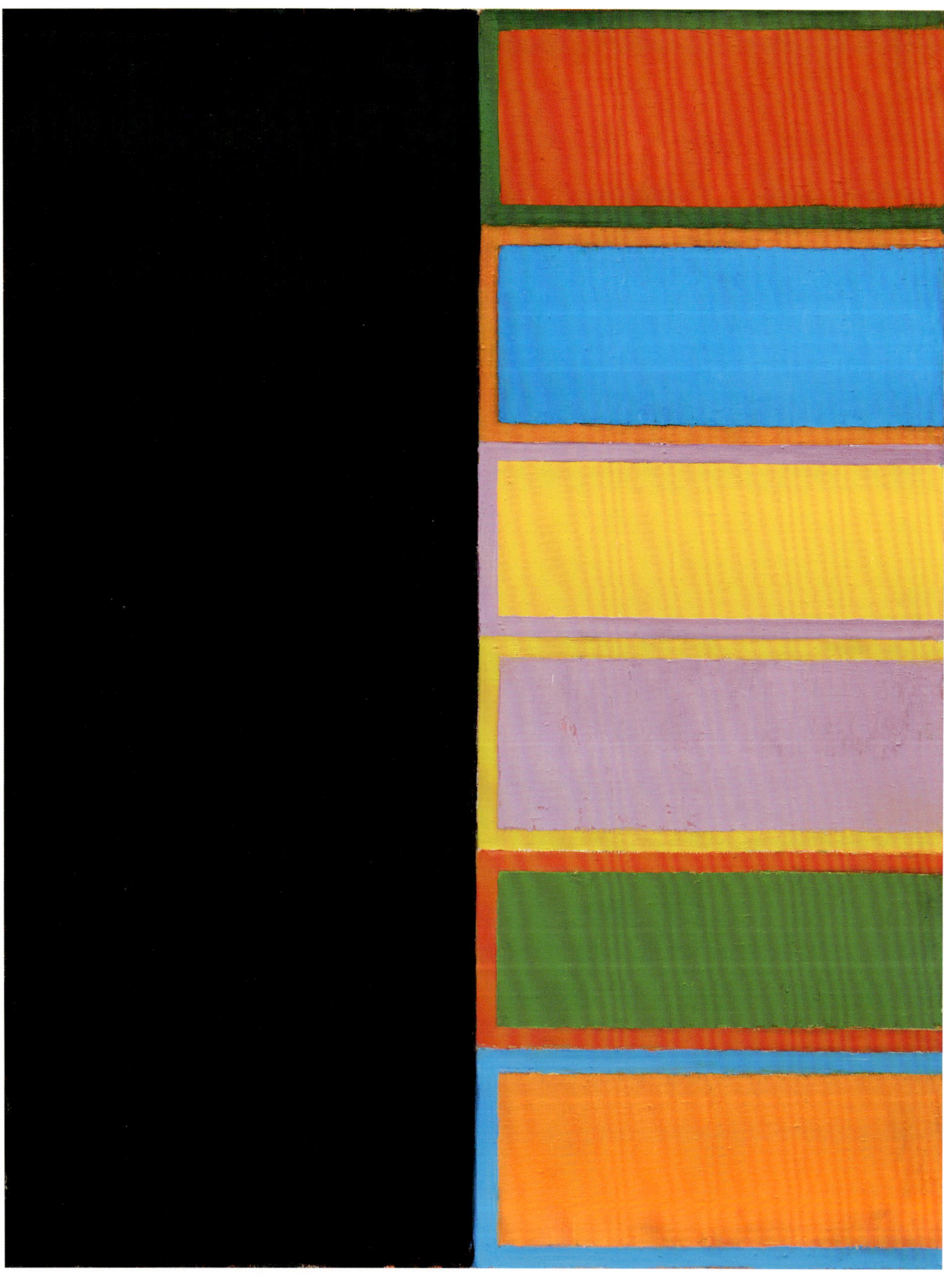

Painting DCCCXLIII, 2007
Oil on canvas
100 x 92 cm

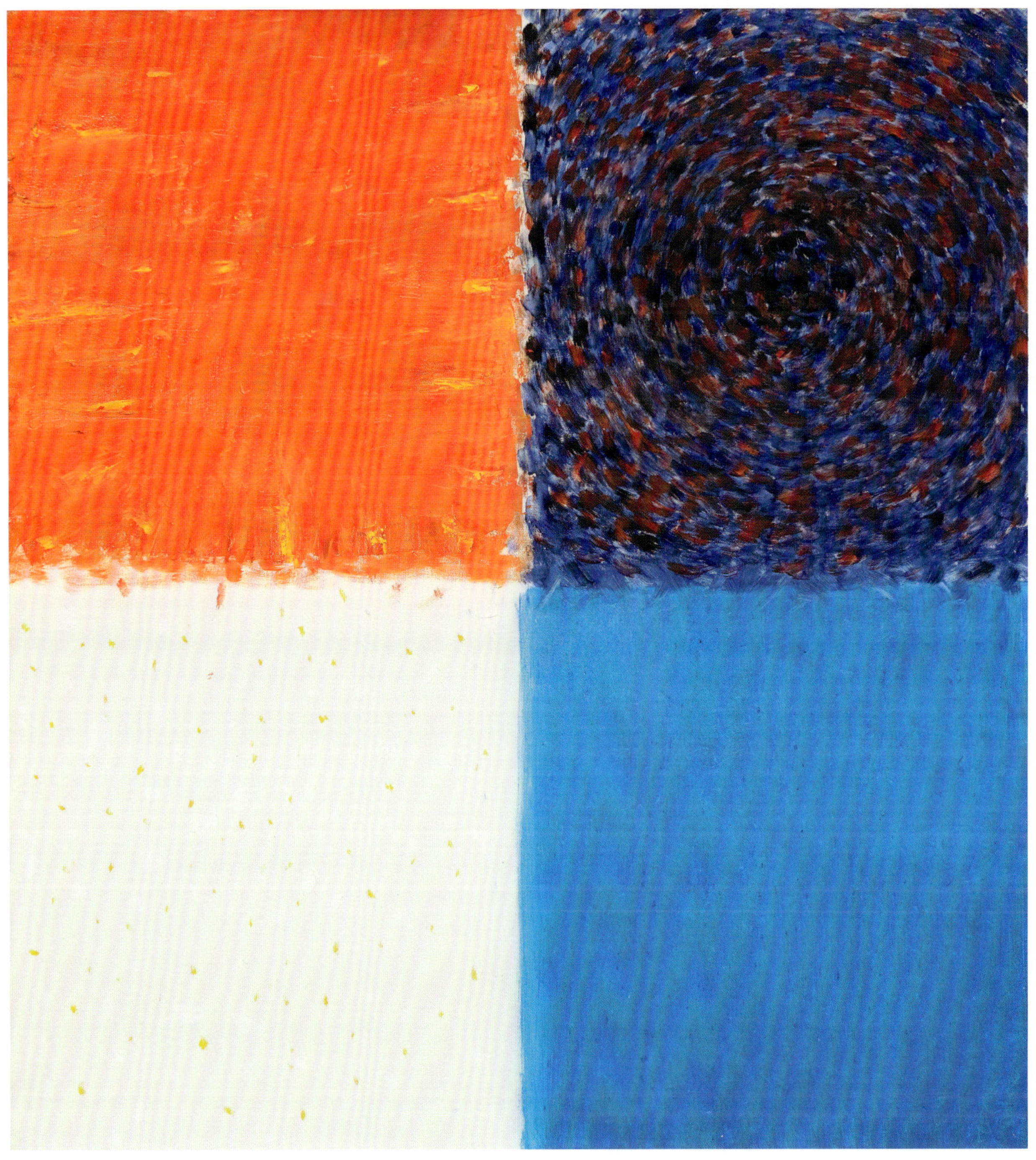

Painting DCLXVI, 1993
Oil on canvas
134.5 x 99.5 cm

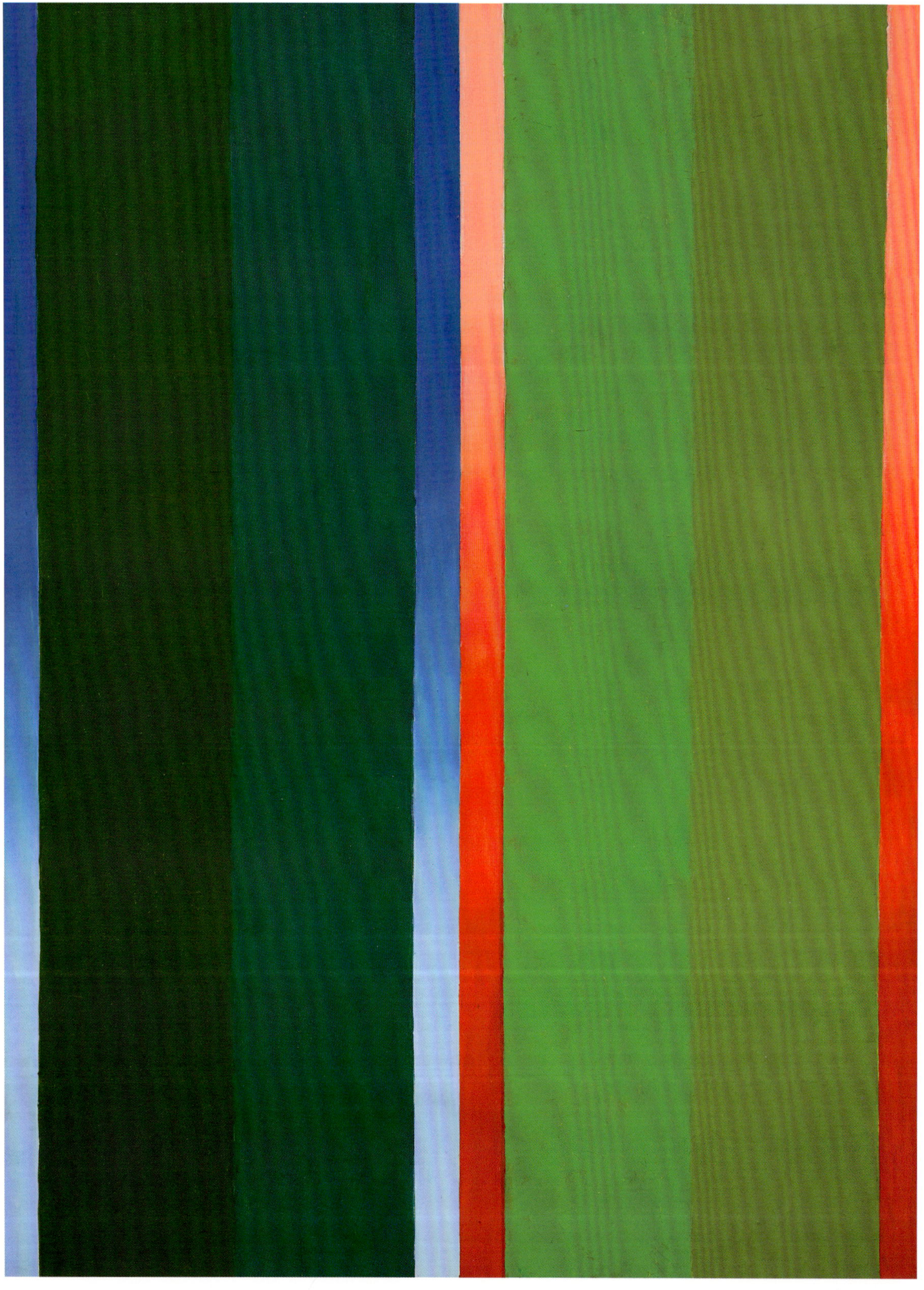

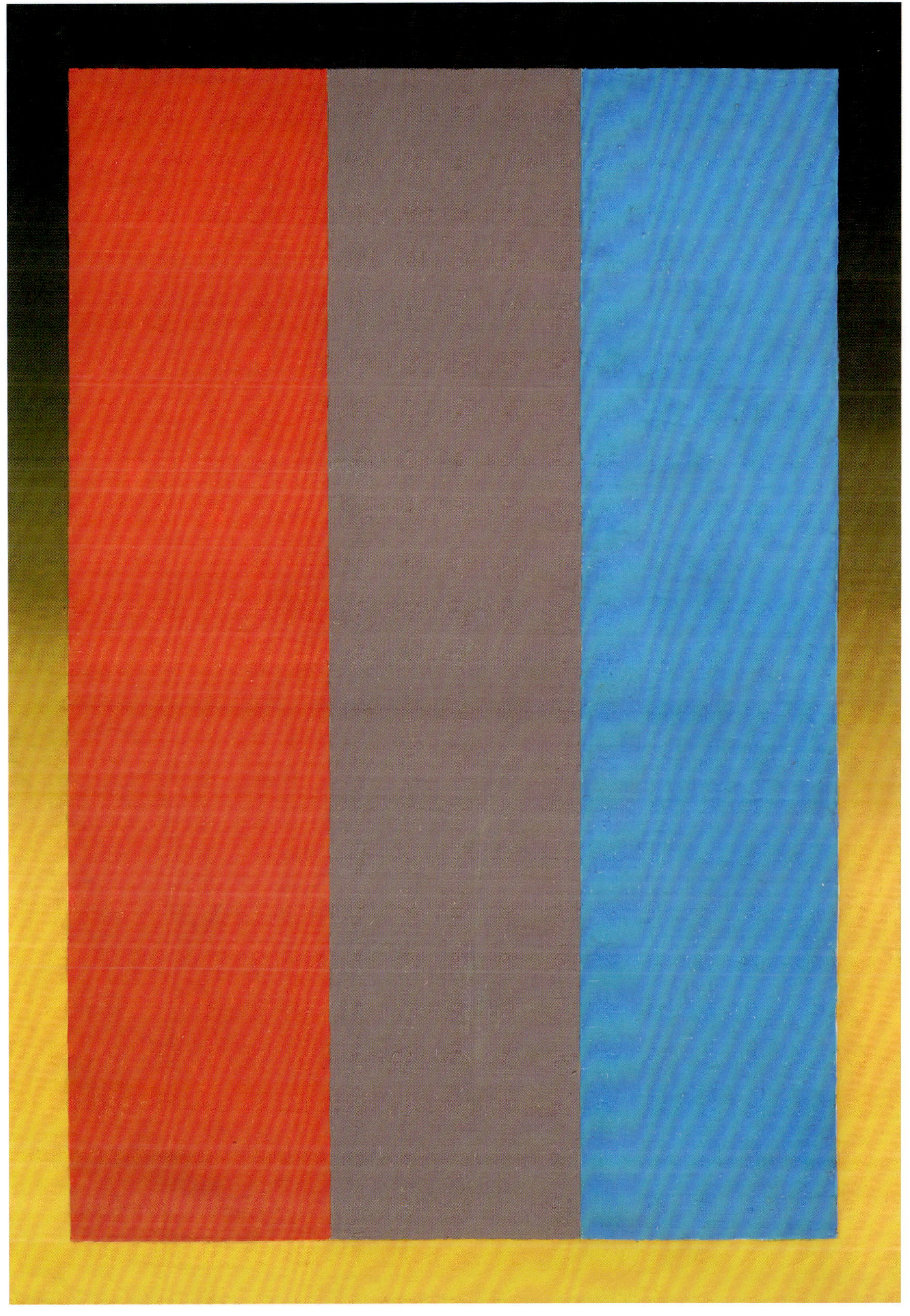

Painting DCI, 1989
Oil on canvas
140.5 x 99.5 cm

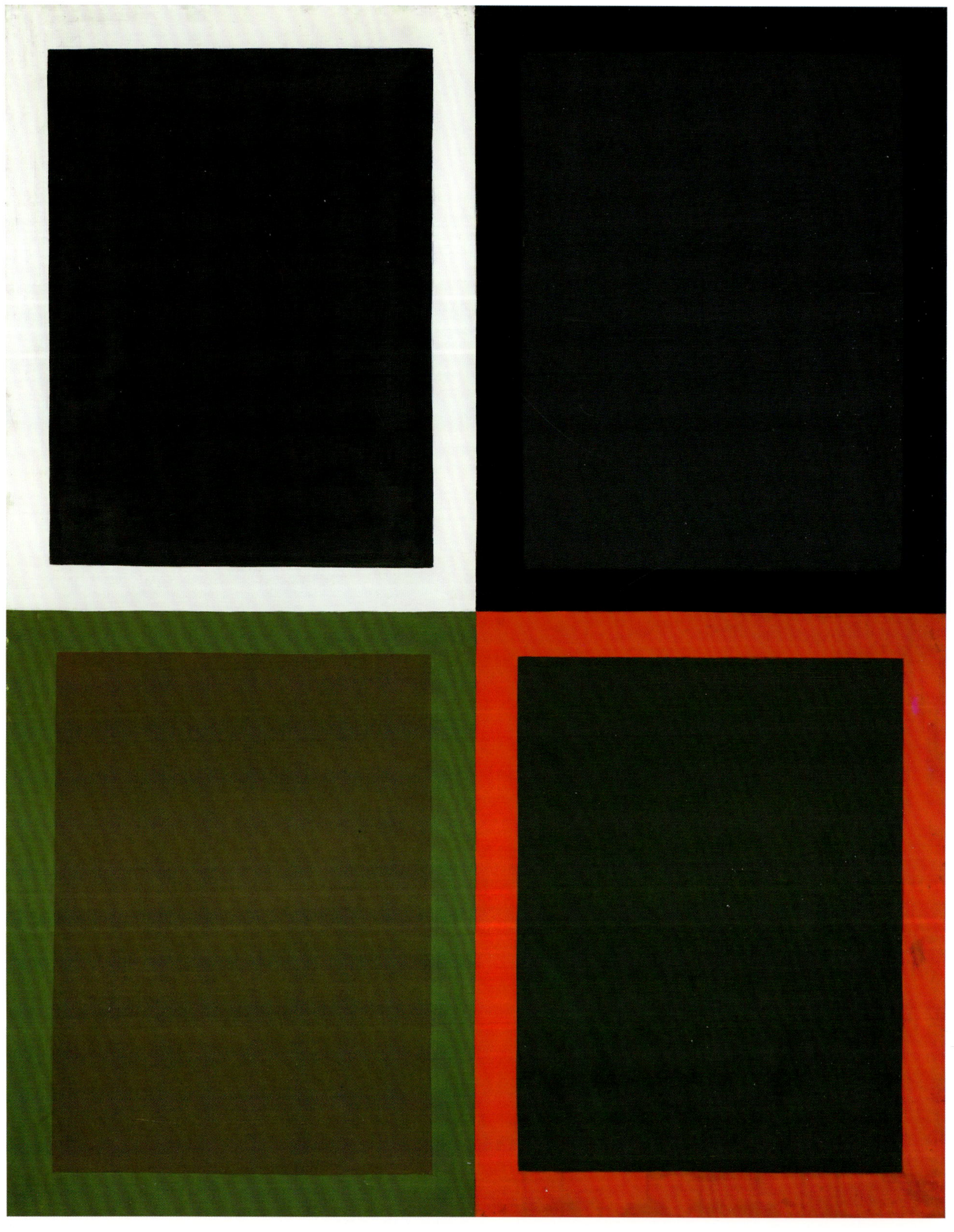

Painting CCCXXXIV, 1975
Oil on canvas
138 x 110.5 cm

Painting CCCXXXII, 1975
Oil on canvas
140 x 100 cm

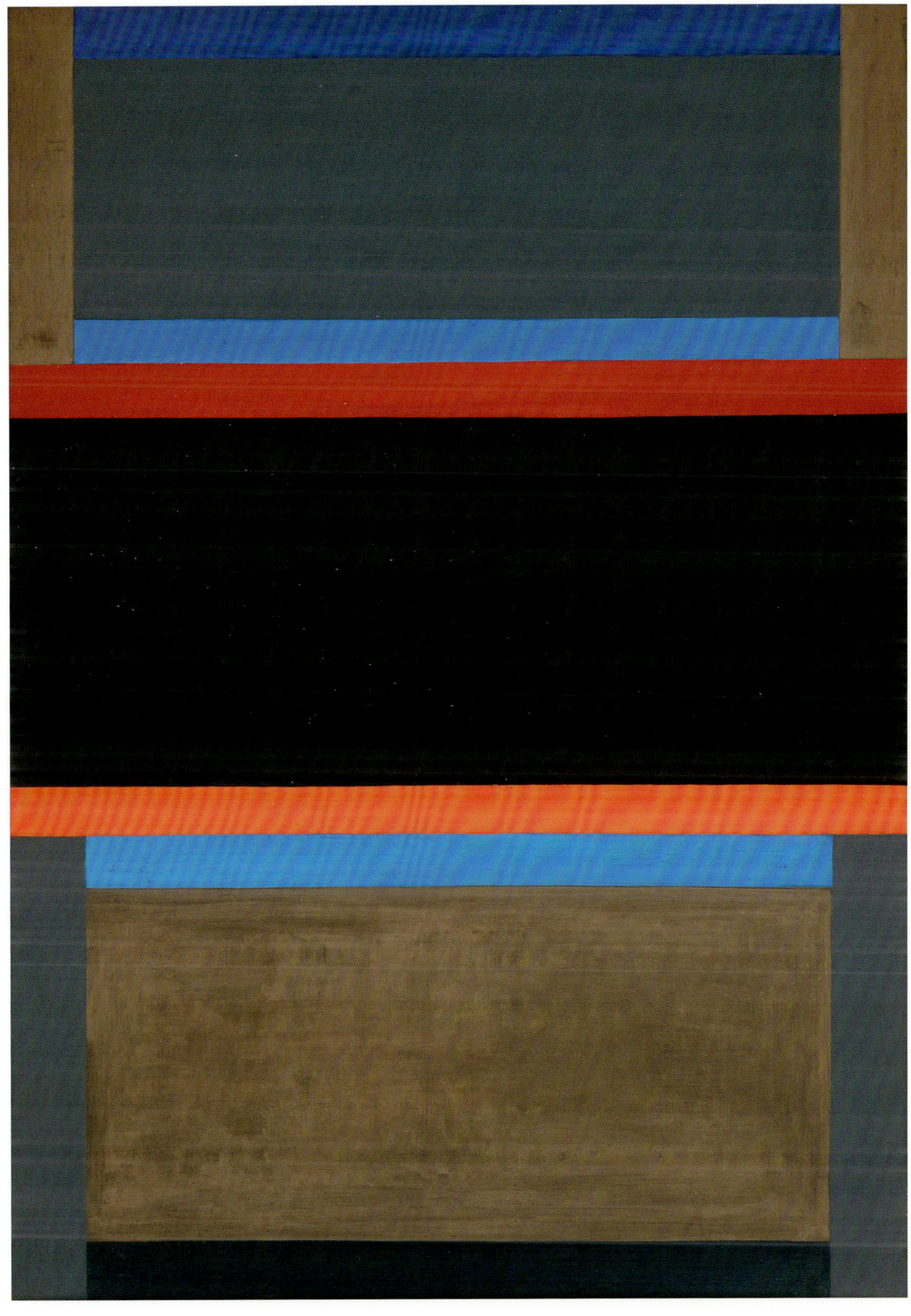

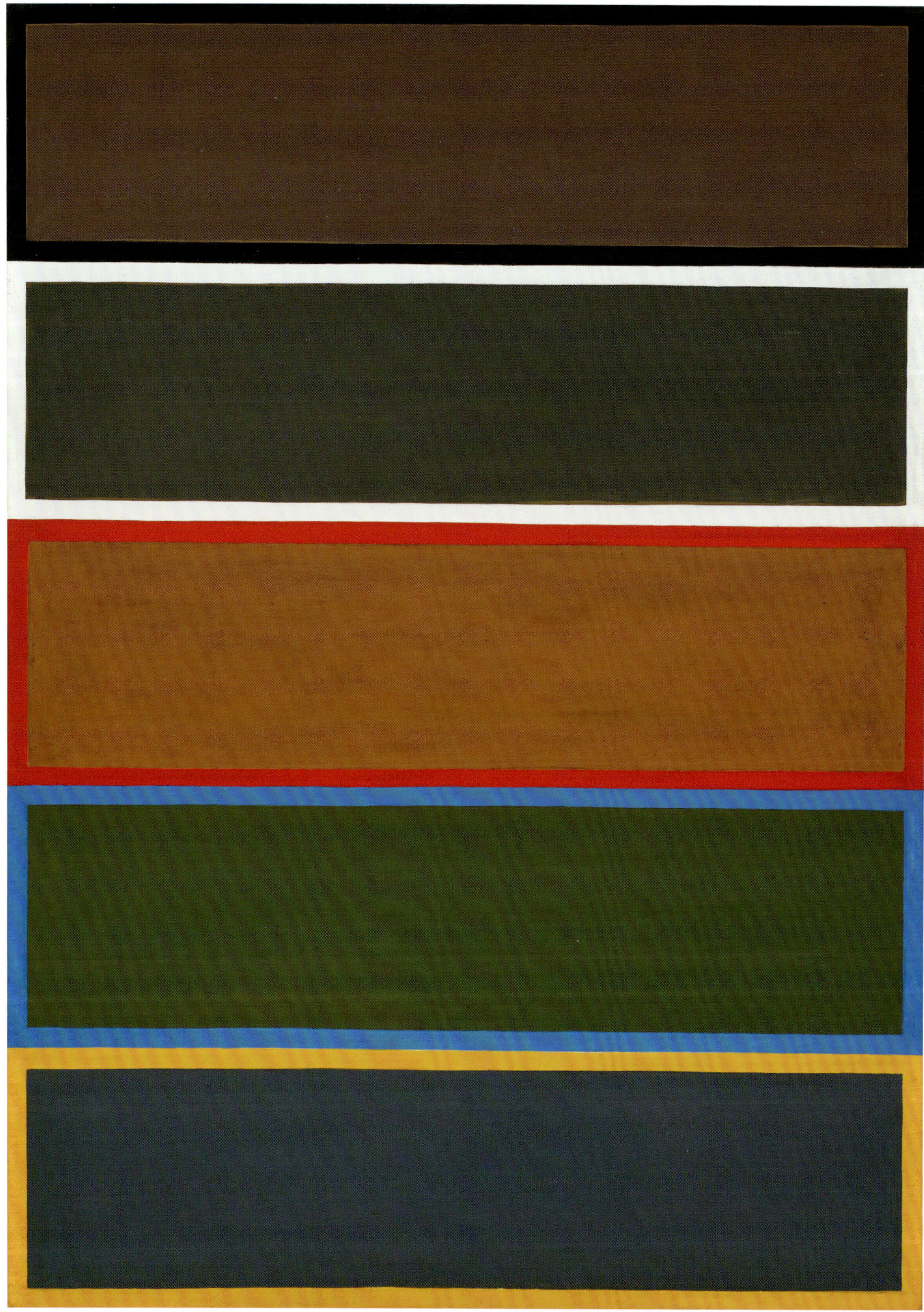

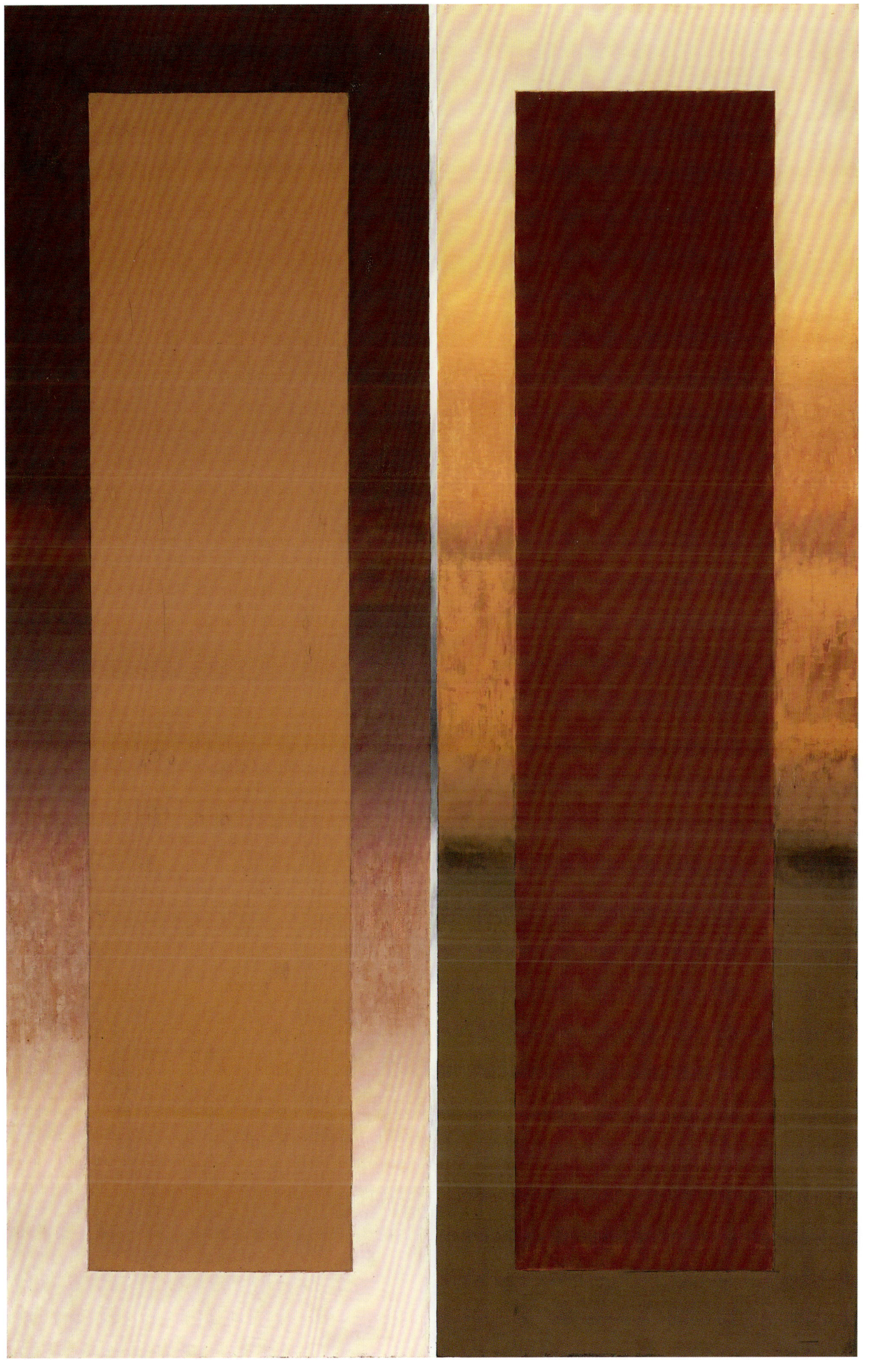

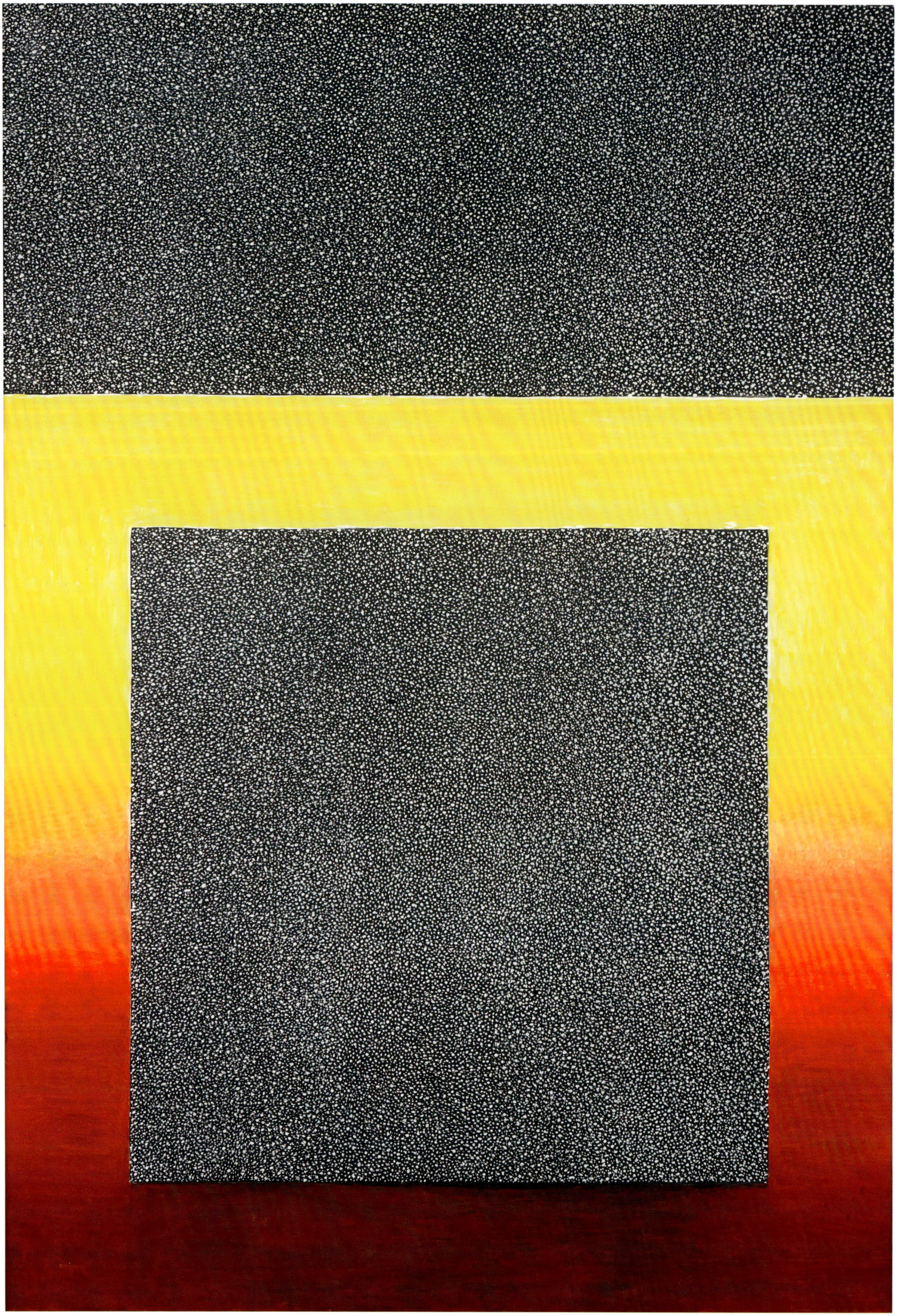

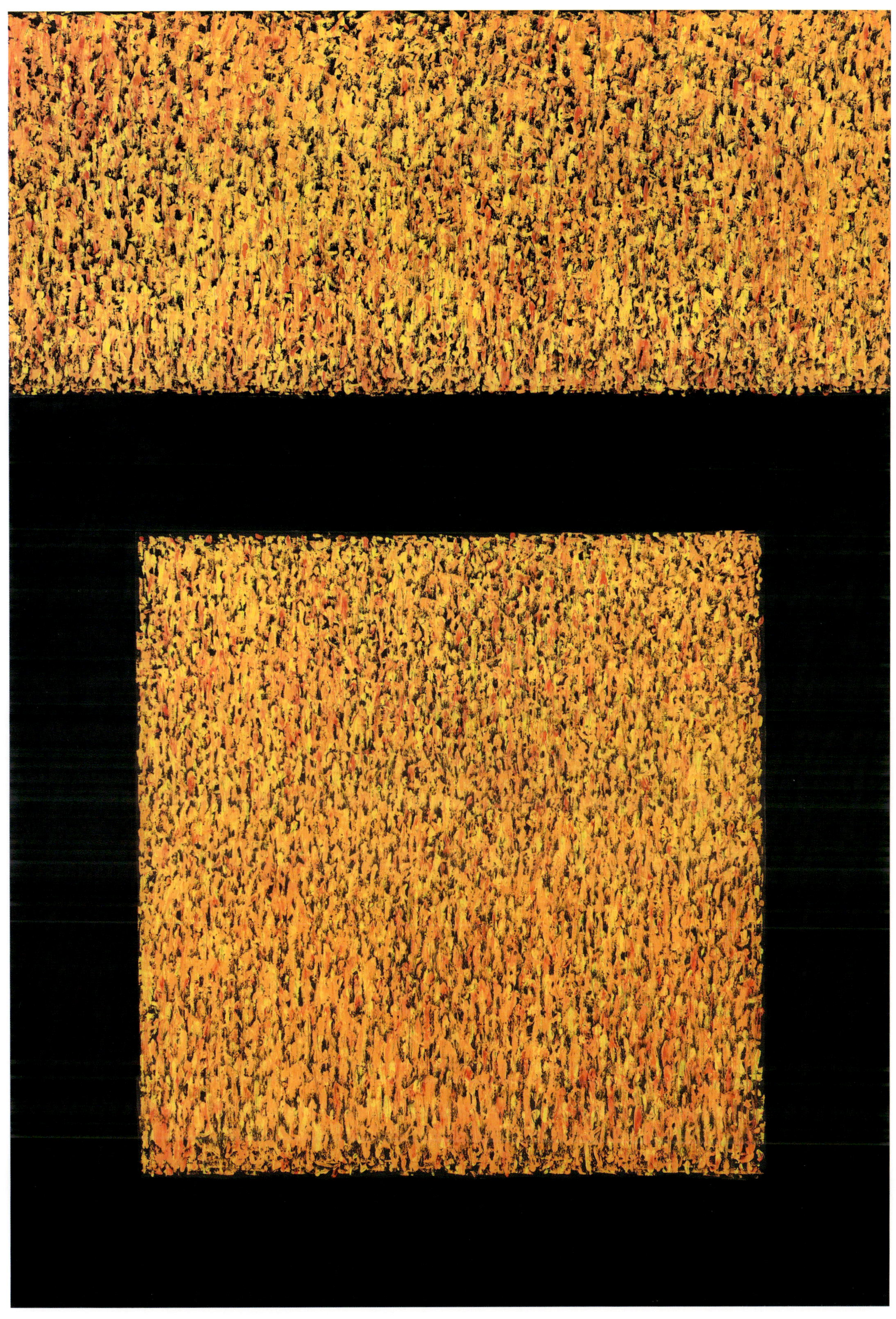

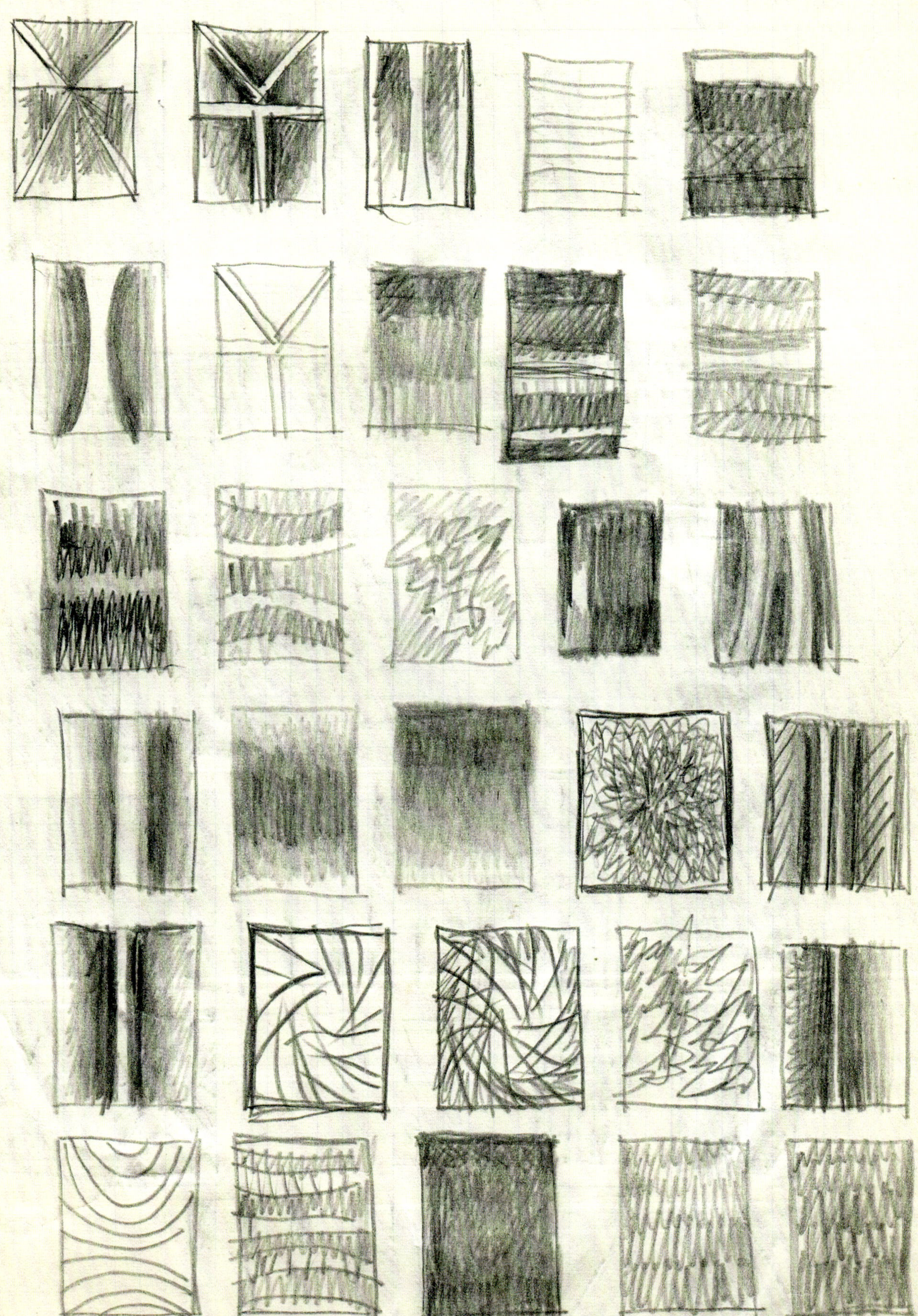

Notions

When does green cease to be a green paint and becomes instead a notion of green, or a void, or perhaps an element?

When one colour/element kills another, this is part of the notion of killing. Or the silence of colour space and the aggression of noise.

Notions are ambiguous when they become themes of painting, but also of imagination.

To paint means to ponder the significance of matter, colour, and form. The question is to what extent words can be replaced with colours.

Void as a physical concept, my void of the picture.
How to decipher it? How to paint to decipher the void?

Stefan Gierowski

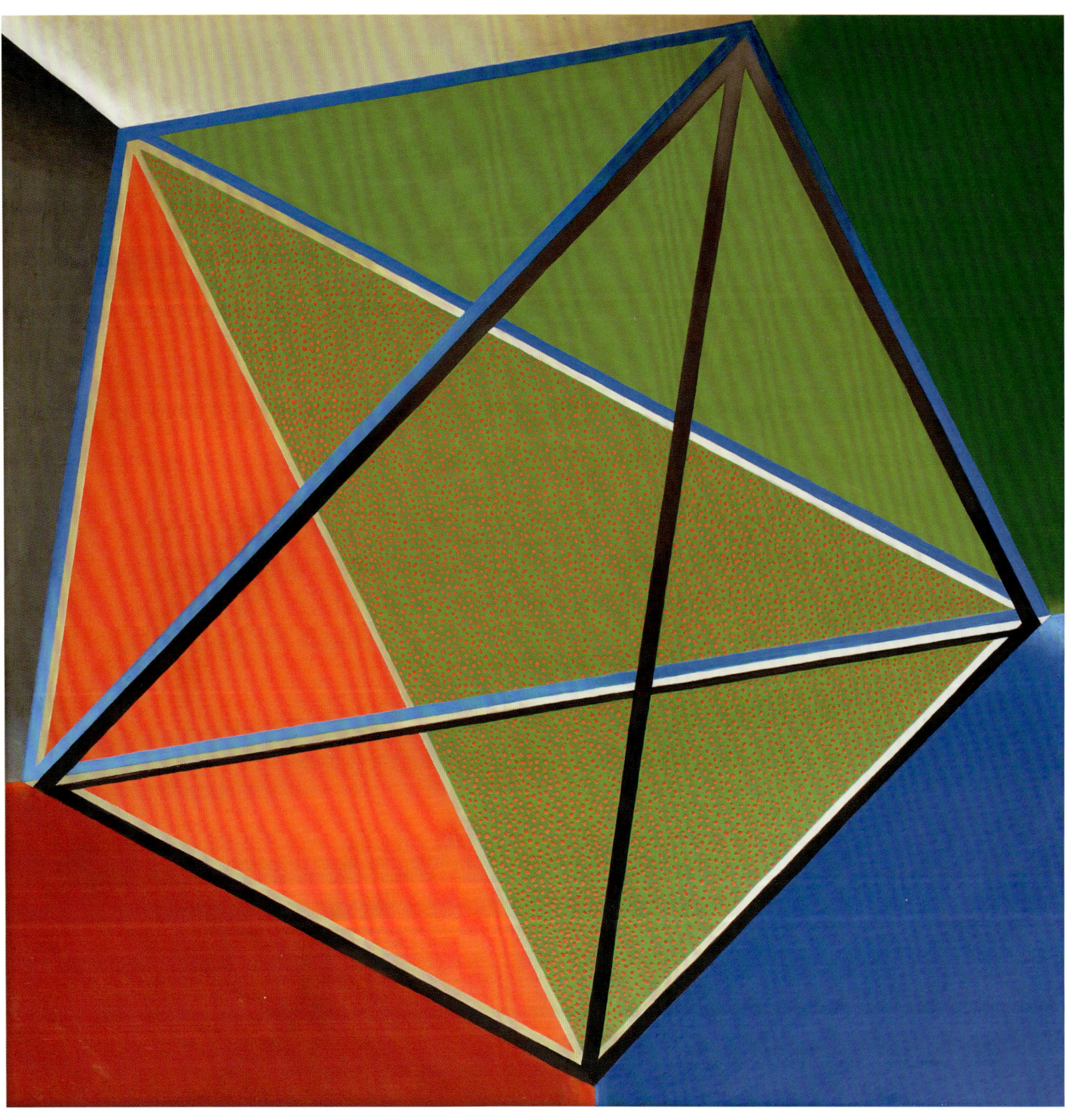

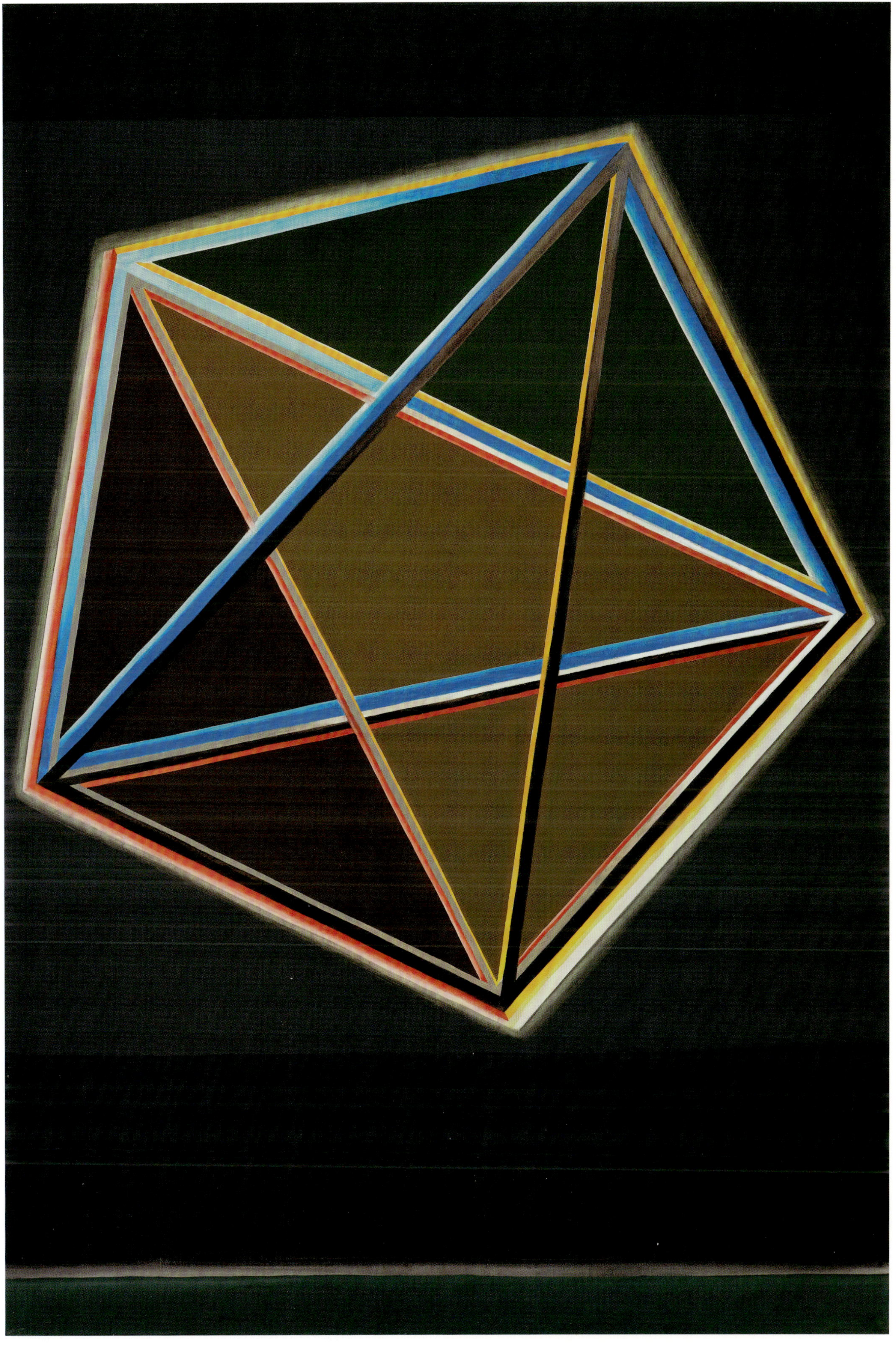

Painting DXLVII, 1985
Oil on canvas
130 x 200 cm
National Museum in Warsaw

Painting DLVI, 1986
Oil on canvas
200 x 130 cm
Museum of Art in Łódź

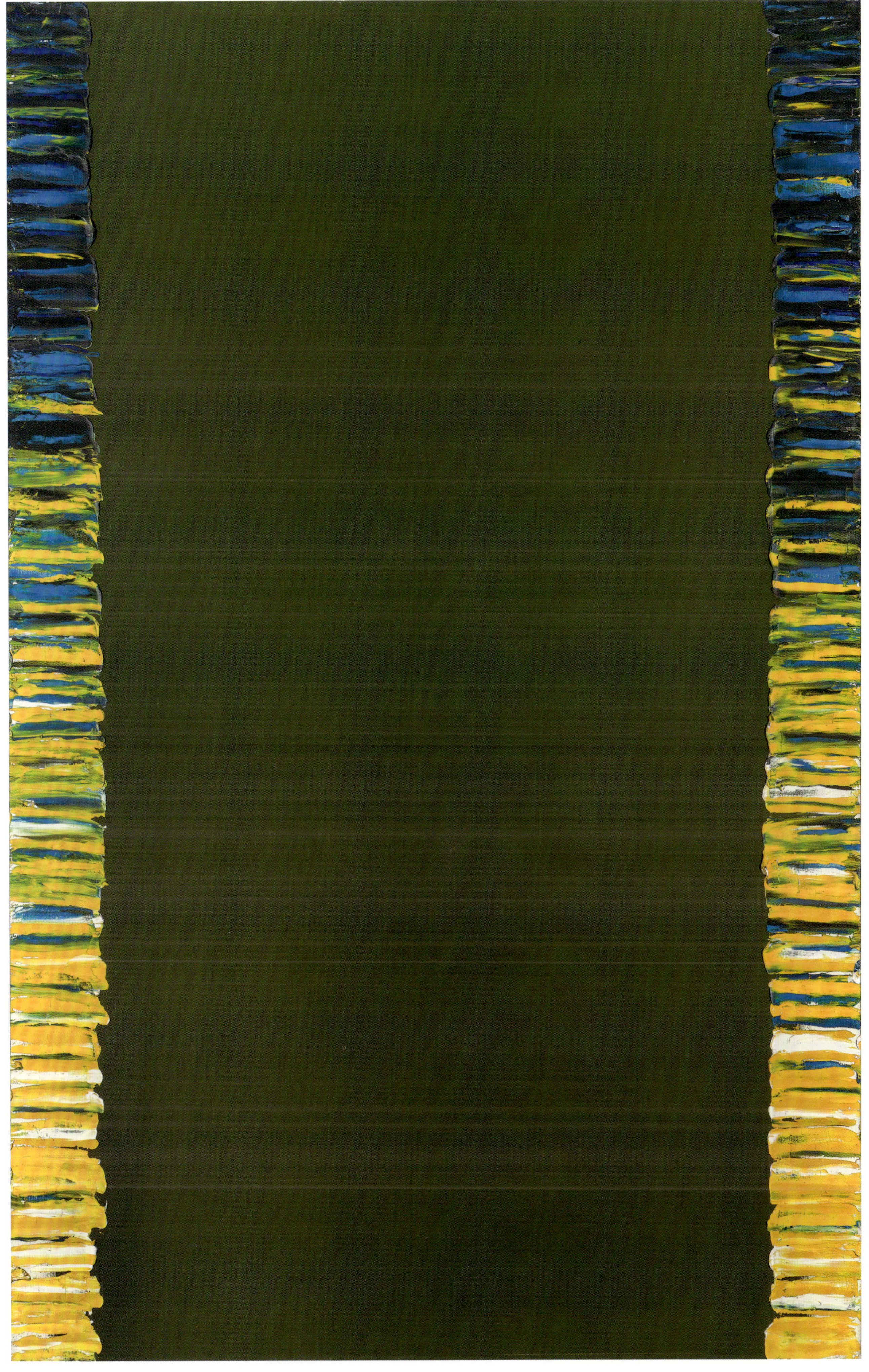

Painting DCXLVI, 1992
Oil on canvas
200 x 70 cm

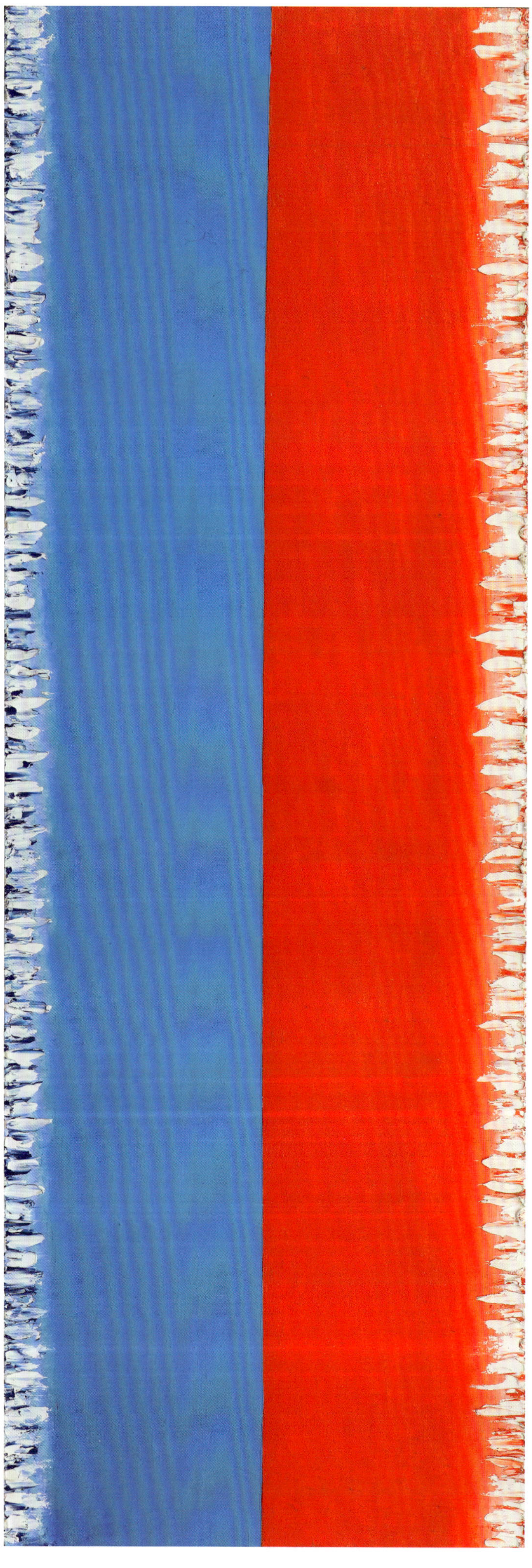

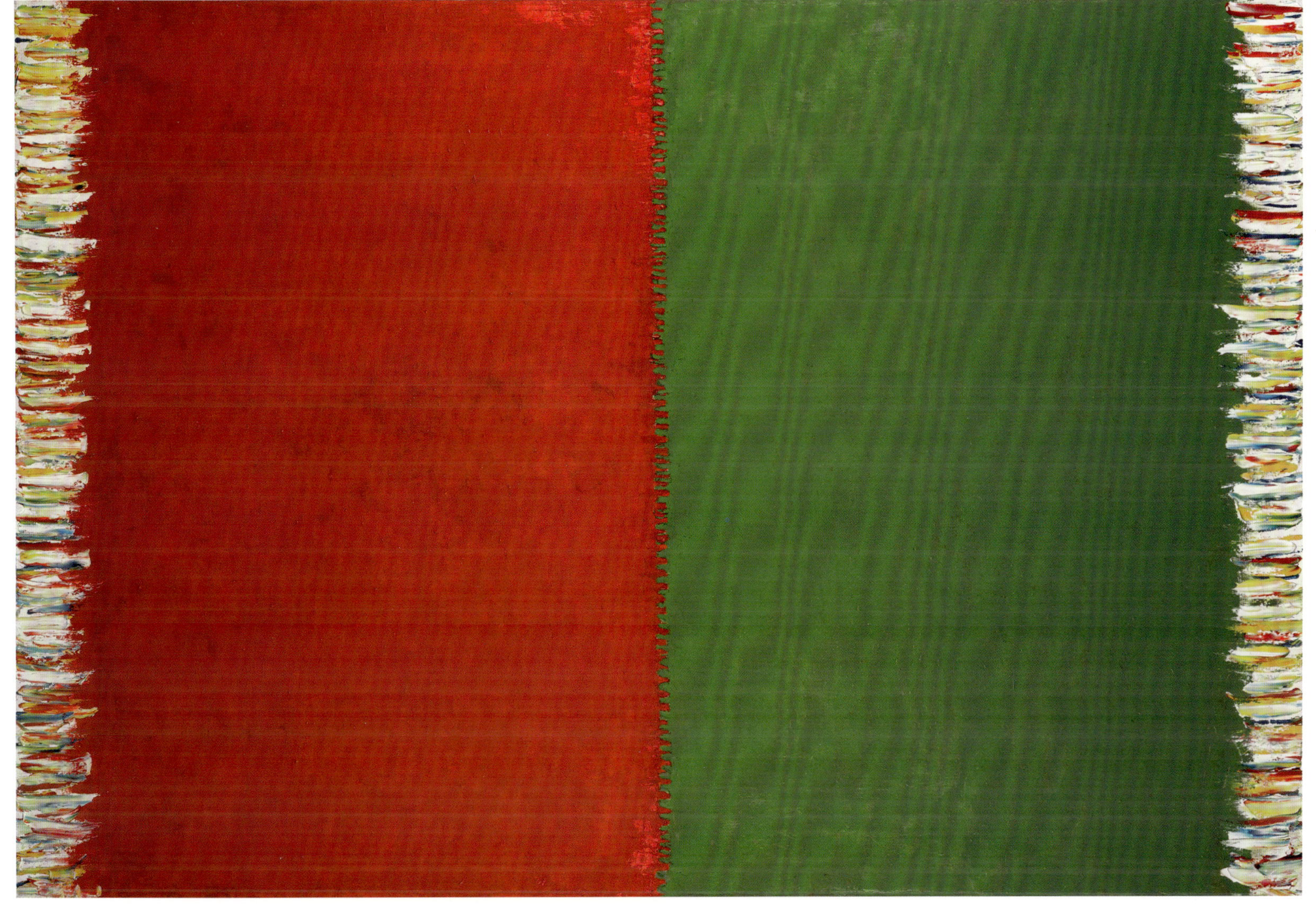

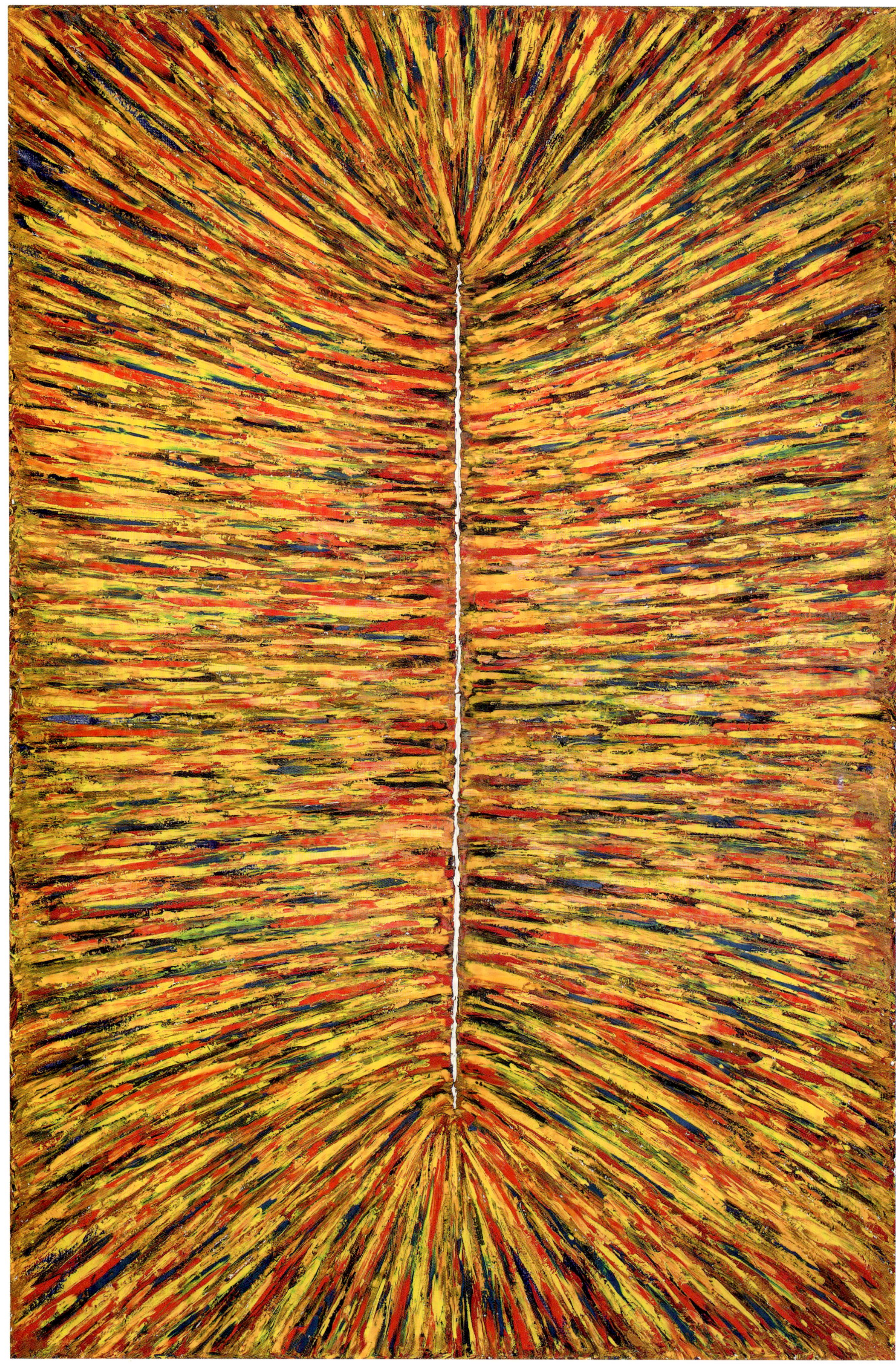

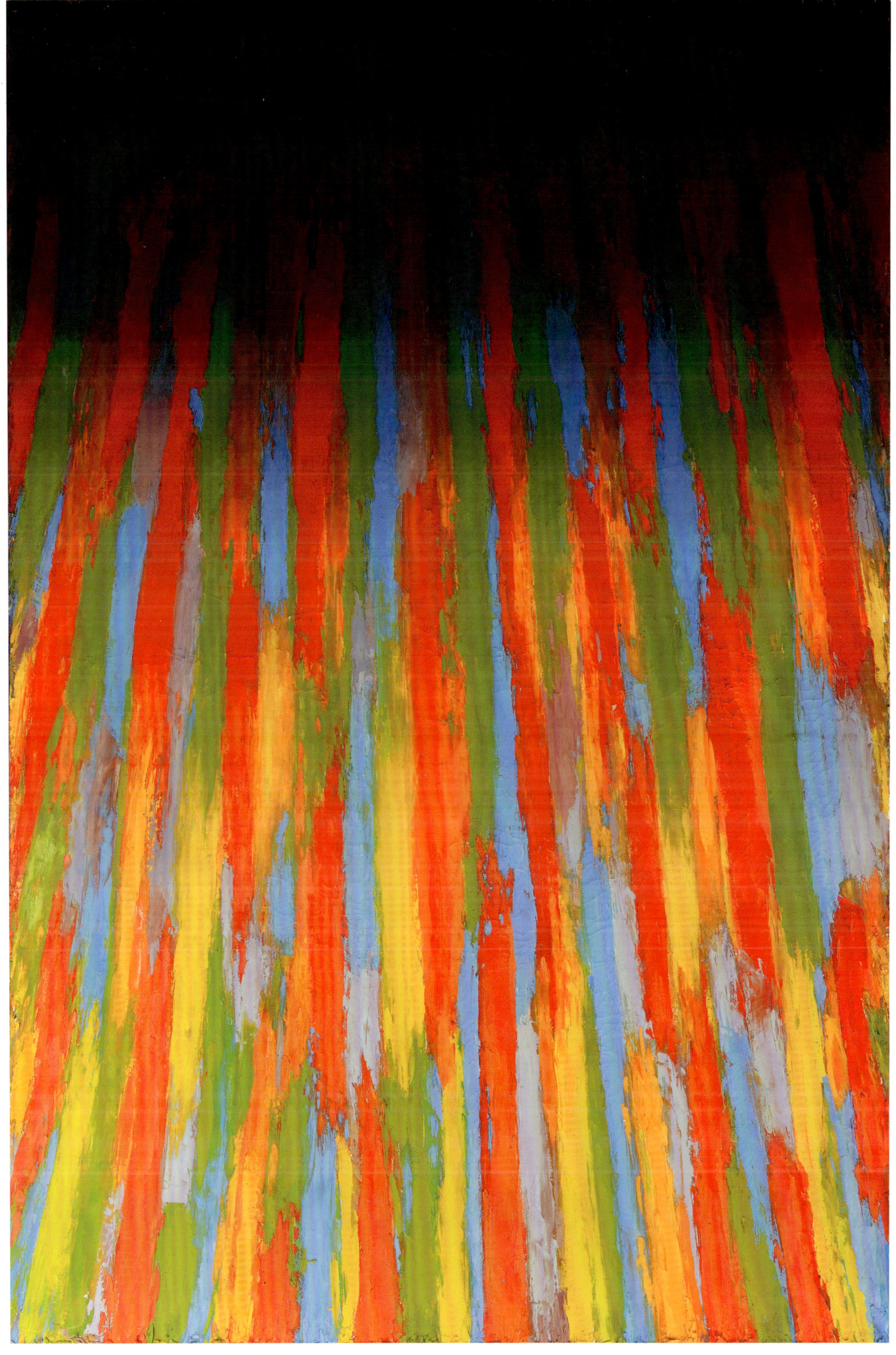

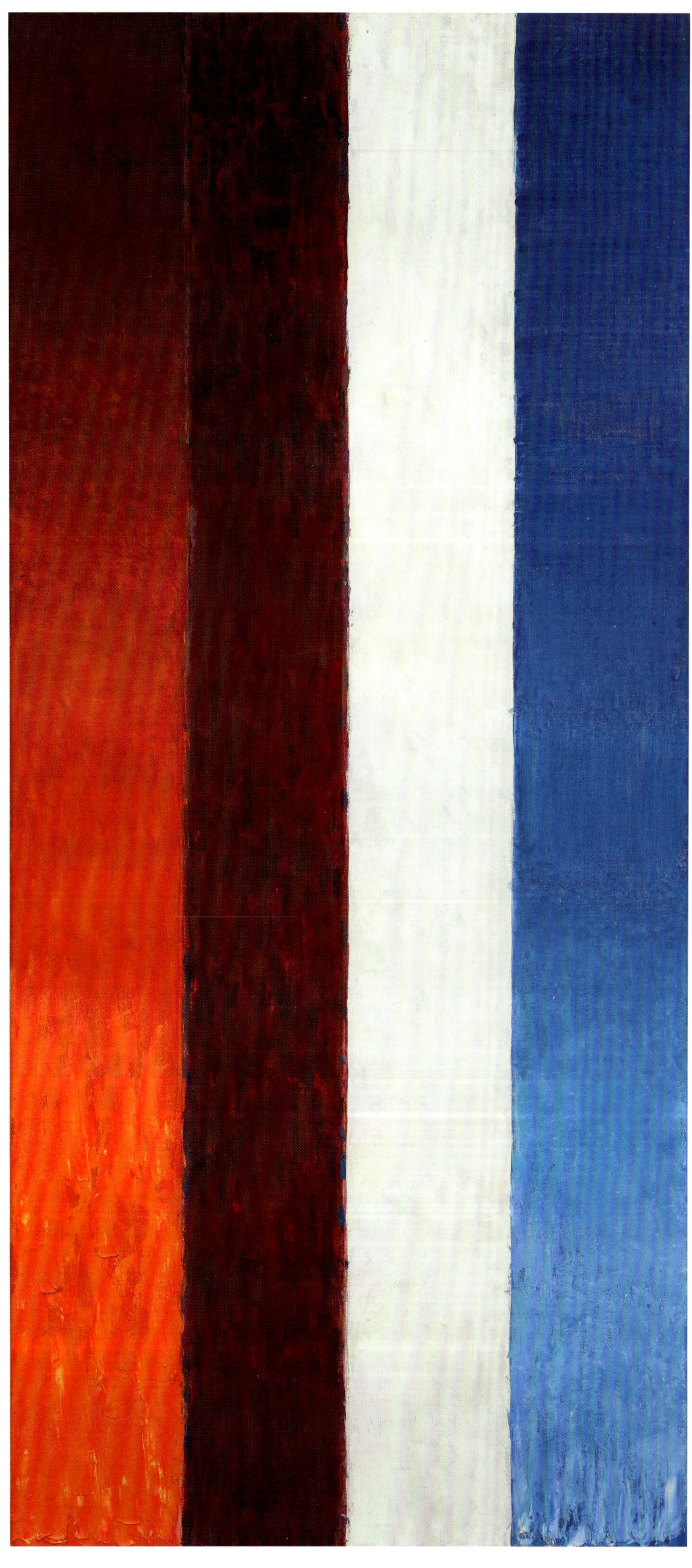

Painting DCCCXLVI, 2008
Oil on canvas
280 x 128 cm

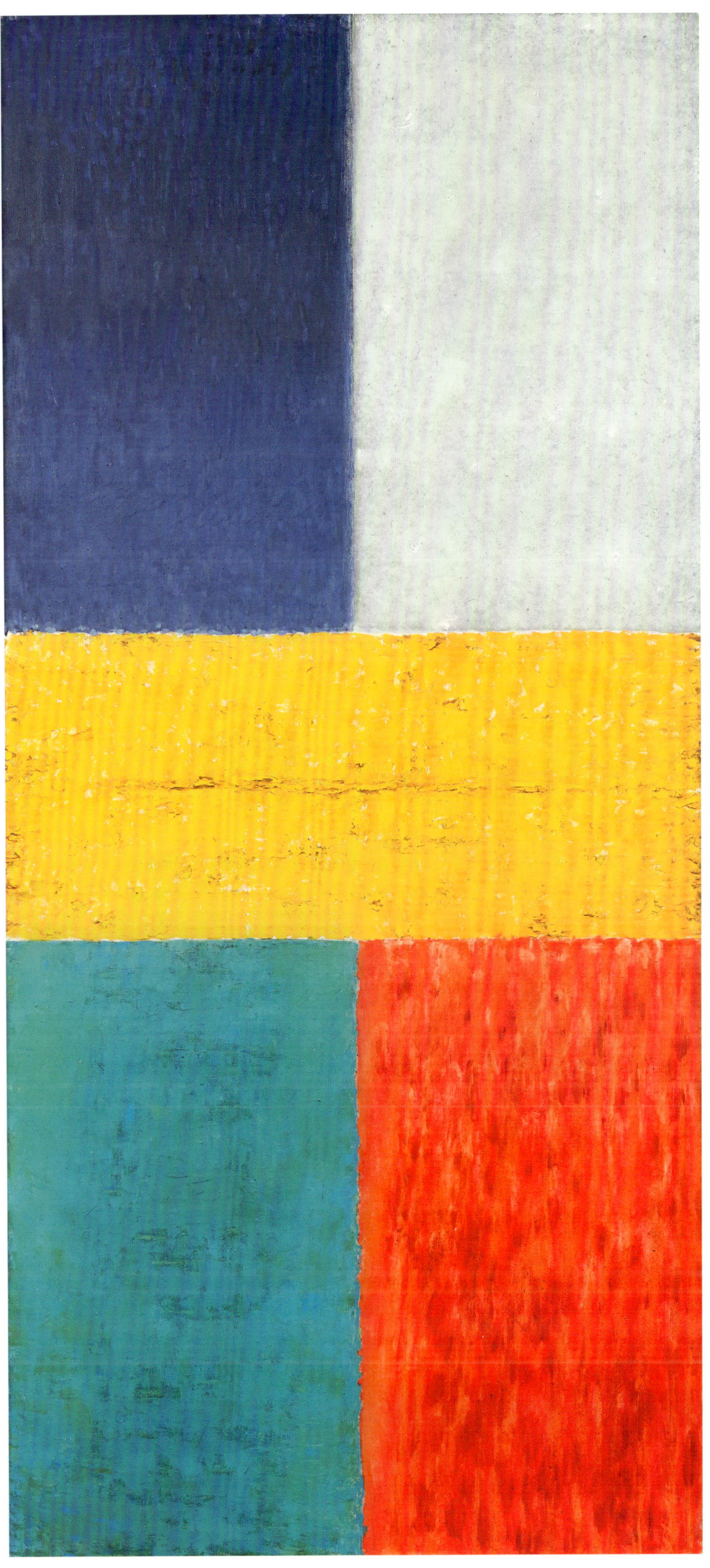

Painting DCCCXLV, 2008
Oil on canvas
280 x 130 cm

Painting DCLXXXIX, 1995
Oil on canvas
100 x 100 cm

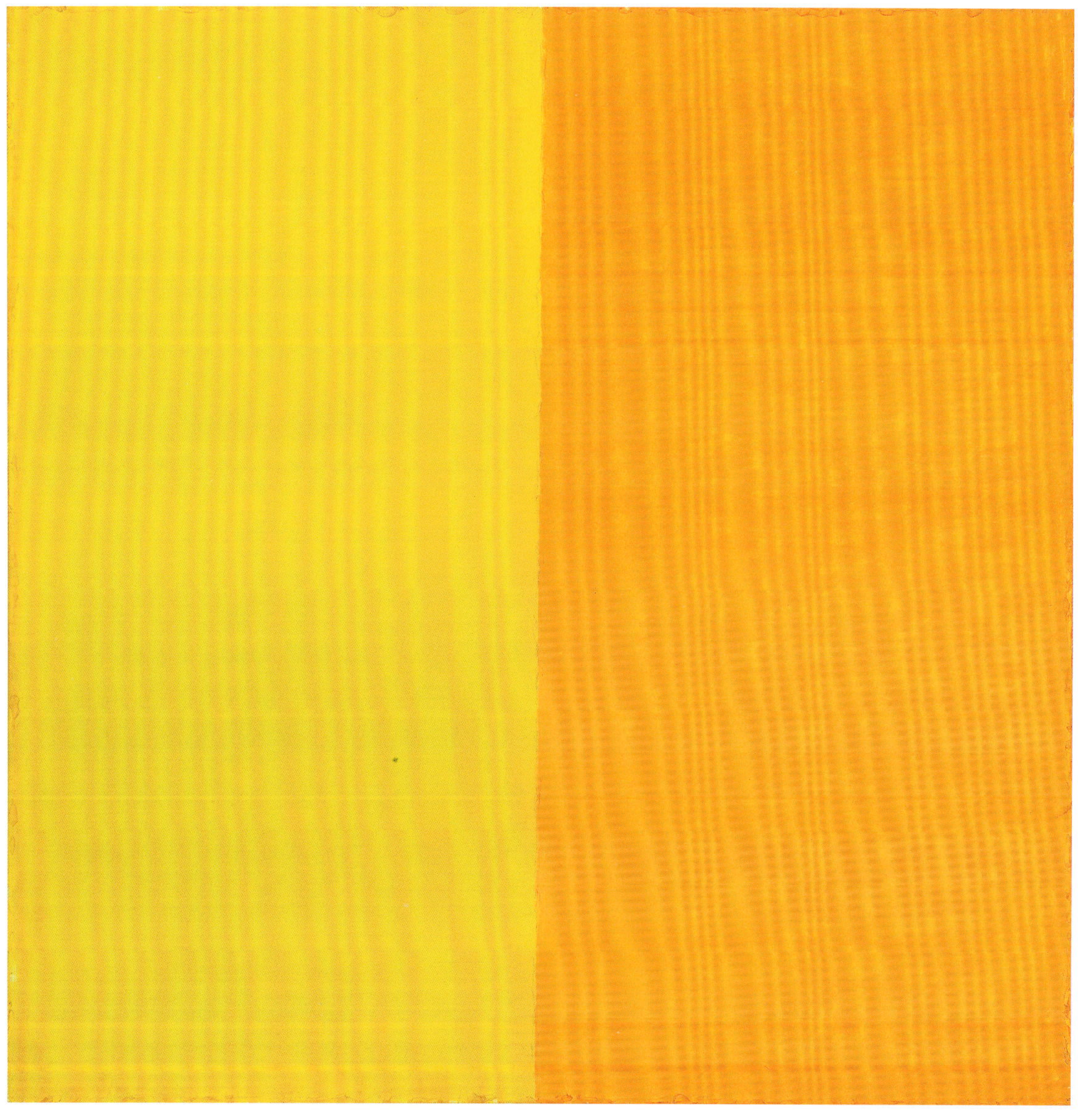

Painting DCCXLII, 1999
Oil on canvas
155 x 155 cm

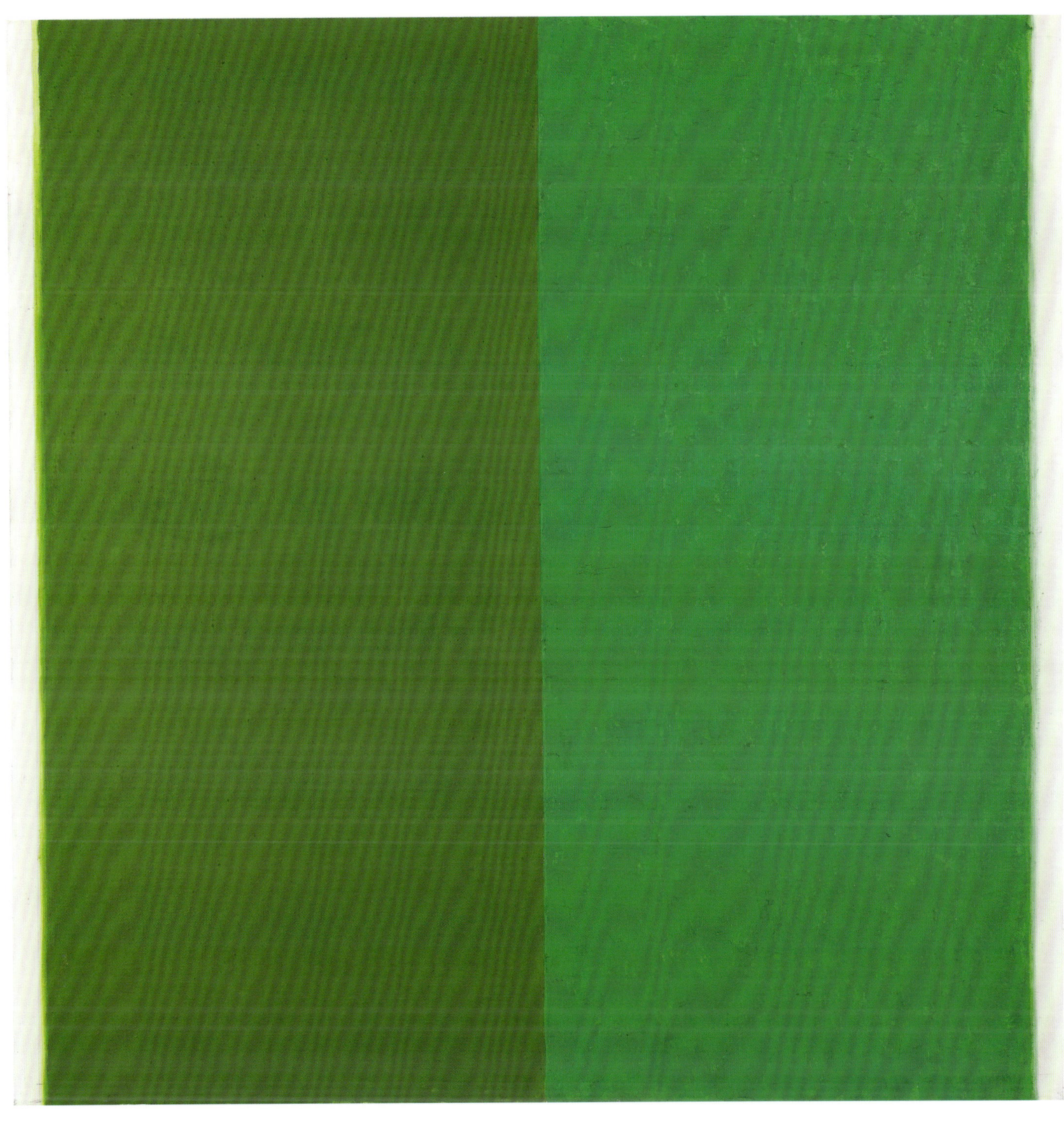

Painting CDLXIX, 1981
Oil on canvas
200 x 70 cm

Painting CDLXXI, 1981
Oil on canvas
200 x 70 cm

Painting DLXVIII (Thou shalt
not kill), 1986
Oil on canvas
200 x 130 cm

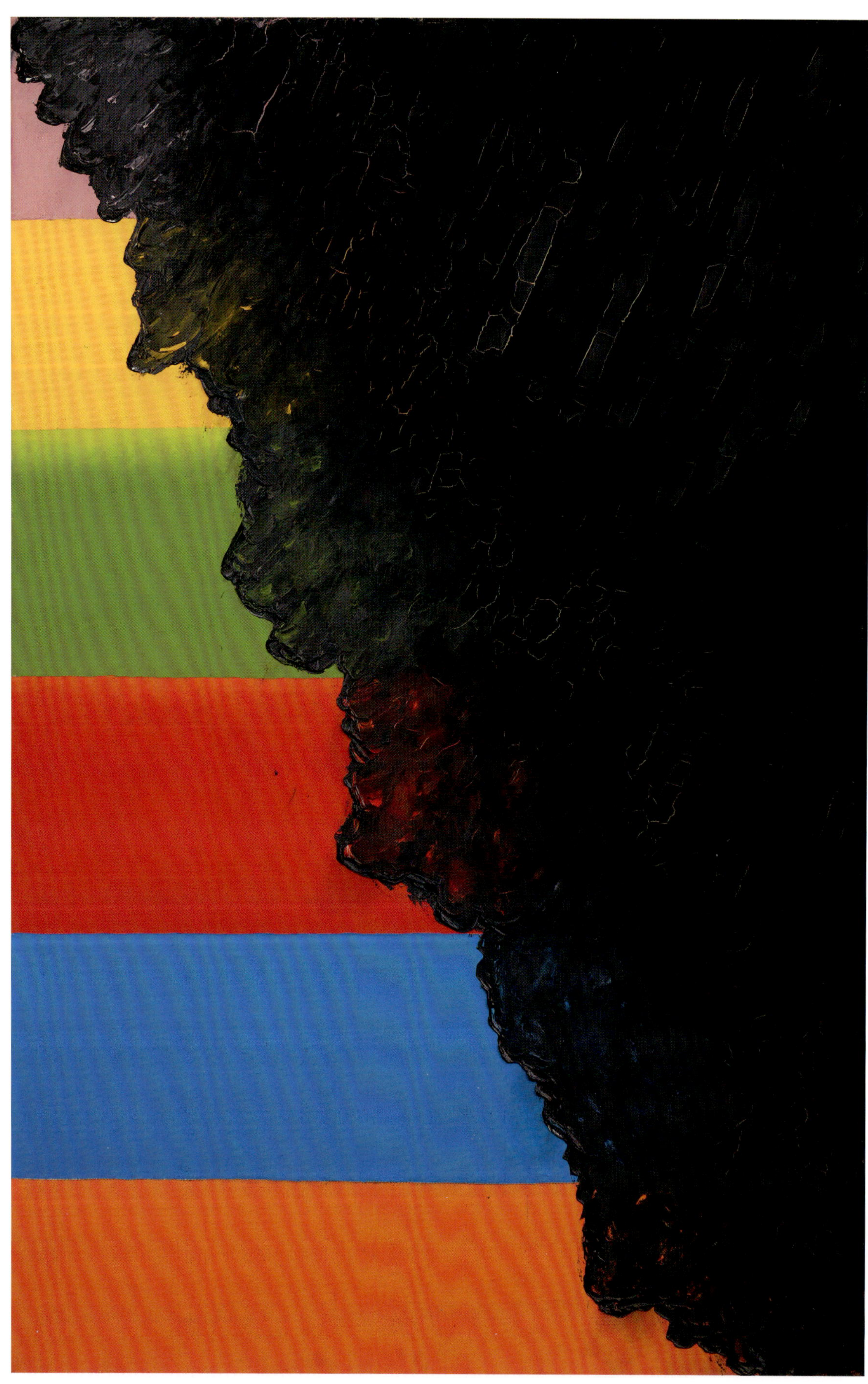

Painting DLXIX (*Thou shalt not commit adultery*), 1986
Oil on canvas
200 x 130 cm

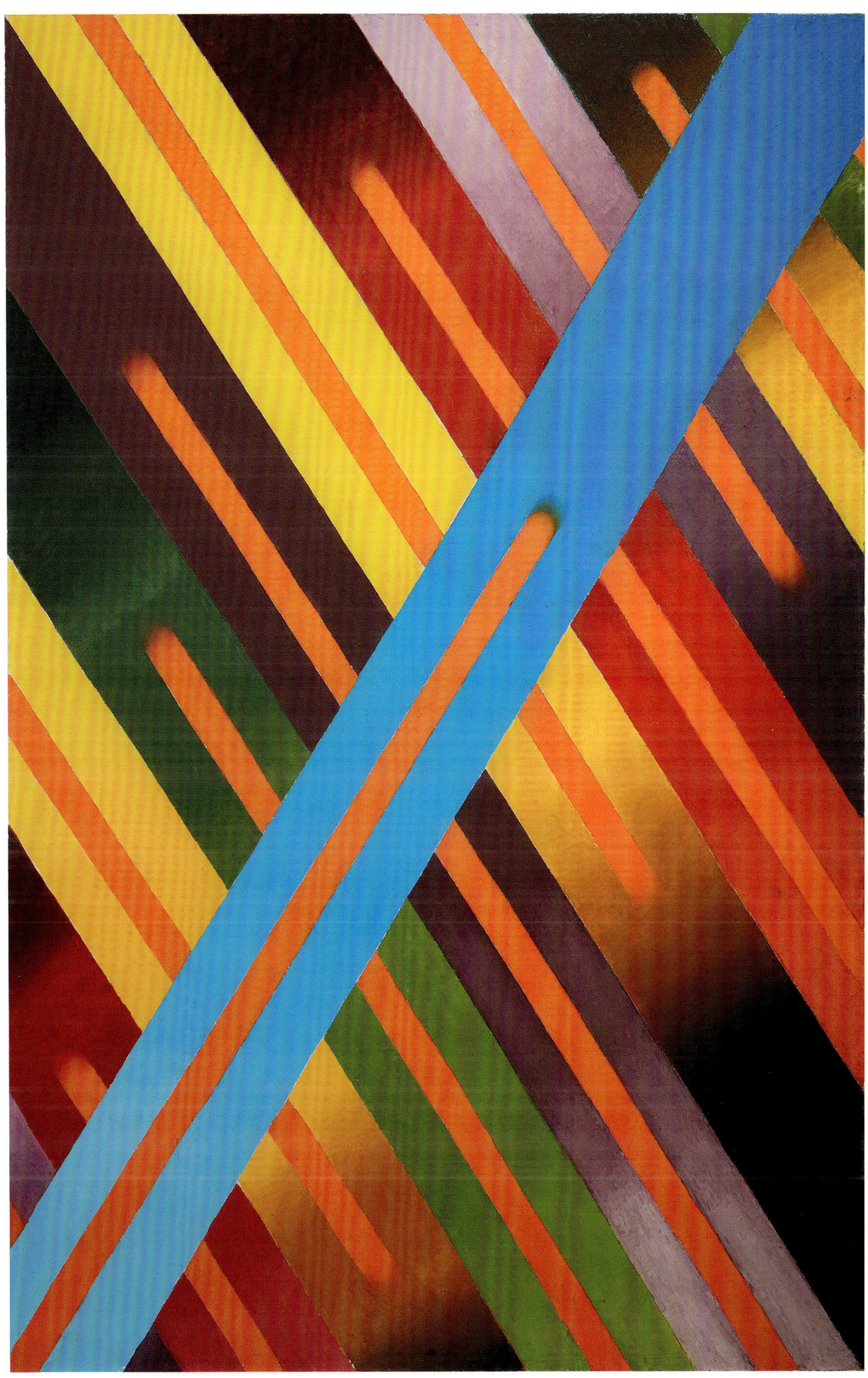

Painting DLXXIII (Thou shalt
not covet thy neighbour's
house), 1987
Oil on canvas
200 x 140 cm

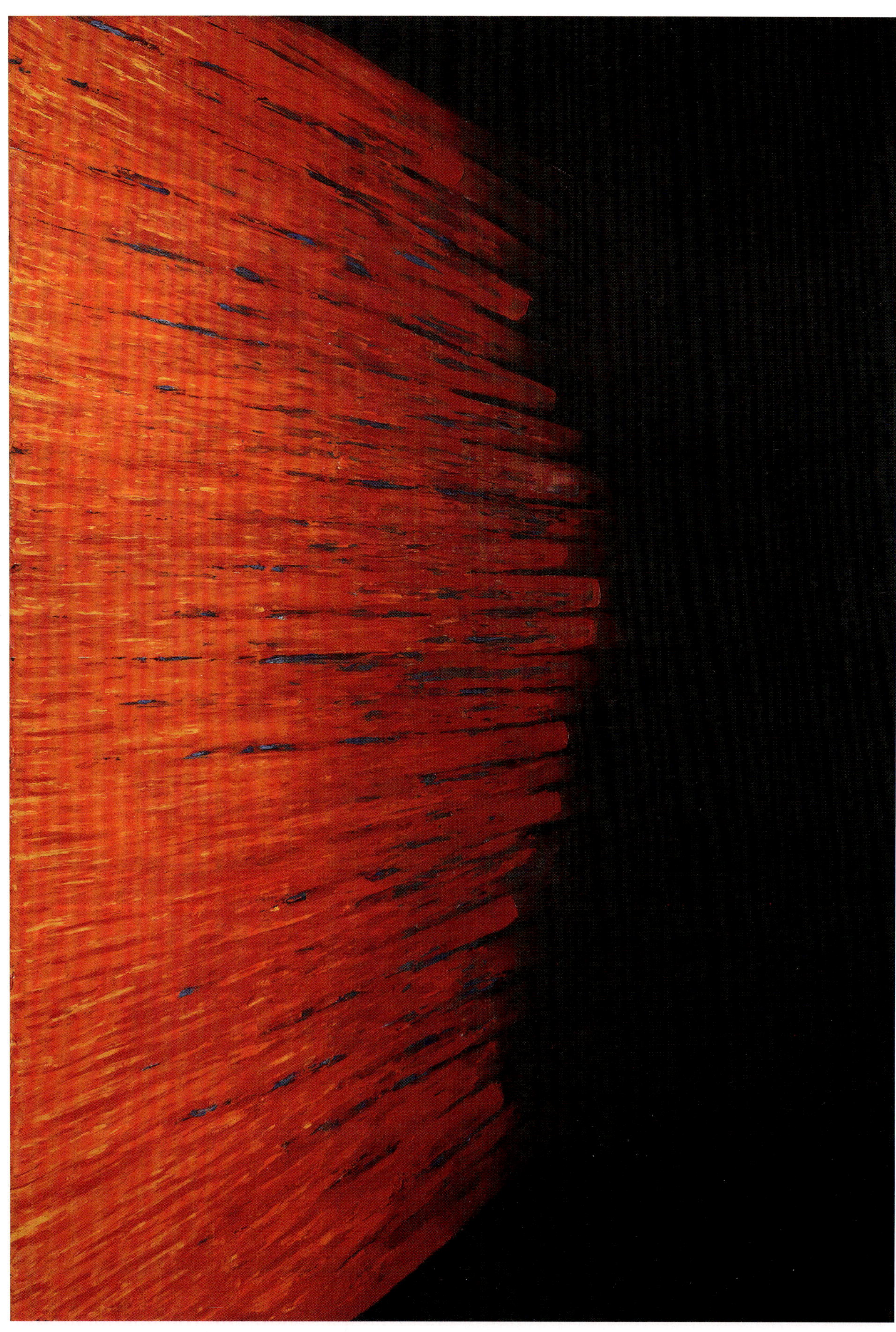

Painting the Ten Commandments,
1986–87
Exhibition view, St. Mary's Church,
Gdańsk, 2015

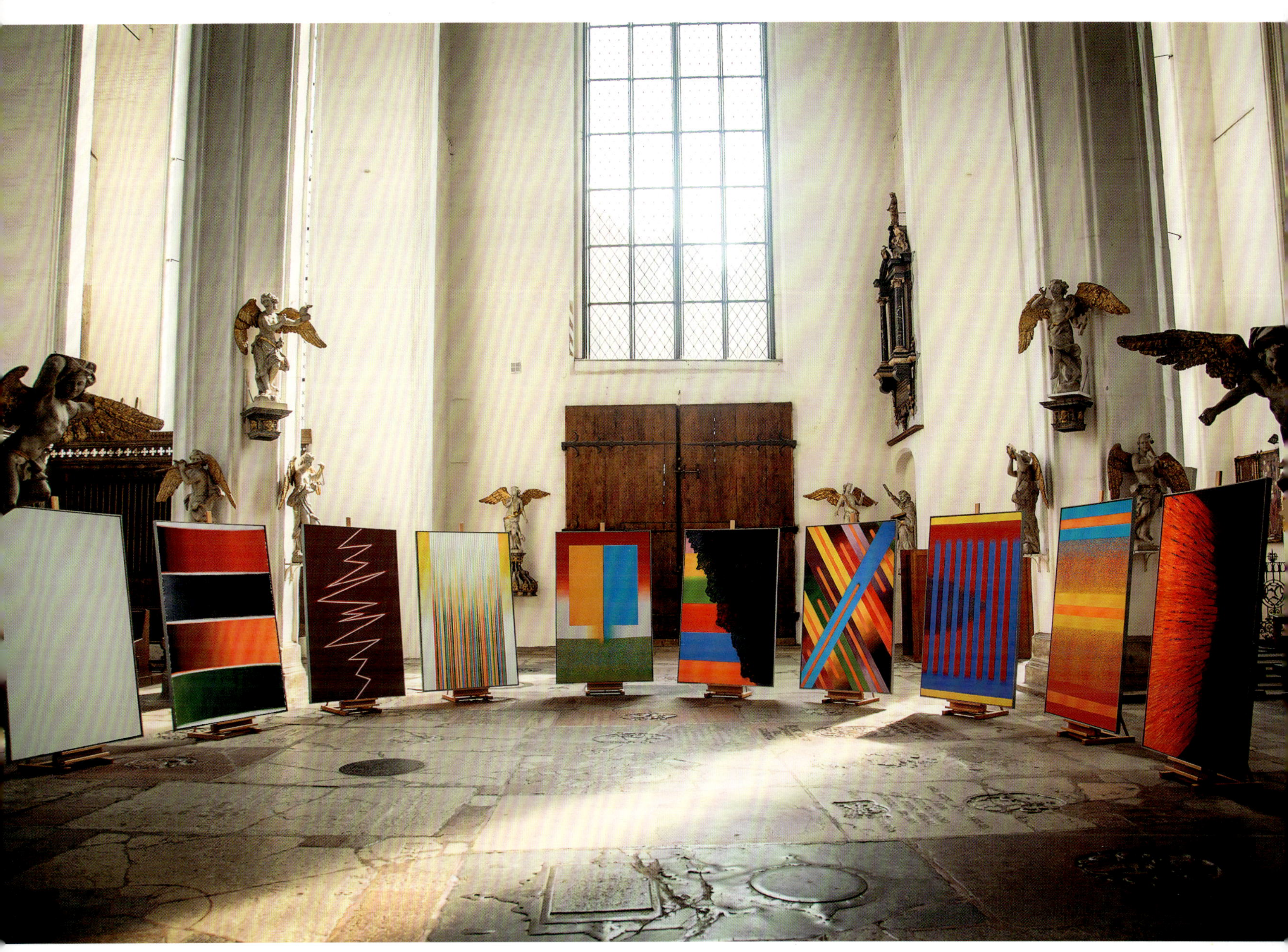

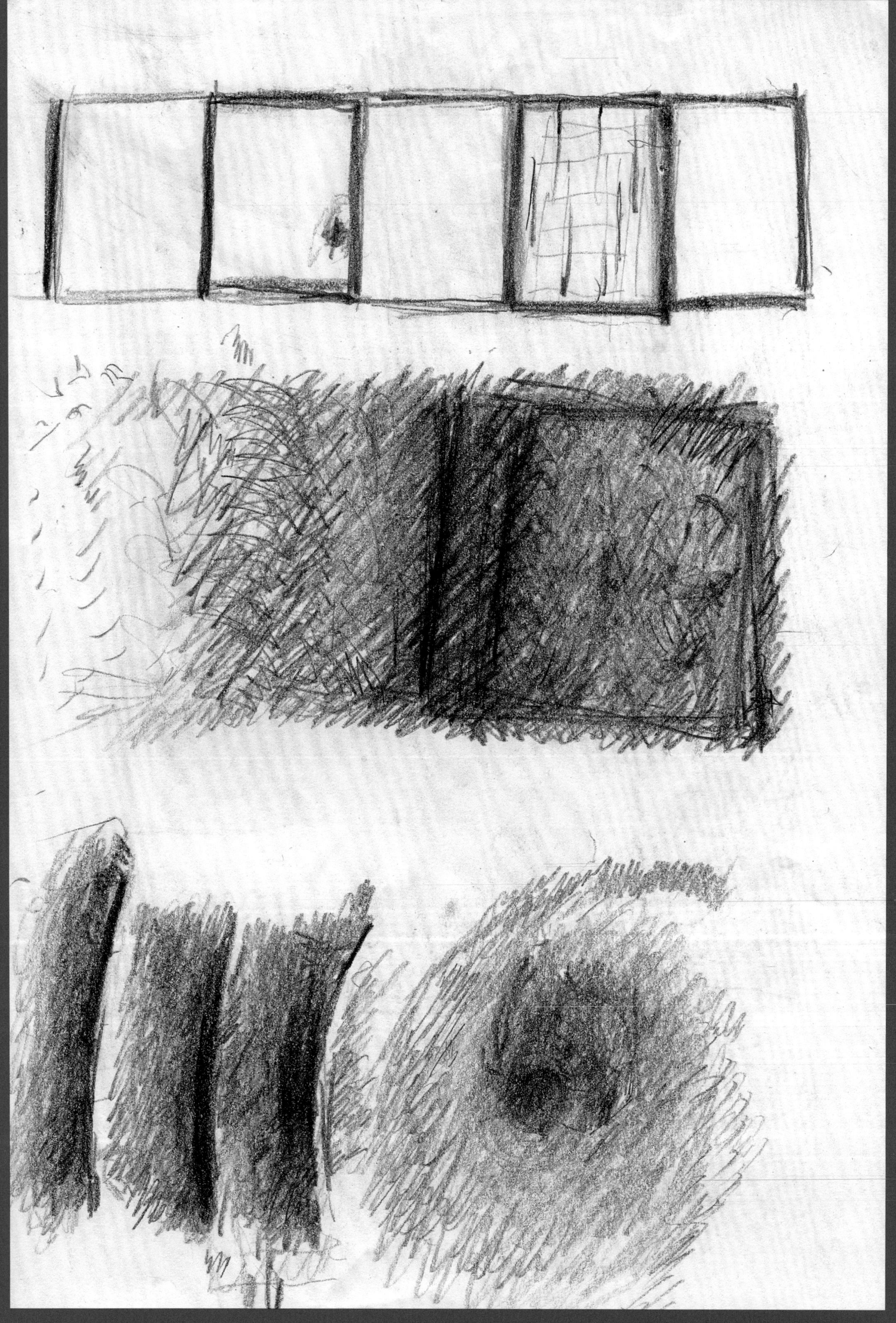

Sketch, 2000s
Pencil on paper
29.7 x 21.2 cm

Beginning and End

Black and white, grey in the middle. Colours are rejected
or absorbed. Grey occupies a special place. The white flat,
not spatial. The black deep, mysterious. There are different
whites and different blacks. The contour of the black
and white – sharp and seemingly extremely strong.
Wherever things must be expressed in the simplest manner,
only black and white are close to truth. It's always about
a truth, but what is it, how to recognize it? Beginning
and end – but is the beginning black or white?

Black and white: two colours of void.
Void = everything.

Stefan Gierowski

Painting CXX, 1962
Oil on canvas
80 x 99 cm

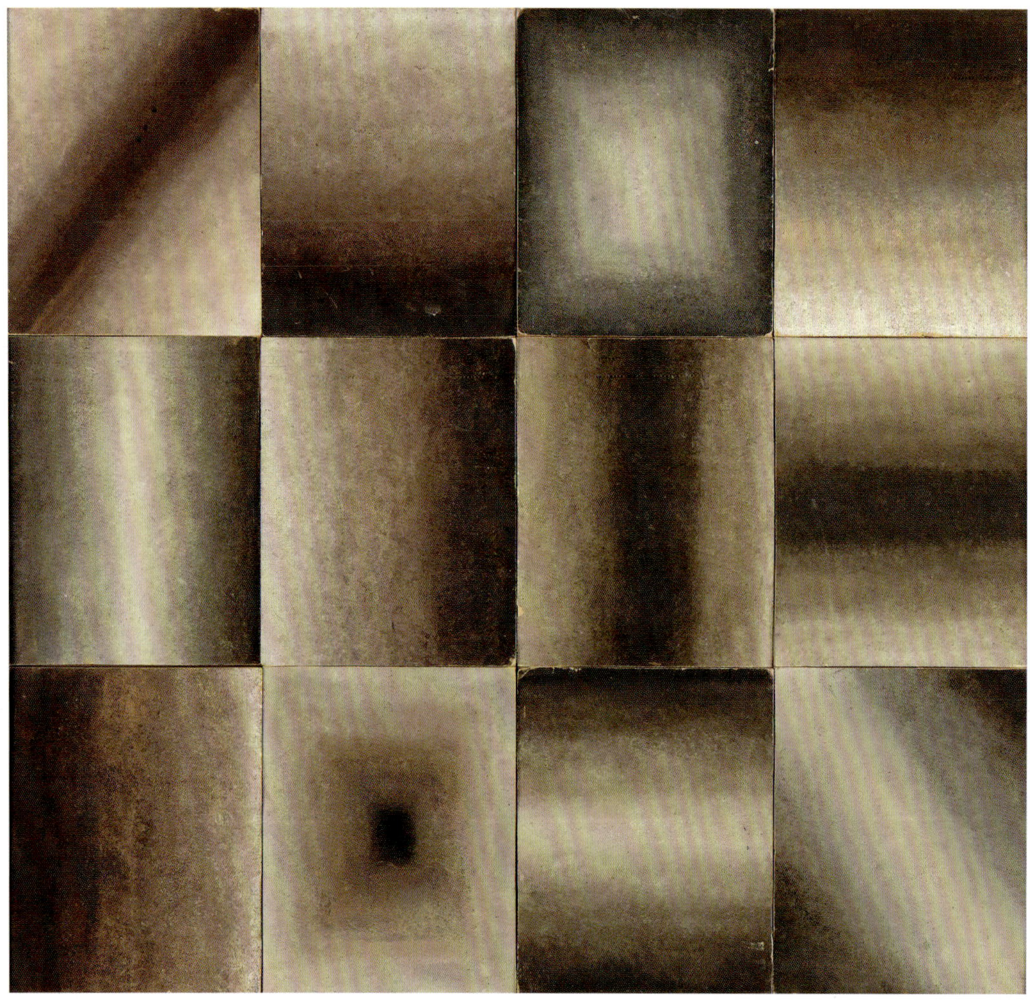

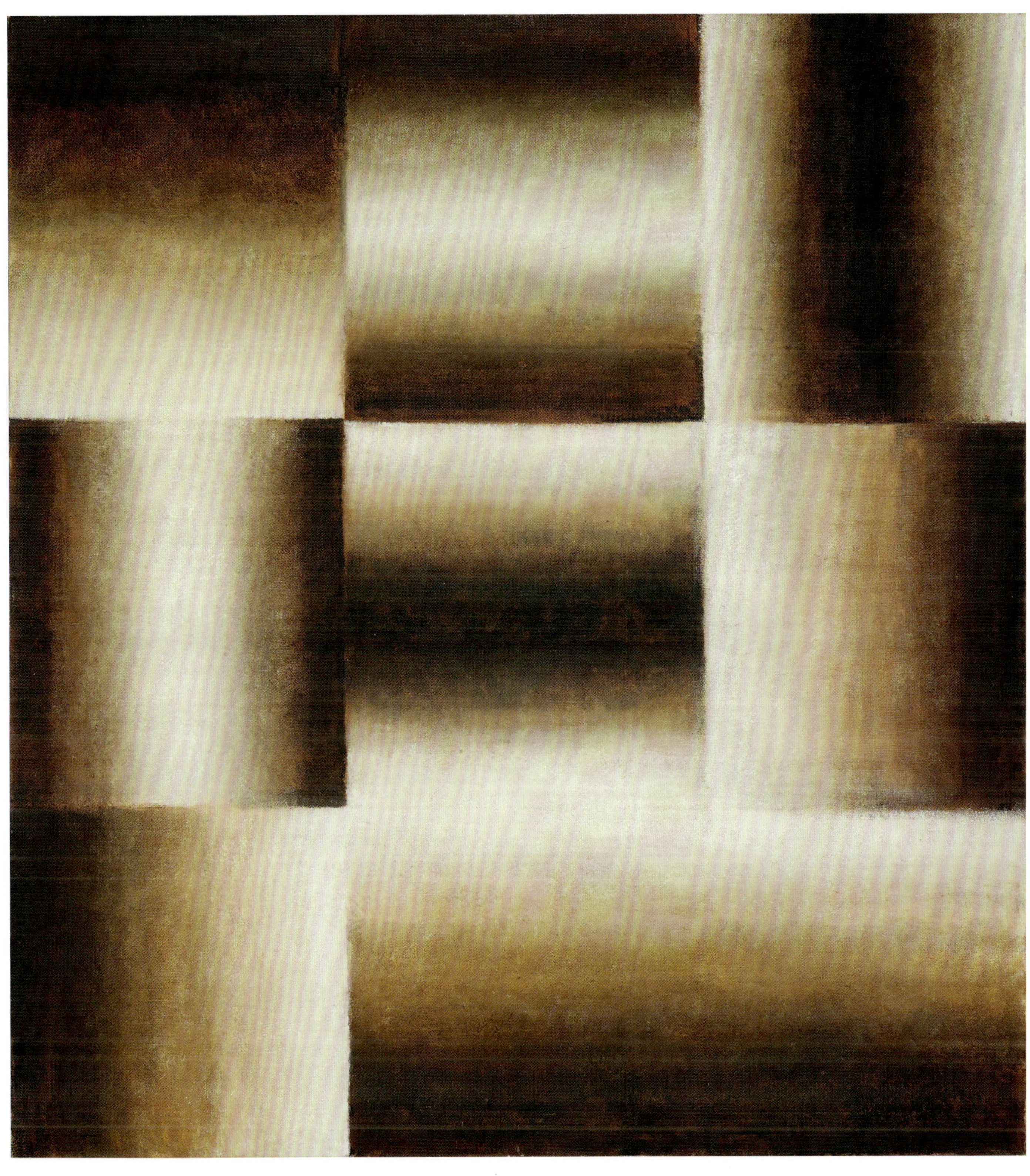

Painting CXLII, 1963
Oil on canvas
155 x 142 cm

Painting CLI, 1963
Oil on canvas
134 x 84.5 cm
Courtesy of Waldemar
Andzelm

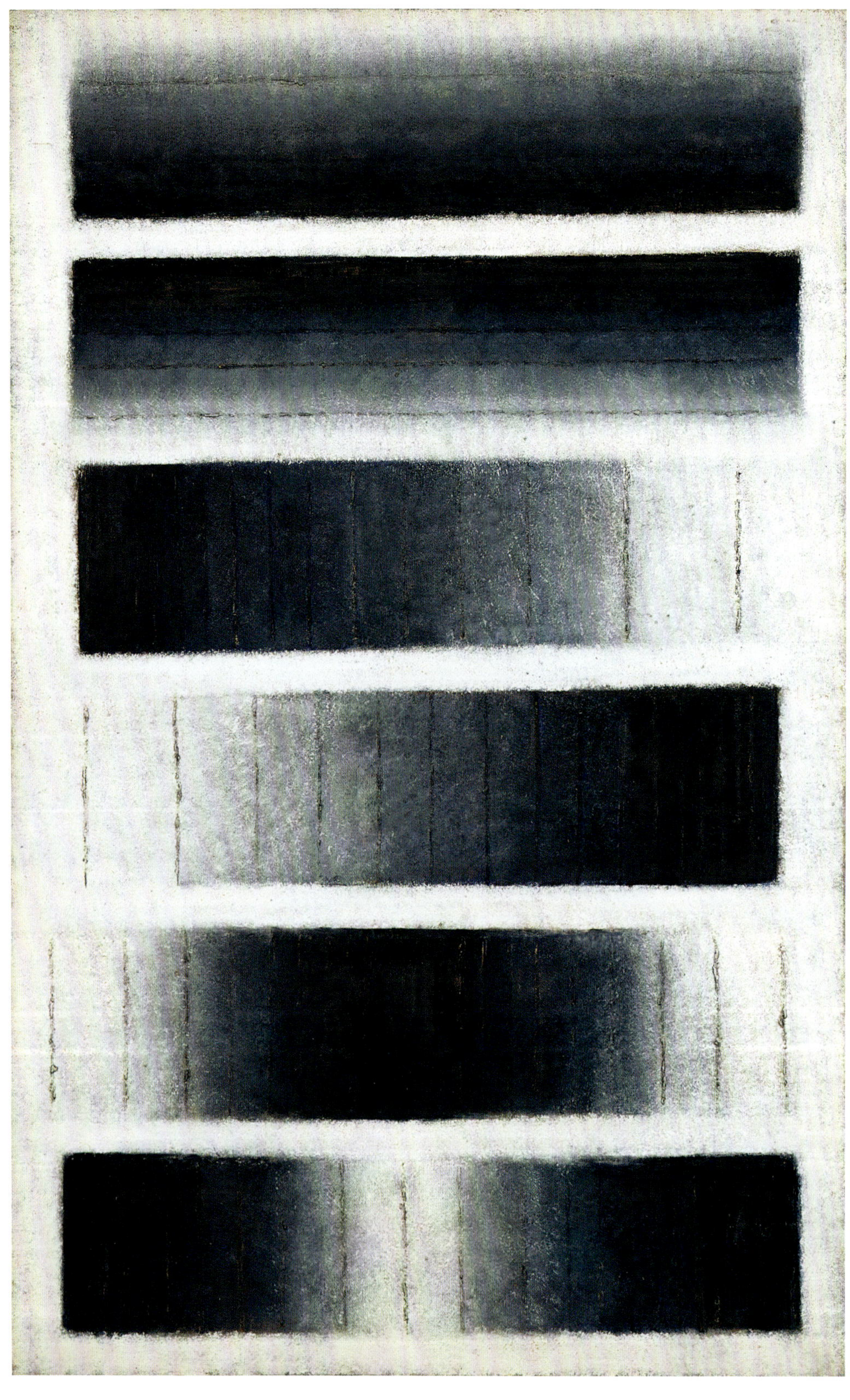

Painting CCCXCIV, 1977
Oil on canvas
100 x 70 cm

Painting DCCCXCVIII, 2012
Oil on canvas
120 x 100 cm

Painting CCCLXXXIV, 1977
Oil on canvas
200 x 75 cm

Painting CDXVII, 1977
Oil on canvas
59 x 45 cm

Painting DCCXCI, 2002
Oil on canvas
92 x 72.5 cm

Painting DCCCXC, 2011
Oil on canvas
92 x 92 cm

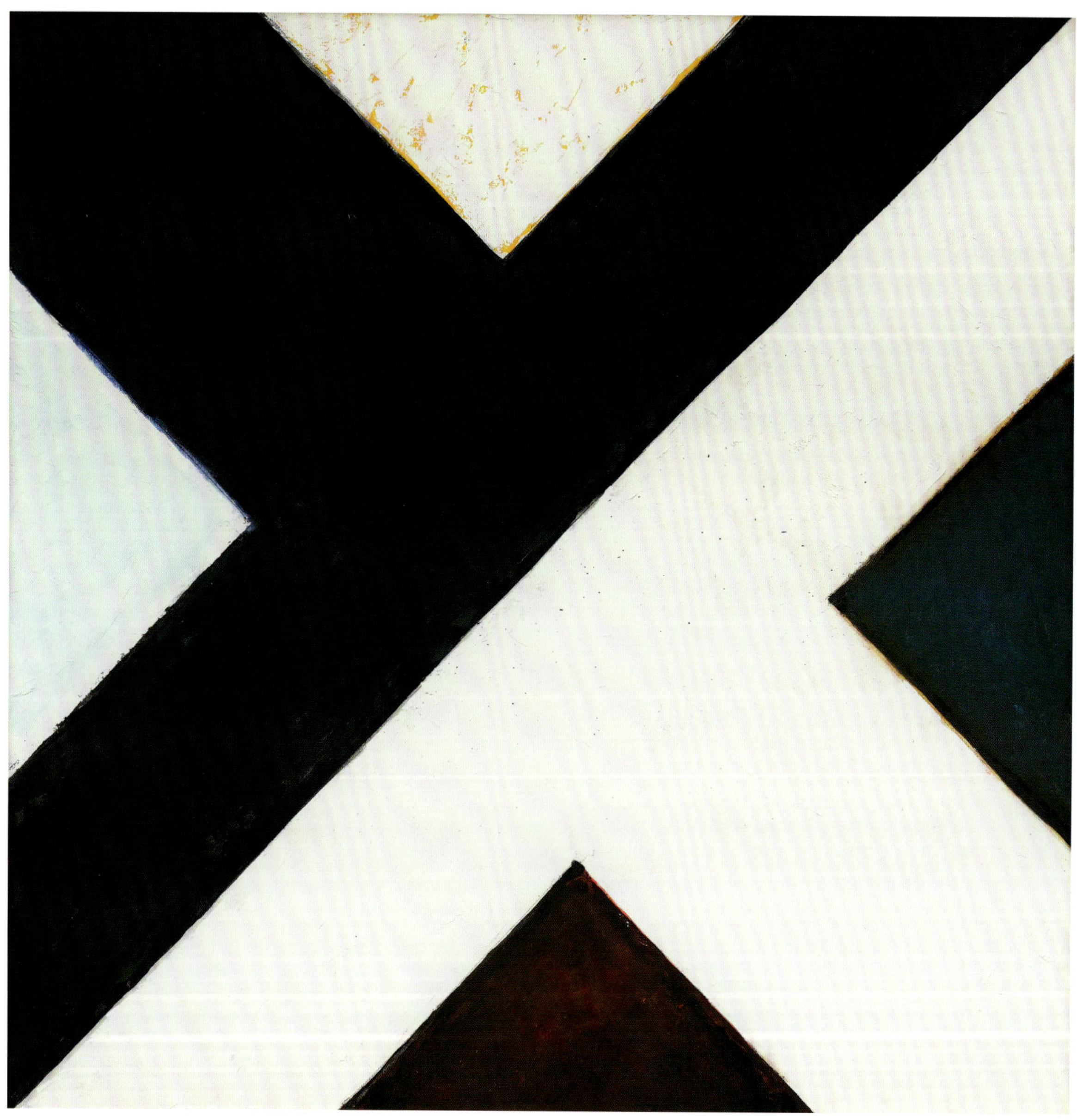

Painting DCCCLXXXVIII, 2011
Oil on canvas
73 x 73 cm

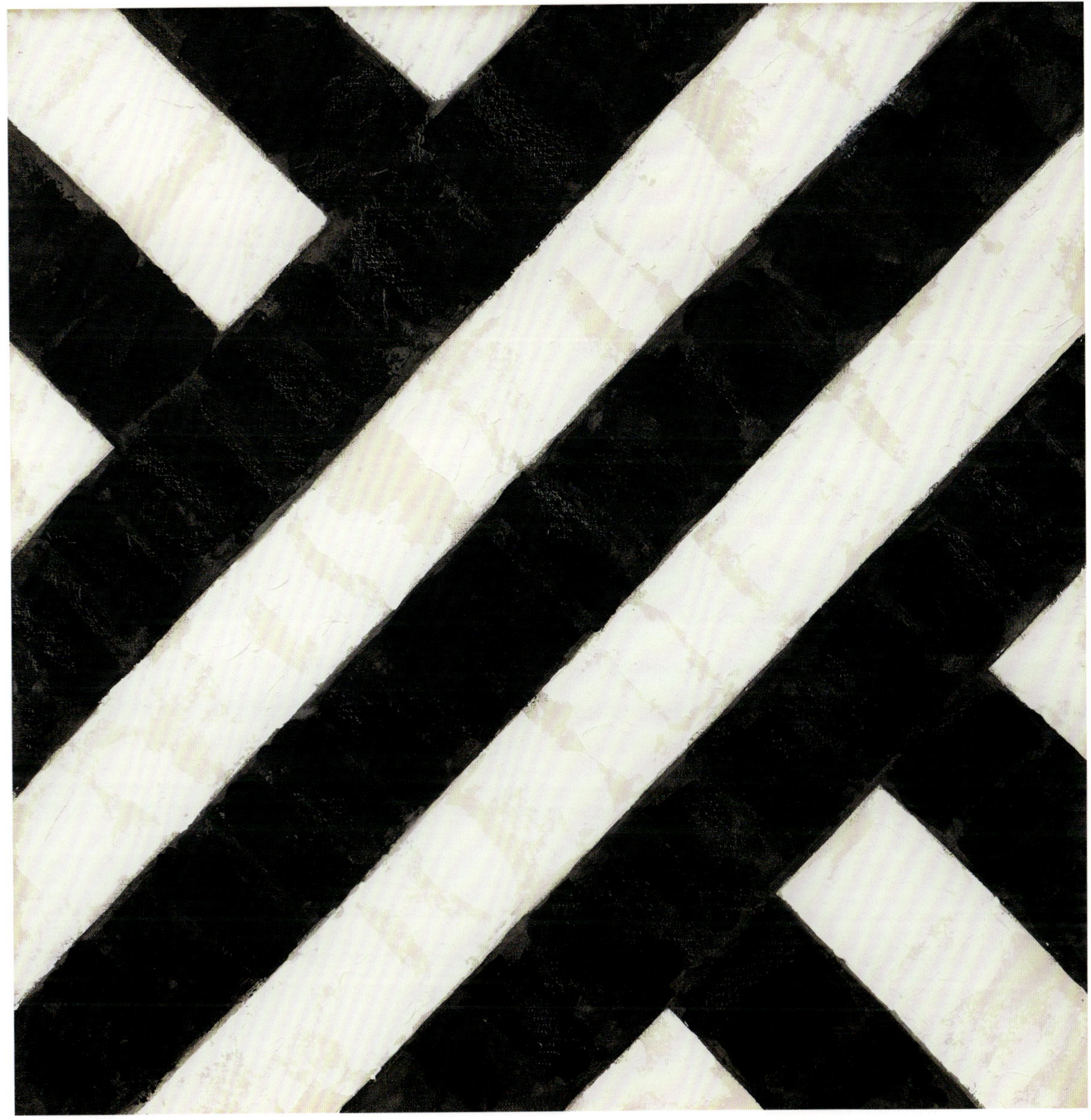

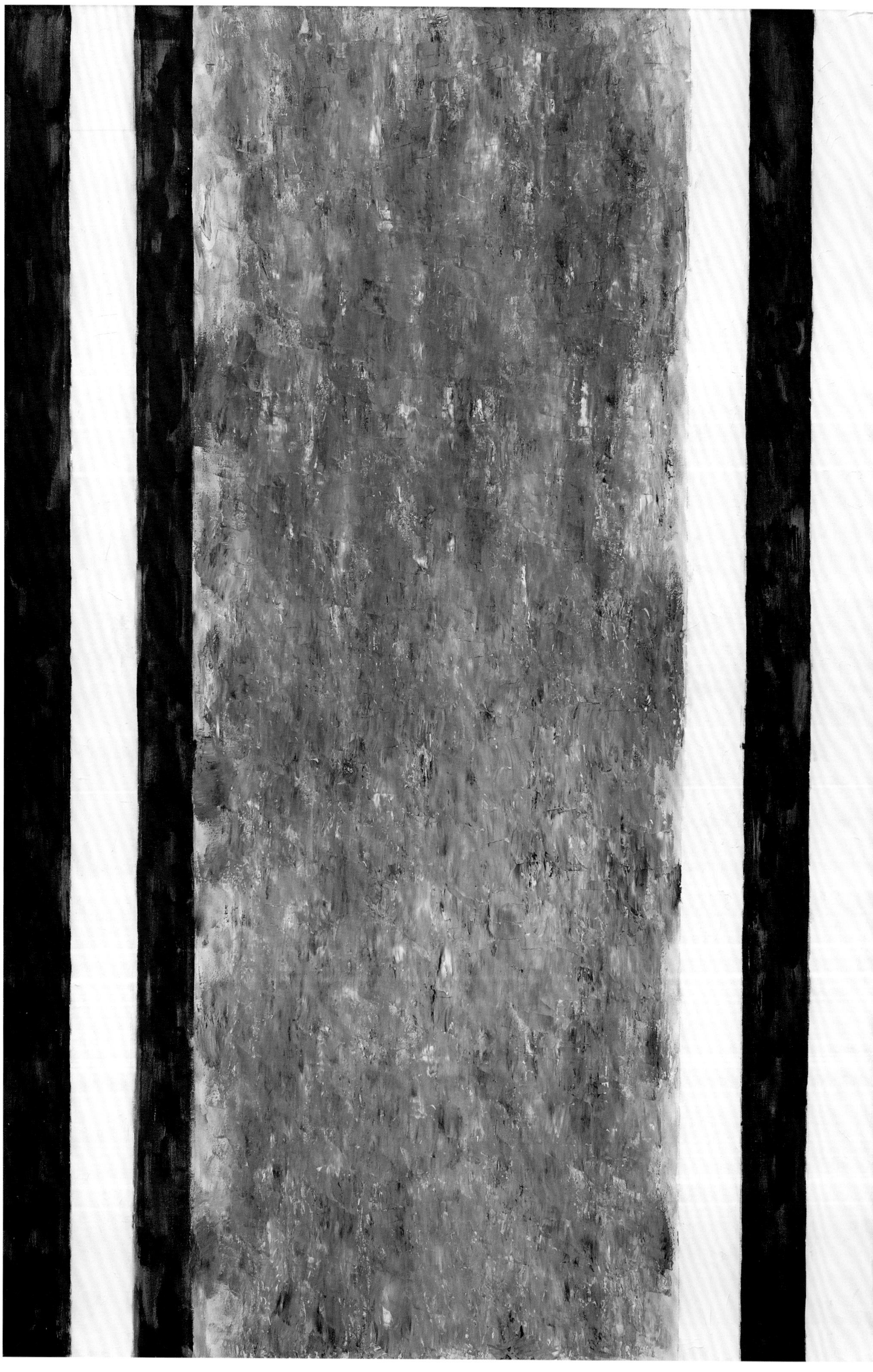

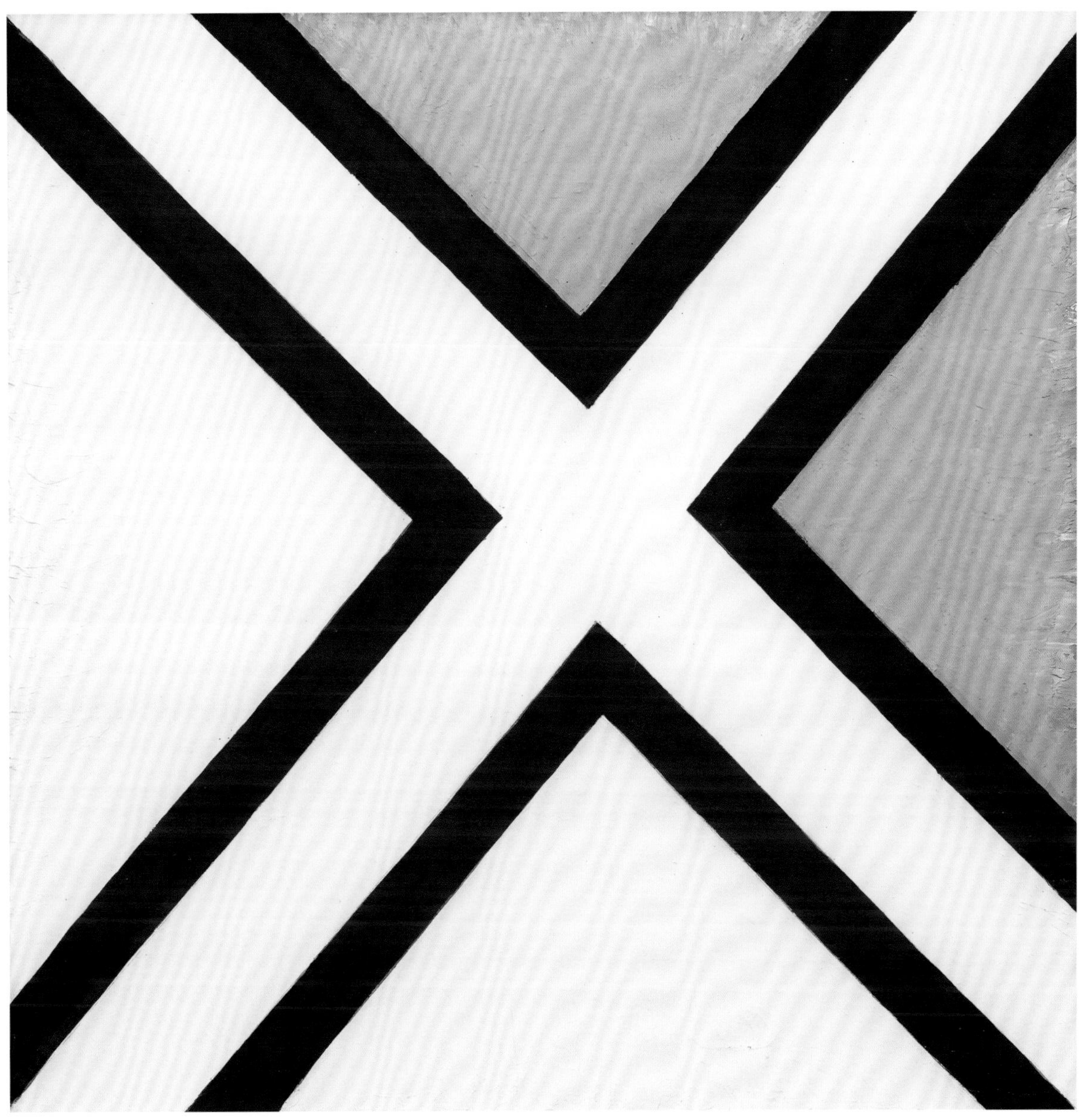

Painting DCCCLXXXIX, 2011
Oil on canvas
150 x 100 cm

Painting DCXCVIII, 1996
Oil on canvas
81 x 81 cm

Painting LXXIV, 1959
Oil on canvas
135 x 96 cm
The Leon Wyczółkowski
Regional Museum in
Bydgoszcz

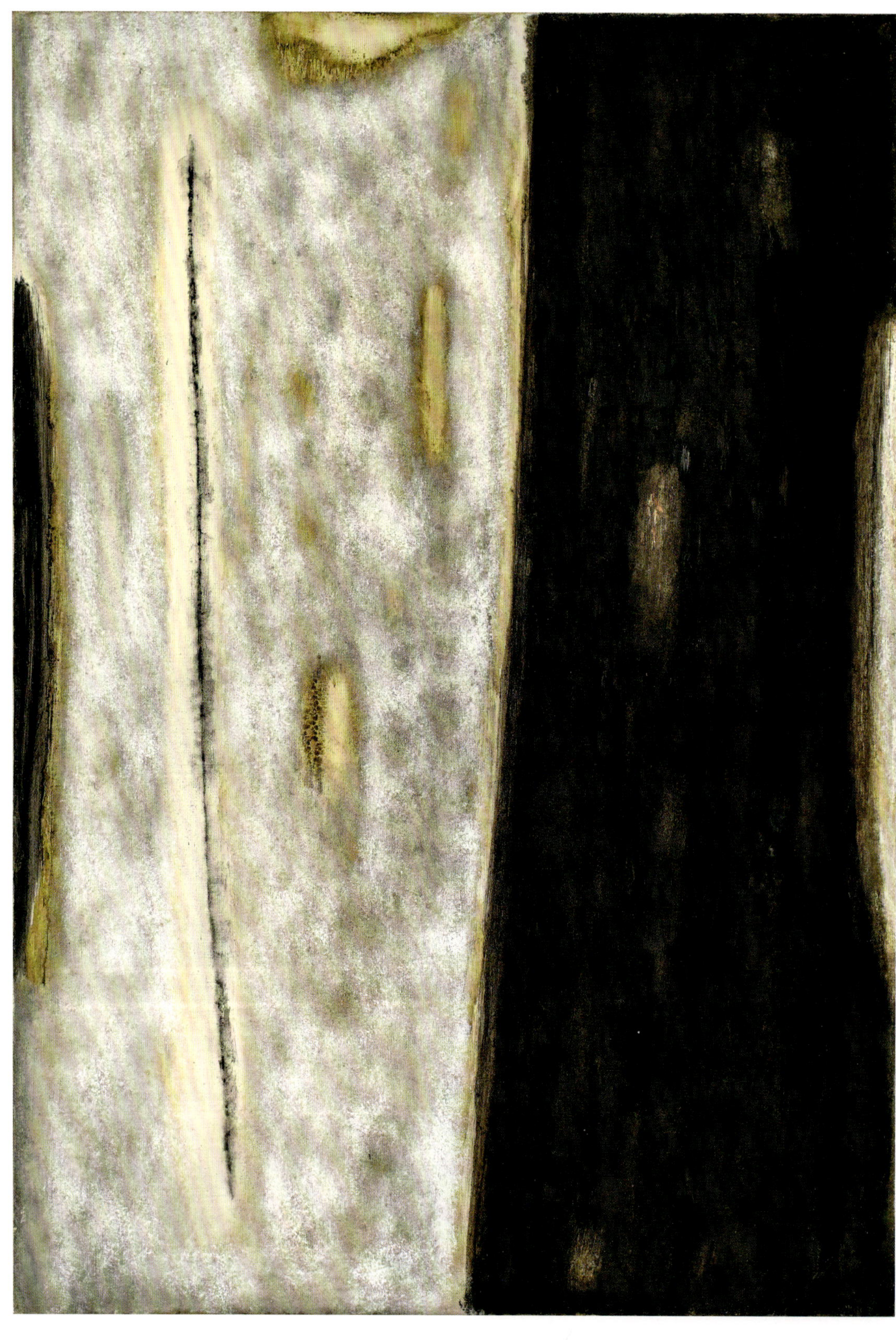

Painting DCCCXCI, 2012
Oil on canvas
100 x 81 cm

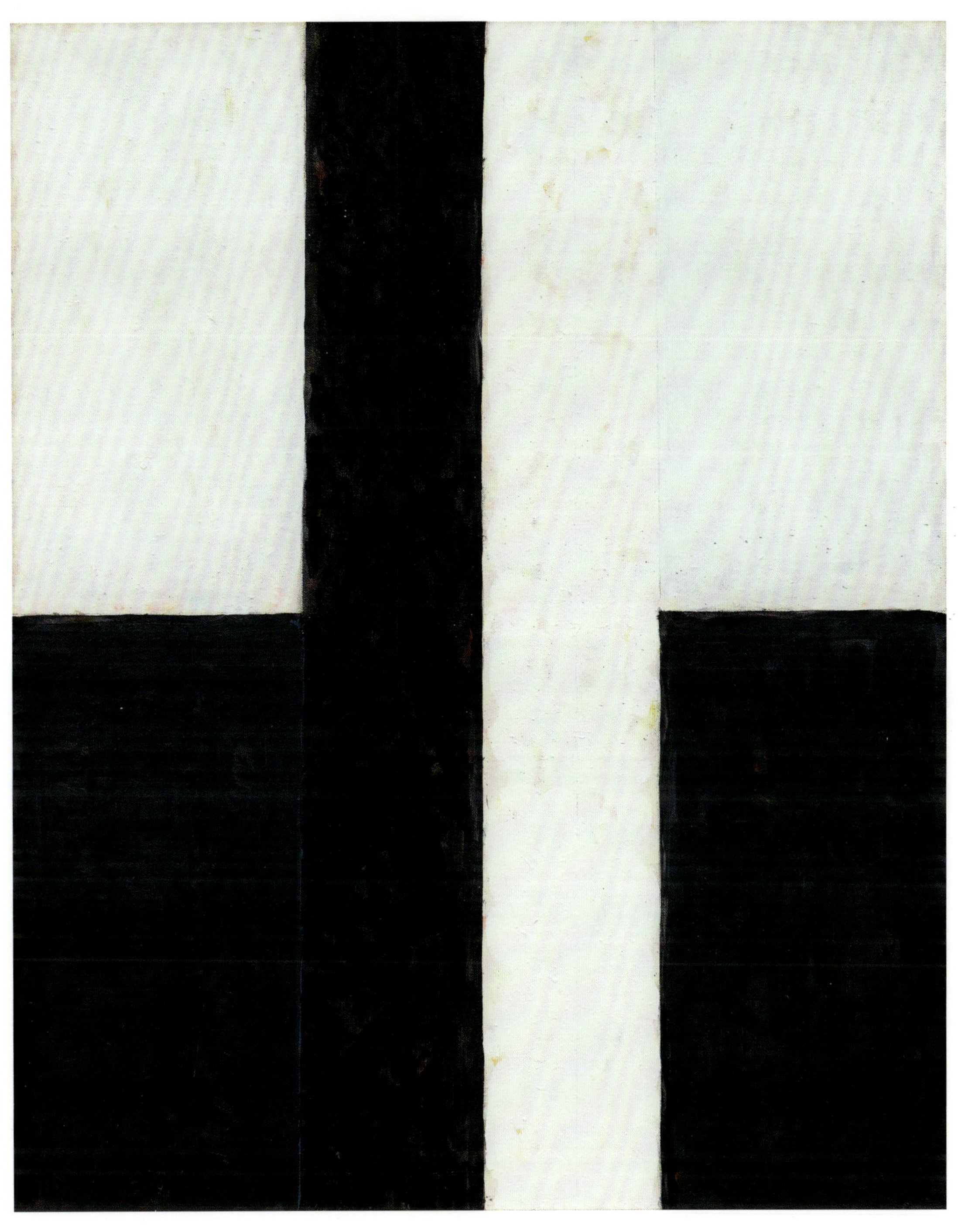

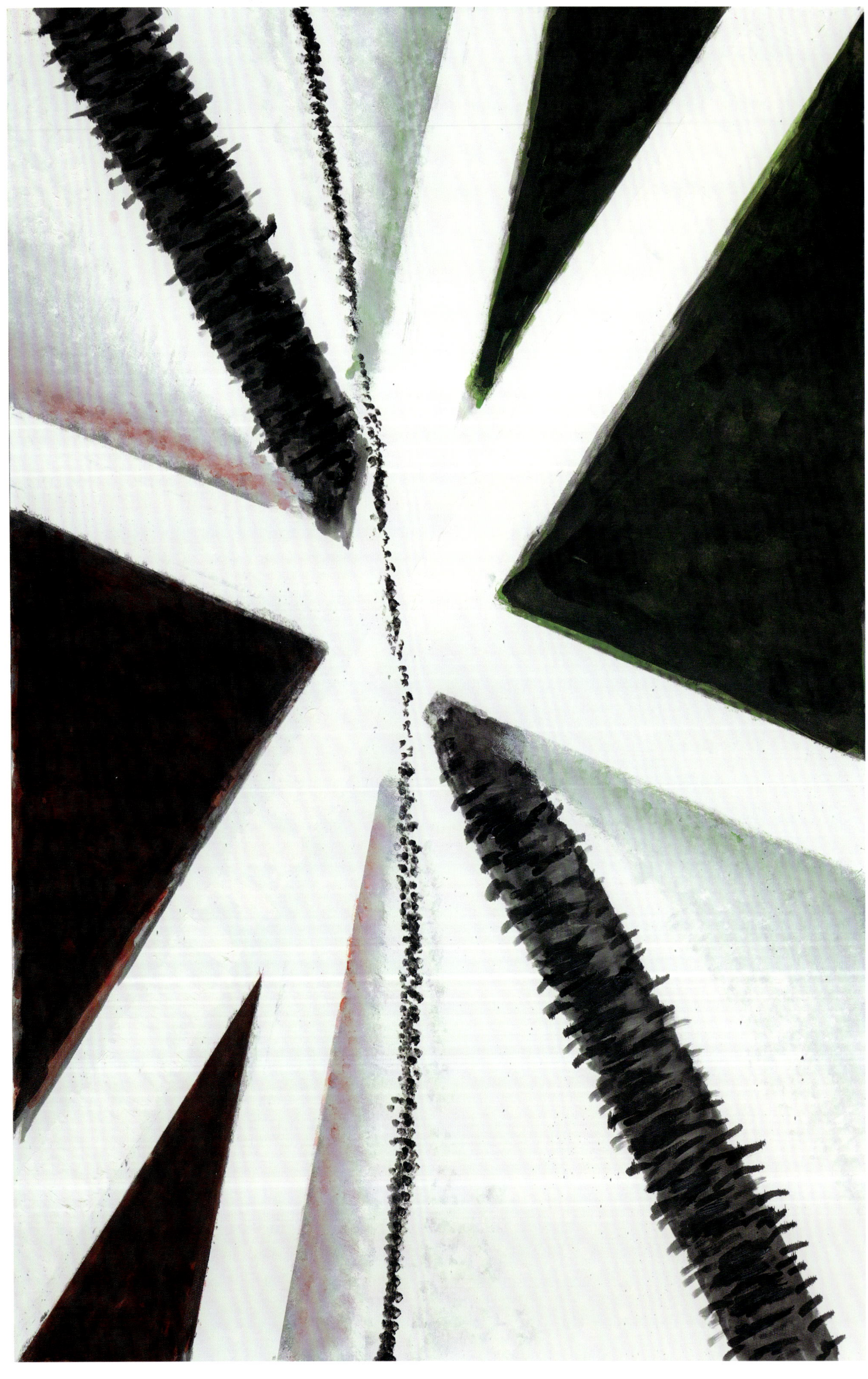

Stefan Gierowski, 1965

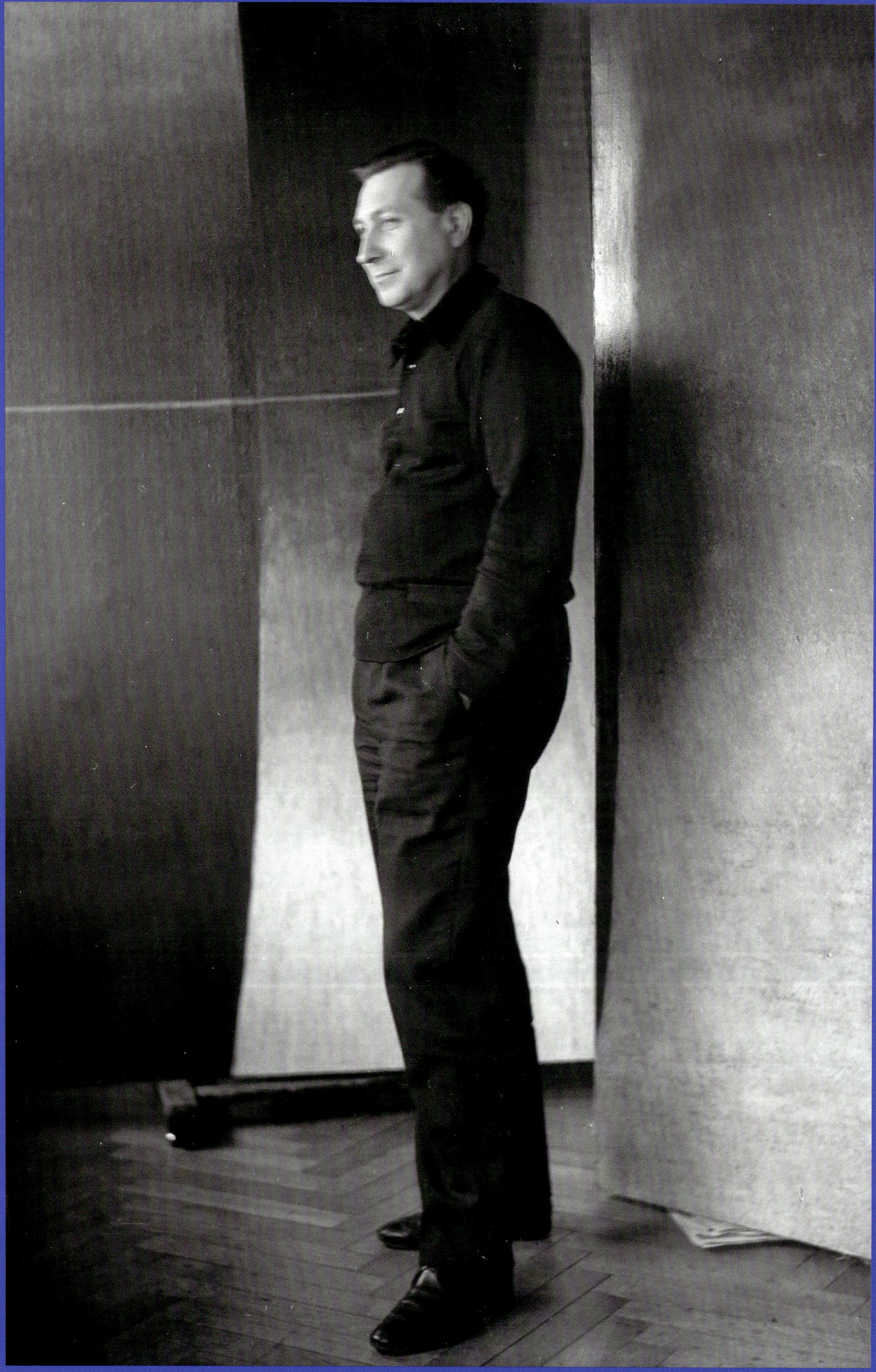

Abstraction

The term "abstract painting" opens up the way for imagination and intellect to work in a particular mode. What happens on the picture plane is a specific reality, formed to stimulate thinking in the abstract world.

Stefan Gierowski

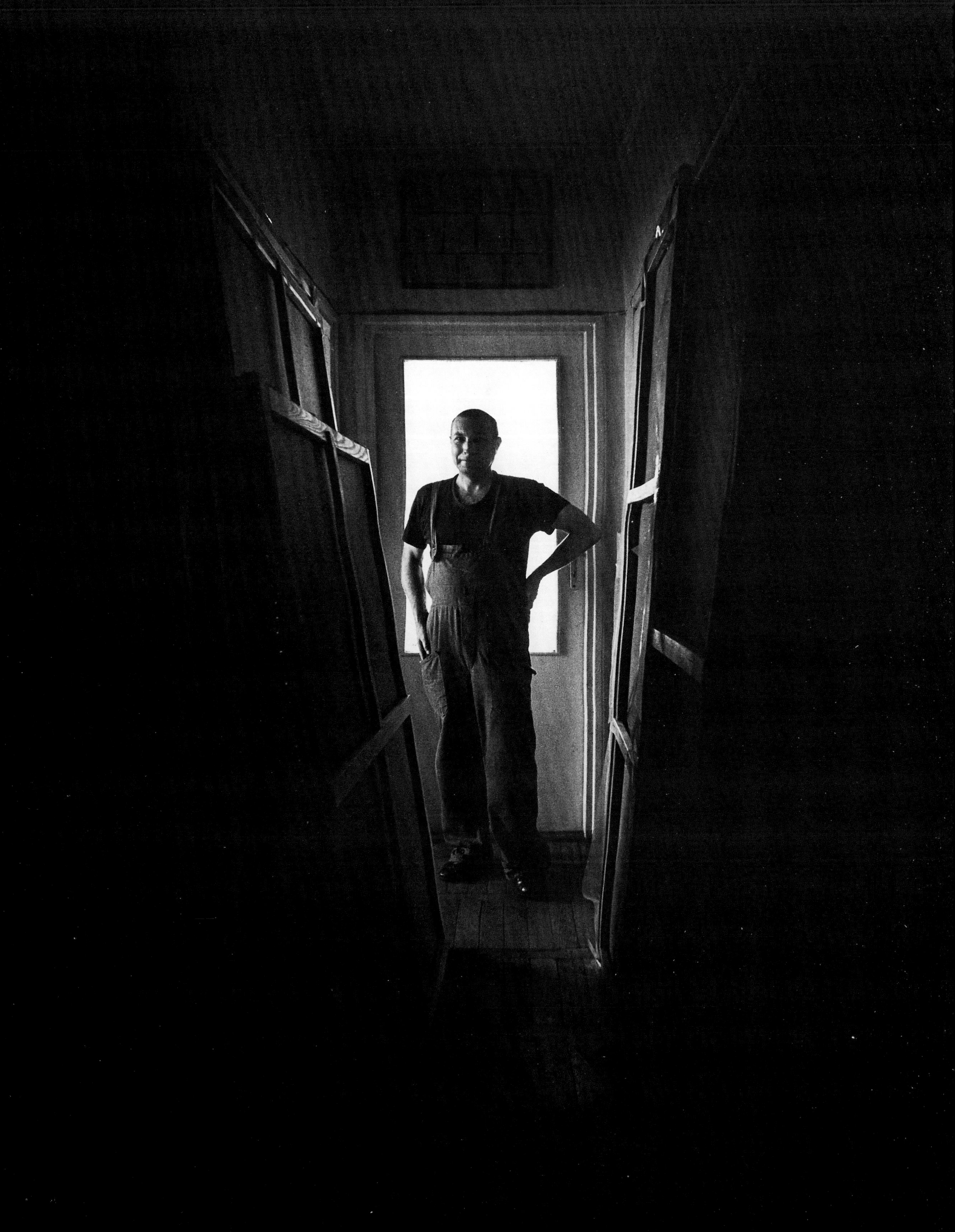

Biography

Early years

Stefan Gierowski was born on 21 May 1925 in Częstochowa. His family lived in Kielce, where he spent his childhood. From an early age, he displayed an interest in painting and wanted to train in the craft. His father, Józef Gierowski, a doctor and a painting enthusiast, played an important role in fostering his son's artistic vocation. His mother, Stefania née Wasilewska, had studied gardening and also encouraged the young Stefan to develop his artistic talents. The creative principle manifested itself in the family also through Józef's uncle, Antoni Gierowski, a nineteenth-century painter and draughtsman. Patriotic traditions were an important part of the young artist's formation.

When the Second World War broke out, Stefan, alongside his mother, joined the Armed Struggle Organization (ZWZ) and then the Home Army (AK), where he participated in underground activities under the nom-de-guerre "Hubert". In 1941, at the age of sixteen, he started studying art clandestinely with Andrzej Oleś, a recognized Kielce-based watercolourist. Three years later, having been transferred to the Home Army's inspectorate in Częstochowa, he had to discontinue his studies.

Student period

After the Home Army's dissolution in early 1945, Gierowski moved to Kraków, where he enrolled simultaneously at the Academy of Fine Arts and the Faculty of Art History at Jagiellonian University. His knowledge of art history proved crucial for his reflections on the possibilities and prospects of painting, opening him up to modernity. Under the supervision of Wojsław Mole, he wrote a seminar paper entitled "Impressionism as Part of French Culture."

At the Academy of Fine Arts, he initially studied in the class of Professor Władysław Jarocki, but when his clandestine studies with Oleś were officially recognized, he was transferred directly into the third year of the course. He trained under Zbigniew Pronaszko, an ex-Formist, as well as in the class of Karol Frycz, where he studied painting in architecture and designed stage sets. His training and conversations with Frycz acquainted him with modernist Young-Poland art. In Pronaszko's class, his fellow students included Zbigniew Grzybowski, Jerzy Panek, Stanisław Wójcik, and Andrzej Wróblewski.

During his studies, Gierowski struck up a collaboration with the literary-cultural magazine *Wieś*, publishing articles on art and illustrating a number of issues.

Art community and teaching

In 1948, having completed his studies, Gierowski returned to Kielce, where he started working as a specialist in the fine arts at the Department of Culture of Kielce Province. He also ran an arts class at the local branch of the Association of Polish Artists and Designers (ZPAP).

In 1949, offered a permanent position as technical editor of *Wieś*, Gierowski moved to Warsaw. On behalf of the periodical, he participated in a conference on artistic education held by the Ministry of Culture and Art in Poznań. In June that year, he met Władysław Strzemiński at the National Museum in Poznań. Also that month, the ZPAP Congress convened in Katowice, with Gierowski as delegate of the Kielce branch; on this occasion, the organisation's takeover by the communist Polish United Workers' Party (PZPR) began, leading to restriction of Gierowski's rights as a member.

The following years saw Gierowski devote himself to family life, with his marriage to Anna Golka and the birth of their two children, Magda and Józef. During this time, besides remaining active in the field of painting, the artist illustrated novels by his friend and fellow Kielce native Edmund Niziurski, such as *Księga urwisów* (The Book of Urchins). But financially it was a difficult period: living in a "kolkhoz" flat and not exhibiting because his paintings did not meet the criteria of Socialist Realism, they survived on his wife's modest salary as a dentist. In late 1951, Gierowski got a job in the Portfolios and Art Books section of the publishing company Wydawnictwo Artystyczno-Graficzne. He maintained an acquaintance with Marek Włodarski, through whom he later met the members of the painting collective Grupa 55.

In 1955, with the Stalinist order already thawing, he took part in the International Young Art Exhibition at Zachęta gallery in Warsaw, where his painting *I Love Life* won second prize. This put him in the spotlight and led to his recognition as a leading painter of the new generation. This reputation was reaffirmed by

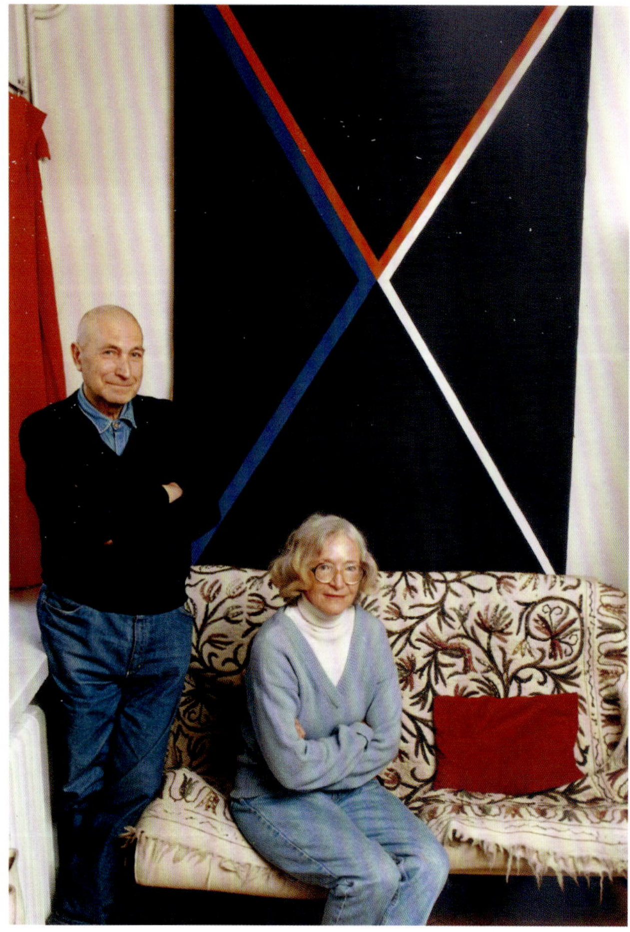

the work *Pigeon-house* (1955), which was shown at the Sixth Warsaw District Exhibition that year, winning critical acclaim. Still in 1955, Gierowski participated in the Nationwide Exhibition of Young Visual Artists *Against War – Against Fascism* at the Arsenal in Warsaw, which proved to be a generational show of artists opposed to the aesthetics of Socialist Realism. The participants would soon become leading figures in the art of their generation as well as Gierowski's long-time friends.

In January 1957, the artist exhibited for the first time at Galeria Krzywe Koło, thus initiating what would be several years of fruitful collaboration with Marian Bogusz and the associated milieu. In February, at the ZPAP General Congress, Gierowski was elected the Union's executive secretary. Together with the newly appointed management board, which was led by his friend Jan Cybis as president, he began working on a new statute for ZPAP, which rejected all political references and socialist terminology to refocus instead on the reorganisation of exhibition structures and art centres. As a result of Gierowski's efforts, several dozen ZPAP-affiliated exhibition spaces were opened around the country. Also in 1957, a year that proved pivotal for his career, Gierowski embarked on a series of paintings designated by Roman numerals. The first of these featured in the Second Exhibition of Modern Art at Zachęta, earning him wide critical acclaim, including from Julian Przyboś and Zbigniew Herbert.

In the following years, alongside Aleksander Wojciechowski and Marian Bogusz, Gierowski was included in the organisational committee of *Confrontations 1960*, a Krzywe Koło event that was recapitulated on 8 September 1960 during the Seventh Congress of the International Association of Art Critics (AICA). With Bogusz and Wojciechowski, he was responsible for the programme of *Confrontations* as well as exhibiting his works in one of the shows.

In the late 1950s and early 1960s, Gierowski frequently exhibited abroad: among others, he participated in the First International Biennale of Young Artists in Paris (1959), the Fifth International Biennale of Contemporary Art in São Paulo (1959), and the exhibition *15 Polish Painters* at the Museum of Modern Art in New York (1961). Following the success of the Polish presentation at the Paris Biennale, he was invited to stage a

solo show at Galerie Lacloche, which opened in April 1961. The same year, at the urging of Marian Wnuk and Jan Cybis, he joined the faculty of the Academy of Fine Arts in Warsaw to teach painting in architecture in the department headed by Aleksander Kobzdej.

Soon after, in 1965, he was granted permission to start his own class. His teaching style was friendly and open, with a curriculum based on general painterly issues such as colour and genre. Over a hundred students graduated from his class, including such figures as Marian Czapla, Jerzy Kalina, Łukasz Korolkiewicz, Ryszard Ługowski, Jarosław Modzelewski, Marek Sobczyk, Antoni Starowieyski, Krzysztof Wachowiak, and Apoloniusz Węgłowski. In 1975–81, Gierowski served as dean of the Faculty of Painting and in 1983 was appointed rector of the Academy, but the authorities objected and he never took up the post. He served on the Organisational Committee of the Congress of Polish Culture in 1981. In 1982–88, he was a member of the Chief Council of Science and Higher Education and president of the Council of Higher Artistic Education. He was promoted to full professor in 1986.

Ten years later he retired from teaching, and has since lived and worked in Konstancin-Jeziorna near Warsaw.

In 2014, the Stefan Gierowski Foundation was inaugurated. Besides popularizing and protecting the artist's oeuvre, it supports young painting through the annual Foundation Prize. It is also an active exhibition venue, organising survey exhibitions devoted to various aspects of contemporary and twentieth-century painting.

Exhibitions

Solo exhibitions

1955
• Klub SARP (Association of Polish Architects' Club), Warsaw
1957
• *Exhibition of Stefan Gierowski's Works*, Galeria Krzywe Koło, Warsaw
1959
• *Exhibition of Stefan Gierowski's Painting*, Galeria Krzywe Koło, Warsaw
1960
• *Stefan Gierowski*, Galeria Krzywe Koło, Warsaw
1961
• Galerie Lacloche, Paris
1963
• Galeria SPAM, Warsaw
1965
• *Gierowski: Géométries Spatiales*, Galerie Lacloche, Paris
1967
• *Exhibition of Stefan Gierowski's Painting*, Centralne Biuro Wystaw Artystycznych, Warsaw
• Galeria BWA, Olsztyn
1968
• Galerie Numaga, Auvernier, Neuchâtel
1970
• *Stefan Gierowski: Painting*, Galeria Współczesna, Warsaw
• Galeria Pryzmat, Kraków
1971
• Galeria ZPAP (Union of Polish Artists and Designers), Gdańsk
1973
• Galeria BWA, Piastów
• Muzeum Kazimierza Pułaskiego, Warka
• Galeria Zapiecek, Warsaw
1974
• Galeria BWA, Lublin
• Muzeum Ziemi Chełmskiej, Chełm
1975
• Galeria Sztuki Nowoczesnej, Nowa Huta, Kraków
1976
• Galerie Numag, Auvernier, Neuchâtel
1977
• *Stefan Gierowski: Painting*, Salon Sztuki Współczesnej BWA, Łódź
• Galerie Simone van Dormael, Brussels
1980
• Galeria BWA, Wrocław
1981
• *Exhibition of Stefan Gierowski's Painting, Winner of the 1980 Jan Cybis Award*, Dom Artysty Plastyka ZPAP (Union of Polish Artists and Designers), Warsaw
1984
• Galeria SHS, Warsaw
• Galeria STUDIO, Warsaw
1986
• Galeria Piotra Nowickiego, Warsaw
• Galeria SHS, Warsaw
• Galeria SARP, Warsaw

1987
• Galerie Numaga, Auvernier, Neuchâtel
1989
• Galeria Zapiecek, Warsaw
1989–90
• *Painting the Ten Commandments in Tribute to a 15th-Century Gdańsk Master*, Muzeum Archidiecezjalne, Warsaw
• Muzeum Uniwersyteckie, Lublin
1990
• *A Couple of Paintings*, Galeria Dziekanka, Warsaw
1991
• *1958–1991 Paintings*, Galeria Zderzak, Kraków
• *Painting the Ten Commandments in Tribute to a 15th-Century Gdańsk Master*, Stowarzyszenie Wspólnota Polska, Kraków
• Galeria BWA, Kielce
1992
• Państwowa Galeria Sztuki Zachęta, Warsaw
1993
• *Paintings*, Państwowa Galeria Sztuki Zachęta, Warsaw
• Galeria Gest, Łódź
1995
• Galeria BWA, Zamość
1996
• Galeria Gest, Łódź
• Galeria Zderzak, Kraków
1997
• Galeria Zapiecek, Warsaw
1998
• Muzeum Górnośląskie, Bytom
2000
• Muzeum Narodowe w Poznaniu, Poznań
• Państwowa Galeria Sztuki Zachęta, Warsaw
2003
• Galeria Piekary, Poznań
2004
• *Black and Other Colours*, Galeria Zderzak, Kraków
2005
• Państwowa Galeria Sztuki, Sopot
• Muzeum Okręgowe im. Leona Wyczółkowskiego, Bydgoszcz
• Galeria Prezydencka, Warsaw
• *The Line – Striving*, Andzelm Gallery, Lublin
• Galeria Pryzmat, Kraków
2006
• *The Process of Creation*, Galeria Art NEW Media, Warsaw
2007
• Galeria Zapiecek, Warsaw
2008
• *Three Landscapes and Four Metas*, Galeria Zderzak, Kraków
2010
• *Painting the Ten Commandments in Tribute to a 15th-Century Gdańsk Master*, Biblioteka Uniwersytecka, Warsaw

• *Hue – Brightness – Saturation*,
Galeria aTAK, Warsaw
• *Paintings from the 1950s and 1960s*,
Akademia Sztuk Pięknych, Warsaw
• *Gabinet Wybitnych Częstochowian*,
Muzeum Częstochowskie,
Częstochowa
2011
• *Painting the Ten Commandments
in Tribute to a 15th-Century Gdańsk
Master*, Kuria Diecezji Radomskiej,
Radom
• *The Space of Paint – the Curiosity of
Emptiness*, Andzelm Gallery, Lublin
2013
• Teatr Wielki, Galeria Opera, Warsaw
2014
• *Painting the Ten Commandments
in Tribute to a 15th-Century Gdańsk
Master*, Galeria Współczesnej Sztuki
Sakralnej, Kielce
2015
• *Painting the Ten Commandments
in Tribute to a 15th-Century Gdańsk
Master*, Muzeum Okręgowe im. Leona
Wyczółkowskiego, Bydgoszcz
• *XC: 16 Paintings from the Fibak
Family Collection*, Galeria Fibak,
Warsaw
• *Painting the Ten Commandments
in Tribute to a 15th-Century Gdańsk
Master*, Bazylika Mariacka, Gdańsk
2016
• *Painting the Ten Commandments
in Tribute to a 15th-Century Gdańsk
Master*, Muzeum Archidiecezjalne,
Katowice
• *Stefan Gierowski: From the Stefan
Gierowski Collection*, Atlas Sztuki, Łódź
• *Stefan Gierowski: Watercolours*,
Przestrzeń dla Sztuki, Nowohuckie
Centrum Kultury, Akademia Sztuk
Pięknych, Uniwersytet Ekonomiczny,
Kraków
• *Prof. Stefan Gierowski: Painting*,
Akademia Techniczno-Humanistyczna,
Bielsko-Biała
A Key, Galeria Zderzak, Kraków
2017
• *Fragment I*, Fundacja Stefana
Gierowskiego, Warsaw
• *Fragment II*, Fundacja Stefana
Gierowskiego, Warsaw
2018
• *Fragment III*, Fundacja Stefana
Gierowskiego, Warsaw
• *Overview of Works about Line under
the Care of the Foundation*, Fundacja
Stefana Gierowskiego, Warsaw
• *Stefan Gierowski: Line in Painting*,
Galeria Bielska BWA, Bielsko-Biała
• *For Marta Instead of Dinner*, Galeria
Zderzak, Kraków
2019
• *Emptiness and Light: The Thing About
Colour*, Galeria BWA, Olsztyn
• *Fragment IV*, Fundacja Stefana
Gierowskiego, Warsaw

• *Fragment V*, Fundacja Stefana
Gierowskiego, Warsaw
2019–20
• *Fragment VI*, Fundacja Stefana
Gierowskiego, Warsaw
2020
• *Stefan Gierowski: Thoughts Drawn
Not Fully Seen*, Fundacja Stefana
Gierowskiego, Warsaw
• *Fragment VII*, Fundacja Stefana
Gierowskiego, Warsaw

Group exhibitions

1946
• *Poland 1939–1945*, Kielce
1949
• Exhibition of ZPAP Division, Kielce
1955
• *Against War – Against Fascism*,
Arsenal, Warsaw
*International Post-Competition
Exhibition for the Fifth Festival of Youth
and Students in Warsaw*, Centralne
Biuro Wystaw Artystycznych, Warsaw
1956
• *Junge Generation: Polnische
Kunstausstellung*, Grassi
Kunstgewerbemuseum, Berlin
• *Ten Polish Painters*, Galerie Georges
Giroux, Brussels, Musée de Liège,
Ghent
1957
• *Modern Art: Exhibition*, Centralne
Biuro Wystaw Artystycznych, Warsaw
• *Modern Polish Art*, Belgrade,
Ljubljana, Zagreb, Skopje
• *Young Painting and Sculpture
Exhibition*, BWA Pawilony, Sopot
1958
• *Salon Marcowy Festival*, Zakopane
• *5 pittori polacchi d'oggi*, Galleria del
Milione, Milan, Unione Culturale-
Palazzo Carignano, Turin, Galleria
La Loggia, Bologna, Galleria L'Attico,
Rome, Galleria d'Arte Minerva, Naples
(1959)
• *Ausstellung Polnischer Künstler von
der Modernen Galerie und Kulturhaus
Warschau*, Galerie Palette, Wuppertal,
Stuttgarter Hausbücherei, Munich,
Deutsche Bücherbund, Bonn, Karlsruhe,
Frankfurt, Essen, Hannover, Düsseldorf
• *Modern Art Exhibition of Krzywe Koło
Gallery*, Galerie Palette, Wuppertal,
Duisburg, Soest
1959
• *Paris Biennale*, Paris
• *V Bienal Internacional de Arte São
Paulo*, São Paulo
• *Art Polonais – Poolse Kunst*, Palais
des Beaux-Arts, Brussels
• *Second Salon Marcowy Festival*,
Zakopane, Centralne Biuro Wystaw
Artystycznych, Warsaw
• *50 ars polskt malerei*, Kungliga
Konstakademien, Stockholm

• *Third Exhibition of Modern Art*,
Centralne Biuro Wystaw Artystycznych,
Warsaw
• *Mostra di pittura polacca
contemporanea*, Sala Napoleonica,
Venice
• *Poland: 50 Years of Painting*, Musée
d'Art et d'Histoire, Geneva
1960
• *Confrontations 1960*, Galeria Krzywe
Koło, Warsaw
1961
• *12 Modern Polish Painters*, Musée
d'Art Moderne de la Ville de Paris
• *Six Contemporary Polish Painters*,
Galerie Chalette, Chicago, New York
• *Gallery Painters*, Galerie Lambert,
Paris
• *15 Polish Painters*, The Museum
of Modern Art, New York, Carnegie
Institute, Pittsburgh, Minneapolis
Institute of Arts, Washington
University, St. Louis, William Proctor
Institute, Utica Munson (1962),
Museum of Fine Arts, Montreal,
National Gallery of Canada, Ottawa
• *Polsk Maleri*, Nasjonalgalleriet,
Oslo
1962
• *Polnische Malerei*, Folkwang
Museum, Essen
• *Confrontations 1956–1962*, Galeria
Krzywe Koło, Warsaw
• *Arguments 1962*, exhibition of
Polish and Czechoslovakian painters
organized for the Sixth
Warsaw Autumn International Festival
of Contemporary Music, Galeria
Krzywe Koło, Warsaw
• *Polish Painters*, Galerie La Calade,
Avignon, Galerie Lambert, Paris
1963
• *Arguments 1963*, Galeria Krzywe
Koło, Warsaw
1964
• *Profile IV: Polnische Kunst Heute*,
Stadtische Kunstgalerie, Bochum
• *The Function of Record:
Contemporary Language of Art*,
Stowarzyszenie Polskich Artystów
Muzyków, Warsaw
• *Marian Bogusz, Tadeusz Dominik,
Stefan Gierowski, Rajmund Ziemski*,
Gasleria Krzywe Koło, Warsaw
• *Second Festival of Polish
Contemporary Painting*, BWA Zamek
Książąt Pomorskich, Szczecin
• *1964 Pittsburgh International
Exhibition of Contemporary Painting
and Sculpture*,
• Carnegie Institute Museum of Art,
Pittsburgh
• *Third International Young Artist
Exhibition Europe–Japan*, Tokyo
1965
• *Image – Seeing – Imagination:
Painting – Drawing – Sculpture*, Galeria
Współczesna, Warsaw

• *V Biennale Internazionale d'Arte Contemporanea*, San Marino
• *Arte actual de Polonia: Pintura, tapicerias y arte gráfico*, Centro de Artes Visuales del Instituto Torcuato Di Tella, Buenos Aires, Salon de Bellas Artes, Montevideo, Museo de Arte Moderno Bosque de Chapultepec, Mexico City (1966), Casa de la Cultura, Guadalajara, Museo Michoacana, Morelia, Palacio de Bellas Artes, Havana (1967)
• *Comparisons*, 18th Festival of Visual Arts, Sopot
Second Visual Exhibition of Złote Grono Symposium, Muzeum Okręgowe / Galeria BWA, Zielona Góra
• *37 Polish Contemporary Artists*, Tel Aviv Museum of Art

1966
• *17 Polish Painters*, D'Arcy Gallery, New York
• *Space – Motion – Light*, Muzeum Sztuki Aktualnej, Wrocław
• *100 Malningar av Polska Konstnärer*, Sveagalleriet, Stockholm
• *Tokyo International Exhibition of Art 1966 (AIAP)*, Keiô Department Store, Tokyo

1967
• *Polské soudobné malířství*, Galerie ULUV, Prague
• *2. Internationale der Zeichnung*, Mathildenhöhe, Darmstadt
• *1967 Pittsburgh International Exhibition of Contemporary Painting and Sculpture*, Carnegie Institute Museum of Art, Pittsburgh
• *Polish Contemporary Painting: Collections of Leon Wyczółkowski Museum in Bydgoszcz*, Musée des Beaux-Arts, Nancy
• *Space – Motion – Light*, Muzeum Sztuki Aktualnej, Wrocław

1968
• *34. Biennale di Venezia,* Polish Pavilion, Venice
• *Triennale India*, New Delhi
• *Moderne Malerei in Polen (1917–1967)*, Kunsthalle, Kiel

1969
• *Exhibition of Contemporary Polish Art*, Scottish National Gallery of Modern Art, Edinburgh
• *Moderne polnische Malerei und Graphik 1959–1969*, Nationalgalerie, Berlin

1970
• *Elektra 70*, New York
• *Painting in the People's Republic of Poland*, Muzeum Narodowe w Warszawie, Warsaw

1972
• *Puolalaisia kuvia – Polska Bilder*, Helsingin Taidehalli, Helsingfors Konsthall, Helsinki, Konstmuseet, Tampere
• *Arta plastićă contemporană din Republica Populařa Polonă*, Sala Dalles, Bucharest

• *Modern Lengyel Művészet*, Műcsarnok, Budapest
• *Deutsch-Polnische Ausstellung II*, Von der Heydt Museum, Wuppertal

1973
• *Mote med Kopernikus: Modern Polsk Konst*, Malmö

1974
• *Pintura Polaca Contemporanea*, Museo de Bellas Artes, Caracas
• *Nationale Ausstellung Polen 74*, Gruga Park, Essen

1975
• *Polonia en Mexico Festival de las Formas / Pintura Contemporanea*, Museo de Arte Moderno, Mexico City
• *Polish Painting Today*, Hastings Art Gallery, Museum and Art Gallery Mansfield, Crescent Gallery, Mansfield, Crescent Gallery, Scarborough
• *Zeitgenössische polnische Kunst*, Ausstellungshalle, Dortmund
• *1960 Confrontations – 1970*, Galeria Zapiecek, Warsaw

1976
• *Sixth Festival of Fine Arts: Homage to Xawery Dunikowski on the 100th Anniversary of His Birth*, Centralne Biuro Wystaw Artystycznych, Warsaw
• *Pintura polaca contemporanea*, Museu Nacional Soares dos Reis, Porto, Fundação Gulbenkian, Lisbon, Palacio de Velázquez, Madrid (1977), Museo Histórico Municipal, Fundació Joan Miró, Barcelona

1977
• *The Romantic Spirit in Polish 19th- and 20th-Century Painting*, Grand Palais, Paris
• *In a Circle of Friends: Exhibition of Aleksander Wojciechowski's Collection of Paintings*, Galeria ZPAP, Warsaw
• *Inheritors and Contesters in Polish 19th- and 20th-Century Art*, Galeries Nationales du Grand Palais, Paris
• *Modern Lengyel Festészet*, Magyar Nemezeti Galéria, Budapest

1978
• *Seventh Festival of Fine Arts*, Narodowa Galeria Sztuki, Warsaw
• *Arsenał: Artistic Formation 1955–1977*, Muzeum Okręgowe, Gorzów Wielkopolski

1979
• *Modern Polish Art*, Galerie Asbæk, Copenhagen
• *Sávremeno pőljsko slikarstvo*, Umentnički Pavilijon Collegium Artisticum, Sarajevo, Muzej na Savremenato Umetnost, Skopje, Moderna Galerija, Titograd
• *Winners of National Awards and the Minister of Culture and Art on the 35th Anniversary of the People's Republic of Poland*, Centralne Biuro Wystaw Artystycznych, Warsaw

• *Polish Contemporary Painting: Winners of National Awards*, Institut Polonais, Paris
• *25 Polish Contemporary Artists*, Centre d'Echanges de Perrache, Lyon
• *25 Years of Painting in the People's Republic of Poland*, Muzeum Narodowe w Warszawie, Warsaw

1980
• *75 Years of the Academy of Fine Arts in Warsaw: Creative Tendencies of Teachers*, Muzeum Narodowe w Warszawie, Warsaw
• *Polalaisia kuvia – maalauksia, piirustuksia ja taidegrafiikkaa*, Porin Taidemuseo, Hämeenlinnan Taidesmuseo

1981
• *Polish Painting from the Collections of the Regional Museum in Bydgoszcz*, Centralne Biuro Wystaw Artystycznych, Warsaw

1982
• *Presence*, Kościół św. Aleksandra, Warsaw

1983
• *The Sign of the Cross*, Parafia Miłosierdzia Bożego, Warsaw
• *Reality and Imagination: Exhibition of the Polish Contemporary Art Collection of the National Museum in Wrocław*, Centralne Biuro Wystaw Artystycznych, Warsaw
• *Artist's Thought*, Pałac Sztuki, Kraków
• *Through the Seen to the Unseen*, Kościół Nawiedzenia NMP, Warsaw

1984
• *Contemporary Art Collection of the Regional Museum in Bydgoszcz*, Galeria BWA, Wrocław
• *Visual Artists for Shipyard Workers: Exhibition of Visual Works on the Anniversary of September 1980*, Bazylika św. Mikołaja oo. Dominikanów, Gdańsk

1985
• *New Sky and New Earth?*, Parafia Miłosierdzia Bożego, Warsaw
• *Polnische Kunst '85: zu gast bei Steyer–Daimler–Puch*, Vienna

1986
• *Gruppe rbk Wuppertal: 27 Künstler aus 7 Ländern – Malerei, Graphik, Skulptur*, Ausstellungshalle Alte Rathaus, Schweinfurt, Kulturzentrum Wilhelm Morgner Haus, Soest
• *Masters of Contemporary Art in Poland*, Herbert F. Johnson Museum of Art, Cornell University, Ithaca
• *Pittura contemporanea polacca*, Centro Studi di Arte e Cultura, Naples

1987
• *Painting in the Warsaw Academy Circle*, Galeria EL, Elbląg, former Norblin factory, Warsaw
• *Freiraum: Ver Generationen Konstrukivischer Strömungen in der polnischer Kunst*, Kunstation, Kleinsassen

1988

• *Polnische Malerei seit 1945 aus der Sammlung des Bezirksmuseums Bydgoszcz*, Galerie der Stadt Esslingen, Villa Merkel, Esslingen, Kunsthalle, Wilhelmshaven

• *Geometria és metafora: Kiállítás a Chelmi Kőrzeti Múzeum Anyagából*, Budapest Galéria, Budapest

1989

• *Freiraum 2*, Villa Toscana, Gmunden

• *Vision and Unity*, Van Reekum Museum, Apeldoorn

• *In the Image, After the Likeness*, former Norblin factory, Warsaw

1990

• *Krzywe Koło Gallery: A Retrospective*, Muzeum Narodowe w Warszawie, Warsaw

1991

• *20th-Century Art Collection in the Art Museum in Łódź*, Państwowa Galeria Sztuki Zachęta, Warsaw

• *Epitaph and Seven Spaces*, Państwowa Galeria Sztuki Zachęta, Warsaw

• *Eyeshot: Within the Field of Vision*, Nikolaj Gallery, Copenhagen

1992

• *Reduktivismus: Abstraktion in Polen, Tschechoslowakei, Ungarn 1950–1980*, Museum Moderner Kunst Stiftung Ludwig, Vienna

• *Circle of Arsenał 1955: Painting, Graphics and Drawing from the Regional Museum in Gorzów*, Państwowa Galeria Sztuki Zachęta, Warsaw

• *10 Years Later: Exhibition of Polish Contemporary Drawing*, Muzeum Sztuki Współczesnej, Radom, Galeria BWA, Kraków, Galeria BWA, Częstochowa, Państwowa Galeria Sztuki, Łódź (1993)

• *Art Museum in Łódź 1931–1992: Collection – Documentation – Actuality*, Musée d'art contemporain de Lyon + ELAC, Lyon

• *Polnische Avantgarde 1930–1990*, Neuer Berliner Kunstverein, Staatliche Kunsthalle, Berlin

1993

• *From the Nooks and Crannies*, Galeria Rzeźby, Warsaw

• *OdNOWA Gallery 1964–1969*, Muzeum Narodowe w Poznaniu, Poznań

• *Vector of Art*, Galeria Miejska Arsenał, Poznań

1994

• *Collection 2*, Centrum Sztuki Współczesnej Zamek Ujazdowski, Warsaw

• *Widerstand und Aufbruch / Resistance and Breakthrough: Polish Art 1980–1993*, churches in Stuttgart

• *Europa, Europa: Das Jahrhundert der Avantgarde in Mittel- und Osteuropa*, Kunst- und Ausstellungshalle der Bundesrepublik Deutschland, Bonn

• *Contemporary Classics*, Muzeum Narodowe w Warszawie, Warsaw

1995

• *Drawing: The First Record (from the ateliers of 60 artists)*, Królikarnia, Warsaw

• *Lines – Linien*, Muzeum im. Xawerego Dunikowskiego w Królikarni, Warsaw

• *To Cybis, to Samborski…*, Akademia Sztuk Pięknych, Warsaw

1996

• *Kunst und Natur / Art towards Nature*, BASF-Feierabendhaus, Ludwigshafen, Państwowa Galeria Sztuki, Zachęta, Warsaw

• *Collection 3*, Centrum Sztuki Współczesnej Zamek Ujazdowski, Warsaw

• *The Thaw: Art Around 1956*, Muzeum Narodowe w Poznaniu, Poznań

• *The Contemporary Warsaw Masters*, Society for Arts Gallery, Chicago

• *Attitudes: Warsaw Artists' Works*, Galeria STUDIO, Warsaw

1997

• *Painting's Limits*, Centrum Sztuki Współczesnej Zamek Ujazdowski, Warsaw

• *Question about Metaphor*, Galeria Aula, Akademia Sztuk Pięknych, Warsaw

• *25 Years Ago and Now: An Attempt to Reconstruct*, Galeria STUDIO, Warsaw

• *Generations*, Państwowa Galeria Sztuki Zachęta, Warsaw

• *Art from Poland 1945–1996*, Műcsarnok, Budapest, Vilnius šiuollaikino meno centras, Makslas muzeja Arsenals, Riga, Tallinna Kunstihoone

1999

• *Generations: Polish Art at the Turn of the Centuries*, Manege Central Exhibition Hall and Pushkin Muzej, Saint Petersburg

2000

• *Kraków Meetings 2000: From To*, Bunkier Sztuki, Kraków

• *Verteidigung der Moderne: Positionen der Polnischen Kunst nach 1945*, Museum Wurth, Kunzelsau

2001

• *International Collection of Contemporary Art*, fourth edition: permanent exhibition, Centrum Sztuki Współczesnej Zamek Ujazdowski, Warsaw

• *In Between: Art from Poland 1945–2000*, Cultural Center, Chicago

• *Jan Cybis, Stefan Gierowski: Chromatic Paintings*, Galeria Zderzak, Kraków

2002

• *100% Painting*, Galeria Zderzak, Kraków

• *Fijałkowski/Gierowski: Painting Visions*, Państwowa Galeria Sztuki, Sopot

• *Abstract Painting – Light*, Galeria Sztuki Współczesnej BWA, Olsztyn

2003

• *White Paintings*, Galeria Stefan Szydłowski, Warsaw

• *Gierowski and Krzywe Koło Gallery*, Muzeum Sztuki, Łódź

2004

• *Euroart 1*, Biennale of Art, former Prussian barracks, Świnoujście

• *Painting Classics, Part 1: In Commemoration of the 100th Anniversary of the Academy of Fine Arts in Warsaw*, Galeria Aula, Akademia Sztuk Pięknych, Warsaw

• *Malewicz in Poland*, Galeria Arsenał, Białystok

2006

• *Warsaw in Berlin: Contemporary Polish Painting*, Kommunale Galerie, Berlin

• *Warsaw in Sofia: Contemporary Polish Painting and Graphics*, Sofia

2008

• *Three Looks: Łapiński, Gierowski, Tarasin*, Galeria ESTA, Gliwice

2009

• *Clashes*, Galeria ESTA, Gliwice

2010

• *Berdyszak – Gierowski – Kałucki – Kamoji*, Galeria Wojewódzkiej Biblioteki Publicznej, Lublin

• *Fijałkowski / Gierowski / Sempoliński*, Galeria Art NEW Media, Warsaw

• *Behind the Iron Curtain: Official and Independent Art in the Soviet Union and Poland 1945–1989*, Fundacja Polskiej Sztuki Nowoczesnej, Warsaw

2013

• *Polish Art Now*, Saatchi Gallery, London

2016

• *Meeting of Generations: Warsaw Academy Painters from Krzysztof Musiał's Collection*, Academy Hall, Akademia Sztuk Pięknych, Warsaw

• *Imagines Medii Aevi*, Muzeum Narodowe w Poznaniu, Poznań

2016–17

• *The Magic of the Square*, Państwowa Galeria Sztuki, Sopot

2018

• *After Cybis, What?*, Narodowa Galeria Sztuki Zachęta, Warsaw

• *Cybis = Painting*, Galeria DAP, Warsaw

2019

• *Deep Impact: Stefan Gierowski and European Avant-Gardes in the 60s*, Fundacja Stefana Gierowskiego, Warsaw

• *Art Values: From the PKO Bank Polski Collection*, Muzeum Narodowe w Warszawie, Warsaw

• *Abstraction and Geometry*, Galeria Retroavangarda, Warsaw

2020

• *Zauberberg*, Galeria Zderzak, Kraków

• *Colours of Change*, Państwowa Galeria Sztuki, Sopot

Biographies
of the
Authors

Dr David Anfam is Managing Director of Art Exploration Consultancy Ltd, London, as well as Senior Consulting Curator at the Clyfford Still Museum, Denver. His diverse books include *Abstract Expressionism* (Thames & Hudson, 1990; second edition 2015); *Mark Rothko: The Works on Canvas – Catalogue Raisonné* (Yale University Press, 1998; sixth printing 2019) and *Anish Kapoor* (Phaidon Press, 2009). Since 1990, Anfam has contributed essays to more than seventy exhibition catalogues, ranging in subject from David Smith and Pier Paolo Calzolari to Max Beckmann and Wayne Thiebaud. His exhibition *Abstract Expressionism* (Royal Academy of Arts, London, 2016–17) was the largest survey of its kind ever held in Europe. Most recently, Anfam curated *Lynda Benglis: In the Realm of the Senses* (NEON, Athens, 2019–20).

Michel Gauthier has been since 2010 curator at the Centre Pompidou in Paris, where he deals with post-war painting and sculpture and where he recently curated exhibitions devoted to Sheila Hicks, Victor Vasarely, Martin Barré and Farid Belkahia. In 2019, he curated the exhibition *Deep Impact. Stefan Gierowski and European avant-gardes in the 60s* at the Stefan Gierowski Foundation in Warsaw. He is the author of numerous studies and some twenty books, including publications devoted to Gerhard Richter, Mohamed Melehi and Claude Rutault. He taught art history at the Sorbonne University from 2007 to 2019.

Stach Szabłowski (b. 1973) is an independent curator, art critic, and commentator. Having earned an MA in Art History at the University of Warsaw, he was closely associated with the Ujazdowski Castle Centre for Contemporary Art in Warsaw in 1998–2016. He has curated several dozen exhibitions, public-art festivals and various artistic projects. His research interests revolve around narrative mechanisms in the visual arts, the intersections of art and cinema, and the anthropology of visuality. He is a regular contributor to art magazines and periodicals, editor of catalogues, author of essays published in books and monographs.